KU-161-568

LEGAL FOUNDATIONS

LEGAL FOUNDATIONS

Keir Bamford LLB, Solicitor

Sheila L Bramley, Solicitor

Kevin Browne LLB, Solicitor

Lesley King LLB, Dip Crim (Cantab), Solicitor

Anthony Morgan LLB, Solicitor

Sarah Pooley BA, MLitt, Solicitor

Matthew Trigg LLB, Solicitor

Published by

College of Law Publishing,
Braboeuf Manor, Portsmouth Road, St Catherines, Guildford GU3 1HA

© The College of Law 2008

All rights reserved. No part of this publication may be reproduced, stored in a retrieval system, or transmitted in any way or by any means, including photocopying or recording, without the written permission of the copyright holder, application for which should be addressed to the publisher.

British Library Cataloguing-in-Publication Data
A catalogue record for this book is available from the British Library.

ISBN: 978 1 905391 57 8

Typeset by Style Photosetting Ltd, Mayfield, East Sussex
Printed in Great Britain by Ashford Colour Press Ltd, Gosport, Hampshire

Preface

This book is divided into five Parts, the first four each dealing with one of the topics which pervade the syllabus of the Legal Practice Course. These topics are: revenue law, professional conduct, EC law and human rights. Part V deals with the core subject, Probate and Administration. The material contained in this book is intended to be an introduction to the pervasive and core topics, and is designed for those with little or no previous knowledge of the subjects. It has been written primarily to support and complement the Legal Practice Course undertaken by trainee solicitors. The approach taken to the subjects is essentially practical and is enhanced by worked examples showing the application of the topics in a practical context.

For the sake of brevity, the masculine pronoun is used to include the feminine. To refer to 'he or she' on every occasion when such a reference was necessary would have added many extra pages to an already lengthy book.

We would like to thank our colleagues at The College of Law for their help in the preparation of this book, particularly Michael Hughes, Jane Chapman, Paula McWhirter and Hellen Revenko, who wrote the first edition of parts of the Revenue section. Thanks are also due to Andrea Cartledge and Richard Halberstadt, who co-wrote the Professional Conduct and Financial Services section in previous years, and to Martin Norris. Matthew Trigg would like to thank Gayle for her support, and Halflab for their good humour and facilities.

The law is stated as at May 2008.

KEIR BAMFORD
SHEILA BRAMLEY
KEVIN BROWNE
LESLEY KING
ANTHONY MORGAN
SARAH POOLEY
MATTHEW TRIGG
The College of Law

Contents

Table of Cases

D

E

F

G

H

Table of Statutes

Table of Statutory Instruments and Codes of Practice

Table of European and International Legislation

International legislation

Table of Abbreviations

AEA 1925	Administration of Estates Act 1925
AEA 1971	Administration of Estates Act 1971
AIM	Alternative Investment Market
APR	annual percentage rate
ATP	authorised third persons
CCS	Consumer Complaints Service
CFI	Court of First Instance
CGT	capital gains tax
COB Rules 2001	Solicitors' Financial Services (Conduct of Business) Rules 2001
COREPER	Committee of Permanent Representatives
CPR	Civil Procedure Rules 1998
CTM	Community trade mark
CTO	Capital Taxes Office
DIB	discrete investment business
DPB	designated professional body
EAT	Employment Appeal Tribunal
ECA 1972	European Communities Act 1972
ECHR	European Convention for the Protection of Human Rights and Fundamental Freedoms 1950
ECJ	European Court of Justice
ECSC	European Coal and Steel Community
ECtHR	European Court of Human Rights
EEA	European Economic Area
EEIG	European Economic Interest Grouping
EFTA	European Free Trade Agreement
EIS	Enterprise Investment Scheme
ESC	Economic and Social Committee
EurAtom	European Atomic Energy Community
EWCs	European Work Councils
FPO 2005	Financial Services and Markets Act 2000 (Financial Promotion) Order 2005
FSA	Financial Services Authority
FSMA 2000	Financial Services and Markets Act 2000
HMRC	HM Revenue & Customs
HRA 1998	Human Rights Act 1998
ICTA 1988	Income and Corporation Taxes Act 1988
IHT	inheritance tax
IHTA 1984	Inheritance Tax Act 1984
IP	intellectual property
I(PFD)A 1975	Inheritance (Provision for Family and Dependants) Act 1975
IPDI	immediate post-death interest
ISA	Individual Savings Account
ITA 2007	Income Tax Act 2007
ITEPA 2003	Income Tax (Earnings and Pensions) Act 2003
ITTOIA 2005	Income Tax (Trading and Other Income) Act 2005
LCS	Legal Complaints Service
LCT	lifetime chargeable transfer
LPA 1925	Law of Property Act 1925
MEP	member of the European Parliament
MEQR	measure equivalent to a quantitative restriction
NCPR 1987	Non-Contentious Probate Rules 1987
non-DIB	non-discrete investment business
OEICs	open-ended investment companies
PA	personal allowance
PAYE	Pay As You Earn
PEP	Personal Equity Plan
PET	potentially exempt transfer
PIA	personal investment authority
PR	personal representative

PTP	permitted third party
QLTT	Qualified Lawyers Transfer Test
RAO 2001	Financial Services and Markets Act 2000 (Regulated Activities) Order 2001
RPB	Recognised Professional Body
RPI	Retail Prices Index
Scope Rules 2001	Solicitors' Financial Services (Scope) Rules 2001
SIB	Securities and Investment Board
SIBR 1995	Solicitors' Investment Business Rules 1995
SLA 1925	Settled Land Act 1925
SRA	Solicitors Regulation Authority
SRO	self-regulating organisation
TA 1925	Trustee Act 1925
TA 2000	Trustee Act 2000
TEU	Treaty on European Union
TIA 1961	Trustee Investments Act 1961
TLATA 1996	Trusts of Land and Appointment of Trustees Act 1996
VATA 1994	Value Added Tax Act 1994
VCT	Venture Capital Trust

Part I

REVENUE LAW

Chapter 1

Value Added Tax

1.1 Introduction

1.1.1 Sources of VAT law

The main charging statute relating to Value Added Tax (VAT) is the Value Added Tax Act 1994 (VATA 1994), as amended by later Finance Acts and certain statutory instruments. Detailed provisions implementing the Act are to be found in the VAT (General) Regulations 1995 (SI 1995/2518) and other statutory instruments. In addition, HM Revenue & Customs (HMRC) issues VAT Notices which, although lacking legal force, express its views on the law. Value added tax was introduced in 1973 in order to harmonise UK law with European Community law, therefore EC Directives 67/227 and 77/338 are also relevant. The standard practioner's work is De Voil, *Indirect Tax Service* (Butterworths, looseleaf).

1.1.2 Charge to tax

Generally, VAT is charged whenever a business supplies goods or services. The business charges the customer VAT at 17.5% on the value of the goods or services. This is known as 'output tax'. The business deducts from the output tax which it collects any VAT it has paid ('input tax') on goods or services received and pays the difference to HMRC.

	Value of goods (£)	VAT charged to buyer (£)	VAT paid to HMRC (£)
(a) A manufacturer buys raw material costing £200 plus VAT from a producer	200	35	
Producer pays to HMRC			35
(b) The manufacturer sells finished article to a retailer for £1,000 plus VAT	1,000	175	
Manufacturer pays to HMRC			140 (175 – 35)
(c) The retailer sells the finished article to a consumer for £2,000 plus VAT	2,000	350	
Retailer pays to HMRC			175 (350 – 175)
Total paid to HMRC			350

Note: (a) VAT does not cost the business anything as any VAT paid is recouped from VAT charged.

(b)   Each business accounts for VAT on the 'value added' to the goods whilst in the possession of the business. The value added by the manufacturer is £800 (£1,000 – £200). 17.5% of £800 is £140, the sum paid to HMRC.

(c)   The ultimate burden falls on the consumer, who pays £2,000 plus £350 VAT for the product. The £350 VAT has been paid to HMRC in three stages.

1.2   Charge to VAT

1.2.1   Definition

Value added tax is 'charged on any supply of goods or services made in the United Kingdom where it is a taxable supply made by a taxable person in the course or furtherance of any business carried on by him' (VATA 1994, s 4(1)). Tax will be charged on the 'value of the supply' (VATA 1994, s 2(1)). The elements of this charge are defined widely, in order both to prevent avoidance and to comply with the Directives, and are dealt with in outline below.

1.2.2   Supply of goods or services

1.2.2.1   Supply of goods

Any transfer of the whole property in goods is a supply of goods (VATA 1994, Sch 4). As well as more obvious transactions like the sale of consumer goods, this includes a supply of power or heat, the grant of an interest in land, and even a gift of goods.

1.2.2.2   Supply of services

Anything that is not a supply of goods but which is done for a consideration is a supply of services (VATA 1994, s 5(2)). This includes the provision of a solicitor's services for a fee, but not a gratuitous supply of services.

1.2.3   Taxable supply

Any supply of goods or services (other than an exempt supply) is taxable (VATA 1994, s 4(2)). Exempt supplies are listed in VATA 1994, Sch 9 and include supplies of residential land, insurance, postal services, education and health services.

1.2.4   Taxable person

A taxable person is a person who makes or intends to make taxable supplies and who is or is required to be registered under the Act (VATA 1994, s 3(1)). A person is required to register if he makes taxable supplies in a defined period which have exceeded a limit, which is set each year, or will exceed that limit. Currently, a person must register if the value of his taxable supplies in the preceding 12 months exceeded £67,000.

Any person who makes taxable supplies is entitled to be registered if he so requests (see **1.3.4**). A person who makes only exempt supplies cannot register.

Once registered, a taxable person (individual, partnership or company) receives a VAT number which is issued for all businesses operated by that person.

1.2.5 Course of business

'Business' includes any trade, profession or vocation (VATA 1994, s 94). A supply in the course of business includes the disposal of a business or any of its assets.

1.2.6 Value of supply

Value added tax is charged on the value of the supply of goods or services. This is what the goods or services would cost were VAT not charged and is often shown as part of the price. For example, a television may be advertised as costing '£400 plus VAT'. £400 is the value of the supply.

If the supply is shown as being for a VAT inclusive amount (eg, a television costs '£235'), the value of supply is 'such amount as, with the addition of the tax chargeable, is equal to the consideration' (VATA 1994, s 19(2)). In the case of the television, the value of supply would be £200 and the VAT £35. A price is deemed to include VAT unless the contrary is stated.

If the supply is not for a consideration in money, the value of supply is taken to be its market value (VATA 1994, s 19(3)).

1.2.7 Rate of tax

The standard rate of VAT is 17.5%. However, there is a large category of supplies which are taxed at 0%. 'Zero-rated' supplies are listed in VATA 1994, Sch 8 and include food, other than food supplied in the course of catering, water, books and newspapers, transport and construction of dwellings. A reduced rate of 5% is applied to certain supplies, including domestic fuel, installation of energy-saving materials and child car seats (VATA 1994, Sch 7A).

1.2.8 Time of supply

A taxable person must account for VAT one month after the end of each quarter (see **1.3.1**). The time of supply (tax point) determines the accounting period within which a supply of goods or services falls.

In the case of goods, the basic tax point is the time goods are removed, or the time they are made available to the person to whom they are supplied. In the case of services, the basic tax point is the time the services are performed (VATA 1994, s 6).

The basic tax point can be varied in a number of cases. For example, it can be brought forward, if the supplier issues a tax invoice (see **1.3.5**) or receives a payment, to the time when the invoice is issued or payment received. It can be delayed, if the supplier issues a tax invoice within 14 days after the basic tax point, to the time when the invoice is issued. Thus the time for accounting for VAT may be brought forward or delayed.

1.3 Tax payable to HM Revenue & Customs

1.3.1 Introduction

A person who is registered for VAT must send a return to HMRC showing the VAT payable by him, together with a cheque for this amount, generally within one month after the end of each quarter.

The amount payable is the VAT he has charged on all supplies of goods and services in the course of his business ('output tax'), less any VAT he has paid in the course of his business ('input tax'). If input tax exceeds output tax, the person will receive a rebate.

1.3.2   Zero-rated and exempt supplies

Zero-rated and exempt supplies are similar to each other, in that the customer does not pay any VAT. However, a person who makes zero-rated supplies will be able to reclaim the VAT he has paid from HMRC. A person who makes only exempt supplies cannot register (see **1.2.4**) and so cannot reclaim VAT.

Example

A baker and a doctor in private practice are converting premises into a shop and a surgery respectively. They will both pay VAT on the cost of their conversions. The baker, who makes zero-rated supplies of food, will be able to reclaim the VAT; the doctor, who makes exempt supplies of health services, will not be able to do so.

1.3.3   Taxable and exempt supplies

Where a person makes both exempt and taxable supplies, for example a doctor in private practice who also acts as an expert witness in personal injury claims, only part of his input tax will be deductible from the output tax charged on the fees for acting as an expert witness (see the VAT (General) Regulations 1995, SI 1995/2518).

1.3.4   Voluntary registration

A person who makes taxable supplies of less than £67,000 per annum is not required to register and charge VAT. This can be an advantage as such a supplier may be able to undercut larger rivals who are obliged to charge VAT.

However, only those people who are registered can reclaim any input tax they have paid. For example, a builder with a small business who bought a van could not reclaim VAT payable on the purchase of the van if he were not registered.

When deciding whether to register voluntarily, people in business must weigh up the advantage of being able to reclaim VAT against the disadvantage that customers might be put off by higher prices.

1.3.5   Tax invoices

A person making a taxable supply to a taxable person must provide him with a tax invoice. A tax invoice is an ordinary invoice or bill which contains specified information about the transaction, such as the VAT number, the tax point, the value of supply and the rate of tax charged.

The tax invoice is important because a person who is claiming to deduct input tax must have tax invoices in respect of all the tax claimed.

1.4   Penalties

1.4.1   Introduction

A person who fails to comply with the VAT legislation is liable to a range of criminal and civil penalties in addition to being required to pay any unpaid tax with interest. There are very few defences to these provisions, although, apart from the default surcharge (see **1.4.5**), the civil penalties may be mitigated. A number of these penalties are dealt with in outline below.

1.4.2   Fraudulent evasion of tax

A person knowingly concerned in the fraudulent evasion of tax is liable, on conviction on indictment, to an unlimited fine and imprisonment for a term not exceeding seven years (VATA 1994, s 72).

1.4.3 Failure to register

Where a person who is liable to register fails to do so, he will be liable to a civil penalty of a percentage of the tax for which he was liable during the period when he should have been registered. This percentage rises from 5% to 15% where the failure lasts more than 18 months (VATA 1994, s 67).

1.4.4 Breaches of regulations

Regulations impose many obligations on taxable persons. Breach of a regulation will lead to a civil penalty. There is a penalty of £500 for failure to keep certain records. Other breaches attract a penalty calculated at a daily rate over the period of the breach (VATA 1994, s 69).

1.4.5 The default surcharge

A person who fails to send a return (see **1.3.1**) is regarded as being in default. If he is persistently in default he becomes liable to a surcharge rising to 15% of the tax for any period in which he was in default (VATA 1994, s 59).

Chapter 2

Income Tax

2.1 Introduction

2.1.1 The importance of income tax

Income tax is the tax which produces the greatest revenue for the UK Government. For example, in the most recent year for which figures are available (2007/08), income tax generated £150.5 billion. Income tax is, therefore, a vital source of revenue from which public services such as health, education, welfare, transport and defence can be funded. Income tax is collected by HM Revenue & Customs (HMRC) (see **2.8**).

2.1.2 Sources of income tax law

2.1.2.1 Statute

The charging statute for income tax is the Income Tax Act 2007 (ITA 2007) as amended by later Finance Acts. Also of importance are the Income Tax (Trading and Other Income) Act 2005 (ITTOIA 2005) and the Income Tax (Earnings and Pensions) Act 2003 (ITEPA 2003).

Income tax is an annual tax renewed each year by Act of Parliament.

2.1.2.2 Case law

The meaning and extent of the statutory provisions are decided by the judiciary.

An appeal by a taxpayer against an assessment to tax is heard either by a tribunal of General Commissioners, or by Special Commissioners. An appeal is usually heard by the General Commissioners unless the case is particularly complicated, technical or lengthy. Appeals from the decision of the Commissioners on a point of law are made to the High Court. There is a right of appeal from the High Court to the Court of Appeal and, with leave, to the House of Lords. Alternatively, the 'leapfrog' procedure may be used to appeal direct to the House of Lords.

2.1.2.3 Official Statements

There would be an impossible workload if all questions as to the meaning and extent of tax legislation were taken to court. Official Statements made by HMRC are therefore an important source of information. The two most important types of statement are Extra-Statutory Concessions and Statements of Practice.

Extra-Statutory Concessions

These are published by HMRC in a booklet. If a taxpayer satisfies the terms of an Extra-Statutory Concession, HMRC waives its right to collect tax which would otherwise be due.

Statements of Practice

These are announced by press release and published in the professional journals. They indicate what view HMRC will take of particular tax provisions.

Note that these Official Statements do not bind the courts.

2.1.3 What is income?

There is no statutory definition of 'income' and the courts have failed to impose a judicial definition. A distinction must be made between income and capital profits: the former is subject to income tax; the latter are subject to capital gains tax. Generally, money received will be income if there is an element of recurrence, for example, a salary or partnership profit share received every month, or interest paid on a bank or building society account every quarter.

2.1.4 Who pays income tax?

The following are liable to pay income tax:

(a)   individuals;

(b)   partnerships (partners are individually responsible for the tax due on their share of partnership profits);

(c)   personal representatives (who pay the deceased's outstanding income tax and income tax chargeable during the administration of the estate); and

(d)   trustees (who pay income tax on the income produced by the trust fund).

Companies pay corporation tax (see *Business Law and Practice*).

Charities are generally exempt from paying tax. There are tax efficient ways of giving money to charities, for example, Gift Aid.

2.1.5 The tax year

Income tax is paid with reference to the 'tax year' or 'year of assessment', which runs from 6 April until 5 April. It is referred to by the calendar years which it straddles: for example, the tax year beginning on 6 April 2008 is referred to as the tax year 2008/09. So, in the simple tax calculation below at **2.1.7**, Amy's salary received between 6 April 2008 and 5 April 2009 will be charged to tax in the tax year 2008/09.

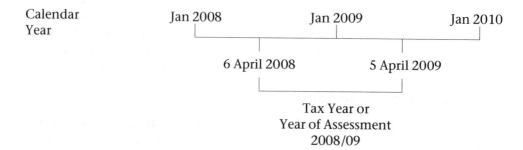

Calculating Income Tax

2.1.6 How much income tax is payable?

The steps to work through to calculate the amount of tax payable are as follows:

Step 1:   Calculate the total income

↓

Step 2:   Deduct any allowable reliefs

↓

The resulting sum is net income

↓

Step 3:   Deduct any personal allowances

↓

The resulting sum is taxable income

↓

Step 4:   Calculate the tax on the taxable income at the applicable rate(s) (starting rate, basic rate and higher rate)

↓

Step 5:   Add together the amounts of tax from Step 4 (to give the overall income tax liability)

Note: As explained below, income tax is charged on an individual's taxable income for 2008/09 at a variety of rates ranging from 10% to 40% (depending on the amount and type of income).

2.1.7 Simple income tax calculation

The five steps may be used to carry out a simple tax calculation. For example, Amy has the following income for 2008/09: £60,000 salary as an executive and £8,835 from writing learned articles. She is liable to make interest payments of £2,000 per annum on a qualifying loan. Amy is a single person. Amy's income tax may be calculated as follows:

		£
STEP 1	Calculate the total income	
	Salary	60,000
	Learned articles	8,835
	TOTAL INCOME	68,835
STEP 2	Deduct any allowable reliefs (interest)	2,000
	NET INCOME	66,835
STEP 3	Deduct any personal allowance	6,035
	TAXABLE INCOME	60,800
STEP 4	Calculate the tax at the applicable rate(s)	
	£34,800 at 20%	6,960
	£26,000 at 40%	10,400
	£60,800	
STEP 5	Add together the amounts of tax from Step 4	
	OVERALL INCOME TAX LIABILITY	17,360

The calculation above indicates the principles used to establish an individual's liability to income tax. The remainder of this chapter will consider each step of the calculation in more detail.

2.2 Total income

Total income is the aggregate of the taxpayer's income from all sources which is charged to income tax.

2.2.1 What income is charged to income tax?

2.2.1.1 The chargeable sources of income

Income is charged to income tax if it comes from a source specified by the ITTOIA 2005 and the ITEPA 2003. The most important sources are listed below.

Location	Source
ITTOIA 2005	
Part 2	Trading income (Profits of a trade, profession or vocation. Part 2 therefore charges the self-employed and applies to sole traders, trading partnerships, sole practitioners and professional partnerships)
Part 3	Property income (Rents and other receipts from land in the UK)
Part 4	Savings and investment income (Interest, annuities and dividends)
Part 5	Certain miscellaneous income (Annual income not otherwise charged)
ITEPA 2003	Employment and pensions income (Income arising out of employment and including social security payments such as sick pay and maternity payments)

2.2.1.2 How do the chargeable sources of income work?

If income is shown to be derived from one of the sources, it will be charged to income tax. For example, if an individual receives rent from land, he will pay income tax under Part 3 of the ITTOIA 2005. Income not having a chargeable source cannot be charged to income tax at all.

2.2.1.3 Why is it divided into chargeable sources?

Each Part of the ITTOIA 2005 and the ITEPA 2003 has its own rules for calculating the amount of income. For example, under Part 3 of the ITTOIA 2005 (which taxes income from land) the charge is on rents and other receipts, but the landlord may deduct expenses such as repairs on the property, ie expenses of an income nature. This means that income tax is charged on the profit element rather than the gross income.

Further details of how the ITTOIA 2005 and the ITEPA 2003 operate can be found in *Business Law and Practice*.

2.2.2 Exempt income

Certain items are free of income tax. They include:

(a)   certain social security benefits (eg child benefit);

(b)   interest on National Savings Certificates;

(c)   scholarships;

(d)   interest on damages for personal injuries or death;

(e)   income from investments in an individual savings account (ISA) (see **5.3**);

(f)   dividends paid in a Personal Equity Plan (PEP): no further subscriptions permitted after 5 April 1999;

(g)   gross income up to £4,250 a year from letting a furnished room;

(h)   annual payments under certain insurance policies, for example, where insurance benefits are provided in times of sickness; and

(i)   premium bond winnings.

Most of the above items are set out in the ITTOIA 2005, Part 6 (Exempt Income). In addition, a number of items are exempted from tax because of Extra-Statutory Concessions (see **2.1.2.3**).

2.2.3   Calculating the total income

It should now be possible to calculate the total income.

The total income is the aggregate of chargeable income computed according to the rules of the various chargeable sources. To work out the total income of a taxpayer it is necessary to find out what sources of income he has, calculate the income arising under each source and then add all the '*gross*' income together. For example:

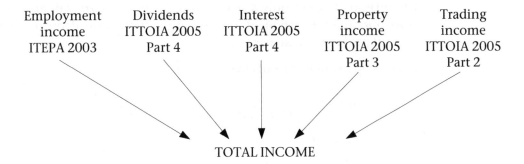

| Employment income ITEPA 2003 | Dividends ITTOIA 2005 Part 4 | Interest ITTOIA 2005 Part 4 | Property income ITTOIA 2005 Part 3 | Trading income ITTOIA 2005 Part 2 |

TOTAL INCOME

Some types of income are received by the taxpayer without any tax having been deducted prior to receipt. These types of income are said to be received 'gross'. The principal types of income received gross are:

(a)   trading income (ITTOIA 2005, Part 2); and

(b)   property income (ITTOIA 2005, Part 3).

2.2.3.1   Grossing up

For certain types of other income, tax will have been deducted at source. The payee receives the net amount, not the gross amount. This is to ensure a steady flow of tax to HMRC and then on to central government to fund public services throughout the year. The three principal types of income that suffer this deduction of tax at source are:

(a)   interest (ITTOIA 2005, Part 4);

(b)   dividends (ITTOIA 2005, Part 4); and

(c)   employment income (ITEPA 2003).

Any sum received after deduction of tax at source must be grossed up to find the original sum from which the tax was deducted. This gross figure must be entered into the payee's calculation of total income. This is because the tax calculation is a way of checking that, overall, the taxpayer pays the right amount of tax.

At the end of the tax calculation the tax that has already been paid will be credited to the taxpayer so that he will owe HMRC only the outstanding amount.

2.2.3.2 Interest

Interest received is assessable under ITTOIA 2005, Part 4. If the interest is paid by banks and building societies to individuals or personal representatives, it is paid after deduction of income tax at 20%, ie the interest is paid net.

Gross amount £100

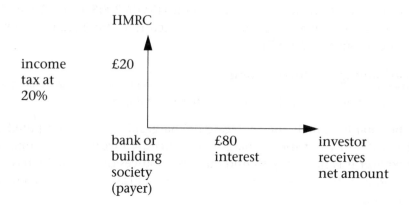

The investor receives only a net amount (and a written statement showing the gross amount of the payment, the amount of income tax deducted and the actual amount paid to the taxpayer).

To gross up a simple formula may be used:

$$\text{interest} \times \frac{100}{(100 - \text{rate at which tax deducted})}$$

=   net interest of

$$£800 \times \frac{100}{(100 - 20)}$$

= $$£800 \times \frac{100}{80}$$

=   £1,000 gross interest

Another way of grossing up at 20% is to divide the sum received by 4 and then multiply by 5, for example:

$$£800 \times \frac{5}{4} = £1,000 \text{ gross interest}$$

2.2.3.3 Salaries and other employment income

Salaries and other employment income are assessable under ITEPA 2003 using the Pay As You Earn system (PAYE). Under the PAYE system, the employer deducts from the employee's salary and then pays to HMRC income tax at the appropriate rate at the time the salary is paid. The PAYE system also takes account of personal allowances.

Gross amount £100

Employment income cannot be grossed up using a simple formula because deduction at source may not be just at one single rate. Under the PAYE scheme, income tax at various rates will be deducted from salaries by the employer using tables and information supplied by HMRC and taking into account the employee's personal reliefs. A certificate of tax paid (P60), showing the gross figure, is given by the employer to the employee on a yearly basis and he can put this figure into his tax return. A taxpayer must complete a tax return if he has other sources of income.

2.2.3.4 Dividends

Dividends from companies are assessed under ITTOIA 2005, Part 4. The dividend paid to the shareholder carries a tax credit. The rate of credit is determined by reference to the 'tax credit fraction' which is initially fixed at one-ninth. This is equivalent to a tax credit of 10% of the sum of the dividend and the credit. For example, if a company pays a dividend of £900 on 1 June 2008 the credit will be £100 (one-ninth of £900) which is 10% of £1,000 (£900 plus the credit of £100).

The ITTOIA 2005, Part 4 income assessable is the sum of the dividend and the tax credit (£900 plus the credit of £100).

To gross up a simple formula may be used:

$$\text{dividend} \times \frac{100}{(100 - \text{tax credit rate})}$$

$$= \text{net dividend of } £900 \times \frac{100}{(100 - 10)}$$

$$= £900 \times \frac{100}{90}$$

= £1,000 gross dividend

Another way of grossing up at 10% is to divide the sum received by 9 and then multiply by 10. For example:

$$£900 \times \frac{10}{9} = £1,000 \text{ gross dividend}$$

Once the gross figures have been calculated for the relevant Parts of the ITTOIA 2005, the aggregate of those figures forms the total income of the taxpayer.

2.3 Allowable reliefs

2.3.1 Net income

Net income is total income less certain specified commitments known as allowable reliefs, for example interest on qualifying loans. Allowable reliefs remove sums of money from the income tax calculation.

2.3.2   Interest payments on qualifying loans

Most interest payments receive no tax relief at all, for example ordinary bank overdrafts, credit card interest and hire purchase interest payments. The borrower pays the interest out of taxed income.

However, in certain cases, tax relief may be available for interest paid on money borrowed. A taxpayer obtains income tax relief for certain interest payments by deducting them from his total income as an allowable relief. To obtain tax relief, interest must be payable on a 'qualifying loan'.

Qualifying loans include the following.   *Relief against tax.*

2.3.2.1   A loan to buy a share in a partnership or to contribute capital or make a loan to a partnership

Example

Dawn, a partner, has total income of £25,000. She borrows £10,000 to make a loan to the partnership to be used wholly and exclusively for partnership business. The interest rate on the loan is 7% per annum. Dawn's net income is:

	£
Total income	25,000
Deduct any allowable reliefs (interest on qualifying loan)	700
Net income	24,300

See *Business Law and Practice* for further details.

2.3.2.2   A loan to invest in a close trading company

See *Business Law and Practice*.

2.3.2.3   A loan to personal representatives to pay inheritance tax

See **30.6.3.5**.

2.4   Personal allowances

Personal allowances are deducted from net income to obtain the taxpayer's taxable income. This means that a certain amount of income is tax free each year.

A summary of the personal allowances available for 2008/09 is set out below:

	£
Personal allowance (PA)	6,035
Aged 65 but under 75	9,030
Aged 75 or over	9,180
Blind person's allowance	1,800
Income limit for age-related allowances	21,800

It can be seen that the availability of allowances depends not on the type of income involved but on the taxpayer's personal circumstances, for example age or disability. The taxpayer must claim his allowances each year in his income tax return. If personal allowances exceed the net income of the taxpayer, the surplus is unused and cannot be carried forward for use in future years.

The principal allowances available and deducted at this stage are as follows.

2.4.1 Personal allowance

This allowance may be claimed by taxpayers resident in the UK, male or female, adult or child, married or single. It may be set against income of any kind. The personal allowance is increased where the taxpayer is aged 65 or over and has only a limited net income. It is increased further when the taxpayer is aged 75 or over (subject to the same net income limit).

Husband and wife are treated as separate single people. Each spouse is independently liable for tax on his or her own income with his or her own personal allowances.

2.4.2 Blind person's allowance

A taxpayer who is a registered blind person receives this relief. If a husband and wife are both registered blind they can each claim the blind person's allowance.

2.5 Rates of tax

2.5.1 Types of income

The taxable income is taxed at the appropriate rate or rates. The rates are different for the various types of income. Before the rates can be applied, therefore, the different types of income must be separated from one another into two categories. The categories are:

(a)   Non-savings/dividend income, comprising all sources of income except savings/dividend income.
(b)   Savings/dividend income comprising interest and dividends.

To find out how much taxable income is comprised of non-savings/dividend income and how much of savings/dividend income, the following calculation is required:

Taxable income
Less **Gross** savings/dividend income
=   Non-savings/dividend income

(This calculation ensures that the taxpayer gets the maximum allowed benefit from any deductions of any allowable reliefs and the personal allowance as non-savings/dividend income is taxed at a higher rate than savings/dividend income.)

2.5.2 Non-savings/dividend income

Once the non-savings/dividend income has been calculated, it is taxed at the basic rate and higher rate. These rates are fixed annually, and for the tax year 2008/09 the rates are as follows:

'Basic rate' of 20%	£0–£34,800
'Higher rate' of 40%	over £34,800

Example

Timothy has a taxable income of £60,500, of which £20,000 is gross savings/dividend income. Timothy's non-savings/dividend income amounts to:

Taxable income	£60,500
Less Gross savings/dividend income	£20,000
Non-savings/dividend income	£40,500

Timothy's non-savings/dividend income will be taxed as follows:

£34,800 @ 20%	£6,960
£5,700 @ 40%	£2,280
£40,500	£9,240

2.5.3 Savings/dividend income

Any savings/dividend income is taxed after any non-savings/dividend income. Savings/dividend income is, therefore, treated as the top slice of taxable income. Dividends are treated as the top slice of savings/dividend income (see diagram below).

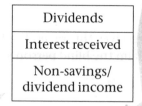

Savings/dividend income

2.5.3.1 Interest received

Interest received is taxed at the starting rate for savings, basic rate and higher rate. For the tax year 2008/09 the rates are as follows;

'Starting rate' for savings of 10%	£0–£2,320
'Basic rate' of 20%	£2,321–£34,800
'Higher rate' of 40%	over £34,800

Having first taxed the non-savings/dividend income, any interest received which falls below the starting rate limit is taxed at 10%. Interest received which falls between the starting and basic rate limits is taxed at the basic rate of 20%; any excess over the basic rate limit is taxed at the 40% higher rate.

Example 1

An individual with taxable income (after allowances and reliefs) of £2,320, of which £1,820 is non-savings/dividend income and £500 is interest (including the tax deducted at source), will be liable to tax:

(a)   at the basic rate of 20% on the first £1,820 of non-savings/dividend income; and

(b)   at the starting rate for savings of 10% on the 'top slice' of £500 of savings income.

Example 2

An individual with taxable income (after allowances and reliefs) of £5,000 of which £4,500 is non-savings/dividend income and £500 is interest (including the tax deducted at source), will be liable to tax:

(a)   at the basic rate of 20% on the first £4,500 of non-savings/dividend income; and

(b)   at the basic rate of 20% on the 'top slice' of £500 of savings income.

Example 3

An individual with taxable income (after allowances and reliefs) of £36,000, of which £26,000 is non-savings/dividend income and £10,000 is interest (including the tax deducted at source), will be liable to tax:

(a)   at the basic rate of 20% on the £26,000 of non-savings/dividend income.

(b)   The savings income will be taxed:

(i)   at the basic rate of 20% to the extent that it falls below the basic rate limit of £34,800, so £8,800 (£34,800 – £26,000) will be taxed at 20%; and

(ii)   at the higher rate of 40% on the remaining £1,200.

2.5.3.2 Dividends

Dividend income is treated as the top slice of taxable income in priority to interest received. To the extent that dividend income falls within the basic rate limit, it is taxed at 10% (dividend ordinary rate). To the extent that dividend income exceeds the basic rate limit, it is taxed at 32.5% (dividend upper rate).

Example 1

An individual with taxable income (after allowances and reliefs) of £5,000, of which £4,500 is non-savings/dividend income and £500 is dividend income (including the tax credit), will be liable to tax:

(a) at the basic rate of 20% on the first £4,500 of non-savings/dividend income; and

(b) at the dividend ordinary rate of 10% on the 'top slice' of £500 of dividend income.

Example 2

An individual with taxable income (after allowances and reliefs) of £36,000, of which £26,000 is non-savings/dividend income and £10,000 is dividend income (including the tax credit), will be liable to tax:

(a) at the basic rate of 20% on the £26,000 of non-savings/dividend income.

(b) The dividend income will be taxed:

    (i) at the dividend ordinary rate of 10% to the extent that it falls below the basic rate limit of £34,800, so £8,800 (£34,800 – £26,000) will be taxed at 10%; and

    (ii) at the dividend upper rate of 32.5% on the remaining £1,200.

2.6 Calculating the tax due

The five steps described above will enable a taxpayer to calculate his overall tax liability for a tax year. There are, however, several deductions that can be made before the amount owing to HMRC is finalised.

2.6.1 Tax deducted at source

When payments are received by the taxpayer after deduction at source, the tax due from the payee will be reduced by the tax already paid on his behalf by the payer, ie the amount of the tax deducted operates as a reduction in the taxpayer's liability to income tax. Most commonly this will apply to the following.

2.6.1.1 Salaries and other employment income

Tax is deducted at source using the PAYE system (see **2.2.3.3**). The amount of tax paid (shown in a taxpayer's P60) is deducted from the taxpayer's overall tax liability. If the tax paid exceeds that liability, a refund will be due.

2.6.1.2 Interest received

The 20% tax deducted at source (as calculated as part of the grossing-up calculation – see **2.2.3.1**) is deducted from the taxpayer's overall tax liability. Again, a refund will be payable if the tax paid exceeds that liability.

2.6.2 Tax credits

2.6.2.1 Dividends

The 10% tax credit for dividends is deducted from the taxpayer's overall tax liability, but tax credits are not reclaimable if they exceed the overall tax liability.

2.7 A full income tax calculation

Frederick carries on a business in partnership and his total income from the partnership's trade for 2008/09 is £31,500. However, to buy his share of this partnership he took out a loan from the Blankshire Bank, and the interest on that loan is £1,665 per annum.

Frederick also has an account at the Guildfleet Building Society on which he receives net interest of £2,000 in 2008/09. He also owns shares in a company and receives dividends of £9,000 net in 2008/09.

To calculate Frederick's tax bill for 2008/09:

	Net	Gross	Tax credits
	£	£	£
Step 1: Calculate total income			
Trade profits (ITTOIA 2005, Part 2)		31,500	
Interest (ITTOIA 2005, Part 4)	2,000	2,500	500
Dividends (ITTOIA 2005, Part 4)	9,000	10,000	1,000
Total Income		44,000	1,500
Step 2: Deduct allowable reliefs			
Loan interest to Blankshire Bank		1,665	
Net Income		42,335	
Step 3: Deduct personal allowances			
Personal Allowance		6,035	
Taxable Income		36,300	

Step 4: Calculate tax at the applicable rate(s)

The gross amount of Frederick's interest received is £2,500.

The gross amount of Frederick's dividends is £10,000

The non-savings/dividend element of his taxable income is:

Taxable income	£36,300
Less Gross savings/dividend income	£12,500
= Non-savings/dividend income	£23,800

	£		£
Non-savings/dividend income	23,800	@ 20% =	4,760

(This non-savings/dividend element of Frederick's taxable income falls £11,000 short of the £34,800 basic rate limit. The interest received therefore falls within the basic rate limit, so it is taxed at the basic rate of 20%.)

Savings income:

	£		£
Interest received	2,500	@ 20% =	500

(To the extent that dividend income falls within the remaining basic rate limit of £34,800, it is taxed at the dividend ordinary rate of 10%; the excess over the basic rate limit is taxed at the dividend upper rate of 32.5%.)

Dividend income	8,500	@ 10% =	850.00
	1,500	@ 32.5% =	487.50
	10,000		
	36,300		

Step 5: Add together the amounts of tax from Step 4

OVERALL INCOME TAX LIABILITY   6,597.50

Less
Tax credits (£500 + £1,000)   1,500.00

Income tax to pay   5,097.50

Although Frederick's total income is £44,000, because of the deduction of reliefs and allowances he pays tax only on £36,300 and is able to deduct from his overall tax liability the tax deducted at source and the 10% tax credit for dividends.

2.8   Collection of income tax and dates for payment

2.8.1   HM Revenue & Customs

Before considering the collection of income tax (see **2.8.2**), it is worth noting that HMRC is also responsible for:

(a)   administering corporation tax, capital gains tax, petroleum revenue tax, inheritance tax, stamp duties, VAT, customs duties and excise duties;

(b)   collecting National Insurance contributions;

(c)   advising on tax policy;

(d)   advising on valuation policy and providing valuation services;

(e)   enforcing the National Minimum Wage; and

(f)   recovering student loan repayments.

2.8.2   Collection of income tax: deduction at source

There are two methods of collection of tax: deduction at source and the self-assessment regime.

As explained above (see **2.2.3**), for certain types of income, tax is deducted at source. The payer of the income acts as a tax collector by deducting from the payment the appropriate amount of income tax and handing it to HMRC. The taxpayer therefore receives the payment net of income tax.

2.8.3   Collection of income tax: self-assessment

The self-assessment regime covers all income tax due. There is a set of payment dates for all sources of income and a single tax bill for the year. However, where income tax has been deducted at source, the taxpayer will declare this income on his tax return and his overall tax liability will be reduced by the amount of income tax already paid.

Examples of when income will be declared on a tax return and the appropriate amount of income tax collected under the self-assessment regime are:

(a)   Trading profit (ITTOIA 2005, Part 2). Any income profits of a trade which a taxpayer has made will be assessed under ITTOIA 2005, Part 2 and collected under the self-assessment regime.

(b)   Rent (ITTOIA 2005, Part 3). A landlord (taxpayer) receiving gross rent from the tenant will be assessed to tax under ITTOIA 2005, Part 3 and any income tax payable will be collected under the self-assessment regime.

The self-assessment method assumes that the taxpayer has actually received the sum on which he is to pay tax and can send part of it to HMRC to satisfy his income tax liability. There is a risk that the taxpayer will spend the income received before HMRC can claim its share.

2.8.3.1   The tax return

Under the self-assessment regime, the taxpayer completes an annual tax return, which includes computation pages to enable the taxpayer to calculate his own income tax. Tax returns are issued soon after 5 April. There are different returns for different types of income.

Even if a taxpayer does not normally receive a tax return, there is a statutory obligation to notify HMRC that he has income that is liable to tax. This must be done within six months of the end of the relevant tax year. There is a penalty for default.

2.8.3.2   Dates for payment

The tax return and any payment must be filed by 31 January following the tax year to which the return relates. If the taxpayer would rather have HMRC calculate his liability, he must submit his return by 30 September following the tax year, and a paper return must be submitted no later than 31 October in any event.

The taxpayer is automatically required to make two payments on account towards the income tax due for any year, and then a third and final balancing payment to meet any tax still outstanding. The first payment on account is due on 31 January in the tax year in question. The second payment on account is due on 31 July after the end of the tax year. Any balancing payment is due on the next 31 January.

Each payment on account should be approximately one half of the income tax liability for the year. They are calculated by reference to the previous year's income tax liability, and are reduced to give credit for tax deducted at source. No payments on account are required if this 'relevant amount' is below a certain limit. This limit is set at a level that ensures most employees and pensioners (and others who receive the bulk of their income after deduction of income tax at source or who have relatively small outstanding tax liabilities) do not have to make payments on account.

Example

Josie's income tax liability for 2007/08 came to £15,000, of which £7,000 was deducted at source. Her return for 2008/09 will be issued in April 2009 and must be submitted to HMRC by 30 September 2009, or by 31 January 2010 at the latest. For 2008/09 she will make interim payments on account of $\frac{1}{2} \times$ (£15,000 – £7,000) = £4,000 on 31 January 2009 and 31 July 2009. Her final adjustment for 2008/09 is due on 31 January 2010.

Taxpayers have the right to claim a reduction or cancellation of payments on account where they have grounds for believing that payments based on the tax liability for the previous year will lead to an overpayment of tax in the current year.

2.8.3.3   Penalties for default

Interest is charged on any amount of tax unpaid at the due date for payment whether that tax is due as a payment on account or as a balancing payment. There are also fixed penalties for late or non-payment.

Throughout the self-assessment regime the onus is on the taxpayer, and there is a statutory requirement to maintain adequate records to support the return, backed up by a penalty for default. HMRC has extensive powers, for example random audits and specific enquiries, to check the accuracy of any return. Appeals against assessments and determinations are made to the General Commissioners or Special Commissioners.

2.9 Chapter summary

There is no statutory definition of income but income payments and receipts have an element of recurrence.

Income tax is payable by individuals, partners, PRs and trustees.

Income tax is payable on income only if it derives from a source specified in either ITTOIA 2005 or ITEPA 2003. Income, which does not derive from one of these sources, is not taxable and some income is specifically exempted from tax.

Income tax is paid on income received during a tax year. The tax year runs from 6 April to 5 April.

There are five steps to be used to calculate a taxpayer's income tax liability.

Step 1: Calculate total income

This is achieved by adding together all the taxpayer's *gross* income arising under each source. Some income (eg interest received and dividends) is received net and will have to be grossed up before being added to the gross income from other sources.

Step 2: Deduct any allowable reliefs to give net income

Interest on a qualifying loan is an example of a payment which may be deducted at this stage.

Step 3: Deduct any personal allowance to give taxable income

Generally, the only allowance which may be deducted at this stage is the personal allowance of £6,035.

Step 4: Calculate the tax at the applicable rate(s)

Before applying the tax rates, separate the non-savings/dividend income from the gross savings/dividend income. This is achieved as follows:

	Taxable income
LESS	<u>*Gross* savings/dividend income</u>
	Non-savings/dividend income

First, tax the non-savings/dividend income as follows:

Basic rate	£0–£34,800 @ 20%
Higher rate	over £34,800 @ 40%

Next, tax the savings/dividend income, starting with any interest received.

To the extent that the starting rate for savings and basic rate bands remain available after taxing the non-savings/dividend income, interest received is taxed as follows:

Starting rate for savings	£0–£2,320 @ 10%
Basic rate	£2,321–£34,800 @ 20%
Higher rate	over £34,800 @ 40%

Finally, tax any dividend income element of the savings/dividend income.

To the extent that the dividend ordinary rate band remains available after taxing the non-savings/dividend income and any interest received, dividends are taxed as follows:

Dividend ordinary rate	£0–£34,800 @ 10%
Dividend upper rate	over £34,800 @ 32.5%

Step 5: Add together the amounts of tax from Step 4 to give the taxpayer's overall tax liability

Having calculated the taxpayer's overall liability, reduce that liability by any income tax deducted at source (and therefore paid direct to HMRC) and by any 10% tax credits in respect of dividend income. The resulting figure is the income tax which the taxpayer is obliged to pay to HMRC.

The taxpayer will submit a tax return to HMRC by 31 January following the tax year to which the return relates. The taxpayer will make payments on account on 31 January in the tax year in question and on 31 July after the end of tax year in respect of his income tax liability. Any balancing payment must be made by 31 January after the end of the tax year.

Chapter 3

Capital Gains Tax

3.1 Introduction

3.1.1 Sources of capital gains tax law

The principal charging statute is the Taxation of Chargeable Gains Act 1992.

3.1.2 The charge to tax

Capital gains tax (CGT) is charged on the chargeable gains made by a chargeable person on the disposal of chargeable assets in a tax year (6 April to following 5 April).

3.1.3 Chargeable assets

Sterling EXCLUDED

All forms of property are treated as assets for CGT purposes, including such things as debts, options, incorporeal property and property created by the person disposing of it. Sterling is excluded from the definition so disposals of cash do not attract CGT liability. The legislation does provide for a limited category of non-chargeable assets, the main example being private motor vehicles. The legislation also provides that certain assets which are not non-chargeable shall be wholly or partly exempt from CGT – see **3.4**.

Who pays CGT?

Chargeable persons are:

(a)   individuals;

(b)   partners (each partner is charged separately for his share of the partnership gains when there is a disposal of a chargeable partnership asset);

(c)   personal representatives (who pay CGT when there is a disposal of the deceased's chargeable assets);

(d)   trustees (who pay CGT when there is a disposal of a chargeable asset from the trust fund).

Companies pay corporation tax (see *Business Law and Practice*). Charities are generally exempt from paying tax.

3.1.4 How much CGT will an individual pay?

The steps required to calculate the amount of CGT payable are as follows:

3.1.4.1 Step 1: Disposal of a chargeable asset

It is first necessary to identify the disposal of a chargeable asset, for example the sale of land.

3.1.4.2 Step 2: Calculation of the gain

This, in basic terms, will be the consideration received when the asset is sold less cost.

3.1.4.3 Step 3: Consider reliefs

Various reliefs may be available (see **3.4**). Early examples assume that none of these apply for the sake of simplicity.

3.1.4.4 Step 4: Deduct annual exemption

An individual does not pay tax on all the gains he makes. There is an exemption for the first £9,600 of total net gains made by an individual in the current tax year.

3.1.4.5 Step 5: Apply the appropriate rates of tax

Gains realised from 6 April 2008 will be taxed at a flat rate of 18%.

Example

Sarah sells land for £89,600. The land cost her £40,000. It is her only disposal during the tax year.

Step 1:	Identify the disposal	
	Sale of land	
Step 2:	Calculate the gain	
	Proceeds of disposal	£89,600
	Less: Cost	£40,000
		£49,600
Step 3:	Consider exemptions and reliefs	Nil
Step 4:	Deduct annual exemption	£9,600
	Chargeable gain	£40,000
Step 5:	What is the rate of tax?	
	CGT at 18% on £40,000 is £7,200.	

3.1.5 Assessment and payment of CGT

CGT is assessed on the aggregate net gain of the current tax year and so it is necessary to consider all the disposals made during the tax year. Tax for individuals is payable on or before 31 January following the end of the tax year (or 30 days from the making of an assessment if later).

The above example shows the principles used to establish an individual's liability for CGT. The remainder of this chapter will consider each step of the calculation in more detail.

3.2 Disposals

3.2.1 The sale or gift of a chargeable asset

There must be a disposal of a chargeable asset. Disposal is widely defined and includes a sale or a gift. If a gift is made then HM Revenue & Customs (HMRC) taxes the gain the taxpayer is deemed to have made on the disposal. This is done by using the market value of the asset at the time of the gift instead of consideration received.

Market Value NOT consideration

Example

Barbara makes a gift of a Ming vase worth £269,600. She had bought the vase for £180,000. It is her only disposal during the tax year.

Step 1:	Identify the disposal	
	Gift of vase	
Step 2:	Calculate the gain	
	Market value of vase	£269,600
	Less: Cost	£180,000
		£89,600
Step 3:	Consider exemptions and reliefs	Nil
Step 4:	Deduct annual exemption	£9,600
	Chargeable gain	£80,000
Step 5:	What is the rate of tax?	
	CGT at 18% on £80,000 is £14,400.	

3.2.2 The disposal of part of an asset

A sale of part of an asset or a gift of part of an asset is a disposal, for example the sale of part of a field. This is considered in detail in **3.8**.

3.2.3 The death of the taxpayer

On death there is no disposal by the deceased, so there is no charge to CGT. The personal representatives acquire the deceased's assets at the market value at the date of death. This has the effect of wiping out gains which accrued during the deceased's lifetime so that these gains are not charged to tax.

Example

Christopher dies owning shares worth £150,000. He had bought the shares for £60,000. Since death is not a disposal, there is no charge to CGT when Christopher dies. His personal representatives will acquire the shares at the market value at his death, ie at £150,000. The gain of £90,000 is wiped out and is not charged to tax. The £90,000 is the difference between the cost of the shares and the market value of the shares at the date of death.

3.3 Calculation of gains

The basic aim is to tax the gain in value that the asset has realised from the date of acquisition to the date of disposal. Consequently, the gain is generally the consideration for the disposal (or market value if the taxpayer gives away the asset) less any of the following expenditure incurred by the taxpayer:

Initial expenditure

(a) The cost price of the asset (or its market value at the date of acquisition if the asset was given to the taxpayer) plus incidental costs of acquisition. Examples of incidental costs of acquisition are legal fees, valuation fees, stamp duty.

(b) Expenditure wholly and exclusively incurred in providing the asset. An example is the cost of building a weekend cottage.

Subsequent expenditure

(a) Expenditure wholly and exclusively incurred to enhance the value of the asset, which is reflected in the value of the asset at the time of disposal. An example is the cost of building an extension to a house. The cost of routine maintenance, repairs and insurance, on the other hand, is not deductible.

(b) Expenditure wholly and exclusively incurred in establishing, preserving or defending title to the asset. An example is the cost of legal fees incurred to resolve a boundary dispute.

Incidental costs of disposal

Examples are legal fees and estate agent's fees.

Note that expenditure which is deductible for income tax purposes cannot be deducted when calculating a capital gain.

Example

Paul sells his holiday cottage for £183,800. He bought the cottage for £50,000 and spent £700 on a survey and £1,300 on legal fees when he purchased it. He spent £8,000 improving the cottage. Legal fees when he sells the cottage are £800 and the estate agent's commission is £3,400.

Step 1:   Identify the disposal
          Sale of holiday cottage

Step 2:   Calculate the gain
          Proceeds of disposal   £183,800

Less:

Incidental costs of disposal
    Legal fees   £800
    Estate agent's commission   £3,400
                                                            £4,200
Net proceeds of disposal   £179,600

Less:

Initial expenditure
    Cost   £50,000
    Survey fee   £700
    Legal fees   £1,300
                                          £52,000

Subsequent expenditure
    Cost of improvements   £8,000
                                                            £60,000
GAIN   £119,600

Step 3:   Consider exemptions and reliefs   Nil

Step 4:   Deduct annual exemption   £9,600
          Chargeable gain   £110,000

Step 5:   What is the rate of tax?
          CGT at 18% on £110,000 is £19,800.

3.3.1   The indexation allowance

For gains realised before 6 April 2008, an indexation allowance was used when calculating the gain on an asset which had been owned for any period between 31 March 1982 and 5 April 1998. The purpose of the indexation allowance is to remove inflationary gains from the CGT calculation so that a smaller gain is charged to tax. Inflation is measured by reference to the Retail Prices Index (the RPI). The indexation allowance is calculated by applying to the initial and subsequent expenditure the percentage increase in the RPI from the date the expenditure was incurred to the date of disposal (or April 1998 if earlier). Tables published by HMRC express this information as an indexation factor for ease of calculation.

The allowance still has some relevance to gains, the charge to which has been deferred before 6 April 2008 by the use of various roll-over or hold-over reliefs – see **3.4**. This is because, on a subsequent disposal after 6 April 2008, the rolled-over or held-over gain will be reduced by the appropriate amount of indexation allowance, provided the relevant assets were owned for some time between 31 March 1982 and 5 April 1998.

The same point applies to inter-spouse disposals made before 6 April 2008 – see **3.9**.

3.3.2 Assets owned on 31 March 1982

Where a taxpayer disposes of an asset which he owned on 31 March 1982, special rules are applied. The aim of these rules is to exclude from the tax calculation the part of the gain that accrued before 31 March 1982, so that no CGT is paid on that part of the gain.

As a result, the gain on such assets is calculated by using the market value of the assets on 31 March 1982, rather than actual expenditure.

3.3.3 Losses

The formula 'consideration received (or market value) less cost' can produce a capital loss.

Example

Christine bought shares for £10,000 three years ago. She sells them for £9,000. She has made a loss of £1,000.

The treatment of losses will be considered at **3.6** and **3.7**.

3.4 Reliefs

After calculating the gain, the next step is to consider whether any reliefs apply. Generally, reliefs may be available due to the nature of the asset being disposed of. The majority of reliefs are aimed at smaller businesses, to encourage investment in this sector of the economy.

The following is a non-exhaustive list of CGT reliefs.

3.4.1 Tangible moveable property

Wasting assets (ie assets with a predictable life of less than 50 years) are generally exempt. Most consumer goods will fall into this category, for example televisions and washing machines. Cars are also exempt.

Not all items of tangible moveable property are wasting assets. Some will go up in value, for example antiques. However, they will be exempt from CGT if the disposal consideration is £6,000 or less.

3.4.2 Private dwelling house

A gain on the disposal by an individual of a dwelling house, including grounds of up to half a hectare, will be completely exempt, provided it has been occupied as his only or main residence through his period of ownership (ignoring the last three years of ownership).

For most people, their home is their most valuable asset. The effect of this relief is that the house can be sold (or given away) without CGT liability being incurred.

For Reliefs see BCP!

3.4.3   Damages for personal injury

The recovery of damages or compensation may amount to the disposal of a chargeable asset; however, the receipt of damages for personal injury is exempt.

3.4.4   Hold-over relief

Hold-over relief enables an individual to make a gift of business assets without paying CGT. However, if the donee disposes of the asset, the donee will be charged to tax not only on his own gain but on the donor's gain as well. Because hold-over relief defers the charge to tax until a disposal by the donee, there must usually be an election by donor and donee to claim hold-over relief.

3.4.5   Relief for replacement of business assets ('roll-over' relief)

This relief encourages expansion and investment in business assets by enabling the sale of those assets to take place without an immediate charge to CGT, provided the proceeds of sale are invested in other business assets. The charge to CGT is postponed until the disposal of the new asset.

3.4.6   Roll-over relief on incorporation of a business

This relief again defers a CGT charge. It is applied (subject to conditions) when an individual sells his interest in an unincorporated business (sole trader, partnership) to a company. The gain is rolled over into the shares received as consideration for the interest being sold to the company. The CGT charge is postponed until the disposal of the shares.

3.4.7   Relief for re-investment in certain unquoted shares

To encourage investment in small company shares, it is possible for an individual to defer payment of CGT on any chargeable gain provided the proceeds of sale are re-invested in certain shares in an unquoted trading company. This is dealt with in **5.4**.

3.4.8   Entrepreneurs' relief

From 6 April 2008, relief is available on gains made by individuals on the disposal of certain assets, including:

(a)   all or part of a trading business the individual carries on as a sole trader or in partnership;

(b)   shares in a trading company, provided the individual's holding is at least 5% of the ordinary voting shares of the company (ie, it is his 'personal' trading company);

(c)   assets owned and used by the individual's personal trading company or trading partnership.

The first £1 million (the lifetime limit) of gains that qualify for relief will be charged to CGT at a rate of 10%. Thereafter, gains above the lifetime limit will be charged at the normal rate of 18%, but disposals on or before 5 April 2008 do not count towards the lifetime limit.

3.4.9   Taper relief

For gains realised before 6 April 2008, an individual, a trustee or a personal representative was able to claim taper relief. The effect of the relief was to make only a percentage of the gain subject to CGT. The relief came into effect on 6 April 1998 as a replacement for the indexation allowance.

The relief was abolished for any gains realised from 6 April 2008 onwards.

3.5 The annual exemption

The annual exemption is applied to make exempt the first slice of the taxpayer's net capital gain for the tax year. Unlike the reliefs referred to in **3.4** it is not applied to any particular disposal but is rather a general deduction from the total net gain. As explained in **3.1.5.4**, the amount of the exemption for tax year 2008/09 is £9,600. If a taxpayer's net gain is smaller than the annual exemption the unused part of the exemption cannot be carried forward to the following tax year.

Personal representatives and trustees of settlements are also entitled to an annual exemption; see **Part V: Probate and Administration**.

3.6 CGT calculation where there is more than one disposal in a tax year

Where a number of chargeable assets are disposed of by a taxpayer in the same tax year, the gain (or loss) on each disposal must be calculated separately. The results are then aggregated (with any losses being set against gains) to find the aggregate net gain (or loss) for the tax year. Where there is an aggregate gain the annual exemption is then deducted from the total to find the chargeable gain.

Example 1

Gordon made the following disposals during 2008/09.

On 17 May 2008, he sold his 3% shareholding in Pibroch Ltd for £11,600. He bought it for £4,000 on 16 April 1997.

On 12 August 2008, he sold his holiday cottage, 'Landseer Lodge', for £190,000. He acquired it on his mother's death on 11 January 1990, when its market value was £30,000.

On 8 January 2009, he sold his units in TVT Unit Trust for £5,000. He had purchased them on 16 May 2001 for £9,000.

Note: For the sake of simplicity, the example ignores incidental costs of acquisition and disposal on all of the transactions and it is assumed that no reliefs are available on any of the disposals.

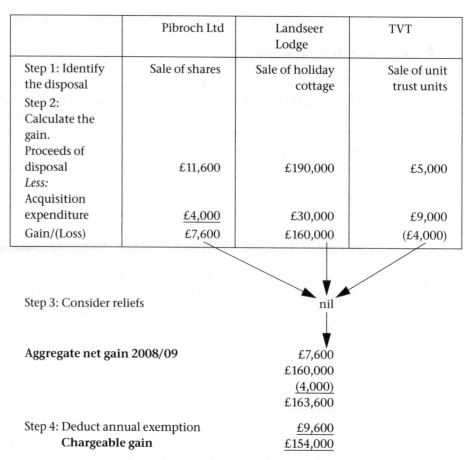

	Pibroch Ltd	Landseer Lodge	TVT
Step 1: Identify the disposal	Sale of shares	Sale of holiday cottage	Sale of unit trust units
Step 2: Calculate the gain. Proceeds of disposal	£11,600	£190,000	£5,000
Less: Acquisition expenditure	£4,000	£30,000	£9,000
Gain/(Loss)	£7,600	£160,000	(£4,000)

Step 3: Consider reliefs   nil

Aggregate net gain 2008/09   £7,600
                                                                  £160,000
                                                                  (4,000)
                                                                  £163,600

Step 4: Deduct annual exemption   £9,600
       Chargeable gain   £154,000

Step 5: What is the rate of tax?
        CGT at 18% on £154,000 is £27,720.

3.7 Unabsorbed losses

It is, of course, possible that a taxpayer's CGT losses in a tax year may exceed his overall CGT gains. If so, setting the losses against the gains will wipe them out completely and the taxpayer will have no CGT to pay. In such a situation, the setting-off of current year losses to wipe out the gains entirely means that the taxpayer loses the use of his annual exemption. The exemption cannot be carried forward to use against gains of future tax years.

If, after setting losses against gains, there are still unabsorbed losses, these may be carried forward to future years and then used to the extent necessary to reduce gains to the limit of the annual exemption. Unabsorbed losses can be carried forward indefinitely. The approach should be:

(a)   work out the gain or loss on each disposal made during the tax year;

(b)   deduct any losses of the current year from gains;

(c)   deduct any losses brought forward from previous years to reduce any remaining gains to the limit of the annual exemption;

(d)   deduct the annual exemption from any remaining gains.

Example 2 *(continued from 3.6)*

Year of loss

In 2007/08, the year before the **3.6** scenario, Gordon made gains of £30,000, and losses of £70,000. He had no unused losses from previous years.

Gains for the year	£30,000
Less: losses for the year	£70,000
Net loss for the year	£40,000

The £30,000 gain is wiped out, and the unused loss of £40,000 is carried forward to next year.

As there is no net gain for 2007/08, the annual exemption cannot be used in this year and it cannot be carried forward to later years.

Year following year of loss

In 2008/09 Gordon's loss of £40,000 carried forward from 2007/08 would be set against the net gains of £163,600 (ie after deducting the current year loss of £4,000). This will reduce the net gains further for 2008/09 to £123,600.

Gordon's CGT position would now be:

	£
2008/09 aggregate net gains	7,600
	160,000
	(4,000)
	(40,000)
	123,600
Less: annual exemption	9,600
2008/09 taxable gains	114,000

Further example

If Gordon's unabsorbed loss in 2007/08 had been greater, eg £180,000, it would be carried forward and used in 2008/09 as follows:

After the deduction of the current year loss of £4,000, the aggregate net gains would be £163,600. The brought-forward loss of £180,000 would then be set against the remaining gains until the gains are reduced to the limit of the annual exemption of £9,600. The balance of the loss (£26,000) remains unused and can be carried forward to set against gains of future years.

	Loss carried forward £	2008/09 gains £
2007/08 loss	180,000	
2008/09 aggregate net gains		7,600
		160,000
		(4,000)
Use part loss	(154,000)	(154,000)
		9,600
Less: annual exemption		9,600
2008/09 taxable gains		nil
Balance of loss to be carried forward	26,000	

3.8 Part disposals

Where the disposal is of only part of the asset the initial and subsequent expenditure are apportioned when calculating the gain.

Example

Anna bought a large plot of land for £100,000 in 1995. She sells part of it for £90,000 in October 2008. The remaining land is worth £360,000. This is her only disposal in the tax year.

Identify the disposal: sale of part of the land.

Calculation of the gain on the land sold:

The consideration received is £90,000.

What is the cost of the part sold?

The total value of the two pieces of land is £450,000, ie £90,000 plus £360,000.

The part sold is worth $\frac{1}{5}$ of the total value, ie £90,000 is $\frac{1}{5}$ of £450,000.

Therefore, take $\frac{1}{5}$ of the cost as the relevant figure for the calculation, ie $\frac{1}{5}$ of £100,000, that is, £20,000.

	£
Proceeds of disposal	90,000
Less:	
Apportioned cost	20,000
Gain	70,000
Deduct annual exemption	9,600
Chargeable gain	60,400

What is the rate of tax?

CGT at 18% on £60,400 is £10,872

3.9 Husband and wife

3.9.1 Disposals between spouses

Where spouses are living together, a disposal by one to the other is treated as being made for such a consideration as to provide neither a gain nor a loss. (As from 5 December 2005, the same rule applies to civil partners living together). This means that a spouse can dispose of property to the other without paying CGT on the disposal. The donor's gain is not wiped out but merely deferred. If the donee disposes of the asset, the donee will be charged to tax not only on the donee's gain but on the donor's gain as well.

Example

(Assume all ownership periods are after 1998, so there is no indexation allowance.)

David gives a portrait to his wife Jane. David will not pay CGT on this disposal.

The portrait was worth £100,000 at the time of the gift. It cost David £80,000 three years ago.

Usually, when a gift is made the acquisition cost of the donee is the market value at the time of the gift (£100,000) but because the portrait was a gift from her husband, Jane will acquire it with a value of £80,000, ie the amount David paid for the painting.

If Jane disposes of the asset, she will have a lower acquisition cost to set against her gain and she will be charged to tax on both her own gain and her husband's gain.

Assume Jane sells the painting for £150,000, five years later.

The calculation will be:

Consideration received	£150,000
Less: Cost	£80,000
	£70,000

If Jane had not acquired the painting from her husband, so that the ordinary rules applied, the calculation would have been:

Consideration received	£150,000
Less: Cost	£100,000
	£50,000

A comparison of the above calculations shows that a larger gain is produced on Jane's disposal where she acquired the portrait from her husband; but, of course, David avoided any CGT charge at the time of the gift to Jane.

3.9.2 Tax planning point: using the annual exemptions of both spouses

Husband and wife are each entitled to an annual exemption of £9,600. If, for example, the husband's annual exemption will not be used while the wife's annual exemption will be used in full, it may be beneficial to transfer some assets to the husband so that he disposes of them and makes the gain. The aim is to make use of both annual exemptions so that tax is saved on a further £9,600. As discussed at **3.9.1**, there will be no charge to tax when the assets are transferred to the husband.

Chapter 4

Inheritance Tax

4.1 Introduction

This chapter explains the basic principles of inheritance tax (IHT).

Inheritance tax is governed principally by the Inheritance Tax Act 1984 (IHTA 1984). The Act may be found in the *Yellow Tax Handbook 2008-2009* (LexisNexis Butterworths), with explanation in *Revenue Law – Principles and Practice*, 26th edn (Tottel, 2008). Suggestions for further reading are listed in the **Appendix to Part I**.

There are three main occasions when IHT may be charged:

(a) on death;

(b) on gifts made within seven years of death;

(c) on gifts into a trust.

4.1.1 Death

As its name implies, IHT is primarily a tax that takes effect on death. When an individual dies, IHT is charged on the value of his estate (broadly, his assets less his liabilities) subject to various exemptions and reliefs.

4.1.2 Gifts made within seven years of death

If IHT were limited to a charge on death, one way to avoid tax would be to reduce the size of one's estate by making lifetime gifts. Inheritance tax is therefore also charged on certain lifetime gifts or 'transfers' if the donor dies within seven years of making them. Such gifts are called 'potentially exempt transfers', because at the time when the transfer is made no IHT is chargeable; the transfer is 'potentially exempt'. If the transferor survives for seven years, the transfer becomes exempt. If he dies within that period, the transfer becomes chargeable.

4.1.3 Gifts into a trust

Inheritance tax might also be avoided by the use of a trust. Since 22 March 2006, trusts created during the settlor's lifetime are specially treated for IHT purposes, and gifts into them do not qualify as potentially exempt transfers. A lifetime gift into a trust is immediately chargeable to IHT at the time when it is made, unless the trust is for a disabled person.

4.2   The main charging provisions

Inheritance tax is charged on 'the value transferred by a chargeable transfer'. The term 'chargeable transfer' is defined as 'a transfer of value which is made by an individual but is not an exempt transfer' (IHTA 1984, ss 1, 2).

This charge may apply in any of the three situations outlined above, because the term 'chargeable transfer' may refer to:

(a)   the transfer on death; or

(b)   a lifetime transfer which is potentially exempt when it is made but becomes chargeable because the transferor dies within seven years; or

(c)   a lifetime transfer which is immediately chargeable at the time when it is made.

In each case, the method by which tax is calculated is broadly similar, and may be approached by applying a sequence of logical steps.

4.2.1   Step 1: Identify the transfer of value

A lifetime transfer of value is any disposition which reduces the value of the transferor's estate. On death, tax is charged as if the deceased had made a transfer of value of his estate.

4.2.2   Step 2: Find the value transferred

For a lifetime transfer, this is the amount of the reduction in the transferor's estate. On death, it is the value of the estate.

4.2.3   Step 3: Apply any relevant exemptions and reliefs

Some exemptions apply both to lifetime transfers and to the transfer on death (eg transfers to spouse or civil partner). Others are more restricted, and many apply only to lifetime transfers (eg annual exemption).

The main reliefs are business and agricultural property relief, which may apply both to lifetime transfers of such property and to the transfer on death.

4.2.4   Step 4: Calculate tax at the appropriate rate

Each individual has a 'nil rate band' (currently £312,000) for IHT purposes. This is a sum which, in any given seven-year period, an individual may transfer without payment of IHT, because the rate of tax is 0%. The rate of tax that applies to transfers in excess of the nil rate band varies according to the type of transfer (details are given in context below).

In order to calculate the tax on any transfer, whether during lifetime or on death, one must first look back over the seven years immediately preceding the transfer. Any chargeable transfers made by the transferor during that period must be taken into account in order to determine how much of the nil rate band is available. This process is known as 'cumulation'.

This chapter will consider the detailed application of the steps outlined above to each of the three types of transfer in turn. Note that, for ease of reference in the examples provided, any mention of the nil rate band assumes that the band has always been £312,000. In fact, it has increased over the years to its current level. In real calculations one may have to identify the previous bands.

4.3 Transfers on death

The steps outlined at **4.2** above apply as follows.

4.3.1 Step 1: Identify the transfer of value

When a person dies, he is treated for IHT purposes as having made a transfer of value immediately before his death, ie there is a deemed transfer of value. The value transferred is the value of the deceased's 'estate' immediately before his death.

4.3.1.1 Definition of 'estate'

A person's estate is defined by IHTA 1984, s 5(1) to mean all the property to which he was beneficially entitled immediately before his death, with the exception of 'excluded property'.

Property included within this definition falls into three categories, as set out below.

(a) Property which passes under the deceased's will or on intestacy. The deceased was 'beneficially entitled' to all such property immediately before he died.

(b) Property to which the deceased was 'beneficially entitled' immediately before his death but which does not pass under his will or intestacy. This applies to the deceased's interest in any joint property passing on his death by survivorship to the surviving joint tenant.

(c) Property included because of special statutory provisions. By statute, the deceased is treated as having been 'beneficially entitled' to certain types of property which would otherwise fall outside the definition. These rules apply to certain trust property and to property given away by the deceased in his lifetime but which is 'subject to a reservation' at the time of death, as explained below.

4.3.1.2 Trust property included in the estate for IHT purposes

In certain circumstances, a person who is entitled to the income from a trust is treated for IHT purposes as 'beneficially entitled' to the capital which produces that income. This means that where a beneficiary who is entitled to all the income from such a trust dies, the trust fund is taxed as if it were part of the beneficiary's estate.

Before 22 March 2006 this principle applied to any trust where the beneficiary had an 'interest in possession', that is, an interest under which the beneficiary is entitled to claim the income as of right, with no power on the part of the trustees to decide whether or not he should receive it. Where such an interest arises on or after 22 March 2006, the rule only applies in limited circumstances. The main example is where the interest is an 'immediate post-death interest' (IPDI). An IPDI is, broadly, an interest in possession arising on the death of the settlor under his will or intestacy.

> #### Example 1
> Gina died in January 2008. In her will, she left all her estate to her executors/trustees, Tom and Tessa, on trust to pay the income to Gina's son, Simon, for life with remainder to Rose absolutely. Both Simon and Rose are over 18 years old.
>
> Tom and Tessa must invest the property to produce income. Simon is entitled to the income during his life. Tom and Tessa must pay it to him. Thus Simon, the life tenant, has an interest in possession.

When Simon dies, his rights under the trust cease. Under the terms of the trust instrument (Gina's will), Rose is now entitled to the trust fund, and Tom and Tessa must transfer all the trust property to her.

For IHT purposes, Simon had an interest in possession which qualified as an IPDI. Although he was entitled only to the income from the trust property and had no control over the disposition of the fund on his death, he is treated for tax purposes as 'beneficially entitled' to the whole trust fund. The fund is taxed on his death as part of his estate. The tax on the trust property will be paid from the trust fund.

Example 2

The facts are as in Example 1, except that Gina did not die in January 2008. Instead, she created the trust on that date by transferring the funds to Tessa and Tom and signing a declaration that they were to hold on trust for Simon for life with remainder to Rose. While the beneficiaries' rights under the trust will be exactly the same as in Example 1, the trust will not be an IPDI. Instead it will be taxed under the 'relevant property' regime. Details of this regime are outside the scope of this chapter.

4.3.1.3   Property subject to a reservation

The Finance Act 1986 contains provisions designed to prevent people from avoiding tax by giving property away more than seven years before death but continuing to enjoy the benefit of the property. The rule applies where the deceased gave away property during his lifetime but did not transfer 'possession and enjoyment' of the property to the donee, or was not entirely excluded from enjoying the property. If property is subject to a reservation at the time of the donor's death, the donor is treated as being 'beneficially entitled' to the property.

Example

In 1998, Diana gave her jewellery, worth £100,000, to her daughter Emma, but retained possession of it. Diana dies in 2008, when the jewellery (still in her possession) is worth £120,000. Although the jewellery belongs to Emma, tax is charged on Diana's death as if she were still beneficially entitled to it. The jewellery, valued at £120,000, is taxed as part of Diana's estate. The tax on the jewellery will be borne by Emma.

4.3.1.4   Property outside the estate for IHT purposes

Property to which the deceased was not 'beneficially entitled' immediately before his death falls outside the definition. Thus if the deceased took out a life assurance policy written in trust for a named beneficiary the proceeds are not part of his estate for IHT purposes. Similarly, a discretionary lump sum payment made from a pension fund to the deceased's family is not part of the estate for IHT purposes.

4.3.1.5   Excluded property

Certain property which would otherwise be included in the estate for IHT purposes is defined in IHTA 1984 as 'excluded property'. Excluded property is not part of the estate for IHT purposes. One example of excluded property is a 'reversionary interest'. For IHT purposes this means any future interest under a settlement, for example an interest in remainder under a trust.

4.3.2   Step 2: Find the value transferred

4.3.2.1   Basic valuation principle

Assets in the estate are valued for IHT purposes at 'the price which the property might reasonably be expected to fetch if sold in the open market' immediately before the death (IHTA 1984, s 160).

This means that the value immediately before death of every asset forming part of the estate for IHT purposes must be assessed and reported to HMRC. Some assets, such as bank and building society accounts and quoted shares, are easy to value. Others, such as land, may be more difficult. Negotiations may be required (in the case of land, with the district valuer) in order to reach an agreed valuation.

The value of an asset agreed for IHT purposes is known as the 'probate value'.

4.3.2.2 Modification of the basic valuation principle: s 171

The IHTA 1984, s 171 provides that, where the death causes the value of an asset in the estate to increase or decrease, that change in value should be taken into account.

Example

Brian has insured his life for £50,000. The benefit of the policy belongs to him (ie the policy is not written in trust). Immediately before Brian's death, the value of the policy to him is its 'surrender value'. This will be considerably less than its maturity value of £50,000. Under s 171, the effect of Brian's death on the value of the policy is taken into account: its value for IHT purposes is £50,000.

4.3.2.3 Quoted shares

The value of quoted shares is taken from the Stock Exchange Daily Official List for the date of death (or the nearest trading day). The list quotes two prices. To value the shares for IHT, take one-quarter of the difference between the lower and higher price and add it to the lower price.

Example

John died owning 200 shares in ABC plc. On the date of John's death the quoted price per share is 102p/106p. The value of each share for IHT is 103p, and so the value of John's holding is £206.

4.3.2.4 Debts and expenses

Liabilities owed by the deceased at the time of death are deductible for IHT purposes provided that they were incurred for money or money's worth (IHTA 1984, s 505). Thus debts such as gas and telephone bills may be deducted. In addition, the deceased may not have paid enough income tax on the income he received before he died; this amount may also be deducted.

Reasonable funeral expenses are also deductible (IHTA 1984, s 162).

4.3.3 Step 3: Apply any relevant exemptions and reliefs

The main exemptions applicable on death depend on the identity of the beneficiary. Reliefs depend on the nature of the property in the estate. Thus it is important to see who is entitled to the property on death and whether the property qualifies for a relief.

4.3.3.1 Spouse or civil partner exemption

IHTA 1984, s 18 provides as follows:

> A transfer of value is an exempt transfer to the extent that the value transferred is attributable to property which becomes comprised in the estate of the transferor's spouse or civil partner.

Any property included in the estate for IHT purposes is exempt if it passes to the deceased's spouse or civil partner under the deceased's will or intestacy or, in the case of joint property, by survivorship.

The rule applicable to 'immediate post-death interest' (IPDI) trusts is that IHT is charged as if the person with the right to income owned the capital (see **4.3.1.2**). This rule applies for the purpose of spouse exemption, both on creation of the trust (whether by will or on intestacy) and on the death of a life tenant.

Example

In his will, Dan leaves his estate worth £300,000 to trustees on trust for his wife, Jane, for life with remainder to their children. Although Jane only has the right to the income from Dan's estate for her lifetime, the trust is treated for IHT purposes as if Jane owned the capital. On Dan's death, his whole estate will be spouse exempt.

4.3.3.2 Charity exemption

The IHTA 1984, s 23(1) provides as follows:

Transfers of value are exempt to the extent that the values transferred by them are attributable to property which is given to charities.

Any property forming part of the deceased's estate for IHT purposes which passes on death to charity is exempt. The exemption most commonly applies to property which passes to charity under the deceased's will. However, if the deceased had a life interest in trust property which passes under the terms of the trust to charity, the charity exemption applies.

A similar exemption applies to gifts to certain national bodies and bodies providing a public benefit, such as museums and art galleries, and to political parties.

4.3.3.3 Business and agricultural property relief

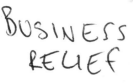
BUSINESS RELIEF

Business property relief applies to reduce the value transferred by a transfer of 'relevant business property' by a certain percentage, provided that the transferor owned the property for the two years immediately before the transfer.

The reduction is 100% for:

(a)   a business, or an interest in a business (such as a share in a partnership); and

(b)   unquoted shares.

The reduction is 50% for:

(a)   quoted shares which gave the transferor control of the company; and

(b)   certain land, buildings and machinery owned by the transferor but used in his company or partnership.

Agricultural property relief applies in a similar manner to reduce the agricultural value of agricultural property.

Further details of these reliefs are given in *Business Law and Practice*.

4.3.4   Step 4: Calculate tax at the appropriate rate

If the deceased has made no chargeable transfers in the seven years before death, the rate of tax on the first £312,000 of his estate (the 'nil rate band') is 0%. If his estate exceeds £312,000, IHT is charged on the excess at 40%.

If the deceased died on or after 9 October 2007 having survived a spouse or civil partner, any part of the nil rate band which was not used on the death of that spouse or civil partner may be claimed by the deceased's estate.

Example

Emily, a widow, dies on 21 August 2008. Her husband Guy died three years earlier leaving all his estate to Emily. There was no tax to pay on Guy's death as his whole estate was spouse exempt, and his nil rate band was not used. Guy's nil rate band is transferred to Emily's estate, so that the rate of tax on the first £624,000 of her estate is 0%.

If the deceased did make any chargeable transfers in the seven years before death the cumulation principle outlined at **4.2.4** will apply. The effect is that the lifetime transfers use up the deceased's nil rate band first, reducing the amount available for the estate. Most lifetime gifts are potentially exempt from IHT and become chargeable only if the transferor dies within seven years. Less commonly, the deceased may also have made gifts in the seven years before death which were immediately chargeable to IHT at the time they were made, eg a gift into a trust. The cumulation principle applies to both types of transfer.

The 'values transferred' by such transfers must be aggregated. This means that any lifetime exemptions or reliefs which operate to reduce the value transferred are taken into account.

Example

In 2005, David made a gift to his daughter. The value transferred (after exemptions and reliefs) was £162,000.

In August 2008, David dies leaving his estate, valued at £200,000, to his son.

The 2005 transfer was potentially exempt from IHT but has now become chargeable. David's cumulative total is £162,000

The nil rate band applicable to David's estate on death is	312,000
less cumulative total	162,000
	150,000

Tax on David's estate:

£150,000 @ 0% =	nil
£50,000 @ 40% =	£20,000

For further details of the effect of the cumulation principle, see **4.6**.

4.3.5 The estate rate

The term 'estate rate' means the average rate of tax applicable to each item of property in the estate for IHT. When tax on the estate has been calculated, it may be necessary for various reasons to work out how much of the tax is attributable to a particular item of property in the estate. For example:

(a)   since tax on certain types of property, such as land, may be paid in instalments, the personal representatives (PRs) must calculate how much of the tax relates to that property;

(b)   the PRs may not be liable to pay all the tax on the estate. If the estate for IHT purposes includes trust property, the trustees are liable to pay the tax attributable to that property;

(c)   the will may give a legacy 'subject to tax'.

The principle is that tax is divided between the various assets in the estate proportionately, according to their value. This may be applied by calculating the average rate of tax on the estate as a percentage, ie the 'estate rate'. For example, if the deceased's nil rate band was completely used up by lifetime transfers, the 'estate rate' would be 40%. However, it is not strictly necessary to calculate the estate rate as a percentage; instead, the amount of tax on a particular item of property in the estate may be calculated by applying to the value of that property the proportion which the total tax bill bears to the total chargeable estate.

Example

Graham, who has made no lifetime transfers, leaves a house, valued at £210,000, to Henry, subject to payment of IHT, and the rest of his estate, valued at £140,000 net to Ian.

Tax on Graham's estate:	£312,000 @ 0%	nil
	£38,000 @ 40%	£15,200

The 'estate rate' is: $\dfrac{£15,200}{£350,000}$ $\dfrac{\text{(total tax bill)}}{\text{(total chargeable estate)}}$

Henry pays tax on the house: £210,000 × $\dfrac{£15,200}{£350,000}$ = £9,120

Ian pays tax on the residue: £140,000 × $\dfrac{£15,200}{£350,000}$ = £6,080

4.3.6   Liability for IHT on death

4.3.6.1   Meaning of 'liability'

The rules that follow concern the question of who is liable to account to HMRC for the payment of the tax due as a result of death. HMRC is concerned with obtaining payment of the tax, and not with the question of who bears the burden of the payment. Payment will usually be obtained from people who are not beneficially entitled to the property but who hold property in a representative capacity (ie PRs and trustees). Those who ultimately receive the property are concurrently liable with such representatives, but in most cases tax will have been paid before the beneficiaries receive the property.

4.3.6.2   The PRs: tax on the non-settled estate

The PRs are liable to pay the IHT attributable to any property which 'was not immediately before the death comprised in a settlement' (IHTA 1984, s 200). This includes:

(a)   the property which vests in the PRs (ie the property which passes under the deceased's will or intestacy); and

(b)   property (other than trust property) which does not pass to the PRs but is included in the estate for IHT because the deceased was beneficially entitled to it immediately before death (eg, joint property which passes by survivorship).

Thus the PRs are liable to pay the IHT on joint property even though that property does not vest in them. Their liability is, however, limited to the value of the assets they received, or would have received but for their own neglect or default.

Concurrently liable with the PRs is 'any person in whom property is vested ... at any time after the death or who at any such time is beneficially entitled to an interest in possession in the property' (IHTA 1984, s 200(1)(c)). This means that tax on property passing by will or intestacy may in principle be claimed by HMRC from a beneficiary who has received that property. Similarly, HMRC may claim tax on joint property from the surviving joint tenant. Such tax is normally paid by the PRs and it is relatively unusual for HMRC to claim tax from the recipient of the property.

4.3.6.3 The trustees: tax on settled property

If the estate for IHT purposes includes any property which was 'comprised in a settlement' immediately before the death, the trustees of the settlement are liable for IHT attributable to that property. This principle is relevant where the deceased had an interest in possession under a trust created before 22 March 2006 or an IPDI under a trust created on or after that date. Again, any person in whom the trust property subsequently vests or for whose benefit the trust property is subsequently applied is concurrently liable with the trustees.

Example

In 1996, Ruth's father died leaving property now worth £300,000 on trust for Ruth for life with remainder to Arthur. Ruth dies leaving property worth £200,000 which passes under her will to Tessa. The trust fund is taxed as part of Ruth's estate as she had made no lifetime transfers. She had made no lifetime transfers.

Tax on Ruth's death:

on	£312,000 @ 0%	nil
on	£188,000 @ 40%	£75,200

The trustees are liable to pay the tax on the trust fund (calculated according to the estate rate):

$$£300,000 \quad \times \quad \frac{£75,200}{£500,000} \quad = \quad £41,120$$

Arthur, the remainderman, is concurrently liable if any of the trust property is transferred to him before the tax has been paid.

Ruth's PRs are liable to pay the tax on Ruth's free estate::

$$£200,000 \quad \times \quad \frac{£75,200}{£500,000} \quad = \quad £30,080$$

4.3.6.4 Additional liability of PRs

Property which the deceased gave away during his lifetime is treated as part of his estate on death if the donor reserved a benefit in the property which he continued to enjoy immediately before death (see **4.3.1**). The donee of the gift is primarily liable to pay tax attributable to the property. However, if the tax remains unpaid 12 months after the end of the month of death, the PRs become liable for the tax.

Where a person dies within seven years of making a potentially exempt transfer (PET), the transfer becomes chargeable and IHT may be payable. The transferee is primarily liable, but again, the PRs become liable if the tax remains unpaid 12 months after the end of the month of death.

In each of the above cases the liability of the PRs is limited to the extent of the assets they actually received, or would have received but for their neglect or default. However, PRs cannot escape liability on the grounds that they have distributed the estate and so they should ideally delay distribution until IHT on any such lifetime gifts has been paid.

4.3.7 Time for payment of IHT on death: the instalment option

The basic rule is that IHT is due for payment six months after the end of the month of death (although PRs will normally pay earlier in order to speed up the administration of the estate).

However, some property, such as land and certain types of business property, attracts the instalment option. Any tax attributable to instalment option property may be paid in 10 equal yearly instalments, the first falling due six months after the end of the month of death. Again, the tax on the estate is apportioned using the estate rate to find how much tax is attributable to the instalment option property.

4.3.7.1 Qualifying property

The instalment option applies to:

(a) land of any description;

(b) a business or an interest in a business;

(c) shares (quoted or unquoted) which immediately before death gave control of the company to the deceased;

(d) unquoted shares which do not give control if either:

    (i) the holding is sufficiently large (a holding of at least 10% of the nominal value of the company's shares and worth more than £20,000); or

    (ii) HMRC is satisfied that the tax cannot be paid in one sum without undue hardship; or

    (iii) the IHT attributable to the shares and any other instalment option property in the estate amounts to at least 20% of the IHT payable on the estate.

4.3.7.2 Interest

Where the instalment option is exercised in relation to tax on shares or any other business property or agricultural land, instalments carry interest only from the date when each instalment is payable. Thus, no interest is due on the outstanding tax provided that each instalment is paid on the due date.

In the case of other land, however, interest is payable with each instalment (apart from the first) on the amount of IHT which was outstanding for the previous year.

4.3.7.3 Sale

If the instalment option property is sold, all outstanding tax and interest becomes payable.

4.3.8 Example of the application of IHT to an estate on death

4.3.8.1 Facts

Veronica dies intestate on 3 August 2008 survived by her partner William (to whom she was not married) and their children Brian (19) and Carla (22). She holds the following property:

	£
House (in joint names with William): value of share	90,000
Bank account (in joint names with William): value of share	5,000
Life assurance policies:	
(1) payable to PRs: maturity value	195,000
(2) written in trust for William: maturity value	30,000
Unquoted shares: 15% holding	15,000
Building society account	19,000
Car and chattels	15,000

There are various debts, including funeral expenses, which total £4,000.

Two years before her death, Veronica made a gift of £198,000 in cash to William. She made no other substantial lifetime gifts.

4.3.8.2 Step 1: identify the estate

Property to which Veronica was beneficially entitled immediately before death:

Passing on intestacy (to children):	life assurance policy (1) unquoted shares building society account car and chattels
Passing by survivorship (to William):	interest in house interest in bank account

(Life assurance policy (2) is not included in the estate for IHT purposes because Veronica was not beneficially entitled to it immediately before her death.)

4.3.8.3 Step 2: value the estate

	£	£
Passing on intestacy:		
life assurance policy (1) (full maturity value)	195,000	
unquoted shares (market value)	15,000	
building society account	19,000	
car and chattels	15,000	
		244,000
Joint property:		
interest in the house	90,000	
interest in the bank account	5,000	
		95,000
		339,000
Less debts (including funeral expenses)		4,000
Value of estate (before reliefs)		335,000

4.3.8.4 Step 3: apply exemptions and reliefs

No exemptions apply to Veronica's estate as she had no spouse and left no property to charity.

The unquoted shares qualify for business property relief at 100%:

	£
100% of £15,000	15,000
Value of estate for IHT	320,000

4.3.8.5 Step 4: calculate tax at the appropriate rate

Cumulate the value transferred by chargeable transfers made in the seven years before death. The gift to William was a PET which has now become chargeable.

	£
Value of gift	198,000
Less two annual exemptions (see **4.4.3**)	6,000
Value transferred	192,000

Only £120,000 of Veronica's nil rate band remains available on her death.

Calculate tax on the estate of £320,000:

| on £120,000 @ 0% | nil |
| on £200,000 @ 40% | £80,000 |

4.3.8.6 Liability

The PRs are liable for tax on the 'free estate', ie the property passing on intestacy and the joint property. This means that the PRs are liable to pay the whole tax bill of £80,000.

4.3.8.7 Time for payment of IHT

Assuming that the PRs deliver the IHT account before 28 February 2009 (six months after the end of the month of death), they must, on delivery of the account, pay the tax on that part of the free estate which does not attract the instalment option.

	£
Free estate	320,000
Less instalment option property:	
share of house	90,000
Tax payable on delivery of account on	230,000

Calculate tax on £230,000 by applying the estate rate:

$$£230,000 \quad \times \quad \frac{£80,000}{£320,000} \quad = \quad £57,500$$

The PRs must pay £57,500 on delivery of the IHT account.

Tax on the house is payable in 10 equal annual instalments.

Tax on the house (£90,000):

$$£90,000 \quad \times \quad \frac{£80,000}{£320,000} \quad = \quad £22,500$$

The first instalment is payable on 28 February 2009 (six months after the end of the month of death).

Subsequent instalments are payable on each succeeding 28 February with interest on the amount outstanding during the previous year.

4.3.8.8 Burden of IHT

IHT on the property passing on intestacy is a testamentary expense, payable from the property before division between the children.

IHT on the joint property (the house and joint bank account) is borne by William, the surviving joint tenant.

IHT on the trust property is borne by the trust fund.

4.4 Lifetime transfers: potentially exempt transfers

The definition of a potentially exempt transfer (PET) includes any gift made by an individual to another individual or into a disabled trust (IHTA 1984, s 3A(1A)), to the extent in either case that the gift would otherwise be chargeable.

This means that all lifetime gifts to an individual are 'potentially exempt' to the extent that no immediate exemption applies.

4.4.1 Step 1: Identify the 'transfer of value'

The term 'transfer of value' is defined to mean any lifetime disposition made by a person ('the transferor') which reduces the value of his estate (IHTA 1984, s 3(1)). In principle, therefore, any lifetime gift falls within the definition.

4.4.2 Step 2: Find the value transferred

The second step is to find the value transferred by the transfer of value. In the case of a lifetime transfer, this is the amount by which the value of the transferor's estate is 'less than it would be but for' the transfer (IHTA 1984, s 3(1)). In other words, the value transferred is the loss in value to the estate of the transferor brought about by the transfer. The transferor's 'estate' is the aggregate of all the property to which he is beneficially entitled (IHTA 1984, s 5).

In practice, the loss to the estate will usually be the market value of the property transferred, although this does not follow in every case.

Example

Vanessa owns a pair of matching bronze statuettes. The market value of the pair together is £80,000, but individually each one is worth £25,000. If Vanessa were to give away one statuette to her son, the loss to her estate would be calculated as follows:

	£
Value of pair	80,000
Less value of remaining statuette	25,000
Loss to estate	55,000

4.4.2.1 Related property

The related property rules are designed to prevent tax avoidance in relation to a group or set of assets. The rules apply most often to property transferred between husband and wife.

Example (*continued*)

Suppose Vanessa gives one of the statuettes to her husband Boris (an exempt transfer to spouse). Without the related property rules Vanessa and Boris would each then own one statuette worth £25,000.

However, the two statuettes owned by Vanessa and Boris are related property. Under the related property valuation rule, the value of each statuette is the appropriate portion of the value of the pair, ie half of £80,000 which is £40,000. If either Vanessa or Boris were to give away their statuette, the value transferred would be £40,000.

4.4.3 Step 3: Apply any relevant exemptions and reliefs

As seen at **4.4**, a gift is potentially exempt only to the extent that it would otherwise be chargeable. At the time when a lifetime gift is made it may be clear that an exemption applies. Some lifetime exemptions, however, may apply to only part of a lifetime transfer, so that the excess is potentially exempt.

The main exemptions and reliefs applicable on death apply also to lifetime transfers. In addition, there are some further exemptions which apply only to lifetime transfers.

4.4.3.1 Spouse or civil partner and charity exemptions

These exemptions, outlined at **4.3.3**, apply to lifetime transfers as well as to the transfer on death. So any lifetime gift to the transferor's spouse or civil partner or to charity is exempt, even if the transferor dies within seven years.

4.4.3.2 Business and agricultural property relief

The reliefs set out at **4.3.3** apply to reduce the value transferred by transfers of business or agricultural property made during lifetime as well as on death. However, if the transferor dies within seven years of the transfer, the relief will generally be available only if the transferee still owns the property when the transferor dies (see **4.6.2**).

4.4.3.3 Order of application of exemptions and reliefs

Spouse or civil partner and charity exemptions are applied before reliefs, since their effect is to make the transfer wholly exempt. If, for example, a transferor gives relevant business property to his wife, business property relief is academic – the transfer is exempt.

The 'lifetime only' exemptions, however, may apply to only part of a transfer. Since the reliefs apply to reduce the value transferred, they should be applied before such exemptions are considered.

4.4.3.4 Lifetime only exemptions

(i) The annual exemption

The annual exemption applies to the first £3,000 transferred by lifetime transfers in each tax year. Any unused annual exemption may be carried forward for one year only, so that a maximum exemption of £6,000 may be available. The current year's exemption must be used before the previous year's exemption can be carried forward.

Example

On 1 May 2006, Annie gives £3,000 to her son Ben. The transfer falls within Annie's annual exemption for 2006/07 and is exempt.

On 1 May 2008, Annie gives £7,000 to her daughter Claire. Annie may apply her annual exemption for 2008/09 and may carry forward her unused annual exemption for 2007/08. Thus £6,000 of the transfer is exempt at the time of the gift. (The remaining £1,000 will be 'potentially exempt', as explained below.)

If a transferor makes more than one transfer of value in any one tax year, then the exemption is used to reduce the first transfer. Any unused exemption is set against the second and any further transfers until it is used up.

Example

Sarah gives £10,000 to Jessica on 30 April 2008 and £10,000 to Kirsty on 1 May 2008. She has made no previous transfers. The annual exemptions for 2008/09 and 2007/08 will be set against the transfer to Jessica and reduce it to £4,000. (The remaining part of Jessica's gift and the whole of Kirsty's gift will be 'potentially exempt', as explained below.)

(2) Small gifts

Lifetime gifts in any one tax year of less than £250 to any one person are exempt. This exemption cannot be set against a gift which exceeds £250.

(3) Normal expenditure out of income

A lifetime transfer is exempt if it can be shown that:

(a) it was made as part of the transferor's normal expenditure (ie there must be regular payments); and

(b) it was made out of the transferor's income; and

(c)   after allowing for all such payments, the transferor was left with sufficient income to maintain his usual standard of living.

Example

Andrew, who is a highly paid company director, has a daughter at drama college. He sends his daughter £100 each month (paid from his income) to assist her with her living expenses. These transfers are exempt as normal expenditure out of Andrew's income (provided Andrew's remaining income is sufficient to support his normal standard of living).

(4) Gifts in consideration of marriage

Lifetime gifts on marriage are exempt up to:

(a) £5,000 by a parent of a party to the marriage;

(b)   £2,500 by a remoter ancestor of a party to the marriage (eg, a grandparent); and

(c) £1,000 in any other case.

4.4.3.5 Potentially exempt transfers

As long as the lifetime transfer is not immediately chargeable (see **4.5**), any value remaining after exemptions and reliefs have been applied is potentially exempt. The transfer will become chargeable only if the transferor dies within seven years. The transferor does not need to take any action at the time when such lifetime transfers are made, and if he survives for seven years they will automatically become exempt. However, if the transferor dies within the seven-year period, his PRs must check whether he made any lifetime transfers in the preceding seven years and declare them. If lifetime transfers exceed the transferor's nil rate band, IHT will be payable on them. In any event, the cumulation principle means that the nil rate band available for the transferor's estate will be reduced, or may have been completely used up. (For further explanation of the effect of death within seven years, see **4.6**.)

Example

On 1 March 2008, Jane gives £130,000 to her brother, Brian. She has made no previous lifetime gifts. The disposition is a transfer of value because the value of Jane's estate is reduced. The value transferred is £130,000, the loss to Jane's estate.

	£
Value transferred	130,000
Less: annual exemptions for 2007/08 and 2006/07	6,000
Potentially exempt transfer	124,000

No tax is payable at the time of the gift. Jane has made a PET, not a chargeable transfer, and so her cumulative total is at present unaffected. If Jane survives until 1 March 2015, the PET will become completely exempt. If Jane dies before that date, the PET will become a chargeable transfer.

4.5   Other lifetime transfers: lifetime chargeable transfers

Any lifetime transfer which does not fall within the definition of a PET (see **4.4**) is an immediately chargeable transfer. The main example is a lifetime transfer made on or after 22 March 2006 into any trust other than a disabled trust. The charge to IHT on lifetime creation of trusts is part of a wider regime under which further charges to tax arise during the existence of the trust and on its ending. The details of these further charges are beyond the scope of this book. The examples below refer to transfers into trusts: in each case it is assumed that the trusts are not disabled trusts.

4.5.1   Calculating tax on a lifetime chargeable transfer

Where an individual makes a lifetime chargeable transfer (LCT), the IHT calculation begins with application of the first three steps as described at **4.4.1**, **4.4.2** and **4.4.3**. Once relevant exemptions and reliefs have been applied, the balance is chargeable to IHT and tax must be calculated by applying step 4.

The rates of tax applicable to LCTs are:

(a)   0% on the first £312,000 (the nil rate band); and

(b)   20% on the balance of the chargeable transfer (this rate being half the rate for transfers which are chargeable on death).

However, chargeable transfers made in the seven years before the current chargeable transfer reduce the nil rate band available to that current transfer. In other words, the value transferred by chargeable transfers made in the seven years before the current chargeable transfer must be 'cumulated' with that transfer.

4.5.1.1   The effect of cumulation

Example 1

In this example, it is assumed that Venetia has used up her annual exemptions in each relevant tax year.

On 1 May 2008, Venetia transfers £50,000 to the trustees of a trust.

She has previously made the following chargeable transfers (after applying relevant annual exemptions):

1 May 2000	£100,000
1 May 2003	£267,000

She has made no other lifetime transfers (and makes no more in the current tax year).

To calculate the IHT due on the chargeable transfer of £50,000, the values transferred by any chargeable transfers made in the seven years prior to 1 May 2008 must be 'cumulated'.

The transfer of £100,000 was made more than seven years ago and can be ignored.

Venetia's cumulative total consists of the £267,000 transferred on 1 May 2003 (less than seven years before the present transfer).

	£
Nil rate band	312,000
less cumulative total	267,000
	45,000

Tax on current chargeable transfer of £50,000:

£45,000 at 0% =	nil
£5,000 at 20% =	£1,000

Example 2

On 1 May 2009, Venetia makes a further transfer of £94,000 to the trustees of the trust. Assuming that the rates of IHT remain the same as for 2008/09, her position for IHT would be as follows:

Nil rate band exhausted by transfers of 1 May 2003 and 1 May 2008.

Tax on current chargeable transfer of £94,000:

£94,000 at 20% = £18,800

Example 3

Venetia makes the following further transfer to the trustees of the discretionary trust:

1 July 2010   £173,000

Assuming the rates of IHT remain the same as for 2008/09, Venetia's position for IHT would be as follows:

The transfer on 1 May 2003 was made more than seven years ago and can be ignored.

Venetia's cumulative total consists of the £50,000 transferred on 1 May 2008 and the £94,000 transferred on 1 May 2009.

	£	£
Nil rate band		312,000
less cumulative total		
1 May 2008	50,000	
1 May 2009	94,000	144,000
		168,000

Tax on current chargeable transfer of £173,000:

£168,000 at 0% = nil

£5,000 at 20% = £1,000

Note that the effect of death on lifetime transfers is considered at **4.6.3**.

4.5.2 Payment of tax

4.5.2.1 Trustees pay

The transferor is primarily liable for IHT, although HMRC may also claim the tax from the trustees. In practice, the trustees often pay IHT out of the property they have been given.

Example

Ahmed transfers £146,000 cash into a trust. His cumulative total is £272,000 and he is entitled to two annual exemptions. Ahmed stipulates that the trustees must pay any IHT.

		£
Value transferred		146,000
Less:	Two annual exemptions	6,000
		140,000
Rate of tax:	Cumulative total £272,000, so £40,000 of the nil rate band is left	
	£40,000 @ 0%	0
	£100,000 @ 20%	20,000
Tax payable by trustees:		20,000

4.5.2.2 Transferor pays: grossing up

If the transferor pays, the amount of tax will be more than it would be if the trustees paid.

This is because IHT is charged on the value transferred, ie the loss to the transferor's estate brought about by the gift (see **4.4.2**). If the transferor pays, the loss is increased by the amount of tax he pays.

Example

Henrietta transfers £80,000 in cash to trustees of a trust. Earlier in the tax year, she gave them £318,000 in cash. She has made no previous chargeable transfers.

The annual exemptions for this tax year and last have already been used by the gift of £318,000 and her cumulative total stands at £312,000. All the current transfer will be taxed at 20%.

If trustees pay IHT:

The loss to her estate is £80,000. Tax payable is 20% of £80,000, which is £16,000.

If Henrietta pays IHT:

The total loss to her estate (ie the value transferred) is £80,000 plus the IHT payable on that transfer.

Therefore, in order to ascertain the value transferred, it is necessary to calculate what sum would, after deduction of tax at the appropriate rate (ie 20%), leave £80,000 (ie the transfer must be grossed up).

Gross up £80,000 at 20%

$$£80,000 \quad \times \quad \frac{100}{80} \quad = \quad £100,000$$

The gross value transferred is £100,000.

Calculate tax on £100,000:

£100,000 @ 20% = £20,000

The tax payable by Henrietta is more than the tax payable by the trustees.

However, if she pays, the trustees are left with the full amount of the property transferred, £80,000, as opposed to £64,000 if they pay.

4.5.2.3 Time for payment

IHT on lifetime chargeable transfers made after 5 April and before 1 October in any year is due on the 30 April in the following year. IHT on lifetime chargeable transfers which are not made between those dates is due six months after the end of the month in which the chargeable transfer is made.

4.6 Effect of death on lifetime transfers

4.6.1 Introduction

The death of a transferor may result in a charge to IHT on any transfers of value which he has made in the seven years immediately preceding his death, whether those transfers were potentially exempt or immediately chargeable when they were made. First, PETs made in that period become chargeable and the transferee will be liable for any IHT payable. Secondly, the IHT liability on lifetime chargeable transfers made in that period is recalculated and the trustees will be liable for any extra tax payable. In either case, as the liability arises on death, the rate of tax, once the nil rate band is exceeded, is 40%.

4.6.2 Effect of death on PETs

Potentially exempt transfers are defined and explained in **4.4**. There is no liability on a PET at the time of the transfer, and it will become wholly exempt if the transferor survives for seven years after the transfer. Many gifts will thus escape a charge to IHT.

A PET will become chargeable only if the transferor dies within seven years of making the transfer. If tax is payable, the transferee will be liable for any IHT.

4.6.2.1 Steps 1–3

As seen at **4.4**, the first three steps are applied to determine the size of the PET. Business property relief and/or agricultural property relief may apply to reduce the value transferred, provided that the transferee still owns the business or agricultural property (see *Business Law and Practice*).

4.6.2.2 Step 4: Calculate tax at the appropriate rate

The final step is to identify the rate or rates of tax applicable to the transfer in question. The value transferred after exemptions and reliefs is taxed at rates determined by the transferor's cumulative total at the time of the PET. This will be made up of any lifetime chargeable transfers made in the seven years before the PET, and also of any other PETs made during that period which have become chargeable because of the death of the transferor within seven years.

The rates of tax applicable to chargeable transfers made within seven years of death of the transferor are:

(a)   0% on the first £312,000 (the nil rate band); and

(b)   40% on the balance.

Example 1

On 5 May 2006, Adam gives a house worth £326,000 to his daughter, Emma.

On 21 September 2008, Adam dies, leaving his estate (consisting of quoted shares and bank deposits worth £200,000) to his son, Matthew. He made no other significant lifetime gifts.

The transfer on 5 May 2006 was a PET which has now become chargeable as the transferor has died within seven years.

(1) Tax on the PET	£
Loss to estate	326,000
Less annual exemptions 2006/07; 2005/06	6,000
	320,000

Adam had made no chargeable transfers in the seven years preceding 5 May 2006, so his nil rate band was intact.

Tax on £312,000 @ 0%	Nil
Tax on £8,000 @ 40%	£3,200 (payable by Emma).

(2) Tax on the estate

The cumulation principle means that Adam's nil rate band has been used up by the chargeable transfer made within the preceding seven years.

Tax on £200,000 @ 40%   £80,000 (payable by Adam's PRs from the estate passing to Matthew)

Example 2

Gina gave the following gifts of cash to her children:

1 September 2002	£166,000 to Claire
25 June 2006	£166,000 to James

Gina died on 30 August 2008 leaving her estate (consisting of her house and bank accounts worth a total of £400,000) to the two children equally. She had made no other significant gifts.

Both gifts were PETs which have now become chargeable as Gina has died within seven years.

(1) Tax on the 2002 PET	£
Loss to estate	166,000
Annual exemptions 2002/03; 2001/02	6,000
	160,000

Gina had made no chargeable transfers in the seven years before 1 September 2002 so her nil rate band was intact.

Tax on £160,000 @ 0%	Nil

(2) Tax on the 2006 PET	£
Loss to estate	166,000
Annual exemptions 2005/06; 2004/05	6,000
	160,000

Gina's cumulative total of chargeable transfers made in the seven years up to 25 June 2006 was £160,000 (the 2002 transfer to Claire). Only £152,000 of Gina's nil rate band remains.

Tax on £160,000

£152,000 @ 0%	Nil
£8,000 @ 40%	£3,200 (payable by James)

(3) Tax on Gina's estate: Gina's nil rate band has been used up by the two chargeable transfers in the last seven years.

Tax on £400,000 @ 40%	£160,000 (payable by Gina's PRs from the property passing to the children)

4.6.2.3 Tapering relief

Where a PET has become chargeable tapering relief is available if the transferor survives for more than three years after the transfer. The relief works by reducing the tax payable on the PET.

Tax is reduced to the following percentages:

(a)   transfers within three to four years before death: 80% of death charge

(b)   transfers within four to five years before death: 60% of death charge

(c)   transfers within five to six years before death: 40% of death charge

(d)   transfers within six to seven years before death: 20% of death charge

Example

1 January 2002	Leonora makes a gift of £96,000 to Isadora
	Leonora's cumulative total before the gift is made is £312,000
1 July 2008	Leonora dies

Effect of death:	£
Transfer of value	96,000
Less: Annual exemptions 2001/02; 2000/01	6,000
PET (which is now chargeable)	90,000

Rate of tax: Cumulative total £312,000 so all £90,000 is in the 40% band

£90,000 @ 40%	36,000

Tapering relief applies. Leonora died within six to seven years of the PET so 20% of this figure is payable

Tax payable by Isadora 20% of £36,000	7,200

4.6.3 Effect of death on lifetime chargeable transfers

If a transferor dies within seven years of making a lifetime chargeable transfer (eg, into a trust), the IHT payable must be recalculated and more IHT may be payable by the trustees. The tax bill may be increased not only because the full death rate of IHT will now apply (subject to tapering relief) but also because PETs made before the lifetime chargeable transfer may have become chargeable. They will increase the cumulative total and so reduce the nil rate band applicable to the lifetime chargeable transfer. If the recalculated bill is lower (which may occur if tapering relief is available), no tax is refunded.

IHT is recalculated in accordance with the rates of tax in force at the transferor's death if these are less than the rates in force at the time of the transfer; if not, the death rates at the time of the transfer are applied. If more than three years have elapsed between the transfer and the death, tapering relief applies to reduce the recalculated tax as for a PET.

Example 1

On 1 May 2005, George transferred £368,000 into a trust on condition that the trustees must pay the IHT. He had made no other lifetime gifts.

(a) On 1 May 2005, George made a lifetime chargeable transfer.

	£
Value transferred	368,000
Less: Annual exemptions 2005/06; 2004/05	6,000
	362,000

Calculate tax.

£312,000 @ 0%	0
£50,000 @ 20%	10,000
Tax payable by trustees	10,000

(b) George dies on 1 September 2008, within seven years of the lifetime chargeable transfer.

Recalculate tax at death rates.

	£
£312,000 @ 0%	0
£50,000 @ 40%	20,000
	20,000

George died between three and four years after the transfer, so apply tapering relief

	£
80% of £20,000	16,000
Less: tax already paid	10,000
Further tax payable by trustees	6,000

Example 2

Drusilla dies on 1 August 2008. During her lifetime she made only the following transfers of value:

1 July 2002	Gift of £133,000 to Rukhsana
1 July 2005	Gift of £319,000 on discretionary trusts

The consequences are as follows:

(a) On 1 July 2002, Drusilla made a PET:

	£
Value transferred	133,000
Less: Annual exemptions 2002/03; 2001/02	6,000
Potentially exempt transfer	127,000

(b) On 1 July 2005, Drusilla made a lifetime chargeable transfer:

Charge to tax on 1 July 2005:

	£
Value transferred	319,000
Less: Annual exemptions 2004/05; 2003/04	6,000
	313,000

Rate of tax	Cumulative total zero	
	£312,000 @ 0%	0
	£1,000 @ 20%	200
Tax payable by trustees		200

(c) Recalculation of tax on death: Drusilla has died within seven years of 1 July 2002, so the PET of £127,000 to Rukhsana has become chargeable. There is no IHT on the transfer as it falls within Drusilla's nil rate band, but her cumulative total is now £127,000.

The tax on the transfer of 1 July 2005 must be recalculated.

Rate of tax: Cumulative total £127,000 so £185,000 of nil rate band left

	£
£185,000 @ 0%	0
£128,000 @ 40%	51,200
£313,000	51,200

Tapering relief applies. Drusilla died between three and four years after the transfer so the recalculated tax is reduced to 80%.

	£
80% of £51,200	40,960
Less: IHT already paid	200
Tax payable by trustees	40,760

(d) In the seven years before her death, Drusilla made two chargeable transfers. Her cumulative total at the time of her death is:

	£
1 July 2002 PET (now chargeable)	127,000
1 July 2005 LCT (lifetime chargeable transfer)	313,000
	440,000

This means that, when calculating tax on Drusilla's estate on death, her nil rate band has been used up, and tax on her estate will be charged at a flat rate of 40%.

4.7 Chapter summary

The main occasions of charge to IHT are:

(a)   on death on the value of an individual's estate;

(b)   on lifetime gifts made by one individual to another where the donor dies within 7 years of the gift;

(c)   on lifetime gifts into a trust.

Lifetime gifts to an individual are only chargeable to IHT if the donor dies within the 7 years after making the gift. At the time such a gift is made it is a 'potentially exempt transfer' (PET). It becomes exempt if the donor survives for 7 years or chargeable if he dies during that period.

Lifetime gifts into a trust are immediately chargeable to IHT at the time they are made. They are known as 'lifetime chargeable transfers' (LCTs).

There are four steps to be used to calculate liability to IHT.

Step 1: Identify the transfer of value

On death this means the value of the estate, ie all the property to which the deceased was beneficially entitled.

For lifetime transfers this means any transaction which reduces the value of the transferor's estate. This includes any gift or a sale at an undervalue.

Step 2: Find the value transferred

On death this means the value of the property in the estate, valued at open market value.

For lifetime transfers this means the amount by which the transferor's estate has been reduced as a result of the transfer.

Step 3: Apply exemptions and reliefs

Transfers to spouse or charity are exempt whether in lifetime or on death.

Some exemptions apply only to lifetime transfers. These include annual exemption (£3,000 pa), small gifts, marriage gifts and gifts made as normal expenditure out of income.

Business Property Relief applies to reduce the value transferred by a transfer of certain types of business property by 100% or 50%. This may apply to transfers made in lifetime or on death.

Step 4: Calculate tax at the appropriate rate

Tax is charged at 0% on the first £312,000 of transfers (the nil rate band).

In order to calculate IHT on any transfer, chargeable transfers made during the preceding seven years must be taken into account. Such transfers will reduce the nil rate band available for the current transfer.

The balance of the transfer in excess of the nil rate band is taxed at 40% if the transfer is on death or 20% for LCTs.

PETs made within 7 years of the transferor's death become chargeable as a result of his death. The rate of tax is 40%, but the amount of tax is tapered if the transferor survived for more than 3 years after the transfer.

If a transferor dies within 7 years of making a LCT, tax must be recalculated at death rates, applying taper if the death was more than 3 years after the transfer.

Chapter 5

Tax-efficient Investments

5.1 Introduction

An individual with high levels of income or capital gains can reduce his exposure to tax by making tax-efficient investments. Depending on which investment vehicle is chosen, it may be possible to:

(a) obtain income tax relief on the investment (and so pay less income tax in the current year);

(b) ensure that future income or capital gains escape tax;

(c) avoid paying CGT on a capital gain by re-investing it.

The rest of this chapter introduces the main features of some investments which meet these objectives. However, no investor should allow a tax advantage to cloud his judgement as to the merits or risk of any particular investment. The list is not comprehensive, but gives examples of the opportunities available. Fuller treatment of these complex matters can be found in *Revenue Law – Principles and Practice*, 26th edn (Tottel, 2008) and *Simon's Direct Taxes* (LexisNexis Butterworths, loose-leaf).

5.2 Investments eligible for income tax relief

5.2.1 Enterprise Investment Scheme (EIS)

This relief is designed to encourage investment in smaller (and riskier) companies. An individual is allowed to subscribe up to £500,000 each tax year in the ordinary shares of qualifying unquoted companies. Broadly, this means trading companies that are not listed on The Stock Exchange, so there is no ready market for their shares. Certain asset-based activities, for example share dealing, property development, farming, shipbuilding and coal and steel production are excluded. During the two years before and three years after the subscription, the individual must not be 'connected with' the company. Thus, the combined shareholdings of the investor and his 'associates' (which includes spouse and close family) must not exceed 30%; neither he nor his associates are normally permitted to be paid employees or directors, although there are exceptions to this rule.

The relief is given by deducting a sum equal to 20% of the amount invested from the shareholder's income tax liability for the tax year of the investment (the maximum deduction is, therefore, £100,000), provided he continues to satisfy the personal qualifying conditions throughout the next three years. A further attraction is that gains on disposal will be exempt from CGT; conversely, if the enterprise fails, the investor's loss on his shares may be set against his income or capital gains.

5.2.2 Venture Capital Trust (VCT)

A VCT is a quoted company run by professional fund managers as a vehicle to hold shares in a range of unquoted trading companies which match the EIS criteria. Smaller enterprises are thus given access to funds and the investor buying shares in the VCT can invest indirectly in smaller businesses, at the same time reducing the risk attendant on investment in a single unquoted company.

VCTs carry tax advantages similar to EISs, but to qualify the shares must be held for five years and the maximum investment each tax year is £200,000. A sum equal to 30% of the amount invested can be deducted from the investor's income tax liability (so the maximum tax deduction in any one tax year is £60,000). Gains on disposal are also CGT exempt. The added feature is that dividend income from a VCT is exempt from income tax.

5.3 Investments producing tax-free income or capital gains

5.3.1 Individual Savings Account (ISA)

This scheme came into effect on 6 April 1999. There are two types of ISA: the Stocks and Shares ISA and the Cash ISA.

In each tax year, an individual aged 18 or above (or 16 for a cash ISA) and resident in the UK can put money into either or both types of ISA. If both types are used, they can be held with different providers. Subscription levels for 2008/09 provide for an overall limit of £7,200.

The whole investment (of up to £7,200) may be in stocks and shares. Alternatively, stocks and shares could be combined with cash (up to a maximum of £3,600).

The tax benefits of ISAs are as follows.

(a) No income tax liability on income produced by the ISA.
(b) No CGT liability on gains arising from ISA investments.
(c) Tax relief is not forfeited when money is taken out of the scheme.

Generally, although money can be withdrawn from either type of ISA at any time without losing the tax benefits, contributions will remain the same for the purposes of calculating the available allowance for that tax year. So, if an individual invests £6,200 in an ISA and, in the same year, withdraws £2,000, the maximum additional investment that he can make into an ISA in that year is £1,000 not £3,000.

As an exception, to encourage investment in shares, transfers may be made from Cash ISAs to Stocks and Shares ISAs and the transfer is treated as if it had initially been paid into a Stocks and Shares ISA. Consequently, further payments into a Cash ISA can still be made up to the maximum of £3,600 (so long as the total allowance of £7,200 is not exceeded). This exception does not apply to transfers from Stocks and Shares ISAs into Cash ISAs.

5.3.2 Enterprise Investment Scheme (EIS)

Capital gains are CGT exempt (see **5.2.1**).

5.3.3 Venture Capital Trust (VCT)

Both income and capital gains are exempt (see **5.2.2**).

5.4 Investment to escape a CGT liability

5.4.1 Deferral relief on re-investment in EIS shares

Unlimited deferral of capital gains arising on the disposal of any asset is available where an individual subscribes wholly for cash for shares in a company which qualifies under the EIS. (As the shares must be acquired for cash, this relief will not usually be available to a partner or sole trader who transfers his business to a company, as the shares acquired following such a transfer are usually in return for the non-cash assets of the business.)

(a) This deferral relief is available where the shares acquired meet the requirements of the EIS (see **5.2.1**).

(b) The relief is complex but, in general terms, the individual's chargeable gain on the disposal of the asset (up to the subscription cost of the shares) is deferred until he disposes of the shares. The deferred gain is taxed at the rate applicable to the taxpayer in the tax year of the disposal of the EIS shares.

(c) The relief is available where the EIS shares are acquired within one year before or three years after the disposal.

(d) As regards the 'true gain' on the disposal of the EIS shares themselves, a slightly different relief applies. Such gains will be exempt from CGT if held for three years, but only if the investor is not 'connected' with the company (see **5.2.1**).

Example

Shares in X Co Ltd (not EIS) have been held by Andrew for two years. He sells them and realises a gain of £60,000. This gain is deferred when he subscribes for shares in Y Co Ltd (an EIS company) for £100,000. Andrew holds the shares in Y Co Ltd for four years and then sells them for £120,000. His deferred gain of £60,000 is now chargeable to CGT. The 'true' gain of £20,000 on the disposal of the shares in Y Co Ltd will be exempt if all the qualifying conditions are met.

A similar relief on reinvestment in VCT shares was withdrawn in the 2004 Budget.

Part I Summaries – Revenue Law

Chapter 2: Income Tax

Topic	Summary	References
Occasions of charge	Individuals, partners, personal representatives and trustees could all incur IT liability on the receipt of taxable income.	
Income or capital?	Income receipts must be distinguished from capital receipts. Only income can be subject to IT; capital gains may be subject to capital gains tax.	2.1.3
Chargeable income	To be chargeable, the income must come from a specified source and not be exempt.	2.2.1 and 2.2.2
	In practice, most income receipts are chargeable. In each tax year, all chargeable income from the different sources are added together to find the taxpayer's total income.	2.2.3
Deduction at source	The payer of some forms of income (eg salaries, interest and dividends) is obliged to deduct the recipient's basic rate IT liability, before payment, and send this direct to HMCR. In such cases, it is necessary to gross-up the payment received by the taxpayer, in order to find his true income from that source. The grossed-up (as opposed to the net) income will be added to his total income.	2.2.3.1 to 2.2.3.4
Allowances and reliefs	The taxpayer may deduct allowable reliefs (eg interest on loans to invest in his business) and relevant personal reliefs (eg personal allowance and blind person's allowance) from his total income. The resulting figure is his taxable income.	2.3 and 2.4
Savings / dividend and non-savings/ dividend income	Interest and dividends are savings/dividend income. All other income is non-savings/dividend income.	2.5.1 to 2.5.3
Rates of tax	Generally, taxable income falls into two bands – the basic rate band and the higher rate band. Within these two bands, however, different rates apply, depending on whether the income is classed as non-savings/dividend income or savings/dividend income. Non-savings/dividend income is taxed first, followed by interest and then dividends.	2.5

Topic	Summary	References
Tax credits	Once the taxpayer's total IT liability is worked out, credit is given for any tax deducted at source (by his employer, bank etc.). The remaining balance is then sent to HMCR, to meet the taxpayer's outstanding liability.	2.6
IT – liability and time for payment	In general terms, the recipient of taxable income must pay the balance of his tax liability to HMCR by 31 January following the tax year in which the income was earned. Special rules apply to the self-employed.	2.8

Chapter 3: Capital Gains Tax

Topic	Summary	References
Occasions of charge	Individuals, partners, personal representatives and trustees could all incur CGT liability when they dispose of chargeable assets.	
Disposals	For CGT to arise there must be a disposal of a chargeable asset. Disposals include gifts, as well as sales, but do not include property passing on death.	
Chargeable assets	Most forms of property are chargeable. The main exemption is sterling. In general terms, depreciating assets are also non-chargeable. This prevents the taxpayer from setting losses on these types of assets against his other chargeable gains.	3.1.3
Calculation of the gain	In basic terms, this is the sale price less allowable expenditure. The main element of allowable expenditure will usually be the acquisition cost of the asset but other expenditure is also deductible.	3.3
	To work out the notional gain made on a gift, the asset is deemed to be disposed of at its market value on the date of the gift.	3.2.1
Reliefs	Various reliefs are available, depending on the circumstances. Most of the reliefs available are aimed at encouraging business investment. Otherwise, a major relief for the ordinary taxpayer is the principal private residence exemption.	3.4.1
Disposals between spouses (and civil partners)	These are treated as being for such consideration as to provide neither a gain nor a loss. On a subsequent disposal by the donee spouse, the gain will be assessed by using the donor spouse's acquisition cost.	3.9.1
Losses	Losses can be set against gains of the same tax year to reduce the net chargeable gain. Unabsorbed losses can be taken forward to set against gains of future tax years, but in such a way that the taxpayer does not lose the use of his annual exemption in future years.	3.7
Rates of tax	After applying an annual exemption to the taxpayer's net aggregate gains, the balance will be taxed at a flat rate of 18%.	3.5 and 3.6

Topic	Summary	References
Liability and time for payment	Any taxpayer still having net aggregate gains after applying his annual exemption, is liable to pay CGT on them by 31 January following the tax year in which the gains were made.	3.1.6

Chapter 4: Inheritance Tax

Topic	Summary	References
Occasions of charge	A charge to IHT can arise on transfers into most types of trust, on other lifetime transfers made within seven years of the transferor's death and on property passing on death.	
Transfer of value	IHT is charged on the value transferred by a chargeable transfer. A chargeable transfer is a transfer of value made by an individual but which is not an exempt transfer. A transfer of value is any disposition which reduces the value of the transferor's estate.	
Value transferred	This is the amount of the reduction in the transferor's estate. On death, it is the value of the estate.	
Exemptions applying to all types of lifetime transfer	Any property passing to a spouse (or civil partner) and to a charity is exempt. Business property relief (and agricultural property relief) may be available on relevant business (and agricultural) property, to reduce the value transferred by either 50% or 100%.	4.3.3.3
	In addition, lifetime transfers may be exempted by a number of other exemptions, including the small gifts exemption, gifts in consideration of marriage and the annual exemption.	4.4.3.4
Transfers into most types of trust	To the extent that exemptions are not available, these are immediately chargeable to IHT and are referred to as lifetime chargeable transfers (LCTs).	4.5
Rate of tax on LCTs at time of transfer	Subject to cumulation (see below), in tax year 2008/09, the first £312,000 of transfers is charged at the nil rate (the nil rate band). All amounts above this are charged at a flat rate of 20%.	
Other lifetime transfers	The main example of these is a gift. To the extent that other exemptions are not available, the transfer is a potentially exempt transfer (PET). As PETs, they are exempt from any IHT charge at the time of the transfer and will become unconditionally exempt if the transferor survives for seven years after the transfer.	4.4

Topic	Summary	References
IHT – effect of death of transferor within seven years of any type of lifetime transfer	To the extent that they do not fall within the nil rate band, LCTs made within 7 years of the transferor's death must be re-assessed at the death rate of 40%.	4.6.3
	Any PETs made within seven years of transferor's death become chargeable transfers (failed PETs) and, to the extent that they do not fall within the nil rate band, are then chargeable at the death rate of 40%.	4.6.2, 4.6.2.1 and 4.6.2.2
IHT – cumulation	To assess the rate of tax on any individual transfer, it is necessary to take into account the value of any other chargeable transfers made within the seven years before the transfer being assessed. The nil rate band is applied to transfers in chronological order, so chargeable transfers within the previous seven years will have taken up some or all of the nil rate band, leaving only the balance for the transfer being assessed.	4.5.1
IHT – tapering relief	If any lifetime transfer (LCT or failed PET) was made between three and seven years before the death of the transferor, any IHT charge to which it is subject is progressively reduced by between 80% and 20% of the full liability.	4.6.2.3
IHT – transfers on death	The deceased is deemed to have made a transfer of value immediately before death. The value transferred is the value of his 'estate' immediately before death. The estate includes all property to which the deceased was beneficially entitled. Property held by the deceased on trust for others does not form part of the estate.	4.3
	Although property held by the deceased as a beneficial joint tenant passes automatically by survivorship to the remaining joint tenant(s), the value of the deceased's share in the property will form part of his estate for IHT purposes. Also included in the estate is property, which the deceased transferred in his lifetime but which he continued to have the use of until his death (gifts with a reservation of benefit).	4.3.1
	Liabilities of the deceased at the time of death and reasonable funeral expenses are deductible from the value of the estate.	4.3.2.4

Topic	Summary	References
IHT – exemptions applicable to death transfers	Any property passing to a spouse (or civil partner) and to a charity is exempt. Business property relief (and agricultural property relief) is available on relevant business (and agricultural) property, to reduce the value transferred by either 50% or 100%.	4.3.3
IHT – rate of tax on death transfers	In tax year 2008/09 (and subject to cumulation with all chargeable transfers (LCTs and failed PETs) in the seven years before death) the first £312,000 of the estate is charged at the nil rate. All amounts above this are charged at a flat rate of 40%.	
IHT – liability and time for payment	Primary liability for IHT falls on the donee of a failed PET, the transferor of a LCT and the personal representatives of the deceased's estate.	
	In the case of lifetime transfers, if the transfer was made between 1 October and 5 April, the date for payment is six months from the end of the month in which the transfer was made. Otherwise, the payment date is on 30 April following the date of the transfer. On death, the general rule is that IHT is payable six months after the end of the month in which the death occurred. However, in the case of certain assets, such as land and shares, the tax may be paid in ten yearly instalments.	

Appendix to Part I

Tax Rates and Further Reading

Summary of rates and allowances for 2008/09

Value Added Tax

Rates:	Standard rate	17.5%
Registration threshold:		£67,000

Income Tax

Rates for non-savings/dividend income

Rates:	Basic rate:	£0–£34,800	20%
	Higher rate:	over £34,800	40%

Rates for savings/dividend income		Interest	Dividends
Rates:	Starting rate	£0–£2,320	10%	10%
	Basic rate	over £2,320–£34,800	20%	10%
	Higher rate	over £34,800	40%	32.5%

Income tax allowances:

Personal allowance	£6,035

Capital Gains Tax

Rates: Individuals, PRs and trustees:	18%
Annual exempt amount:	
Individuals:	£9,600
Trustees (generally):	£4,800

Inheritance Tax

Rates (for transfers on or after 6 April 2008):

£0 to £312,000	nil %
over £312,000	40%

Transfer on death

Full rates apply.

Lifetime transfers

(a) Potentially exempt transfers

Gifts to individuals, and gifts into accumulation and maintenance trusts or trusts for the disabled or trusts with an interest in possession (not otherwise exempt).

(i)   On or within seven years of death

On death, the full rates apply with a tapered reduction in the tax payable on transfers as follows:

Years between gift and death	Percentage of full charge
0–3	100
3–4	80
4–5	60
5–6	40
6–7	20

Note: the scale in force at date of death applies

(ii)   More than seven years before death – gift is exempt therefore NIL tax payable

(b) Chargeable transfers

Gifts into and out of most types of trusts and gifts involving companies.

At the time of gift, half the full rates apply. If the gift also falls within seven years of death, (a)(i) above applies but the lifetime tax will be credited against tax due on death.

Further reading

Yellow Tax Handbook 2008–2009 (Butterworths)

Orange Tax Handbook 2008–2009 (Butterworths)

Tolley's Value Added Tax 2008–2009 (Tolley)

Tolley's Income Tax 2008–2009 (Tolley)

Tolley's Capital Gains Tax 2008–2009 (Tolley)

Tolley's Inheritance Tax 2008–2009 (Tolley)

Revenue Law – Principles and Practice, 26th edn (Tottel, 2008)

Simon, *Simon's Direct Taxes* (Butterworths, loose-leaf)

De Voil, *Indirect Tax Service* (Butterworths, loose-leaf)

Part II

THE PROFESSIONAL CONDUCT

OF SOLICITORS

Author's note

- This Part has been compiled from the Solicitors' Code of Conduct available at the time of writing.
- This book is not intended as a definitive guide to the subject.
- This book is not intended to constitute legal advice. The publisher and author are not responsible or liable for the results of any person acting (or omitting to act) on the basis of information contained within this publication.

Chapter 6

The Legal Profession

6.1 Professional conduct

'Professional conduct' is the term that is often used to describe the rules and regulations with which a solicitor must comply. Solicitors, like every other person, must comply with the laws of the country. However, additional requirements are placed upon solicitors due to the nature of their job.

A solicitor is said to be a member of a profession. Other examples of members of professions include doctors and accountants. The public must be able to place a great deal of trust in such professionals due to the work that they carry out. For example, on a simplistic level, both solicitors and accountants often handle large amounts of clients' money. A client must be able to trust that this money will be safe in the hands of those professionals.

In addition to holding client monies, solicitors must be able to be trusted to act in the best interests of clients. Clients often seek advice from solicitors concerning transactions worth millions of pounds. With that amount of money at stake, the client must be certain that the solicitor will provide honest advice and take every step to protect that client's interests. Equally, clients often seek a solicitor's advice on sensitive matters. The client must be reassured that whatever the matter, the solicitor can be trusted to keep the information confidential and not, for example, sell it to third parties like the press.

Accordingly, in addition to the general law, the Solicitors Regulation Authority publishes a number of rules with which the solicitor must comply at all times. These rules apply to the entire profession, including trainee solicitors and student members. The aim of these rules is to ensure the protection of the public and to uphold the integrity of the profession itself.

Breach of these rules can have severe consequences. For example, where a solicitor breaches certain rules relating to the service provided to clients, he may be ordered to pay the client compensation of up to £15,000. The ultimate sanction for breach of the rules of professional conduct is to be 'struck off'. This effectively ends the solicitor's career and prevents him from acting as a solicitor.

6.2 The Solicitors Regulation Authority

The Solicitors Regulation Authority ('SRA') was established by The Law Society in January 2007 to take over the regulation of solicitors from The Law Society itself. The SRA also controls matters such as training and admission to the profession.

The SRA's own literature states that it is independent and regulates in the public interest. The SRA is governed by a board of 16 members. This board is comprised of nine solicitors and seven lay members. The current Chair is Peter Williamson, a former President of The Law Society. Details of the members of the SRA's board can be found at www.sra.org.uk.

The SRA has a staff of more than 600, based in Redditch and Leamington Spa, and an annual budget of over £50 million. This budget is funded from the practising certificate fee (see **18.1**).

The regulation of the profession is considered in detail in **Chapter 7**.

6.3   The Law Society

6.3.1   Introduction

The Law Society is the representative body for solicitors in England and Wales. It was founded in 1825 to raise the reputation of the profession. Today it fulfils a number of roles.

The Law Society represents solicitors within England and Wales. For example, The Law Society lobbies the Government in respect of changes in the law, and campaigns for better working conditions for solicitors, particularly on behalf of solicitors undertaking publicly funded work. The Law Society also seeks to improve the reputation of the profession as a whole, and to promote the benefits of using a solicitor to the general public.

6.3.2   Membership

After admission, membership of The Law Society is voluntary. However, all members of the profession are bound by the rules of professional conduct whether they are members of The Law Society or not.

Student membership of The Law Society is compulsory in certain cases. For example, students wishing to enrol on the Legal Practice Course (perhaps the most common route of qualifying as a solicitor) must join The Law Society as student members prior to enrolling on the course.

6.3.3   Governance

The Law Society is governed by the Council of The Law Society. The Council delegates many of its powers and decision-making responsibilities to various Boards, such as the Corporate Governance Board and the Law Reform Board.

6.3.4   Local law societies

There are approximately 120 local law societies throughout England and Wales. These often provide representation, training and facilities (such as law libraries) to local firms within their area. They also help to provide a link between The Law Society and local solicitors. Local law societies do not have any disciplinary powers.

6.4   Different aspects of practice

The legal profession is made up of a number of different types of organisations. Within these organisations there are a number of roles that a solicitor may fill.

6.4.1   Sole practitioner

A sole practitioner is a solicitor who chooses to practise on his own. He almost certainly will employ administration staff, such as secretaries, etc, and may also employ other solicitors or paralegals. However, he will own, and therefore be responsible for, the firm in its entirety.

Whilst sole practitioners used to be fairly common, there is a general trend for solicitors to practise in larger organisations. There are a number of reasons for this. One prominent reason is cost. In recent times, a solicitor's practice has become more reliant on information technology. Solicitors firms use such equipment for researching legal issues, for running sophisticated accounts programs, and for the day-to-day management of clients' files. Both the hardware and software required to perform these operations is expensive. Accordingly, it is easier to share this cost out amongst a number of partners, rather than for one person (ie the sole practitioner) to cover the entire cost.

Another reason is practicalities. When a partner, or other fee earner, in a law firm goes on holiday, his clients' matters may temporarily be taken over by another solicitor within the firm. The sole practitioner may not have this option. Accordingly, the sole practitioner may have to arrange for a locum solicitor to supervise his office in his absence.

There is also a growing trend for solicitors to specialise in one particular area of law, for example family law or insolvency. Unless the sole practitioner is running a niche practice, this option is not open to him.

Lastly, the sole practitioner's right to practise on his own is restricted by the SRA's restrictions on who is 'qualified' to supervise an office (see **18.5.1**). In the future it is proposed that the SRA's permission will be required to practise as a sole practitioner (a 'sole solicitor' endorsement).

6.4.2 Partnership

Most solicitors' firms operate as a partnership. The firm is owned and run by the partners, who then employ other solicitors and administration staff to work for them. As the partners own the firm, they are entitled to share the profits generated by the firm between them.

Some large firms have two types of partners – 'equity' partners and 'salaried' partners. A salaried partner is the first step on the partnership ladder. A salaried partner may not be entitled to share in the profits of the firm, but he will receive a salary from the firm in excess of that paid to other non-partner fee earners. After a number of years a salaried partner may be promoted to an equity partner, whereupon he will be entitled to share in the profits of the firm.

The Solicitors' Code of Conduct 2007 ('the Code') imposes various responsibilities upon partners in terms of supervision of, and responsibility for, their firm (see further **Chapter 18**).

6.4.3 Incorporated practices

A solicitors' practice may be incorporated as a company registered under the Companies Act 1985, or be a limited liability partnership (LLP). An incorporated practice must be approved by the SRA as a 'recognised body'.

A recognised body must be controlled by solicitors (or other lawyers subject to Rule 14 of the Code) or other recognised bodies. The directors/shareholders (or members in the case of an LLP) must all be solicitors holding a practising certificate, or other lawyers (see Rule 14).

All the rules, principles and requirements of professional conduct that apply to individual solicitors apply equally to recognised bodies.

Recognition of a recognised body lasts for three years (unless revoked by the SRA within that period).

6.4.4 Multi-national partnerships

Under Rule 12 of the Code, a multi-national practice, consisting of solicitors and registered foreign lawyers/registered European lawyers, may be formed and may operate in England and Wales (subject to certain restrictions).

6.4.5 The future

The Legal Services Bill will introduce the concept of Alternative Business Structures. It is anticipated that these structures will allow non-lawyers to own law firms or become partners in law firms. At the time of writing, it is anticipated that these new Alternative Business Structures will be available from 2011.

Some firms, such as the Automobile Association, have already expressed an interest in taking advantage of such provisions.

The Bill will also introduce Legal Disciplinary Practices (LDPs). These will allow firms to be made up of up to 25% non-lawyers. It is anticipated that these will be allowed from 2009.

6.4.6 Employed solicitors

An 'employed solicitor' is a solicitor who is employed by a non-solicitor employer. He may also be referred to as 'in-house counsel'. A number of large companies have in-house legal departments to advise on issues that arise from their business activities. Law firms often second their solicitors to work for their larger clients on a temporary basis. It is not uncommon for these solicitors to leave their law firm and go on to work for these clients on a full-time basis as employed solicitors.

Employed solicitors are subject to the same rules and regulations as solicitors in private practice. They will also be subject to the additional requirements of Rule 13 ('In-house practice').

6.4.7 Law centres

Law centres are run by solicitors, other legal advisers and community workers, to provide free legal advice and case work to disadvantaged individuals within local communities. The Law Centres Federation acts as a co-ordinating body for law centres nationally.

A solicitor who works for a law centre must still comply with all of the rules of professional conduct.

6.4.8 Legal advice centres

A legal advice centre is a place where the public may attend for legal advice but where no case work is undertaken. In many parts of the country legal advice centres are operated by the Citizens' Advice Bureaux and solicitors will attend to give free legal advice either as honorary legal advisers, or on a rota scheme. The College of Law itself runs legal advice centres, staffed by its students under the supervision of a qualified solicitor.

6.4.9 Duty solicitor schemes

The police station duty solicitor scheme aims to provide advice and assistance to people at police stations who otherwise would not be legally represented.

The court duty solicitor scheme aims to provide emergency legal representation at magistrates' courts on a rota basis to those who are not otherwise represented.

In both cases, the scheme is staffed by contracted solicitors on a rota basis, with fees being paid by the Legal Services Commission.

6.5 Chapter summary

(1) A solicitor is said to be part of a profession. Accordingly, a higher standard of behaviour is expected of him than of a member of the public.

(2) The Solicitors Regulation Authority regulates the legal profession. It publishes rules and regulations with which a solicitor must comply in addition to the general law.

(3) These rules must be obeyed by all solicitors, whether they are members of The Law Society or not.

(4) The Law Society represents the legal profession.

(5) The legal profession is made up of a number of different types of practices.

Chapter 7

Regulating the Profession

7.1 Introduction

The previous chapter looked at the legal profession and the fact that a higher standard of behaviour is expected from the profession than from an ordinary citizen. This is because solicitors are often trusted with large amounts of client money and/or a client's confidential information.

This chapter will consider who is responsible for specifying the rules which ensure that this higher standard of behaviour is met, and also how these rules are enforced.

7.2 How the profession regulates itself

7.2.1 The Solicitors Regulation Authority

As was noted in **Chapter 6**, the Solicitors Regulation Authority ('SRA') was created by The Law Society in January 2007 to deal with the regulation of solicitors in England and Wales. However, a separate organisation, the Legal Complaints Service, is often the first point of contact for the public when complaining about solicitors (see **7.4.2**).

The SRA was created in anticipation of the Legal Services Bill. Once the Bill becomes law, the regulation of the profession will continue to be undertaken by the SRA, which will be overseen by a newly created Legal Services Board.

The SRA can publish and enforce rules governing how solicitors behave and conduct their business. The most important of these rules are contained in the Solicitors' Code of Conduct 2007 (the main subject of this Part) and the Solicitors' Accounts Rules 1998.

From time to time, the rules that govern the conduct of solicitors are replaced by a newer version. For example, the Solicitors' Code of Conduct 2007 replaced the 8th edition of the Guide to the Professional Conduct of Solicitors, which was published in 1999. The rules are updated regularly and it is important to refer to the most recent version. The current version of the rules is published on the SRA's website.

7.2.2   Aim of the Code

The aim of the Code is to ensure that the profession is able to meet the needs of its clients and society. For example, the overarching principles of the Code are contained in the Core Duties, which are considered in **Chapter 8**. The SRA's guidance notes to the Core Duties state that the solicitor will serve society by upholding the rule of law, and serve his clients by making the clients' business his first concern.

These rules are binding on all solicitors, regardless of whether or not they are members of The Law Society. The Code is also binding (subject to certain limitations) on Registered European Lawyers and Registered Foreign Lawyers (see Rule 23 for further details).

The Code is comprised of the Rules and guidance. The SRA has stated that the guidance is not mandatory and does not form part of the Code. However, the guidance does provide an insight into how the Rules themselves will be interpreted, and so should be followed at all times. Accordingly, the following chapters highlight both the Rules and guidance.

The Rules themselves are considered in detail in the following chapters. However, due to the volume of material covered by the Code, no publication can set out to cover all eventualities. Accordingly, the aim of this Part is to highlight the main areas of difficulty that may arise in practice. If it doubt, the practitioner should consult the SRA's Professional Ethics Helpline. Throughout this section of the book, unless otherwise advised, references to Rules are to Rules of the Code of Conduct.

7.3   The pervasive nature of conduct

Conduct is said to be a pervasive subject – it cannot be viewed in isolation. It pervades all aspects of a solicitor's life and work, regardless of the area of work in which the solicitor chooses to practise. The topics covered in this book are of general application.

7.4   Complaints against solicitors

7.4.1   Complaints procedures

Every principal of a firm must ensure that the firm has a written complaints procedure and that complaints are handled in a prompt, fair and effective manner in accordance with that procedure (Rule 2.05).

The client must be told in writing at the outset that he is entitled to complain and to whom complaints should be addressed. Firms will have a designated complaints officer who will deal with such matters. The client is also entitled to a copy of the complaints procedure upon request.

Once a client has made a complaint, the firm must explain in writing how the complaint will be handled and when the client is likely to receive a response.

Any breach of Rule 2.05 may lead to the firm being found guilty of providing an inadequate professional service (see **7.6**).

7.4.2 The Legal Complaints Service

If a complaint cannot be resolved by the firm, the client must be given the details of the Legal Complaints Service ('LCS') (formerly the Consumer Complaints Service).

One major way in which the rules of professional conduct are enforced is as a result of complaints made by the public against solicitors. The LCS exercises some of the SRA's powers in relation to the handling of complaints. The LCS is part of The Law Society, and operates independently from premises in Leamington Spa.

The LCS is the sole point of receipt for complaints concerning solicitors. The LCS itself will deal with any matters regarding solicitors providing their clients with a substandard service (termed an 'inadequate professional service'). However, where the issues reportedly concern allegations of professional misconduct (eg, breach of confidentiality), they will be passed to the SRA.

A client's complaint concerning professional misconduct must be received by the LCS within six months of that alleged conduct. A client's complaint concerning an inadequate professional service must be received within six months of the end of the work that the solicitor completed, or within six months of the solicitor's final response to the complaint. The solicitor must make the client aware of these deadlines.

The powers of the SRA and the LCS depend upon whether the subject of the complaint concerns a breach of professional conduct, or the provision of an allegedly inadequate professional service.

7.5 Breach of professional conduct

7.5.1 Professional misconduct

'Professional misconduct' primarily concerns breaches of the rules set out in the Solicitors' Code of Conduct 2007. For example, if a solicitor gave an undertaking (see **Chapter 14**) to post his client's witness statement to another solicitor on 1 May and then failed to do so, he would breach Rule 10.05 and so would be said to breach the rules of professional conduct.

7.5.2 The Solicitors Regulation Authority

Although all complaints from the general public are received through the LCS, complaints primarily concerning a breach of professional conduct will be dealt with by the SRA.

The role of the SRA is to protect the public. Accordingly, having received a report of a breach of a conduct rule, the SRA must assess the risk to the general public posed by the solicitor. If the breach is a minor breach and is it unlikely that it will be repeated, the SRA may choose to deal with the matter by way of a letter of advice to the solicitor concerned.

If the SRA considers that there is a more serious case to answer, both the complainant and solicitor will be invited to submit their views on the matter, together with any supporting documentation. A report will then be compiled based on the submissions of both parties.

The report will be considered by an adjudicator or adjudication panel, who will exercise the statutory powers delegated to them by the Council of The Law

Society. The adjudication panel is made up of solicitors and lay members of the public.

The adjudication will take place purely on the basis of the adjudication report and any supporting documentation. Very rarely will the solicitor and complainant be allowed to present any evidence in person.

The standard of proof applied by the adjudicator or adjudication panel will be a flexible civil standard of proof. For example, less serious allegations would need to be proved on the balance of probabilities, whereas serious allegations, such as allegations of dishonesty or deceit, would need to be proved beyond reasonable doubt. There is no formal system of precedent by which the adjudicator/adjudication panel will be bound.

As from 1 January 2008, the SRA has made its regulatory decisions public. This allows the general public to search under the name of the solicitor they propose to use to establish whether he or she has been subject to any regulatory sanction.

7.5.3 Powers of the SRA – professional misconduct

Where a finding of professional misconduct is made, the adjudicator/panel may discipline the solicitor in the following ways.

7.5.3.1 Make no order

The adjudicator/panel may decide that although a finding of misconduct is warranted, the solicitor should not be punished.

7.5.3.2 Reprimand

The adjudicator/panel may reprimand the solicitor. This is not done in person by the adjudicator, but the record of the breach of conduct and sanction will be kept on the solicitor's file by the SRA and may have further repercussions on the solicitor's career.

7.5.3.3 Refer the matter to the Solicitors Disciplinary Tribunal

The SRA has a duty to ensure that no solicitor remains on the Roll who is guilty of conduct which renders him unfit to practise. Where the allegation made against the solicitor is sufficiently serious, or the solicitor has a past record of breaching the rules of professional conduct, the adjudicator/panel may therefore decide that the powers available to them are insufficient to deal with the alleged breach. In these cases, the adjudicator/panel will not make a finding of misconduct but will refer the matter to the Solicitors Disciplinary Tribunal (see **7.7**).

The SRA does not have the power to award compensation, or direct that the solicitor pays compensation, to the complainant in respect of a breach of the rules of professional conduct.

7.6 Inadequate professional services

7.6.1 Introduction

The expression 'inadequate professional services', as you might expect, denotes a situation where the solicitor has provided a service to his client which is inadequate, ie not of a standard which it is reasonable to expect of a solicitor. This service may be inadequate because of the level of service the solicitor has provided to the client (ie organisational incompetence), because the solicitor has failed to advise the client adequately, or because the solicitor has failed to comply with the Code of Conduct concerning client care and costs.

The following may warrant a finding of 'inadequate professional service':

(a)   delay;

(b)   failure to follow instructions;

(c)   failure to respond to client's correspondence;

(d)   failure to keep the client informed (eg, as to costs or other matters);

(e)   failure to advise.

7.6.2   Conciliation

A large number of complaints concerning allegations of inadequate professional services are dealt with by conciliation without the need for any formal adjudication. A caseworker at the LCS, or a Local Conciliation Officer appointed by the LCS, will act as a mediator between the solicitor and the complainant client.

A solicitor may offer to pay the client compensation to resolve the complaint. If the LCS believes that the level of compensation offered by the solicitor is reasonable then it may close the file and decline to take any further action on the matter, even if the complainant does not wish to accept the offer.

In 2004, the CCS (the LCS's predecessor) resolved 34% of complaints concerning service issues by mediating to an informal agreement between the solicitor and the client.

7.6.3   Non-conciliation cases

Complaints which the LCS is unable to resolve by conciliation are adjudicated upon by the LCS in the same manner as those concerning professional misconduct which go before the SRA.

7.6.4   Powers of the LCS – inadequate professional services

Allegations of the provision of inadequate professional services are addressed to the solicitor's firm, rather than to the solicitor personally. Where a finding of 'inadequate professional service' is made, the LCS has the power to order the firm of solicitors to:

(a)   waive the bill;

(b)   waive the right to recover a fee;

(c)   refund any money that has been paid;

(d)   rectify any mistakes at the firm's own expense;

(e)   compensate the client up to £15,000.

Guidance is provided on the LCS's website (www.legalcomplaints.org.uk) as to the level of compensation that is likely to be awarded. This information is provided to the public so that clients and solicitors have realistic expectations as to the level of redress they are likely to experience on the resolution of complaints.

The guidance states that the LCS attempts to classify the inadequate professional service received by the client as falling into one of four categories, depending on the inadequate service itself and the distress and inconvenience it has caused to the client. These categories range from 'Modest' (with an average award of compensation of less than £250) to 'Extremely serious' (with an award of compensation up to the maximum £15,000). Examples of awards given by the LCS are provided on its website.

The LCS can also take into account any financial loss suffered by the client as a result of the solicitor's actions or inactions.

A solicitors' firm's indemnity policy must cover awards for inadequate professional services within the terms of the policy (see **18.3**). However, frequently such awards will fall within the policy's excess, and the partners of the firm will therefore have to meet the award from the firm's funds.

Where the allegations of inadequate professional services are particularly serious, or the firm of solicitors has a past record of similar behaviour, the LCS may also consider the matter to involve a breach of professional conduct and refer it to the SRA (see **7.5.2**).

7.6.5   Distinction between inadequate professional services and negligence

A solicitor owes a duty of care to his client in the law of tort. Where the solicitor breaches this duty and the client suffers loss as a result, the solicitor may be sued by the client for negligence (see further **7.12** below).

The client does not have to suffer any loss for the solicitor to be guilty of providing an inadequate professional service. The mere fact that the solicitor has provided services which are not of the quality reasonably to be expected of a solicitor is enough. For example, a solicitor may miss a deadline in respect of issuing proceedings, which would then deprive his client of the opportunity to pursue the matter in court. This would be an inadequate professional service, as the service provided would be below what it is reasonable to expect from a solicitor. However, it would also constitute negligence, as the solicitor has breached his duty of care to his client and as a result the client has suffered a foreseeable loss (ie, he won't be able to pursue his matter in court and recover damages).

The LCS and the SRA have no power to adjudicate upon issues of negligence in a legal sense, ie they are not courts and so do not have the power to adjudicate on legal issues. However, where there is an overlap between negligence and the provision of inadequate professional services, the LCS may adjudicate on the basis of the inadequate professional services where its powers of redress would be adequate to compensate the client.

7.7   The Solicitors Disciplinary Tribunal

7.7.1   Introduction

The Solicitors Disciplinary Tribunal hears and determines applications relating to allegations of unbefitting conduct and/or breaches of the rules of professional conduct by solicitors. Most applications to the Disciplinary Tribunal are made on behalf of the SRA. However, except where the Solicitors Act 1974 expressly provides otherwise, any person may make an application directly to the Tribunal without first making a complaint to the SRA.

The Disciplinary Tribunal was established by s 46 of the Solicitors Act 1974 and is independent of The Law Society and the SRA. The members of the Disciplinary Tribunal are appointed by the Master of the Rolls. There is no statutory maximum on the number of members, and at the time of writing it comprised 20 solicitor members and 10 lay members. The solicitor members must have been admitted for at least 10 years, and the lay members must be neither solicitors nor barristers.

The Disciplinary Tribunal sits in divisions of three members, each made up of two solicitors and one lay person. The decisions of the Disciplinary Tribunal may be delivered by a single member.

7.7.2 Tribunal procedure

The Disciplinary Tribunal has power, exercisable by statutory instrument, to make rules governing its procedure and practice. These rules are made with the concurrence of the Master of the Rolls. The SRA maintains a panel of solicitors in private practice who prosecute applications before the Disciplinary Tribunal on its behalf. In most cases, either the SRA's own advocates or the panel solicitor will present the case before the Disciplinary Tribunal. In complex cases, counsel may be instructed to present the case.

7.7.3 Application to the Tribunal

An application to the Disciplinary Tribunal must be made by a Statement of Allegations, supported by evidence (this will be prepared by the panel solicitor, or the SRA's advocate where the applicant is the SRA). The Disciplinary Tribunal will consider the application and, if satisfied that there is a case to answer, will fix a hearing date. Either party may be represented at the hearing by a solicitor or counsel. Evidence is given on oath and witnesses may be called.

The decisions of the Disciplinary Tribunal are called 'Findings' and 'Orders'. The Order itself, together with brief reasons for the decision, is made available at the end of the hearing. The Findings must be made in writing, setting out the facts which the Disciplinary Tribunal found to be substantiated, and must contain its Order. The Findings are usually given eight or so weeks after the hearing. The Findings and Order are then filed with the SRA and take immediate effect, except where an appeal against the Order has been lodged, when the effect of the Order may be suspended until the appeal is determined.

Where (unusually) an application is made directly to the Disciplinary Tribunal, the Tribunal may refer the matter to the SRA for investigation before proceeding with the application. Where in such a case the SRA investigates the complaint and finds it to be substantiated, it may take over the application on the applicant's behalf (or deal with the matter by using the powers of the SRA/LCS discussed at 7.5 and 7.6 above).

7.7.4 Powers of the Tribunal

The Solicitors Act 1974, s 47 gives the Disciplinary Tribunal power to make such order as in its discretion it thinks fit, including the following:

(a)   striking a solicitor off the Roll;

(b)   suspending a solicitor from practice;

(c)   imposing a fine not exceeding £5,000 (in respect of each allegation) which is forfeit to Her Majesty;

(d)   reprimanding the solicitor;

(e)   requiring the payment by any party of costs or a contribution towards costs.

7.7.5 Restoration to the Roll

Once struck off the Roll of solicitors, the Tribunal may also restore a solicitor to the Roll.

7.7.6 Appeals

Appeal from a decision of the Disciplinary Tribunal is made, with a limited number of exceptions, to the High Court.

7.8 The Legal Services Ombudsman

7.8.1 Introduction

The post of Legal Services Ombudsman was created by the Courts and Legal Services Act 1990, s 21. The Ombudsman, appointed by the Secretary of State, holds office for a renewable term of three years; he cannot be an authorised advocate, authorised litigator, licensed conveyancer, authorised practitioner or notary. His function is to investigate any allegation made about the manner in which a complaint has been handled by the professional body of an authorised advocate, authorised litigator, licensed conveyancer, registered foreign lawyer or notary, or employees of such persons. Solicitors are 'authorised advocates' and 'authorised litigators' within the meaning of the Courts and Legal Services Act 1990.

7.8.2 Complaints to the Ombudsman

As noted above, complaints against solicitors are made to the LCS which, with the SRA and the Solicitors Disciplinary Tribunal, has power to investigate and to impose sanctions on a solicitor where the complaint is upheld. A complainant who is dissatisfied with the way in which the LCS or SRA has handled a complaint may refer the matter to the Legal Services Ombudsman.

The Legal Services Ombudsman is thus not a point of first referral for a complaint. His function is to investigate a complaint which has already been made to one of the relevant professional bodies, where there is an allegation that the complaint was not properly handled by the professional body itself.

Complaints cannot be investigated by the Ombudsman where the issue which is the subject of the complaint is being, or has already been, determined by a court, the Solicitors Disciplinary Tribunal, the Disciplinary Tribunal of the Council of the Inns of Court, or any other tribunal specified in regulations made by the Secretary of State.

The Ombudsman's report may include one or more of the following recommendations:

(a)   that the professional body concerned should reconsider the complaint;

(b)   that the professional body should consider the exercise of its powers over the person who was the subject of the complaint;

(c)   that a specified amount of compensation should be paid to the complainant either by the professional body, or by the person who was the subject of the complaint.

When a report is sent to any of the persons listed above, there is a duty on the recipient to have regard to the report's conclusions and recommendations, and to notify the Ombudsman within three months of the receipt of the report of the action taken or proposed to be taken to comply with the recommendations. The Ombudsman may, if he thinks it appropriate, order (rather than recommend) the SRA/LCS, or the solicitor who was the subject of the complaint, to pay compensation.

7.9 Legal Services Complaints Commissioner

On 28 October 2004, the Secretary of State launched the office of the Legal Services Complaints Commissioner. The Commissioner's stated role is to improve how the SRA and LCS deal with complaints about solicitors. The Commissioner is appointed by the Secretary of State and is independent.

The Commissioner does not deal with complaints concerning solicitors; rather he agrees and monitors performance targets and plans concerning complaints handling with which the SRA and LCS must comply. Should they fail to comply with the agreed performance targets or plans, the Commissioner has the power to levy a fine. The amount of the fine will be the lower of 1% of The Law Society's annual income or £1,000,000. The Law Society was fined £250,000 during 2006.

7.10 Other powers of the Solicitors Regulation Authority

7.10.1 The investigation of accounts

In order to monitor a solicitor's compliance with the Solicitors' Accounts Rules 1998, the SRA may require a solicitor to produce his financial accounts, and any other relevant documents, to the SRA (Solicitors' Accounts Rules 1998, Rule 34).

7.10.2 Intervention

Where the public is at risk, the SRA may take control of a solicitor's files and client monies. This is generally referred to as an 'intervention'. The SRA appoints another firm of solicitors to act as its agents to close down the practice. Intervention may also occur where a sole practitioner is unable to continue his practice through ill health, an accident or death.

7.10.3 Delivery of files

In order to investigate complaints of misconduct, the SRA has the power, under s 44B of the Solicitors Act 1974, to serve a notice on a solicitor requiring the delivery of a file or documents in the possession of the solicitor to the SRA.

7.11 Powers of the court

A solicitor is an officer of the court. Accordingly, the court has jurisdiction to discipline the solicitor in respect of costs within any matter before the court. The court may order the solicitor to pay costs to his own client, or to a third party (see CPR, rr 44 and 45).

7.12 Negligence

7.12.1 Introduction

In addition to or instead of the actions that the SRA or LCS may take, a solicitor may be sued by his client in the tort of negligence. A solicitor owes his clients a duty of care. Where a solicitor breaches this duty, and the client suffers loss as a result of that breach, the solicitor may be sued in negligence. Firms must carry compulsory indemnity insurance against such actions (see **18.3**).

7.12.2 Steps to be taken on discovery of a claim

Rule 20.07 provides that if a solicitor discovers an act or omission which would justify a claim by a client or third party against him, he must:

(a)   inform the client that independent advice should be sought (unless the loss to the client is trivial and can be remedied by the solicitor);

(b)   consider whether the discovery of a claim has caused a conflict of interest, and if so the solicitor should cease acting for the client in that matter. It will be very rare that a conflict of interest does not arise;

(c)   notify his insurer.

However, The Law Society's guidance states that solicitors should respond to complaints even if they believe the allegations concern negligence, and a referral to the firm's insurance provider will be necessary.

Where the solicitor does cease to act for the client, and is asked to hand over the papers to another solicitor who is giving independent advice on the merits of a claim, the solicitor should keep copies of the original documents for his own reference.

7.13   The Compensation Fund

The Compensation Fund is maintained by the SRA under s 36 of and Sch 2 to the Solicitors Act 1974. All practising solicitors, except those who are applying for their first three practising certificates after admission, are required to make a fixed compulsory annual contribution to the Compensation Fund. Payment is made with the annual practising certificate fee. An additional levy may be imposed if the Fund becomes insufficient to meet the claims being made on it.

The Fund exists to make grants to persons who have suffered loss as the result of the dishonesty of a solicitor or a solicitor's employee in connection with the solicitor's practice, or in connection with a trust of which the solicitor is (or was formerly) a trustee. The Fund may also help individuals who have suffered financial hardship as a result of a solicitor failing to account for money received.

Payment from the Fund is made only where the applicant cannot recover his money by other means. For example, if the applicant could recover his money from an insurance policy then the Fund will not pay out. The applicant is also expected to have taken appropriate civil and/or criminal proceedings against the defaulting solicitor before making an application to the Fund.

The SRA has a discretion to refuse a grant out of the Fund which would result in sums exceeding £1 million being paid to or on behalf of an applicant in respect of any individual transaction or matter.

Where payment is made from the Fund, the SRA is subrogated to the rights of the applicant and can therefore take proceedings against the defaulting solicitor in order to recover the amount paid out by the Fund.

In some cases, a loan from the Fund may be made to the partners of a defaulting solicitor to enable them to settle liability to a client. Such a loan is repayable on settlement of the claim under the firm's insurance policy.

7.14   Chapter summary

(1)   The SRA is empowered by the Solicitors Act 1974 to publish rules for the regulation of conduct of solicitors.

(2)   At present these rules are enforced by the SRA and the LCS.

(3)   The SRA deals with breaches of the rules of professional conduct, whereas the LCS primarily deals with allegations of solicitors providing inadequate professional services.

(4)   Inadequate professional services occur when a solicitor provides a service which is not of a quality which it is reasonable to expect from the solicitor. The client does not need to suffer any loss as a result of the poor service in order to raise the issue.

(5)   The SRA may reprimand a solicitor for a breach of the rules of professional conduct, or in serious cases may refer the matter to the Solicitors Disciplinary Tribunal.

(6)   The LCS has numerous sanctions at its disposal in respect of a finding of 'inadequate professional services'. These include directing the solicitor to waive his bill, or directing the solicitor to compensate the client up to £15,000. The SRA/LCS has no power to pay compensation to the client itself.

(7)   The Solicitors Disciplinary Tribunal may fine a solicitor, suspend the solicitor or, as an ultimate sanction, strike the solicitor off the Roll.

(8)   A solicitor will be negligent if he breaches a duty of care to his client and foreseeable loss results as a consequence of that breach. Where the solicitor has been negligent, he may be sued by the client for damages.

(9)   The Compensation Fund is maintained by the SRA. Payment may be made from the Fund when a client has suffered loss as a result of a solicitor's dishonesty. No grant may be made from the Fund until the client has exhausted all other remedies.

Chapter 8

The Core Duties

8.1 Introduction

The profession is regulated by the Government (eg, the Proceeds of Crime Act 2002) and by rules of conduct set out by the Solicitors Regulation Authority ('SRA') itself. The main focus of this Part is the Solicitors' Code of Conduct 2007, published by the SRA.

The starting point for the consideration of the Code is Rule 1 – The Core Duties.

8.2 The Core Duties

The SRA's guidance to the Core Duties states:

> A modern just society needs a legal profession which adopts high standards of integrity and professionalism. As a solicitor . . . you serve both clients and society. In serving society, you uphold the rule of law and proper administration of justice. In serving clients, you work in partnership with the client making the client's business your first concern. The core duties contained in rule 1 set the standards which will meet the needs of both clients and society.

The Core Duties set the basic principles with which all solicitors must comply. Any breach of Rule 1 would be a breach of professional conduct.

The SRA's guidance provides that the Core Duties are the 'overarching framework' for the Rules. For example, the guidance further provides that the Core Duties should help solicitors deal with situations not covered in the detailed rules as 'no code can foresee or address every ethical dilemma'.

8.3 Rule 1.01: Justice and the rule of law

8.3.1 Introduction

Rule 1.01 provides that a solicitor must uphold the rule of law and the proper administration of justice. For example, a solicitor must refuse to act (or cease acting) for a client where to act would involve the solicitor in a breach of the law (Rule 2.01(1)(a)).

The SRA's guidance to Rule 1 states that a solicitor's obligation under this rule extends not only towards his clients, but also to others such as the court and third parties the solicitor may deal with. A solicitor's obligations to the court and third parties are dealt with in **Chapter 16**.

8.3.2 Avoiding discrimination

8.3.2.1 Discrimination

A solicitor's duty to uphold the rule of law will also extend to complying with all anti-discrimination legislation.

He is also under a much wider duty not to discriminate in his professional dealings against any group listed within Rule 6.01. Accordingly, a solicitor must not unlawfully discriminate (directly or indirectly) against any person on the grounds of:

(a)   sex (including marital status);

(b)   race or racial group;

(c)   ethnic or national origins;

(d)   colour;

(e)   nationality;

(f)   religion or belief;

(g)   age;

(h)   sexual orientation; or

(i)   (unless any exception applies) disability.

The SRA's guidance notes define discrimination as occurring where one person is treated less favourably than another would be treated in the same or similar circumstances, and that treatment cannot be justified.

Any finding of discrimination by a court or tribunal will be treated as professional misconduct.

8.3.2.2 Equality and diversity policy

Firms are also obliged to have a written policy for promoting equality and diversity, and avoiding discrimination within the firm (Rule 6.03).

8.4 Rule 1.02: Integrity

This rule (and additional guidance) provides that a solicitor must act with integrity towards clients, the courts, lawyers and the public. A solicitor is in a position of trust, and so must behave in an appropriate manner to reflect that position.

8.5 Rule 1.03: Independence

A solicitor must not allow his independence to be compromised (for example, as a result of pressure from any source, including clients or the court).

A client must be able to rely on the solicitor providing objective and unbiased advice if that client is to have any confidence or faith in the solicitor's ability to act in the client's best interests.

Pressure will include financial pressure. For example, a solicitor may receive a large amount of work from a firm of accountants. Another client may seek the advice of the solicitor as to whether that firm of accountants has been negligent. The solicitor may feel unable to give objective and unbiased advice for fear of offending the firm of accountants and therefore losing its work. In such circumstances, the solicitor must decline to act.

8.6 Rule 1.04: Best interests of clients

Rule 1.04 provides that a solicitor must act in the best interests of each of his clients. The SRA's guidance further provides that a solicitor must 'always act in good faith and do your best for each of your clients'.

This duty means that a solicitor must put his client's interests before his own. For example, a solicitor may have to turn down the opportunity of taking on a lucrative client if this new client's interests conflict with the best interests of an existing client (see **Chapter 13** for further details).

This duty derives from the common law, as a solicitor is said to be in a fiduciary position in relation to his client. This fiduciary relationship is considered further in **Chapter 10**.

8.7 Rule 1.05: Standard of service

Rule 1.05 provides that a solicitor must provide a good standard of service to his clients. This duty extends to providing a good standard of client care (see **Chapter 11** generally) and also a good standard of work (ie, the solicitor is sufficiently competent to complete the work).

This rule is linked to the concept that a solicitor must act in the best interests of a client (see **8.6** above).

For example, imagine that a client is seeking to instruct a solicitor in respect of a complex dispute regarding a contract of insurance. If the solicitor in question knows very little about insurance law then he will be unable to act in the best interests of the client. The best interests of the client in this case would be for the solicitor to refer the client to an expert (ideally this would be a colleague, or alternatively someone in another firm) in the relevant field of law.

Equally, a solicitor must consider whether he has the capacity (in terms of work volume) to take on a particular matter. If a solicitor was to take on work when he did not have the capacity to deal with it effectively, he would not be acting in the client's best interests.

8.8 Rule 1.06: Public confidence

Both The Law Society and the SRA are keen to improve the reputation of the profession in the eyes of the general public. Accordingly, Rule 1.06 provides that a solicitor 'must not behave in a way which is likely to diminish the trust the public places in you or the profession'.

For example, if a solicitor was to use money from his client account to fund the purchase of a new car then he would not only breach the Solicitors' Accounts Rules, but he would almost certainly harm the public's trust in the profession and breach Rule 1.06.

A solicitor may harm the public's trust in the profession by behaviour outside of his solicitors' practice. For example, conviction of a criminal offence would lead the solicitor to breach Rule 1.06. Where a solicitor is convicted of an offence involving dishonesty, it is likely that he will be struck off the Roll of solicitors.

8.9 Chapter summary

(1)   The SRA sets out rules concerning professional conduct.

(2)   The starting point for consideration of the Code of Conduct 2007 is Rule 1 – The Core Duties.

(3)   The Core Duties set out the fundamental requirements which solicitors must satisfy in practice.

(4)   Breach of the Core Duties may constitute professional misconduct.

Chapter 9

Obtaining Instructions

9.1 Introduction

A solicitors' firm is a business, and has much in common with any high street store. Obviously a firm of solicitors sells services rather than goods, but just like a high street store it needs a regular supply of customers to survive. Without clients, a solicitors firm cannot generate income to pay staff salaries, the rent on premises, or for the upkeep of the office equipment. Accordingly, just like a high street store, a firm of solicitors must take steps to try to maintain and increase its market share. The two most common ways of trying to achieve this are through advertising and referrals.

9.2 General principles

As noted above, a solicitors' firm must take steps to try to maintain and increase its market share in order to prosper as a business. However, no matter how urgent these financial pressures may be, a solicitor must at all times comply with the rules of professional conduct, and in particular with the Core Duties (see **Chapter 8**). A solicitor's primary duty is to his client. Accordingly, a solicitor must not do anything that would compromise his independence. Therefore a solicitor must not do anything, or enter into any arrangement, that would restrict him from acting in the best interests of his client.

For example, a firm of solicitors may be offered a large financial incentive to refer all clients requiring advice on financial services to a particular firm of brokers. However, the firm must not accept this offer if it would prevent the solicitors acting in the best interests of their clients.

9.3 Advertising

9.3.1 Introduction

In the past, it was common for solicitors to rely on their personal reputation to obtain work. For example, a solicitor would earn a reputation for a certain type of work (eg, family law) by word of mouth in a town or city. This method of obtaining work is still valuable today. One of the best ways of attracting clients is by personal recommendation of a friend or colleague who has experienced similar problems. There are also publications, such as the Legal 500, which list the names of the 'top' solicitors in a particular legal field and geographical location.

However, in recent times firms have invested a lot of money with a view to attracting new clients through different means. For example, firms will advertise their services in local newspapers, on their websites or through promotional literature. The use of radio and television advertisements has also become more frequent in recent years (particularly in the area of personal injury).

The aim of these advertisements is to increase the general public's awareness of the firm in question, and of the services that the firm offers (ie, how the firm could help the potential client). Therefore, when a potential client needs the services of a solicitor, he will know of which firm to contact.

Another purpose of advertising is to improve the reputation of the profession in the eyes of the general public. For example, during September 2004, the Law Society launched an advertising campaign entitled 'My hero, my solicitor', to remind the general public of the benefits of using solicitors, rather than unqualified individuals, when they have problems in their lives.

Solicitors are generally free to publicise their practice, provided that they comply with:

(a) the general laws on advertising and data protection in force at the time. These include:

    (i)   the British Code of Advertising, Sales Promotion and Direct Marketing,

    (ii) the Data Protection Act 1998, and

    (iii) the Privacy and Electronic Communications (EC Directive) Regulations 2003 (SI 2003/2426);

(b) Rule 7 of the Solicitors' Code of Conduct 2007.

9.3.2   Rule 7

9.3.2.1   General

Rule 7 applies to all forms of publicity, including stationery, advertisements, brochures, websites and media appearances (Rule 7.06).

The Solicitors Regulation Authority ('SRA') considers that there is an imbalance of knowledge between the general public on one hand and the solicitor providing the service on the other. Accordingly, publicity issued by, or on behalf of, law firms must not be misleading or inaccurate (Rule 7.01). This is particularly the case when dealing with publicity relating to solicitors' charges. For example, any estimated fees must not be set at an unrealistically low level. Any charge must be clearly expressed, and the publicity must make it clear whether disbursements and VAT are included (Rule 7.02).

9.3.2.2   Unsolicited visits or phone calls

A solicitor may wish to 'cold call' individuals in order to promote his business. As mentioned above in **9.3.1**, a solicitor must comply with the general law applicable to such marketing. This means that the solicitor must have all consents required by the relevant data protection legislation for the type of marketing he intends to carry out.

The Data Protection Act 1998 also permits all individuals to request that their details are not used for direct marketing purposes, and therefore if a solicitor receives such a request, it should be taken seriously and complied with.

In addition, Rule 7.03 prohibits a solicitor from making unsolicited visits or telephone calls to the general public, unless an exception (such as a call to a client or former client) applies. However, even when such an exception does apply, solicitors should be mindful of complying with the provisions of the relevant legislation. The SRA advises that clients should be given the opportunity to refuse to receive direct marketing materials (such as cold calling or mailshots). It suggests that this opportunity is given to clients in their terms of business letter. This is also a good opportunity to provide clients with the information required by the Data Protection Act 1998, advising individuals about how their personal data will be processed.

9.3.2.3   Mailshots

A solicitor may use mailshots. However, the SRA's guidance provides that when doing so, solicitors should be mindful of the provisions of the Data Protection Act (see **9.3.1** and **9.3.2.2**).

9.3.2.4   Letterheads

A letterhead (including a fax heading) is considered a form of publicity. The SRA specifies the information which the letterhead must contain.

A firm's letterhead must contain the words 'regulated by the Solicitors Regulation Authority', and details of the composition and ownership of the firm. For example, a partnership of 20 or fewer partners must display the names of those partners on the letterhead. The letterhead of a firm with over 20 partners must display either the names of those partners, or a statement that a list of partners is available for inspection at their office (Rule 7.07).

9.3.3   Responsibility for advertising

A solicitor may instruct a third party, such as an advertising agency, to deal with certain aspects of his advertising campaign. However, the solicitor must ensure that any publicity created by the third party complies with the provisions of Rule 7 (Rule 7.05). The SRA's guidance provides that a solicitor must take reasonable steps to withdraw or change any publicity which breaches Rule 7.

9.3.4   Enforcement

Minor breaches of Rule 7 will be dealt with by local law societies bringing the breach to the attention of the firm concerned. Serious or persistent breaches will be dealt with as breaches of professional conduct.

9.4   Referrals of business

9.4.1   Introduction

In addition to targeting the general public, a solicitor may also enter into an agreement with a third party to refer clients to that third party and/or for the third party to refer clients to the solicitor. For example, a solicitor could enter into an arrangement with a local estate agent, so that the agent will 'introduce' to the solicitor's firm any potential house buyers looking for a solicitor to complete their conveyancing.

Any such arrangement must comply with the provisions of Rule 9. Note, however, that Rule 9 does not apply to introductions made between solicitors. Accordingly, where a solicitor cannot act for a particular client due to a conflict of interest with an existing client, the solicitor may refer the new client to a separate firm of solicitors without having to consider the provisions of Rule 9. However, the solicitor must still act in the best interests of the client when making the referral.

9.4.2   Best interests of the client – Rule 9.03

A solicitor must always act in the best interests of the client. Accordingly, a solicitor must not let any referral agreement interfere with this duty.

Rule 9.03 provides that where a solicitor recommends that a client uses a particular third party (eg, for financial advice), that referral must be made in good faith and the particular third party must be chosen based on what would be in the client's best interests.

Where a solicitor refers a client to a business that can only offer products from one source, the solicitor must inform the client of this limitation in writing (Rule 9.03(5)).

Furthermore, a solicitor may not enter into an arrangement which would restrict his ability to recommend any particular firm, business or agency (Rule 9.03(2)). For example, a solicitor could not enter into an arrangement which would bind him to refer all of his clients seeking financial advice to a particular firm of accountants.

This final restriction does not apply to arrangements concerning certain types of investments (see **9.4.9**).

9.4.3   Independence – Rules 1.03 and 9.01(1)

A solicitor must maintain his independence, in order that his judgement concerning what is in the client's best interest is not influenced by any outside source. For example, the SRA's guidance provides that a solicitor must never place himself in a position whereby his advice to a client is affected due to an attempt not to offend a referrer of work. For instance, a solicitor may be very reluctant to advise a client to seek financial advice from Y Bank if 30% of the solicitor's clients are referred to the solicitor by Y Bank's rival, X Bank. The guidance provides that a solicitor should monitor his sources of work to avoid becoming too reliant on one particular referrer.

The solicitor must also retain control of the work he undertakes and must not agree to provide a service on the basis that the solicitor does not communicate or take instructions directly from the client (ie, a third party takes the instructions and then passes them on to the solicitor to complete the work).

9.4.4   Referral fees

During March 2004, the Master of the Rolls lifted the ban on solicitors paying referral fees to third parties introducing clients to solicitors. These arrangements have been used mainly in areas such as personal injury and conveyancing. For example, in April 2005 it was reported that Shoosmiths had agreed to pay a referral fee to the Automobile Association (AA) in respect of the parties' deal that Shoosmiths would act as the exclusive provider of legal services to the AA's customers.

After some uncertainty as to their future, the SRA announced in December 2007 that referral fees would continue to be permitted. However, due to evidence of significant non-compliance with the rules concerning such fees, the SRA has stated that it will explore a number of approaches to improve compliance. These include whether solicitors should be accredited to enter into referral arrangements.

However, the Board did rule out seeking criminal sanctions for breaches of these rules. The issue will be reviewed again in December 2008.

Lastly, the SRA has warned solicitors that they should only deal with claims management companies that are appropriately regulated.

In addition to complying with Rule 9.03 (see **9.4.2**), the conditions with which a solicitor must comply when dealing with referrals depend upon whether the solicitor receives any payment for the referral.

9.4.5   Referrals without payment – Rule 9.01

9.4.5.1   Introduction

Where a solicitor receives or refers work without the receipt of any fee or other consideration, in addition to the solicitor's duty not to compromise his independence by agreeing to act (see 9.4.3), he must draw the introducer's attention to the provisions of Rule 9 and Rule 7 (publicity).

9.4.5.2   Limitations

Regardless of whether a referral fee is being paid or not, a solicitor must not enter into a referral arrangement in respect of claims arising from death or personal injury with any third party who deals with such claims if that third party receives contingency fees from those claims (see Rule 9.01(4)–(6)). Rule 24 defines a contingency fee as 'any sum ... payable only in the event of success' (see **11.9.3**).

9.4.6   Referrals involving a financial arrangement – Rule 9.02

Where the solicitor enters into a financial arrangement with an introducer, the solicitor must comply with additional requirements.

9.4.6.1   Financial arrangement

Rule 9.02 will apply only where the solicitor enters into a 'financial arrangement'. This is defined by Rule 9.02(i) as any payment to a third party in respect of referrals, or any agreement to be paid by a third party introducer to provide services to the third party's customers. 'Payment' is further defined as including 'any other consideration'. For example, this would include the payment of marketing fees or panel membership fees. It does not include giving or receiving normal business expenses, proper disbursements or 'normal hospitality', such as corporate entertainment or business lunches which are proportionate to the relationship.

For example, taking an individual, such as an accountant, out to lunch in return for the accountant referring some work to you would be proportionate. Paying for the accountant to take a world cruise in return for referring some work would not be proportionate and so would be deemed to be a financial arrangement.

9.4.6.2   The requirements

In addition to complying with Rule 9.01, the solicitor must also comply with Rule 9.02, which includes (but is not limited to) the following obligations:

(a)   The agreement with the introducer must be in writing and available for inspection by the SRA.

(b)   The introducer must undertake to comply with Rule 9.

(c)   The introducer and the solicitor must give the client all relevant information in writing, including:

(i)   the fact that a financial arrangement exists; and

(ii)   the amount of any payment to or by the introducer (with reference to the individual retainer or, if the payment is of a more general amount (such as a yearly fee), such information concerning the arrangement that the solicitor is able to give), and

(iii) whether the client must pay anything to the introducer.

(d)   Where the solicitor is accepting a referral from the introducer, the solicitor must also confirm in writing that:

(i)   any advice given will be independent; and

(ii)   the solicitor will not disclose any information to the introducer without the consent of the client; and

(iii) the solicitor may have to cease acting if a conflict of interest arises between the client and introducer (where the firm is also acting for the introducer).

The information must be provided by the introducer before the referral takes place and by the solicitor before he accepts the instructions to act.

The solicitor must also satisfy himself that the client has not been acquired by the introducer as a result of marketing or publicity that, if undertaken by a solicitor, would breach the Solicitors' Code of Conduct (eg, by 'cold calling').

9.4.7   Breach of the Code

A solicitor is under a continuing duty to monitor whether the introducer breaches Rule 9 or Rule 7 (publicity). Solicitors' firms are advised to carry out random checks, for example by asking clients what information the introducer provided to the client and whether the client had been 'cold called'. The solicitor should take all reasonable steps to remedy any breach. The solicitor must terminate the agreement where the introducer continues to be in breach.

A solicitor cannot accept a referral where the client has been obtained as a result of marketing or publicity that would breach Rule 7 (Rule 9.02).

Any breach by the solicitor will be prima facie professional misconduct.

9.4.8   Limitations

A solicitor cannot enter into a financial agreement with an introducer in respect of referrals for criminal proceedings or any matter upon which the solicitor will be publicly funded (Rule 9.02(h)). See also **9.4.5.2** above.

9.4.9   Financial services

A solicitor who carries out a regulated activity without being authorised by the Financial Services Authority or exempt will commit a criminal offence. A regulated activity would include giving advice on a specified investment such as stocks and shares. There are a number of exemptions and exclusions of which a solicitor may take advantage when carrying out a regulated activity (see **Chapter 17**).

However, when a solicitor is carrying out such a regulated activity, he cannot enter into any agreement with another person which would limit his ability to refer the client to any third party (Rule 19.01(1)(c)). For example, a solicitor could not enter an agreement with Monks & Co Financial Advisers to refer all clients seeking financial advice to that firm, as this would restrict the solicitor's ability to refer clients to another suitable firm within the area. The only exception to this rule is where the investment concerns regulated mortgage contracts, general insurance contracts or pure protection contracts. However, where the solicitor takes advantage of this exception he must still comply with Rule 1, in particular the duty to maintain his independence and act in the best interests of his client, and also Rule 9 (referrals).

Furthermore, the solicitor should consider carefully whether referring a client to a tied agent (ie, a financial adviser that contractually may offer the client products only from a certain provider or providers) would be in the best interests of the client. Indeed, Rule 9.03(6) expressly provides that where the client may require an endowment policy (or similar life insurance with an investment element), the solicitor must refer the client to an independent financial adviser rather than a tied agent.

The topic of financial services and solicitors is dealt with in **Chapter 17**.

9.5   Fee sharing

Fee sharing would occur if a solicitor made a payment to a third party in respect of a percentage of fees earned on a particular matter, or a percentage of the solicitor's gross or net fees for a particular period.

The SRA considers that to allow a solicitor to share fees with a non-solicitor may threaten the solicitor's independence and duty to act in the best interests of his clients, as the solicitor's judgement may come under pressure. For this reason the solicitor is (subject to limited exceptions, such as payments to a charity in certain circumstances) prohibited by Rule 8 from sharing his professional fees with any person who is not a solicitor.

A solicitor may share fees (subject to Rule 8), for example, with:

(a)   practising members of other legal professions;

(b)   the solicitor's partners (subject to Rule 12), retired partners or predecessors;

(c)   the solicitor's genuine employee;

(d)   an estate agent who is the solicitor's sub-agent for the sale of property;

(e)   non-lawyers for the sole purpose of facilitating the introduction of capital or services to the solicitor's firm (except in relation to cross-border practice);

(f)   charities (if certain conditions are met).

For example, the SRA's guidance provides that a solicitors firm could make payments to a bank in return for a loan. These payments could be calculated as a proportion of fees under ground (e) above, provided that the arrangement did not constrain the solicitor's professional judgement.

Where a solicitor does enter into a fee-sharing arrangement with a third party, the solicitor must provide to the SRA on request the details of the agreement, together with details concerning the annual percentage of fees being paid to the fee sharer in question.

Where the percentage of all fees shared with non-lawyers exceeds 15%, the SRA may ask for evidence of a risk assessment to demonstrate whether the solicitor's independence is being put at risk by the fee-sharing arrangement(s).

9.6   Chapter summary

(1)   Solicitors should always be independent and impartial when giving advice to a client.

(2)   Solicitors are free to publicise their practice, provided that they comply with the general law on advertising in force at the time and with Rule 7 of the Solicitors' Code of Conduct 2007.

(3)   A solicitor's promotional material must not be misleading or inaccurate.

(4)   A solicitor may enter into a financial arrangement with an introducer, provided that they comply with Rule 9 of the Code of Conduct.

(5)   Subject to limited exceptions, solicitors must not share their professional fees with non-lawyers.

Chapter 10

The Retainer

10.1 Introduction

The contract between a solicitor and his client is often referred to as a 'retainer'. As with any other contract, the relationship between the solicitor and the client is governed by the general law. However, in addition to considering the general law, a solicitor must also comply with obligations placed upon him by the rules of professional conduct.

10.2 Acceptance of instructions

10.2.1 Terms of the retainer

As noted above, many of the terms of the retainer will be implied into the contract either by the law, or by the rules of professional conduct. Some of these terms are considered below. However, the solicitor must ensure that the more basic terms of the retainer are understood by the client. One such critical issue is to ensure that the client understands exactly what work the solicitor has agreed to undertake. Solicitors are obliged to send a 'client care' letter to clients at the start of the transaction (see **11.6**). It is advisable for the solicitor to use this document to confirm to the client exactly what he understands his instructions to be (and also what action, if any, the client must take). This will avoid any misunderstandings at a later date, such as where the client makes a complaint against the solicitor for his failure to complete a certain task which the solicitor was unaware he had been instructed to complete.

It is important that a client's expectations are managed at an early stage of the solicitor–client relationship. If the client knows what the solicitor will and will not be doing for him, there will be less scope for problems to arise at a later date.

10.2.2 Identity of the client

Equally, the solicitor must ensure that he clarifies the identity of his client. For example, a solicitor may be instructed by a director of a company concerning the debts of that company. The solicitor will be obliged to clarify whether he is being instructed by the director in her personal capacity, or by the director on behalf of the company (ie, the company will be the client, not the director personally). As noted below, a solicitor owes many duties to his client, and he can ensure that these duties are met only if he knows the identity of his client.

A solicitor is also under a separate duty to obtain 'satisfactory evidence' of the identity of his clients (ie, are they who they say they are?). This obligation is imposed by the Money Laundering Regulations 2007 (SI 2007/2157), and is considered further at **15.2.3**.

10.2.3   Third party instructions

A solicitor may receive instructions from a third party on behalf of a client. For example, a client's daughter may seek to instruct a solicitor on behalf of her elderly mother, as the mother may have mobility problems in attending the solicitor's office.

Alternatively, a solicitor may receive instructions from one client purporting to instruct the solicitor on behalf of a number of clients. For example, a solicitor may be instructed by Mr Smith to purchase a property on behalf of Mr Smith and Mr Brown.

Where a solicitor receives such third party instructions, he must confirm that all the clients (the mother in the first example; Mr Smith and Mr Brown in the second example) agree with the solicitor's instructions before proceeding with the transaction (Rule 2.01(c)).

When considering whether to accept instructions from or on behalf of a number of clients the solicitor must take into account any actual or potential conflicts of interests, (see **Chapter 13**).

10.3   Refusal of instructions to act

10.3.1   Introduction

Solicitors firms spend thousands of pounds in attempting to attract new clients to their business. They will also try to ensure that they retain their existing clients. However, there will be some clients for whom a solicitor will decline to act. For example, a solicitor may decline to act for a client who is known for not paying his legal fees.

Generally, like any other business, a solicitor is free to decide whether to accept or decline instructions to act for a particular client. However, this discretion is limited by the rules of professional conduct and also by the general law. A solicitor may not decline to act in certain circumstances. Equally, the Solicitors Regulation Authority ('SRA') has prescribed circumstances where a solicitor must decline to act.

10.3.2   Restrictions placed on the refusal of instructions

A solicitor must not unlawfully discriminate against anyone in his professional dealings (Rule 6.01). Therefore, a solicitor must not decline to act for a client based on matters such as the client's sex, race, disability, ethnic origins or nationality.

Further, a solicitor cannot refuse to act as an advocate for a client on the grounds that he finds the nature of the case objectionable, or finds the opinions or beliefs of the prospective client unacceptable (Rule 11.04 – see **16.2**).

10.3.3   Situations where a solicitor must decline to act

A solicitor's freedom to accept instructions is restricted by his duty to obey the Solicitors' Code of Conduct 2007.

Rule 2.01 sets out the circumstances in which instructions must be refused:

(a)   where to act would involve the solicitor in a breach of the law; or

(b)   where to act would involve the solicitor in a breach of the rules of professional conduct;

(c)   where the solicitor has insufficient resources or a lack of competence to deal with the matter; or

(d)   where the solicitor has reasonable grounds for believing that the instructions are affected by duress or undue influence.

10.3.3.1   Where to act would involve the solicitor in a breach of the law

For example, a solicitor instructed to act on the sale of a property might be instructed to draw up a false surveyor's report and send it to the purchaser in order to hide some defects to the structure of the property. If the solicitor agreed, he would be participating in a fraud against the purchaser. Clearly, instructions must be refused here.

Where a solicitor becomes aware that his client is involved in criminal conduct, the solicitor must consider very carefully the obligations placed upon him by the Proceeds of Crime Act 2002 (see **Chapter 15**).

10.3.3.2   Where to act would involve the solicitor in a breach of the rules of professional conduct

For example, a solicitor must cease to act where:

(a)   there is, or is likely to be, a conflict of interest between the solicitor and his client or between two clients (see **Chapter 13**);

(b)   the solicitor holds 'material' confidential information for an existing or former client which would be relevant to a new instruction (see **Chapter 12**);

(c)   the client instructs the solicitor to mislead or deceive the court (see **16.1.1**);

(d)   the instructions involve an agreement preventing an investigation by the SRA or the Legal Complaints Service of the conduct of a solicitor or a member of his firm (see Rule 20.05).

10.3.3.3   Where the solicitor has insufficient resources or a lack of competence to deal with the matter.

The solicitor must act in the best interests of his client (Rule 1.04). A solicitor must also provide a good standard of service to his clients (Rule 1.05). Accordingly, the solicitor must consider the level and quality of service he will be able to provide to the client. Every solicitors firm will have a maximum capacity of work with which the firm can deal effectively at any one time. If the solicitor or firm will not have the time or resources to deal with the client's matter then it would not be in that client's interests to accept the instruction. The obligation of considering whether the solicitor or firm has sufficient resources to deal adequately with the client's matter continues throughout the client's retainer.

Equally, if a solicitor is approached by a prospective client about an area of law of which the solicitor knows very little, it would be in the client's best interests to be referred to another firm which possesses the requisite knowledge.

10.3.3.4   Duress or undue influence

Where a solicitor knows or suspects (on reasonable grounds) that instructions from a client have been affected by duress or undue influence, the solicitor must not carry out those instructions until he satisfies himself that the instructions represent the client's wishes (Rule 2.01(d)).

The SRA's guidance provides that some clients, such as the elderly, or those with language or learning difficulties, are particularly susceptible to undue pressure from others. Where a solicitor suspects that a client's instructions are tainted by duress or undue influence, he should take steps to ensure that the client's instructions are genuine, eg by arranging to interview the client alone, away from any third party such as a relative.

10.3.3.5   Acting where another solicitor is already instructed

The SRA's guidance provides that, 'as a matter of good practice', a solicitor should not act on a matter upon which the client has already instructed another solicitor, unless he receives the consent of that solicitor (or the retainer with the first solicitor is terminated).

Equally, a solicitor may be asked to provide a second opinion on legal advice given by another solicitor. A solicitor may provide this opinion, but must ensure that he has been fully informed about the matter prior to giving the advice.

It is advisable to document the basis of the advice in the advice letter by specifying each item of documentation to which the solicitor has had access prior to giving the advice.

10.4   Duties to the client during the retainer

10.4.1   Introduction

A solicitor will owe the client a number of duties throughout the retainer. These duties are prescribed by the common law and the rules of professional conduct. Some of these duties (such as the duty of confidentiality) will continue even after the retainer has been terminated. The following are examples of some of the duties that solicitors owe to their clients.

10.4.2   Duty of reasonable care and skill

In addition to the solicitor's duty of care in common law, s 13 of the Supply of Goods and Services Act 1982 provides that a supplier of services will carry out those services with reasonable care and skill. This term is implied into the retainer between a solicitor and his client, and therefore the solicitor may be sued for a breach of contract if the term is breached. However, this implied term does not apply to advocacy services provided before a court, tribunal, inquiry or arbitrator (Supply of Services (Exclusion of Implied Terms) Order 1982 (SI 1982/1771), art 2).

Nevertheless, the solicitor may be sued for negligence in both contentious and non contentious proceedings. The House of Lords removed an advocate's protection from negligence claims in *Arthur JS Hall & Co v Simons* [2002] 1 AC 615. Accordingly, a solicitor who acts as an advocate may be sued in the tort of negligence if he breaches his duty of care to his client within court proceedings.

In certain circumstances, a solicitor may owe a duty of care to third parties, such as beneficiaries to an estate (see **16.5.5**).

10.4.3   Duty to act in the best interests of the client

As has been noted throughout this Part, a solicitor must act in the best interests of his client. This duty is taken from the Core Duties of the Solicitors' Code of Conduct, and also from common law.

The solicitor–client relationship is said to be a 'fiduciary relationship'. Under the common law, a fiduciary relationship is one where one party must act in the best interests of the other party. This means that the solicitor must put the interests of his client before his own. Another example of a fiduciary relationship is the doctor–patient relationship. Directors of a company also owe a fiduciary duty to the company itself.

Where such a relationship exists, one party may not make a secret profit at the expense of the other party. For example, a solicitor may be paid commission, say £50, when referring a client to a third party such as an accountant (subject to certain conditions – see **Chapter 9**). As the solicitor owes a fiduciary duty to his client, this £50 must be accounted to the client. This duty to account is also mirrored by the Solicitors' Code of Conduct 2007 (see **11.16**).

Equally, there is a presumption of undue influence where a fiduciary duty exists. This means that in any dealings between a solicitor and his client, there will be a rebuttable presumption that the solicitor has exercised undue influence in persuading the client to enter into that dealing. In order to rebut this presumption, the solicitor would need to show that such influence had not been exercised, for example by making a full disclosure of all relevant facts, ensuring that the client took independent legal advice and understood the transaction, and ensuring that all dealings were fair and at arm's length.

10.4.4   Taking advantage of the client

As a result of the fiduciary relationship between the solicitor and client, the solicitor must not take advantage of the client. The SRA's guidance note 1 to Rule 2 provides that this would include abusing or exploiting the client's vulnerabilities, such as his age, ill health or inexperience.

10.4.5   Confidentiality

A solicitor and his firm have a duty to keep the affairs of their client confidential. This duty continues even after the retainer has been terminated. This topic is considered in detail in **Chapter 12**.

10.4.6   Disclosure

A solicitor owes the client a duty to disclose all relevant information to the client, regardless of the source of this information. This topic is considered in detail in **Chapter 12**.

10.4.7   Client care and costs

A solicitor is obliged to provide information on costs and other issues at the start of and throughout the matter, to enable the client to make informed decisions. A solicitor also has a duty to keep the client informed throughout the transaction and to deal with the client's matter promptly (see **Chapter 11**).

10.5   The client's authority

A solicitor may derive authority from the retainer to bind the client in certain circumstances. This authority can be limited expressly by the client in the terms of the retainer. However, the solicitor should never seek to rely on this implied authority to bind the client. Express instructions should always be taken from the client prior to the solicitor taking any step in the proceedings or matter.

10.6   Termination of the retainer

10.6.1   Introduction

As with any contractual relationship, the retainer may be terminated by either party, or by the general law.

10.6.2   Termination by the client

The SRA's guidance to Rule 2 provides that a client may terminate the retainer at any time for any reason. However, the client is likely to be liable to pay the solicitor's fees for work done up until the point of termination. A solicitor may require his costs to be paid prior to forwarding the file to the client (see **10.7**).

10.6.3   Termination by the solicitor

In contrast to the right of a client to terminate the retainer at will, the Solicitors' Code of Conduct restricts the right of a solicitor to terminate the retainer. Rule 2.01(2) provides that a solicitor may terminate a retainer only with good reason and on reasonable notice.

10.6.3.1   Good reason

Examples given by the SRA of a 'good reason' to terminate include where:

(a)   the solicitor has to terminate the retainer pursuant to Rule 2.01 (eg, the instructions would involve the solicitor in a breach of the law or the rules of professional conduct – see **10.3.3**);

(b)   the solicitor cannot obtain proper instructions from the client;

(c)   there has been a breakdown in confidence within the relationship between the solicitor and client (eg, the client is not willing to accept the advice of the solicitor).

10.6.3.2   Reasonable notice

The SRA's guidance to Rule 2 provides that what amounts to 'reasonable notice' will depend on the circumstances. For example, the guidance states that it would rarely be acceptable to stop acting for the client immediately before a court hearing, where it would be impossible for the client to find someone else to represent him at the hearing.

10.6.4   Termination by law

The retainer will be terminated automatically by law in certain circumstances. These include where the solicitor is declared bankrupt or either party loses mental capacity after the retainer has commenced.

Where the solicitor does not practise as a sole practitioner, his being declared bankrupt or losing mental capacity will have little practical effect, as one of his partners will take over the client's matter.

Where the client loses mental capacity, the SRA's guidance provides that the solicitor must not just leave the client without legal representation. The guidance suggests the solicitor should inform the Court of Protection, or take the appropriate steps to ensure that someone (such as a litigation friend) is appointed to represent the interests of the client.

10.6.5   Responsibilities on termination

A solicitor should confirm to the client in writing that the retainer has been terminated, and take steps to deal with any property of the client which may be held by the solicitor. For example, the solicitor may be holding client monies which, subject to the position on costs, should be returned to the client as soon as possible, together with any interest. The solicitor will also have to deal with the client's paperwork. The SRA's guidance provides that the solicitor should hand over the client's papers (to the client or an appointed third party) promptly, subject to the solicitor's right to exercise a lien for any unpaid costs (see **10.7**).

Where the client's matter is ongoing and the client has instructed another firm of solicitors, it may be advisable to retain a copy of the file. The solicitor should also consider the client's rights and the solicitor's obligations under the Data Protection Act 1998. The Act requires that any personal data in those files are retained only for the purpose for which they were collected, although this will not prevent the solicitor from retaining a copy of the file in order to defend himself from any future claims of negligence.

10.7   Liens

A lien is a legal right that allows a creditor to retain a debtor's property until payment. Accordingly, a solicitor may hold on to property already in his possession, such as client's papers, until his proper fees are paid. The SRA's guidance suggests that where possible an undertaking to pay the costs should be accepted instead of the solicitor retaining the client's papers under a lien.

Example

Mr Hall instructs X & Co solicitors to deal with his business affairs. He is not satisfied with the service he receives and so informs X & Co that he wishes to terminate his retainer and instruct Y & Co. It would be preferable for Y & Co to offer an undertaking to pay any outstanding costs of X & Co, rather than X & Co relying on a lien to hold on to the client's papers until payment. If the undertaking is offered (and accepted), the file may be forwarded to Y & Co as soon as possible. Thus Mr Hall will not be prejudiced by any delay.

The court has the power under s 68 of the Solicitors Act 1974 to order the solicitor to deliver up any papers to the client. The SRA also has a similar power where it has intervened in a solicitor's practice (see **7.10.2**).

Alternatively, a solicitor may apply to court under s 73 of the Solicitors Act 1974 for a charging order over any personal property of the client recovered or preserved by the solicitor within litigation proceedings. The charging order may cover the solicitor's taxed costs for those proceedings.

10.8   Chapter summary

10.8.1   Acceptance of instructions

(1)   The solicitor must ensure that the client understands the extent of the retainer between the solicitor and client.

(2)   Where the solicitor receives instructions from a third party, he must confirm with the client that those instructions accord with the client's wishes.

10.8.2   Refusal of instructions

(1)   A solicitor's ability to accept or decline instructions is limited by the general law and the rules of professional conduct.

(2)   A solicitor must not decline to act for someone on any discriminatory grounds.

(3)   A solicitor must refuse to act where the instructions would involve the solicitor in a breach of the law or the rules of professional conduct.

10.8.3   Duty to the client during the retainer

(1)   The solicitor has a duty to act with reasonable skill and care when providing services (such as legal advice).

(2)   The solicitor has a fiduciary duty to act in the best interests of the client. Accordingly, a solicitor must not take advantage of his client.

(3)   A solicitor owes various duties to the client throughout the retainer, including a duty of confidentiality and a duty of disclosure.

(4)   A solicitor should not seek to rely on any implied authority to bind his client.

10.8.4   Termination of the retainer

(1)   The retainer may be terminated by either party, or by law.

(2)   The solicitor's right to terminate the retainer is restricted by the rules of professional conduct.

(3)   A solicitor should deal promptly with the papers and property of the client within his possession. In certain circumstances a solicitor may exercise a lien over this property until his fees are paid.

Chapter 11

Client Care and Costs

11.1 Introduction

The marketplace for legal services is a very competitive area. From high street firms to large city firms, the competition to work for the best clients in a particular matter is often fierce.

Firms often spend large amounts of money on marketing budgets to attract clients. It is therefore in the firms' best interests to try to keep their clients from instructing other firms by providing a high level of service.

Where a client becomes dissatisfied with his solicitors, it is often due to a lack of information concerning issues such as costs or how the matter is progressing. Accordingly, Rule 2 of the Solicitors' Code of Conduct 2007 sets out the minimum standards of service that a client can expect to receive.

Rule 2 is not prescriptive on exactly how a firm should comply with its obligations under Rule 2, as different law firms will have in place differing client care systems. However, The Law Society does produce detailed practical guidance on how some of the obligations may be complied with. At the time of writing, the latest guidance, entitled 'Your clients – your business', can be found on The Law Society's website.

The aim of Rule 2 could be found in an earlier draft of the Code of Conduct. The now defunct Rule 1.08 made it clear that a firm of solicitors must ensure that a client receives information on costs and other matters in a clear and frequent manner to enable the client to make informed decisions.

This information should be given to the client at a first interview, and be updated throughout the matter.

11.2   Client care – Rule 2.02

11.2.1   The client's objective

The solicitor is under a duty to ascertain exactly what the client wishes to achieve by instructing the solicitor. Once this objective has been identified, the solicitor must give the client a clear explanation of the issues involved in achieving the client's goal (Rule 2.02).

These issues include the consideration of whether the expense or risk involved in achieving the client's objective will justify the objective itself (Rule 2.03(6)). For example, a complaint from clients is often that they were unaware that it would cost so much to achieve so little.

The solicitor is obliged to give the above information, together with the options available to the client, as the client must agree upon the next steps to be taken in the matter. If the client is not fully aware of the issues involved then he will not be in a position to make an informed decision.

11.2.2   Level of service

The solicitor must also agree an appropriate level of service with the client at the start of the matter (Rule 2.02(2)(a)). For example, some clients may want to be updated in writing on a regular basis. On the other hand, a client may want to hear nothing from a solicitor until a certain stage of a transaction has been reached.

11.2.3   Responsibilities

Both the solicitor and the client will have their own responsibilities during a matter. For example, the solicitor will be obliged to keep the client informed of progress and seek the client's instructions where required. The solicitor will also expect the client to keep him updated as the matter progresses. The solicitor is under an obligation to explain these responsibilities to the client at the start of the matter (Rule 2.02(2)(b) and (c)).

11.2.4   Status and supervision

A solicitor must confirm in writing the name and status of the person or people dealing with the matter. The solicitor must also confirm the identity of the person responsible for the overall supervision of the matter (Rule 2.02(2)(d)). This information must be provided to the client as soon as possible after the solicitor agrees to act.

11.2.5   Obligation to update

A solicitor must keep the client informed of progress throughout the retainer (Rule 2.02(1)(d)).

11.2.6   Restrictions on acting

Where a client has been referred to the solicitor by a third party, there may be conditions placed on how the solicitor may act for the client. The Solicitors Regulation Authority's ('SRA's') guidance to Rule 2 gives the example of a client referred to a solicitor by the client's insurer. Under the terms of acting, the solicitor may not be able to issue proceedings without the authority of the insurer (who will be funding any such action).

If any such restrictions apply to a solicitor then the solicitor must explain the limitations to the client (Rule 2.02(2)(e)).

However, a solicitor must not enter into any agreement with a third party under which the solicitor will not be able to act in the client's best interests (see **9.4.2**).

11.2.7 Limitations to client care

A solicitor will not breach Rule 2.02 if he can demonstrate that it was inappropriate to comply with all of the requirements. For example, a client who regularly uses a particular solicitor may not need to be given information concerning the status of the individual as the client will already have the information (Rule 2.02(3)).

11.2.8 Information to be given in writing

The SRA's guidance provides that the information must be provided in a clear and readily accessible form. It is advisable to have a written record of this information. This will enable the client to keep a record of the information provided to him. It will also serve as a written record that the solicitor has complied with Rule 2.02.

11.3 Information about costs – Rule 2.03

11.3.1 Introduction

One of the most important issues for a client is the overall cost of legal services. When an individual goes into a shop to buy something, it is easy for that person to work out how much the thing will cost and therefore whether he wants to spend that amount of money on buying the product.

The provision of legal services often does not work in the same way. Nevertheless, the client must be given the best possible information as to the overall costs of the matter if he is to be able to make an informed decision about whether he wants to go ahead with it.

11.3.2 Best possible information

A solicitor is obliged to provide the client with the best possible information about the likely overall cost of a matter, both at the outset and when the matter progresses.

A solicitor must provide the client with details of the basis and terms of the solicitor's charges. For example, the client may be charged a fixed fee or by reference to an hourly charge-out rate. The solicitor must also inform the client whether payments are likely to be made to any third parties for which he will be liable (and if so, how much). For example, when dealing with a residential conveyancing matter, the solicitor will be obliged to obtain details concerning the property from local authority and Land Registry searches.

It will often be impossible to provide an accurate estimate of the overall cost of a matter at the start. However, just providing the client with details of the solicitor's charge-out rate will rarely be sufficient. For example, if the only information the solicitor provides to a client is that his charge-out rate will be £200 per hour, the client will not know whether he will have to pay £200 for the matter to be finished (if the solicitor puts in one hour's work) or £20,000 (if the solicitor puts in 100 hours' work).

If a precise figure is not possible, the SRA's guidance suggests that the solicitor should explain why the precise figure cannot be given and agree either:

(a)   a ceiling figure, above which the solicitor's costs cannot go, without the client's permission; or

(b)   a review date when the parties will revisit the costs position.

The solicitor is also obliged to inform the client if his charging rates are to be increased.

The solicitor must not forget expressly to include VAT in any hourly rate or quote. For example, a solicitor may quote his hourly rate as £200 plus VAT. If the solicitor fails to quote with VAT, the price the client pays will be deemed to include VAT. Accordingly, if a solicitor were to say that his charge-out rate was £200 per hour, that would be all the client was liable to pay. The solicitor would have to pay the VAT element to the authorities from this £200, and would therefore lose out.

11.3.3   Funding arrangements

A solicitor is obliged to discuss with the client how the client will pay for the legal services (Rule 2.03(1)(d)).

11.3.3.1   Publicly funded work

This obligation includes whether the client may be eligible to apply for public funding (such as Legal Help or Legal Representation) (Rule 2.03(3)). This obligation will still apply where the solicitors firm in question does not complete publicly funded work.

Where a solicitor is acting for a publicly-funded client, the solicitor must explain:

(a)   the effect of the statutory charge (ie, that the client may have to repay money to the Legal Services Commission should the client recover or preserve any assets in proceedings);

(b)   that the client may have to pay a fixed or periodic contribution to the Legal Services Commission, and the consequences of not doing so;

(c)   the circumstances in which the client may have to pay his own legal costs or the costs of the other party; and

(d)   that even if the client is successful, the other party may not be ordered to pay (or be able to pay) his costs in full.

11.3.3.2   Other funding options

The solicitor must also explore whether any other funding may be available to the client. For example, the client may have insurance to cover the costs of any legal action, or his costs may be covered by his trade union.

11.3.4   Costs issues in litigation

A client must be advised of the circumstances in which he will be liable to pay the costs of the other party in a matter (Rule 2.03(1)(f)). For example, in litigation the client may be ordered to pay the costs of the winning party. The solicitor should consider whether these costs might be covered by insurance (Rule 2.03(1)(g)).

Regardless of any costs order the court may make in favour of the client concerning litigation, the client must be advised that he may still be liable to pay his own solicitor's costs. For example, the amount that the losing party in litigation is ordered to pay to the winning party will be assessed by the court, and it is unlikely to cover the entirety of the winning client's legal costs. Where the solicitor wishes to charge the client for any such excess, the solicitor must have entered into a written agreement with the client to that effect (see CPR, r 48.8(1A)).

The client will also remain liable to pay his solicitor's costs where the losing party is unable to meet the costs order. This should be made clear to the client prior to starting any litigious proceedings.

11.3.5 Conditional fee arrangements

Rule 2 also applies to conditional fee arrangements (see **11.9.3**). A solicitor, when acting under a conditional fee arrangement must also explain various additional matters set out in Rule 2.03(2). For example, these include explaining the circumstances under which the client will be liable to pay the solicitor's costs.

11.3.6 Limitations to costs information

A solicitor will not breach Rule 2.03 if he can demonstrate that it was inappropriate to comply with all of the requirements. For example, a client who regularly uses a particular solicitor on agreed terms may not need to have the costs information repeated (Rule 2.03(7)).

11.3.7 Costs information should be in writing

All of the information the solicitor is obliged to provide to the client should be given in a clear manner and confirmed in writing (Rule 2.03(5)).

11.4 Liens

A solicitor must explain to the client that in certain circumstances the solicitor may be able to exercise a lien in respect of any costs the client has failed to pay (Rule 2.03(1)(e)) (see **10.7**).

11.5 Timescale

The solicitor should provide the client with a clear estimate of the time required to complete the client's objectives. The client must be informed if this estimate changes (eg, if there have been any delays), and also informed when the matter has completed.

11.6 Client care letter

The information a solicitor is obliged to provide under Rule 2 should be provided in writing. Accordingly, a firm should send the client a client care letter as soon as possible after the first interview, detailing the issues set out above and the terms of the firm's retainer.

This letter should also contain details of the solicitor's complaints handling procedure (see **7.4.1**).

11.7 Breach of Rule 2

Every firm must have a written complaints procedure (see **7.4.1**). If the matter is referred to the Legal Complaints Service ('LCS') then a breach of any of the provisions of Rule 2 could lead to a finding that a solicitors firm has provided an inadequate professional service. The SRA may seek to take further disciplinary action against firms with a record of repeated breaches of Rule 2.

11.8   Fees and costs

11.8.1   Introduction

The retainer between the solicitor and client is a contract, and so the fees and charges the solicitor will levy for acting for the client will be agreed between the parties at the start of the retainer. However, restrictions are placed upon the fees a solicitor may charge, and also upon how the solicitor will be remunerated by the SRA and the general law. The rest of this chapter offers a summary of the main provisions; it is not intended to be a comprehensive guide.

These restrictions vary depending upon what type of work the solicitor has agreed to carry out for the client. A distinction is made between 'contentious' business and 'non-contentious' business. This distinction is particularly relevant when considering whether, and how, a client can challenge the bill of a solicitor.

11.8.2   Contentious business

Contentious business is defined as 'business done, whether as a solicitor or an advocate, in or for the purposes of proceedings begun before a court or an arbitrator, not being business which falls within the definition of non-contentious business or common form probate business' (Solicitors Act 1974, s 87). Accordingly, contentious business is work done in relation to proceedings. However, contentious business starts only once proceedings have been issued.

For example, a client may seek the advice of a solicitor with a view to suing his previous firm for negligence. The solicitor advises that the client should start proceedings, but suggests that a letter is sent to the previous firm beforehand, giving that firm seven days to offer appropriate compensation. The client is clearly contemplating litigious proceedings, but if the firm makes an acceptable offer before proceedings are issued, the solicitor's work will be classified as non-contentious.

11.8.3   Non-contentious business

Non-contentious business is defined as 'any business done as a solicitor which is not contentious business' (Solicitors Act 1974, s 87). This includes obvious examples such as conveyancing or commercial drafting work. The definition also includes all proceedings before tribunals, except the Lands Tribunal and the Employment Appeals Tribunal.

Non-contentious business is governed by the Solicitors' (Non-Contentious Business) Remuneration Order 1994 (SI 1994/2616).

11.9   Options available for solicitor's fees

A solicitor may agree to charge a client for work done on a number of different bases. Some of these options are considered below. Whichever method of charging the client and solicitor agree, the overall amount of the charge will be regulated by statute and so the client may be able to challenge the bill at a later date (see **11.12**).

11.9.1   Hourly rate

Perhaps the most common method of charging clients is by use of an hourly rate, ie the client is charged for the time spent on the file. The client is informed at the start of the matter which fee earner will be working on the client's files, and the fee earner's respective charge-out rates. However, the SRA's guidance states that merely giving an hourly rate is not acceptable (see **11.3.2**). The solicitor must agree either a ceiling above which the costs cannot go without the agreement of the client, or a date when the solicitor and client will review the costs position.

11.9.2 Fixed fee

Alternatively a solicitor may agree to complete the work for a fixed fee, or a fixed fee plus VAT and disbursements. Fixed fees are often used for conveyancing transactions. If the solicitor agrees to act in return for a fixed fee, this fee cannot be altered at a later date (unless the client agrees) if the work turns out to be more expensive than the solicitor first expected.

11.9.3 Variable fees

A solicitor is permitted, in certain circumstances, to charge a fee which varies according to the outcome of the matter. One such example of a variable fee is a contingency fee. Rule 24 defines a contingency fee as any sum payable only in the event of success. For example, where a solicitor offers to act for the client on the basis that he receives 15% of the client's damages in a matter.

Rule 2.04 prohibits solicitors from entering into a contingency fee agreement for work done prosecuting or defending any contentious proceedings before any court or arbitral hearing, unless it is permitted by the general law. One such permitted agreement is a conditional fee agreement. An example of a conditional fee agreement is the 'no win, no fee' basis of charging that is popular in areas of work such as personal injury. Under such an agreement, the solicitor may agree to charge nothing if the client loses, but will charge his fees plus an agreed 'uplift' (or 'success fee', for example an extra 20%) in the event of success.

In respect of litigation or advocacy services, a solicitor may enter into (and enforce) a conditional fee agreement if it complies with s 58 of the Courts and Legal Services Act 1990. For example, the agreement must be in writing, signed by both the solicitor and the client, and, where a success fee is to be paid, specify the percentage of the success fee. The success fee cannot exceed a percentage specified by the Lord Chancellor (currently 100%). A solicitor cannot enter into a conditional fee agreement for any criminal work or family proceedings.

The conditional fee agreement must also comply with any additional requirements specified by the SRA. To aid compliance, The Law Society has published a model conditional fee arrangement for use by the profession.

If the client instructs a solicitor on a conditional fee arrangement (for example, on a 'no win, no fee' basis), this may not mean that the client will pay nothing if he loses his case. Although he may not be liable to pay his solicitor's fees, he may well have to pay disbursements such as court fees, or more particularly barrister's fees, and also VAT. The client may also have to pay his opponent's costs. A solicitor should explore whether the client can obtain insurance to cover these costs in the event of losing the case.

The SRA's guidance provides that a solicitor may enter into a contingency fee arrangement in respect of non-contentious work, but to be enforceable this must be in the form of a non-contentious business agreement (see **11.13**).

11.9.4 Other methods

A solicitor may agree to be remunerated by some other means. The SRA's guidance suggests that one such example would be a solicitor agreeing to accept shares in a new company in return for his work, rather than costs. However, the guidance provides that in such circumstances the client should be advised to seek independent advice about such a costs agreement.

11.10 Money on account

It is common for a solicitor to require a client to pay a sum of money to the solicitor at the start of the transaction on account of the costs and disbursements that will be incurred.

In contentious business, a solicitor may require a client to pay a reasonable sum to the solicitor on account of costs. If the client does not pay this money within a reasonable time, the solicitor may terminate the retainer (Solicitors Act 1974, s 65(2)).

There is no such statutory right in non-contentious business. Accordingly, where the solicitor requires money on account before starting a matter, the solicitor should make this a requirement of the retainer.

11.11 Solicitor's bill

11.11.1 Introduction

For a solicitor to be able to obtain payment from the client, certain formalities need to be complied with in respect of the solicitor's bill. These matters include (but are not limited to) the following:

(a)   The bill must contain enough information for the client to be satisfied that the bill is reasonable, and also provide details of the period to which the bill relates.

(b)   The bill must be signed by the solicitor or on his behalf by an employee authorised to do so. Alternatively, the solicitor/authorised employee may sign a covering letter which refers to the bill (Solicitors Act 1974, s 69(2A)).

(c)   The bill must be delivered by hand to the client, by post to his home, business address or last known address, or by e-mail if the client has agreed to this method and provided an appropriate e-mail address (Solicitors Act 1974, s 69(2C)).

In a non-contentious matter, the solicitor must also inform the client of the matters set out in art 8 of the Solicitors' (Non-Contentious Business) Remuneration Order 1994 (SI 1994/2616). These matters include (but are not limited to):

(a)   the client's right to challenge the bill, using the remuneration certificate process and/or taxation by the court (see **11.12**). The client must be informed of the time limits relating to the application for a remuneration certificate; and

(b)   the solicitor's right to charge interest on the bill after the period of one month has elapsed after the delivery of the bill.

Where these requirements have not been complied with, the solicitor cannot take any action to recover any unpaid costs (see **11.11.4**).

Whilst there is no obligation to inform a client within contentious proceedings that he has the right to challenge the bill, it is advisable to do so.

11.11.2 Interim bills

A solicitor may wish to bill his client for work done on the client's file before the matter has completed. This will particularly be the case where the client's matter is likely to go on for some months, such as protracted litigation. A solicitor may wish to issue interim bills throughout the matter.

Where a solicitor delivers an interim bill, it will be considered (subject to limited exceptions) an interim 'bill on account' of the final bill which will be delivered at the end of the matter/retainer. A solicitor is unable to sue the client for non-payment of such a bill, and the client cannot apply to have the bill assessed. The solicitor has the right to deliver an interim 'statute bill', upon which he can sue the client for non-payment, in limited circumstances only, such as a 'natural break' in lengthy proceedings.

However, The Law Society recommends that if the solicitor wishes to issue interim 'statute bills' during a lengthy matter, this right should be expressly reserved within the retainer. The Law Society's guidance ('Your clients – your business' – see **11.1**) provides that the solicitor must specify the time limit within which the client must pay the interim bill, and must also expressly reserve the right to terminate the retainer in the event of non-payment.

11.11.3 Interest on bills

In a non-contentious matter a solicitor may charge interest on the whole or the outstanding part of an unpaid bill with effect from one month after delivery of the bill, provided that notice of the client's right to challenge the bill has been given to him. The rate of interest chargeable must not exceed that which is payable on judgment debts. At the time of writing the rate is currently 8%.

In contentious business, The Law Society's guidance provides that a solicitor may charge interest on an unpaid bill where the solicitor expressly reserves this right in the retainer, or the client later agrees for a 'contractual consideration' to pay interest. Alternatively, where a solicitor sues the client for non-payment of fees, the court has the power to award the solicitor interest on the debt under s 35A of the Supreme Court Act 1981 or s 69 of the County Courts Act 1984.

The rate of interest will be the rate payable for judgment debts unless the solicitor and client expressly agree a different rate.

11.11.4 Enforcement

Subject to certain exceptions, a solicitor may not commence any claim to recover any costs due to the solicitor (such as suing the client) until one month has passed since the solicitor delivered his bill (Solicitors Act 1974, s 69). The bill must also be in the proper form (see **11.11.1**).

However, the High Court has the power under s 69 to allow the solicitor to commence such a claim against the client within this one-month period where the court is satisfied that the client is about to leave the country, be declared bankrupt (or enter into a composition with his creditors), or do anything else which would prevent or delay the solicitor obtaining his fees.

11.12   Client's right to challenge the bill

The client may challenge the amount of a solicitor's bill, provided that he complies with certain requirements. These requirements depend upon how the client wishes to go about challenging the bill.

11.12.1 Remuneration certificate

11.12.1.1 Introduction

In non-contentious proceedings, a client may require his solicitor to obtain a remuneration certificate. Where the client requests a remuneration certificate within the specified time limits, the solicitor must apply for such a certificate from the LCS. The LCS will then assess whether the fees charged by the solicitor are reasonable.

The remuneration certificate will state what sum the LCS considers to be reasonable for the work the solicitor has carried out. Where the amount specified in the remuneration certificate is less than the fees the solicitor has charged, the client will be liable to pay only the fees set out in the certificate. The LCS cannot increase the solicitor's fee.

Remuneration certificates are governed by the Solicitors' (Non-Contentious Business) Remuneration Order 1994 (SI 1994/2616).

11.12.1.2 Who can apply?

Generally speaking, only the solicitor's client has the right to apply for a remuneration certificate. In probate matters, residuary beneficiaries (other than those with a contingent interest) may require the solicitor to obtain a remuneration certificate where the personal representatives of the estate are all solicitors.

The remuneration certificate may be used only where the costs of the matter do not exceed £50,000.

11.12.1.3 Time limits

A client must request that the solicitor obtains a remuneration certificate within one month of receiving his bill. However, where the solicitor has failed to inform the client of the information prescribed in art 8 of the Solicitors' (Non-Contentious Business) Remuneration Order 1994 (see **11.11.1**), such as his right to obtain a remuneration certificate, this one-month time limit will run only from the date when the client is given this information.

Where the solicitor has deducted his costs from monies he was holding on behalf of the client and does not inform the client of his right to obtain a remuneration certificate, the client must object to the costs of the solicitor within three months of receiving the bill if he wishes to use the remuneration certificate procedure.

11.12.1.4 Conditions of application

As a condition of applying for a remuneration certificate, the solicitor may require the client to pay 50% of the solicitor's fees, together with all of the disbursements and VAT from the bill. This payment must be made within one month of the client receiving his bill or being notified of his right to apply for a remuneration certificate (if later). The LCS has the power to waive this requirement in exceptional circumstances.

11.12.1.5 Grounds

As noted at **11.12.1.1** above, the remuneration certificate will specify an amount which it is reasonable to charge for the work the solicitor has completed. Costs in non-contentious proceedings are governed by art 3 of the Solicitors' (Non-Contentious Business) Remuneration Order 1994. This provides that a solicitor may charge fees that are 'fair and reasonable' in all the circumstances. In determining what is 'fair and reasonable', the LCS must consider:

(a) the complexity of the matter, or the difficulty or novelty of the questions raised;

(b) the skill, labour, specialised knowledge and responsibility involved;

(c) the time spent on the business;

(d) the number and importance of the documents prepared or perused, without regard to length;

(e) the place where and the circumstances in which the business or any part thereof is transacted;

(f) the amount or value of any money or property involved;

(g) whether any land involved is registered;

(h) the importance of the matter to the client; and

(i) the approval (express or implied) of the entitled person, or the express approval of the testator, to:

(i) the solicitor undertaking all or any part of the work giving rise to the costs, or

(ii) the amount of the costs.

11.12.1.6 Loss of right

A client will lose the right to apply for a remuneration certificate where:

(a) the client has paid the bill (other than by deduction);

(b) the court has ordered the bill to be taxed (see **11.12.2**);

(c) the solicitor and client have entered into a non-contentious business agreement (see **11.13**).

11.12.2 Assessment by the court

A client may apply to have his bill assessed by the court in both contentious and non-contentious proceedings. This is sometimes referred to as a bill being 'taxed'. Accordingly, this process may be used as an alternative to applying for a remuneration certificate in non-contentious proceedings.

The client must apply to have the bill assessed within one month from the date of delivery. Where no application is made within this month, the client may still apply within 12 months of delivery, but will require the leave of the court for the bill to be assessed (Solicitors Act 1974, s 70).

The costs will be assessed by a judge or district judge sitting as a 'costs officer'. The costs officer has the power to assess the fees and disbursements of the solicitor.

The costs will (with certain exceptions) be assessed on an 'indemnity basis'. The court will allow only costs that have been reasonably incurred by the solicitor and which are reasonable in amount. Any doubt as to what is to be considered reasonable is resolved in the favour of the solicitor. However, the client may be ordered to pay the costs of the solicitor arising from the assessment process.

11.12.2.1 Non-contentious proceedings

Where a court is asked to assess a solicitor's bill in non-contentious proceedings, in deciding what is reasonable, the court must have regard to the circumstances outlined at **11.12.1.5** above (Solicitors Act 1974, s 56(7)).

11.12.2.2   Contentious proceedings

The factors the court must take into account when considering whether costs are reasonable are set out in CPR, r 44.5. These include (but are not limited to):

(a)   the conduct of the parties;

(b)   the amount or value of any money or property involved;

(c)   the importance of the matter to the parties;

(d)   the particular complexity of the matter, or the difficulty or novelty of the questions raised;

(e)   the skill, effort, specialised knowledge and responsibility involved;

(f)   the time spent on the case; and

(g)   the place where and the circumstances in which work, or any part of it, was done.

Subject to certain exceptions, a client cannot apply for an assessment of costs where the solicitor and client have entered into a contentious business agreement (see **11.14**).

11.13   Non-contentious business agreements

A solicitor and client may enter into a non-contentious business agreement in respect of the solicitor's remuneration for any non-contentious work. Under this agreement the solicitor may be remunerated by a gross sum, commission, a percentage, a salary, or otherwise.

To be enforceable, the agreement must comply with s 57 of the Solicitors Act 1974. For example, the agreement must:

(a)   be in writing;

(b)   be signed by the client;

(c)   contain all the terms of the agreement (including whether disbursements and VAT are included in the agreed remuneration).

Where the relevant provisions have been complied with, the client will be unable to apply for a remuneration certificate. However, the court may set the agreement aside if the amount charged by the solicitor is unfair or unreasonable.

11.14   Contentious business agreements

A solicitor may enter into a contentious business agreement in respect of his remuneration for contentious work completed on behalf of the client (see Solicitors Act 1974, ss 59–63).

The agreement may provide for the solicitor to be remunerated by reference to a gross sum, an hourly rate, a salary or otherwise. However, the solicitor may not be remunerated by a contingency fee.

In order to be enforceable, the agreement must comply with certain requirements, including:

(a)   the agreement must state it is a contentious business agreement;

(b)   the agreement must be in writing;

(c)   the agreement must be signed by the client; and

(d)   the agreement must contain all the terms.

Where the contentious business agreement is enforceable, the client will be unable to apply to court for an assessment of costs (except where the agreement provides that the solicitor is to be remunerated by reference to an hourly rate.) However, the court may set aside the agreement if it is unfair or unreasonable.

11.15 Overcharging

A solicitor must act in the best interests of the client and must not take advantage of his client. Therefore a solicitor must not overcharge for work done. Where a costs officer (when assessing a solicitor's bill in a non-contentious matter) reduces the amount of the costs by more than 50%, he must inform the SRA. Overcharging the client will be considered a breach of professional conduct.

11.16 Commission

The solicitor–client relationship is a fiduciary relationship (see **10.4.3**), and so a solicitor must not make a secret profit whilst acting for the client. The SRA's guidance defines a commission as:

(a) a financial benefit received by the solicitor by reason of and in the course of the relationship of solicitor and client; and

(b) arises in the context that the solicitor has put a third party and the client in touch with one another.

For example, a client may require specialist tax advice, and so may be referred by the solicitor to a tax consultant. The tax consultant may pay the solicitor commission in return for this referral.

Rule 2.06 provides that where a solicitor receives commission over £20, this commission must be paid to the client. Alternatively, if the solicitor obtains the client's consent (having disclosed full details of the commission), the commission can be deducted from the client's bill or retained by the solicitor.

Where the solicitor is carrying out an exempt regulated activity in respect of financial services (see **Chapter 17**), the solicitor must consider s 327 of the Financial Services and Markets Act 2000. Accordingly, to comply with s 327(3), the solicitor must account to the client for all commission received (even amounts under £20).

11.17 Chapter summary

11.17.1 Client care

(1) A solicitor must maintain appropriate client care procedures as prescribed by the SRA. This information must be given to the client in writing at the start of the matter and be updated throughout.

(2) The solicitor must ascertain what the client wishes to achieve by instructing the solicitor. The solicitor must explain clearly what is involved in achieving this aim, and carry out a costs/benefit analysis.

(3) The client must be given information relating to various matters, such as the responsibilities of the client and solicitor, who will be dealing with (and supervising) the client's matter, and the level of service that the client may expect from the solicitor.

(4) The solicitor must update the client as to progress throughout the matter.

11.17.2   Information about costs

(1)   A solicitor must give his client the best possible information as to the likely overall costs of a matter. This information should be in writing, and be updated regularly.

(2)   This information must include details of the basis and terms of the solicitor's charges. The solicitor must also advise the client of any payments to third parties (such as barristers) which the solicitor may have to make.

(3)   Where it is not possible for a solicitor to provide an accurate estimate of the overall costs, the solicitor should agree dates to review the costs incurred, or agree a level beyond which costs may not go.

(4)   A solicitor must advise the client as to the availability of public funding or insurance to cover the client's costs.

(5)   A solicitor must advise the client whether he may be liable to pay the costs of the other party to the matter.

11.17.3   Fees and costs

(1)   A solicitor and client may agree the level of costs the solicitor may charge. However, this agreement is regulated by statute and the common law.

(2)   A distinction is made between costs in contentious matters and costs in non-contentious matters.

(3)   A solicitor's bill must contain prescribed information in order for the bill to be enforceable.

(4)   A client may challenge the costs of a solicitor both in contentious and non-contentious proceedings.

(5)   Generally, a solicitor may not sue to recover his costs from the client until one month has elapsed since the bill was delivered.

Chapter 12

Confidentiality

12.1 Duty of confidentiality

> You and your firm must keep the affairs of clients and former clients confidential except where disclosure is required or permitted by law or by your client (or former client). (Solicitors' Code of Conduct 2007, Rule 4.01)

12.1.1 Introduction

Confidentiality is a fundamental principle of the solicitor–client relationship. For example, it is important that a solicitor receives all the relevant information from a client in order to give the best possible advice. A client would be dissuaded from informing his solicitor of all the relevant facts if he thought that this information would be released to the public. However, the obligation of confidentiality extends beyond obviously confidential information given to a solicitor by his client and includes all information about a client or matter, regardless of the source of that information.

This duty will continue after the retainer has been terminated. Accordingly, a solicitor will owe a duty of confidentiality to former, as well as existing, clients. The duty also continues after the death of the client, whereupon the right to enforce or waive the duty of confidentiality is passed to the client's (or former client's) personal representatives.

Any breach of Rule 4.01 will be a breach of professional conduct. The solicitor may be disciplined by the Solicitors Regulation Authority ('SRA'), or by the Solicitors Disciplinary Tribunal (see **Chapter 7**). In addition, the client (or former client) may sue the solicitor for any breach of this duty.

12.1.2 Specific examples

The SRA's guidance to Rule 4 gives specific examples of where confidentiality is required. For example, these include the contents of a will (until probate has been granted and the will becomes a matter of public record), the client's address, and the contents of the solicitor's bill.

Another example (not given in the guidance) is the identity of a solicitor's clients. A solicitor will have to take various practical steps to safeguard the identity of his clients. For example, he will have a file, or files, for particular clients and the client's name (and often address and type of matter, such as divorce) may be written on the file. If a solicitor routinely interviews clients at his desk, steps should be taken to ensure that the covers of these files are not left where they could be read by any other clients.

A number of solicitors' firms use the names of their clients in their marketing and publicity to illustrate the quality of clients that instruct their firm. Where solicitors wish to use the names of their clients in marketing materials, they must obtain the consent of these clients beforehand.

12.1.3 Where confidential information may be disclosed

Information which is subject to the duty of confidentiality may be disclosed in the following circumstances:

(a)   where the client, or former client, authorises the disclosure;

(b)   pursuant to a statutory duty, such as the Proceeds of Crime Act 2002;

(c)   where it is necessary to prevent the client or a third party committing a criminal act which is likely to result in serious bodily harm;

(d)   under a court order, or where a police warrant permits the seizure of confidential documentation;

(e)   in certain circumstances where the client is publicly funded;

(f)   where the information is in the public domain.

However, the SRA's guidance stresses that a solicitor should always be mindful of the importance of the duty of confidentiality. The guidance advises that a solicitor should obtain advice from the Professional Ethics Guidance Team, or obtain legal advice, where the solicitor is uncertain as to whether to disclose the confidential information. The solicitor must also bear in mind legal professional privilege (see **12.4**)

Example

While providing instructions to his solicitor on another matter, a client informs his solicitor about a violent mugging which he intends to carry out in the near future. What should the solicitor do?

The SRA's guidance to Rule 4 provides that the solicitor may disclose confidential information where the solicitor believes it is necessary to prevent a criminal act which is likely to result in serious bodily harm. If the solicitor was certain that the information received was accurate (ie, that the information was fact and not just fantasy) then the exception would apply and the solicitor could inform the police. If in doubt as to whether to disclose the information, the solicitor should seek advice from the Professional Ethics Guidance Team.

Whilst this exception might apply where the crime had not yet been committed, and therefore the information could be disclosed as being necessary to prevent the commission of a criminal act that might lead to serious bodily harm, this would not be the case if the client was confessing to a crime which had already been committed. In this case, the information would be subject to the usual obligation of confidentiality as between client and solicitor.

12.1.4 Use of confidential material received by mistake

Due to the volume of information which passes between solicitors on a daily basis, occasionally mistakes may be made and information destined for a third party may be inadvertently disclosed to a solicitor. For example, a solicitor acting for one party in a matter may mis-address correspondence destined for his client to the solicitor acting for the other party. In this case, immediately on becoming aware of the error, the receiving solicitor must return the papers to the originating solicitor without reading them or otherwise making use of the information contained therein.

The SRA's guidance provides that such information should not be disclosed to the client.

12.2 Duty of disclosure

A solicitor is also under a duty, pursuant to Rule 4.02 of the Solicitors' Code of Conduct 2007, to disclose to a client all information which is relevant to that client's matter, regardless of the source of that information.

12.2.1 Limitations

The duty of disclosure does not apply where:

(a)   a disclosure would be prohibited by law;

(b)   a client has expressly waived the duty to disclose; or

(c)   the solicitor reasonably believes that serious physical or mental injury will be caused to any person (including his own client) if the information is disclosed. (Rule 4.02)

12.2.2 Duty of confidentiality overrides duty of disclosure

The duty of disclosure will often conflict with the duty of confidentiality. Consider the following situation:

Example

Mr Smith instructs a solicitor to purchase a derelict plot of land from X Limited in order for him to build a new house. Another one of the solicitor's clients, Mrs Brown, sold the land to X Limited two years ago at a knock-down price as the land is contaminated. This information would be relevant to Mr Smith and so the solicitor would owe a duty to disclose the information to him. However, to do so would be to breach the solicitor's duty of confidentiality to Mrs Brown, even though the solicitor has completed the work for Mrs Brown and she no longer owns the land.

In situations such as this, your duty of confidentiality always overrides your duty of disclosure. The solicitor could tell Mr Smith only if Mrs Brown waived her confidentiality in respect of the information.

12.2.3 Agreeing a lower duty of disclosure

The SRA's guidance provides that it is possible to agree a less stringent duty of disclosure than the duty prescribed by the Code itself (see guidance note 26 to Rule 4). However, a solicitor should consider issues such as professional embarrassment (see **12.3.5**) prior to agreeing a lower duty of disclosure.

12.3 Placing confidential information at risk

12.3.1 Introduction

In order to protect against any accidental disclosure, Rule 4.03 provides that a solicitor must not act in certain situations. A solicitor must act in the best interests of the client and so must not place himself in a situation where any relevant information could be disclosed to another client, as any such disclosure would be against the best interests of the client to whom the solicitor owes a duty of confidentiality.

Accordingly, a solicitor (or firm) must not place confidential information at risk by acting (or continuing to act) where:

(a)   the information might reasonably be expected to be material to another client; and

(b)   one client has an interest adverse to the other client,

unless arrangements are put in place to safeguard the confidential information (Rule 4.03).

For example, where the same solicitor holds confidential information for one of his clients which he knows is relevant to a matter for one of his other clients, he cannot act for both clients unless the clients agree a lesser duty of disclosure.

12.3.2   Is the information material?

Rule 4.03 will prevent you (or your firm) from acting only where the information might reasonably be expected to be 'material'. This is defined by the SRA's guidance as information which is:

(a)   relevant to your client's matter; and

(b)   of more than inconsequential interest to the client (ie, will the decision affect the client's decision-making?).

The question of whether the information is 'material' relates to the client to whom the duty of disclosure concerning the information is owed. In the example at **12.2.2**, the solicitor would need to consider whether the information that Mrs Brown provided to the firm is relevant to Mr Smith's land purchase (eg, Mr Smith will need to be advised to try to reduce the price). If so, this information would be 'material' to Mr Smith.

12.3.3   Do the clients have an 'adverse' interest?

Adversity relates to the relationship between two respective clients. The SRA's guidance provides that this relationship will be said to be adverse where the client to whom the solicitor owes the duty of confidentiality is, or is likely to become, an opposing party in a matter to the client who is owed the duty of disclosure.

This would include a situation where the clients litigate against each other, are involved in mediation, or even if the clients are on opposing sides of a negotiation.

12.3.4   Exceptions

Where the same individual within a firm holds confidential information for one party which is relevant to another client, that particular solicitor will be unable to act for both clients unless a client agrees to a lesser duty of disclosure. This will be the case regardless of whether the two clients have an interest adverse to each other.

However, where a firm of solicitors holds confidential information which is material to another client, and one client has an interest adverse to the other, Rule 4 may still allow the firm to act for both parties if safeguards are put in place. These safeguards are designed to prevent the disclosure of the confidential information. The level of safeguards required will depend on the agreement of the clients involved.

12.3.4.1   Where clients consent – Rule 4.04

Rule 4.04 may allow a firm to act for a new client in a particular matter, or to continue to act for two existing clients, where both clients agree that a number of steps should be taken to protect the confidential information. These steps include the following.

Information barriers

Information barriers are practical steps taken to ensure that confidential information cannot pass from one client to another client. These steps were previously referred to within the profession as 'Chinese walls'. On a practical level they aim to prevent confidential information, given by a client to one part of a firm, from being made available to another part of the same firm.

The SRA has set out a number of measures which will normally be appropriate to protect confidential information. They include:

(a)   that the client who might be interested in the confidential information acknowledges in writing that the information held by the firm will not be given to him;

(b)   that all members of the firm who hold the relevant confidential information ('the restricted group') are identified and have no involvement with or for the other client;

(c)   that no member of the restricted group is managed or supervised in relation to that matter by someone from outside the restricted group;

(d)   that all members of the restricted group confirm at the start of the engagement that they understand that they possess, or might come to possess, information which is confidential, and that they must not discuss it with any other member of the firm unless that person is, or becomes, a member of the restricted group, and that this obligation shall be regarded by everyone as an on-going one;

(e)   that each member of the restricted group confirms when the barrier is established that he has not done anything which would amount to a breach of the information barrier; and

(f)   that only members of the restricted group have access to documents containing confidential information (Solicitors' Code of Conduct 2007, guidance note 45 to Rule 4).

Given the nature of the safeguards, information barriers will not be appropriate in every situation. For example, an information barrier could not be erected in a firm with one fee earner.

Informed consent

The consent of the parties to the firm acting for both clients must be obtained in respect of a number of matters.

(a)   The firm must explain to the client for whom it proposes to act, or for whom it proposes to continue acting (ie, the client to whom it would owe a duty of disclosure), that it holds, or might hold, material information in relation to the client's matter which the firm cannot disclose.

(b)   Another issue that must be agreed with the parties is the conditions under which the firm will act. This agreement must include details of how information barriers will be used to protect the information. The SRA's guidance to Rule 4 specifies a number of practical steps which would normally be necessary in relation to information barriers (see above). However, the guidance expressly recognises that rigid safeguards have not been enshrined in the rules. Therefore the firm may agree measures in addition to the requirements set out in the guidance.

(c)　As part of obtaining the consent of the parties in respect of how the solicitor will act (or continue to act), the parties must effectively consent to the firm acting for the other party. However, this consent must be obtained without providing any information to each of the clients which would breach the firm's duty of confidentiality to the other client (see below).

In obtaining the consent of the parties, the firm must have a 'reasonable belief' that both clients understand the relevant issues. This last condition is concerned with the issue of 'informed consent'. It is not enough that both clients offer their consent. The clients must consent after having understood and considered the risks and rewards involved in the situation.

The SRA considers that 'informed consent' will generally be of use only to 'sophisticated clients', such as large companies with in-house legal advisers or other expertise, who will be able to assess the risks of providing their consent based on the information provided.

The SRA's guidance further provides that for such clients there may be circumstances in which the informed consent could be obtained through the firm's standard terms of engagement at the start of the matter (see guidance note 36 to Rule 4). However, if such an approach is taken, the firm must highlight in the terms of engagement the risk of the firm having to cease to act where, for example, the firm becomes unable to comply with the safeguards it has agreed to act under.

A further problem for the solicitor to consider is whether he is able to disclose enough information about the identity and business of the other client to enable his client to consider the risks of giving such consent. The solicitor needs to provide enough information to enable informed consent to be given by one client, without disclosing information which would breach the duty of confidentiality to the other.

The exception allowing solicitors to act where they are holding confidential information will rarely be of use to, for example, matrimonial clients or personal injury clients.

Is it reasonable to act?

Lastly, the firm of solicitors must consider whether it would be reasonable to act for the new client (or to continue to act for two existing clients) in all the circumstances. The following example is based upon one given by the SRA's guidance notes:

> Shepherd Co Limited approaches your firm to act for it in the purchase of Derkin Co Limited. Derkin Co Limited is a former client of your firm and when acting for Derkin Co your firm obtained confidential information that the company has millions of pounds missing from its accounts. Even if the rules permitted your firm to act for Shepherd Co, your firm must consider whether it would be reasonable to act given the knowledge that the firm holds. You could not disclose the information to Shepherd Co due to your duty of confidentiality to Derkin Co.

Summary – Rule 4.04

Rule 4.04 will permit a solicitors firm to act where:

(a)　the client for whom the firm acts, or proposes to act, knows that the firm may hold material information in relation to the client's matter which the firm cannot disclose; and

(b)   the firm has a reasonable belief that both clients understand the relevant issues after these have been brought to their attention (ie, informed consent); and

(c)   both clients agree the conditions under which the firm will be acting (ie, information barriers, etc); and

(d)   it is reasonable to act in all the circumstances.

12.3.4.2   Where the client's consent cannot be obtained – Rule 4.05

Exceptions are still available where a client's consent cannot be obtained.

There will be a number of situations where the consent of both clients cannot be obtained. For example, the client to whom you owe a duty of confidentiality may simply refuse to give you permission, particularly where the client for whom you propose to act is a commercial rival.

Alternatively, the firm of solicitors may be unable to seek the consent of the client to whom they owe a duty of confidentiality because the client cannot be located. Or the solicitor may be unable to seek the consent of the client as to reveal any details concerning the situation would breach a duty of confidentiality to another client.

In limited circumstances the firm may continue to act on an existing matter in breach of Rule 4.03 as a last resort. In order to do so the firm must comply with a number of requirements set out in Rule 4.05. The main requirement is that any safeguards (ie, information barriers) adopted by the firm to protect the information must comply with the standards that are required by law at the time they are put in place. These standards will be established by case law.

However, the SRA specifies a number of measures which it expects to be implemented in most situations. These measures reflect the desire that firms must adopt an extremely high standard of protection for the confidential information. In addition to the measures outlined above, the SRA's measures include (but are not limited to) the following:

(a)   there must be a physical separation of the restricted group of staff from those acting for the other client, eg in separate buildings or on separate floors and with some form of 'access restriction' being put in place;

(b)   computer systems must be protected by the use of separate computer networks or passwords;

(c)   the firm must issue a statement that it will treat any breach of the information barrier (even an accidental breach) as a serious disciplinary offence;

(d)   the firm must implement systems for the opening of post, faxes and e-mails that will ensure that confidential information is not disclosed to anyone outside the restricted group.

The solicitor must still obtain the informed consent of the client to whom he owes a duty of disclosure that the client is happy for the firm to act without full disclosure, and the solicitor must still act only where it is reasonable to do so.

In the event that the client to whom the duty of confidentiality is owed (and who has withheld his consent) is unhappy that the firm is acting for another party in breach of Rule 4.03, the client may apply to court to seek an injunction to prevent the firm from continuing to act for the other client.

12.3.5   Professional embarrassment

Even where Rule 4 would allow a firm to act for two clients, where the firm held confidential information for one client that was material to the other client's matter, a solicitor might still be obliged to refuse to act on the grounds of professional embarrassment.

A firm should decline to act where the information which it cannot disclose to the client would cause severe embarrassment to the firm if the fact that it had agreed to act in those circumstances ever came out.

The SRA's guidance to Rule 3 provides an example in which a firm agrees to act for a company to draft a contract of employment for a prospective employee, where the firm knows (but is unable to disclose to the client due to confidentiality) that the prospective employee is under investigation for fraud. The embarrassment here would stem from the fact that the firm would know that the client seeking to employ the prospective employee was wasting legal fees on an outcome that (if it knew all the facts) it would not wish to pursue.

The firm should also consider the Core Duties, such as whether it will be able to act in the best interests of the client in question, and public confidence in the legal profession. Acting in the above situation would clearly not be in the best interests of the client, and arguably would also damage the reputation of the profession.

12.3.5.1   Example

In the example at **12.2.2**, Mr Smith instructed a firm of solicitors to purchase a plot of derelict land. Mrs Brown, also a client of the firm, had previously sold the land and had informed the firm that the land was contaminated. The information is material to Mr Smith's matter – information concerning the state of the land is relevant to whether Mr Smith will want to buy it. However, the two clients' interests are not adverse to one another. There is no suggestion that Mr Smith and Mrs Brown are likely to be on opposing sides of a particular matter. Therefore, subject to any conflicts of interest, Rule 4.03 would not prevent the firm acting for both parties. However, the firm could not inform Mr Smith of the contamination – the firm's duty of confidentiality to Mrs Brown would remain. Nevertheless, the firm should decline instructions on the basis of professional embarrassment.

12.4   Confidentiality and privilege

The obligation of confidentiality which a solicitor owes to his client is distinct from the issue of legal professional privilege. While confidentiality prevents a solicitor from disclosing any information relating to a client without that client's consent, legal professional privilege allows a solicitor to withhold specific information which he would otherwise be required to disclose, for example in court proceedings.

Legal professional privilege applies to information which is passed between a solicitor and a client, whether written or oral, directly or indirectly. The rationale behind this right to withhold information, even from the court, is similar to the rationale for the obligation of confidentiality – it exists to enable a client to speak to his solicitor without worrying that the information passed over might be disclosed at a later date.

However, there are limitations in place to prevent legal professional privilege being used as a cloak to hide information which a client does not wish a court to see. One type of legal professional privilege is legal advice privilege. It applies only to information passed between the client and a solicitor *acting in the capacity of a solicitor*. In other words, the communication must relate to the request for, or the provision of, advice to the client by the solicitor. If documents are sent to or from an independent third party, even if they are created for the purpose of obtaining legal advice, they will not be covered by this privilege, and therefore simply 'copying in' a solicitor will not mean the information can be withheld. If the communication is made for the purpose of committing a fraud or a crime, it will not attract privilege (*R v Cox and Railton* (1884) LR 14 QBD 153).

Clients and solicitors may also claim litigation privilege in respect of documents created for the sole or dominant purpose of litigation or other adversarial proceedings which have already commenced or are contemplated. This privilege also extends to communications between a solicitor and third parties. A related issue which also arises in the case of litigation is that anything said by a solicitor whilst speaking in court as an advocate is privileged. Therefore the solicitor cannot be sued for defamation in such circumstances.

A House of Lords case, *Three Rivers DC v Bank of England* [2004] UKHL 48, examines closely the limits of legal professional privilege. It was concerned with advice given in complex matters involving large corporate clients, but left unanswered important questions concerning which representatives of a large corporate client can be regarded as the client for the purpose of claiming privilege. A Court of Appeal case suggests that solicitors will have to take care to identify and restrict those within the client corporation from whom they take instructions and to whom they give advice.

Like the obligation of confidentiality, privilege continues beyond the death of a client (*Bullivant v A-G for Victoria* [1901] AC 196).

The court has power to decide whether or not a particular item is privileged.

12.5 Chapter summary

(1) A solicitor (and his staff) must keep the affairs of his clients confidential. This duty applies regardless of the source of the information.

(2) The duty of confidentiality continues until the client permits disclosure or waives the confidentiality.

(3) The duty of confidentiality can be overridden in exceptional circumstances.

(4) The solicitor also has a duty to disclose to the client all information that is relevant to the client's matter, regardless of the source of that information.

(5) The duty of confidentiality overrides the duty of disclosure.

(6) A solicitor must not risk breaching confidentiality by acting for another client where the solicitor holds information that would be relevant to the other client's matter, unless appropriate safeguards can be put in place.

(7) One of these safeguards is a requirement that the solicitor obtains the informed consent of the parties. In exceptional circumstances a solicitor may act where this consent is not given.

(8) In addition to the duty of confidentiality, a solicitor must also consider legal professional privilege. Where legal professional privilege applies, a solicitor can refuse to disclose communications between himself and a client.

Chapter 13

Conflict of Interests

13.1 Introduction

A solicitor must act in the best interests of his clients. There will be situations where the interests of two clients (or prospective clients) conflict. Where this happens it will be practically impossible for the solicitor to act in the best interests of the two clients simultaneously.

For example, a solicitor is asked to act for Mr Lacey and Mr Roberts, who are suing each other over a boundary dispute (an obvious situation where the interests of the two clients conflict). Both clients will ultimately want to win their case, and so the solicitor will have a duty to act in the best interests of each client and take steps to try to ensure that they are successful in their litigation. However, the solicitor would be placed in an impossible situation, as anything done to help Mr Lacey win his case will be detrimental to Mr Roberts' case (and therefore not in Mr Roberts' best interests).

For this reason, the Solicitors Regulation Authority ('SRA') prohibits solicitors from acting where there is a conflict of interests between two or more clients.

13.2 Rule 3.01: Conflict of interests

> You must not act if there is a conflict of interests (except in the limited circumstances dealt with in 3.02). (Solicitors' Code of Conduct 2007, Rule 3.01)

There are two situations where a conflict of interests may arise:

(a)   a conflict between two or more clients; or

(b)   a conflict between the client's interests and the solicitor's interests.

13.3 Conflict between two or more clients

13.3.1 Introduction

A solicitor is prohibited from acting, pursuant to Rule 3.01, where:

(a)   the solicitor or firm owes separate duties to act in the best interests of two or more clients;

(b)   in relation to the same or related matters; and

(c)   those duties conflict, or there is a significant risk that those duties may conflict.

13.3.2   Former clients – confidential information.

A conflict of interests may arise only between two current clients of the firm. Where a client's retainer has been terminated the firm no longer owes a duty to act in that client's best interests, and so a conflict of interest cannot arise concerning the affairs of a former client.

However, even in the absence of a conflict of interests, a firm may be prevented from acting for a client where it holds confidential information for the former client which would be material to the work done for the new client. See **Chapter 12** for further details.

13.3.3   Same or related matters

It is easy to see how a conflict of interests might arise when advising two clients about the same matter. The first example in this chapter (at **13.1**) concerned two clients involved in the same matter – a court case.

A conflict of interests can also arise concerning different but related matters. A matter will be related if it concerns the same asset or liability (Rule 3.01(3)). For example, you could not act to sell a new house for one client whilst also acting for another client who is alleging that a part of the house has been built on his land. However, there would need to be some reasonable degree of relationship (such as in the above example) for a conflict to arise.

Where the only conflict between the parties is their wider business interests then this will not create any conflict of interest issues. For example, imagine that Isla Cola and Samet Cola are the two main cola distributors in England and Wales. A firm of solicitors could represent Isla Cola on a purchase of a new IT system for their factory, whilst also representing Samet Cola in the purchase of a fleet of cars for their management. Although the interests of Isla Cola and Samet Cola will conflict (as they will both want to sell more cola than the other firm), a solicitors' firm may act for both at the same time without breaching Rule 3.01 as the purchases of the IT system and the cars are not related matters.

13.3.4   Significant risk of a conflict of interests

An actual conflict of interests is not required. A significant risk that your duties to act in the best interests of each client may conflict will be enough to satisfy Rule 3.01.

For example, if Mr and Mrs Rowntree sought to instruct the same solicitor to act for them in their divorce from one another, the solicitor could not act for both of them. This would remain the case even if they explained that their divorce was an amicable one, and they had agreed the division of their assets and what should happen to the children. Even if there was no actual conflict between their interests (an unlikely event), the solicitor could not act, as there would be a significant risk that the duty to act in their best interests might conflict. For instance, Mrs Rowntree might want more of the matrimonial assets once the solicitor has advised her about her legal rights, and Mr Rowntree may not agree to this.

13.3.5 Exceptions

13.3.5.1 Introduction

Where a conflict of interests exists, or where there is a significant risk that a conflict may exist, a firm of solicitors may still act for both parties in defined circumstances and with the consent of both parties.

The following exceptions were introduced by the Law Society following a period of lobbying by parts of the profession to liberalise the previous conflict of interest rules, which prohibited a firm acting where there was a conflict, or where the firm held confidential information for one client which was relevant to another client.

Common interest exception (Rule 3.02(1))

A firm may act for two or more clients where there is a conflict or risk of a conflict, provided the parties have a substantially common interest in relation to a matter (or part of a matter) and all the clients give their informed consent to the firm acting for all the parties.

The SRA's guidance confirms that the solicitor or firm in question must be satisfied that a common purpose exists, and there must be a clear consensus on how it should be achieved. Any areas of conflict must be 'substantially less important' to each client when compared to their common purpose.

The guidance also provides that it must be disproportionate in terms of cost and disruption to require the parties to instruct separate solicitors.

An example of how this exception may be used is where a solicitor is instructed by a group of people who want to set up a company. This example is referred to in the SRA's guidance.

A solicitor or firm should also be careful to consider whether instructions will be taken from each of the parties involved in an equal manner. It would be inappropriate to act where the group of clients includes a 'dominant' client who provides instructions on the matter, to the exclusion of others. The SRA's guidance provides that you must be able to act in an even-handed manner towards and for all of the clients.

The 'commercial' exception (Rule 3.02(2))

A firm of solicitors may act for two or more clients where a conflict exists, or where there is a risk that a conflict exists, where:

(a) the clients are competing for the same asset (and if one client obtains the asset it will be unattainable to the other clients); and

(b) there is no *other* conflict, or significant risk of conflict, between the interests of the clients in relation to that matter; and

(c) the clients provide their informed consent in writing to the firm acting in such a manner, acknowledging that they are aware that the firm is acting (or may act) for the other clients who are competing for the same asset; and

(d) subject to any agreement to the contrary, no one solicitor may act or supervise the work for more than one of the clients.

It is envisaged that this exception will be used for corporate clients only. For example, in 2003 the supermarket chain Safeways was the subject of a bidding war between Morrisons, Tesco, Asda and Sainsburys. It is arguable that this exception would have allowed one firm to act for two or more of the bidders, despite the fact that the obligation to act in the best interests of the two clients would conflict (both would want to buy Safeways, and any step taken by the firm in question to try to make this happen would be detrimental to the interests of the other client).

However, there are limitations to this exception in such a corporate/commercial context. For example, the SRA's guidance states that this exception should not be used for disputes over assets, unless the dispute is concerned with corporate restructuring, or insolvencies.

It is not believed that this exception will become commonly used outside of the corporate/commercial field of law. The SRA advises 'considerable caution' for firms seeking to apply the exemption to categories of work where proposing to work in the above manner is not 'accepted business practice'.

13.3.5.2   Informed consent

One condition common to both exceptions is the concept of informed consent. A client providing consent will not be enough.

The solicitor must:

(a)   draw all the relevant issues to the attention of the clients before the solicitor agrees to act (or, when already acting, as soon as reasonably possible), in such a way that the clients can understand the issues; and

(b)   have a reasonable belief that the clients understand the relevant issues; and

(c)   be reasonably satisfied at the clients are of full mental capacity (Rule 3.02(4)).

As noted in the previous chapter, obtaining informed consent may apply mainly to sophisticated clients such as large companies, perhaps with in-house legal departments, which will have the expertise to appreciate the issues and risks involved, and make a decision based on those risks.

13.3.5.3   Is it reasonable to act?

When considering whether to use one of the above exemptions it also must be reasonable for the firm to act for both parties, considering all the circumstances of the matter (Rule 3.02(3)).

The solicitor should consider whether one client is at risk of prejudice if he is not represented separately (ie by another firm) from the other client(s). This will particularly be the case where one client is vulnerable, or where the parties do not have equal bargaining power.

The SRA's guidance places upon the solicitor or firm a continuing duty to keep under review throughout the duration of the retainer the question whether it remains reasonable to act for both parties.

13.3.5.4   Confidential information

Where a solicitor or firm does decide to act by taking advantage of one of the above exemptions, the firm may well put itself in a position where it holds material confidential information for one client which it has a duty to disclose to another client. Where this is the case, the firm will need to consider whether it should be acting where the confidential information would be placed at risk. See **Chapter 12** for more details.

13.4 Conflict of interests between two existing clients

A solicitor may have agreed to act for two clients where, at the beginning of the transaction, there was no actual conflict or any significant risk of a conflict. However, a conflict may arise during the retainer.

Where such a conflict does arise between two existing clients, a solicitor must have regard not only to the conflict of interest, but also to the issues surrounding confidential information. The solicitor may continue to act for one of the clients only where the solicitor's duty of confidentiality is not put at risk (Rule 3.03).

Pursuant to Rule 4.04(3), the firm can continue to act for one client where the consent of the other client is obtained and Rule 4.04 is complied with (see **12.3.4.1**).

13.5 Conflict between the solicitor's interests and the client's interests

Rule 3.01 would also prevent a solicitor or firm from acting where the solicitor's duty to act in the client's best interests would conflict (or there is a significant risk that it may conflict) with the solicitor's own best interests concerning the same matter or a related matter.

For example, a solicitor could not act for a client suing a company where the solicitor was a major shareholder in that company. The solicitor would be obliged to act in the best interests of the client and take steps to try to ensure that the client was successful in suing the company. In taking those steps the solicitor would be acting to the detriment of the company. If the client was successful, the company would have to pay the client damages and so its share price might drop. This would be detrimental to the company's shareholders – including the solicitor.

The SRA's guidance notes to Rule 3 provide further examples of situations where a solicitor's interest will conflict with that of his client (see guidance notes 41–55 to Rule 3).

A solicitor must act in the best interests of his client. Thus a solicitor must not make a secret profit whilst acting for the client. Rule 2.06 of the Code provides that solicitors must inform their client of any commission exceeding £20 received on the client's matter. The solicitor may keep the commission only if the client consents (see **11.16**).

13.6 Gifts from clients

Pursuant to Rule 3.04, a solicitor must not accept a gift from a client (either in the client's lifetime or on death) for the benefit of the solicitor, any partner, owner or employee of the firm (or any member of their family) where the gift is of a significant amount (unless the client is a member of the beneficiary's – ie, the solicitor's – family).

Whether the gift is of a significant amount relates to the gift itself (for example a gift of £100,000), or to the size of the gift compared to the rest of the client's estate and the reasonable expectations of the prospective beneficiaries of the estate.

Where the solicitor wishes to accept the gift, he must advise the client to seek independent legal advice about whether the gift should be given. If the client declines to do so then the solicitor must refuse to act for the client in relation to the gift.

For example, if a client wished to give £20,000 to one of your firm's secretaries (or her husband) in her will, if the gift was of a significant amount (it certainly would be) then the client should be advised to seek independent legal advice. If the client refused to do so then the solicitor could not act for the client regarding the will.

A solicitor may prepare a will for a family member (and receive a substantial legacy from that will) without the need for that family member to seek independent legal advice. However, the SRA's guidance urges extreme caution in such circumstances.

13.7 Public office: Rule 3.05

There may also be a conflict of interest which precludes a solicitor from acting in particular matters due to a related public appointment or office held by that solicitor, such as being a member of a planning committee or a district judge. The public office may provide the solicitor with confidential information or inside knowledge of, for example, policy, which may affect the solicitor's advice to the client or his approach to the matter.

This 'inside information' may also be available to the solicitor if another individual at the solicitor's practice (whether partner, member or employee) held such an office, or indeed if it was held by a member of the solicitor's family. As such, in these circumstances, the solicitor would still be precluded from acting.

The rationale behind this rule is twofold: not only may a conflict of interests arise, but it is necessary in such matters to ensure that justice is not only done but is seen to be done. It is also important that the behaviour of the solicitor cannot be brought into question and potentially bring the profession into disrepute.

13.8 Professional embarrassment

Even where there is no conflict of interests, nor any significant risk of a conflict, a solicitor may still decline to act for a client due to professional embarrassment. (See also **12.3.5** above.)

A solicitor should consider whether accepting instructions to act for a client would breach one of the Core Duties. One example given by the SRA's guidance notes concerns acting against a former client. There would be no conflict of interest, as a conflict cannot arise between an existing client and a former client. However, the solicitor must consider whether he would feel restricted in doing his best for the existing client on the basis that he was acting against a former client (with whom the solicitor may have built up a good relationship). If so, the solicitor would not be acting in the best interests of the existing client in accepting the instructions.

A solicitor may also take into account his own commercial considerations when deciding whether to accept instructions from a new client. For example, if your firm's major client is Isla Cola and you are asked to act for its major rival on a completely unrelated matter, you might decline to do so if you thought that Isla Cola would instruct another firm as a result.

13.9 Limited retainer

Where a conflict arises between two clients, either at the beginning of or during a transaction, an alternative to relying on one of the exemptions set out above (at **13.3.5**) may be to accept a limited retainer. The solicitor could be retained to act only in relation to those areas where no conflict exists, with each client seeking independent advice on the conflicting areas. It is necessary to make clear the terms of your retainer, and that there are defined areas where you cannot advise.

However, the SRA's guidance provides that a solicitor will rarely be able to act under a limited retainer where there is an unequal bargaining position between the two parties.

13.10 Conveyancing

The area of conveyancing is subject to additional rules regarding acting for more than one party within a transaction. These are considered in more detail in *Property Law & Practice*.

13.11 Chapter summary

(1)   A solicitor must not act where there is a conflict, or significant risk of a conflict, between the interests of two or more clients, or between the interests of the client and the solicitor.

(2)   Where there is a conflict between two clients, a solicitor may act if he can satisfy the requirements of the common interest exception or the commercial exception.

(3)   A solicitor must not accept gifts from clients in certain circumstances without ensuring that the client seeks independent legal advice.

(4)   A solicitor who holds a public office or appointment may be prevented from acting in a matter, particularly if it affects the perception of justice being done.

(5)   Regardless of the rules concerning conflicts of interests, the solicitor must also consider his duty of confidentiality.

(6)   A solicitor may decline to act if he is professionally embarrassed, or for commercial considerations.

(7)   Additional exceptions may apply to allow a solicitor to act in a conveyancing transaction.

Chapter 14

Undertakings

14.1 Introduction

In its Code of Conduct 2007, the Solicitors Regulation Authority ('SRA') defines an undertaking as 'a statement made by you or your firm to someone who reasonably relies upon it, that you or your firm will do something or cause something to be done, or refrain from doing something' (Rule 24, 'Interpretation').

In other words, an undertaking could be said to be an enforceable promise. Any statement made by a solicitor to do or not do something, whether given to a client or to another third party (such as another solicitor), may be an undertaking. Indeed, even if such a promise is made on a solicitor's behalf by a member of his staff, it may constitute an undertaking.

A solicitor must fulfil undertakings given in the course of practice, and also undertakings given outside of practice in the solicitor's personal capacity, if the undertaking was given 'as a solicitor' (Rule 10.05(1)).

It is not necessary to use the word 'undertake' for the undertaking to be binding. Even a promise to give an undertaking will usually be interpreted as an undertaking, and therefore will be binding on the solicitor concerned.

Once the undertaking has been relied upon by the recipient, it can be withdrawn only by agreement.

Given the consequences for breaching an undertaking (see below), the SRA's guidance makes it clear that a solicitor is not obliged to give or accept an undertaking. Indeed, a solicitor should think carefully when considering whether to give an undertaking.

14.2 Why undertakings are necessary

Undertakings are often given by solicitors in order to smooth the path of a transaction. They are a convenient method by which some otherwise problematic areas of practice can be avoided.

Example

Imagine a solicitor is acting for Mr Taylor concerning the sale of his business. Mr Taylor has agreed that he will pay the legal costs of the purchaser if the purchaser buys the business. However, the purchaser of the business wants Mr Taylor to pay this money (an agreed £10,000) up front before the deal takes place, in order to fund the necessary due diligence process (eg, to examine the contracts and leases of the business to establish whether the business is worth the asking price).

The solicitor could give an undertaking to the purchaser's solicitors to pay £10,000 towards the purchaser's costs from the proceeds of sale of the business (assuming that the proceeds of sale would cover the £10,000). If accepted, the purchaser's solicitors might well be happy to complete the due diligence work without any money on account from their client. In the absence of such an undertaking the client would have to fund paying the £10,000 before receiving the proceeds of sale from the business.

14.3   Breach of an undertaking

Where a solicitor gives an undertaking, the terms of that undertaking will be personally binding on the individual solicitor concerned (see Rule 10.05(1)).

For example, a solicitor is acting for a client who is in arrears with his mortgage payments. The client is taken to court by his mortgage company to repossess his house. To prevent the house being repossessed the client offers to pay the arrears (£10,000) within seven days. The mortgage company agrees to withdraw the repossession proceedings, but only on the basis that the solicitor gives an undertaking to pay the mortgage company £10,000 within seven days. If the solicitor agreed to give the undertaking in those terms and the client didn't come up with the money, the solicitor would be personally liable to pay the £10,000.

If a solicitor fails to comply with such an undertaking, the solicitor may be sued personally by the recipient. The solicitor will also breach the rules of professional conduct and will be disciplined by the SRA or the Solicitors Disciplinary Tribunal (see **14.8**).

14.4   Oral and written undertakings

An undertaking will be binding regardless of whether it is given orally or in writing (Rule 24, 'Interpretation'). However, it is advisable to give undertakings in writing, so that there can be no dispute as to the terms of the undertaking. If, however, it is necessary in the circumstances to give an oral undertaking, the solicitor should ensure that an attendance note recording the undertaking is placed on the client's file and that it is confirmed in writing as soon as possible.

14.5   Terms of the undertaking

14.5.1   Introduction

An undertaking is not a contract. For example, there is no obligation for consideration (whether in monetary or other forms) to be present for an undertaking to be enforceable against a solicitor. However, given the binding effect of undertakings, and the consequences for breach, a solicitor should take just as much care in drafting undertakings as he would do when drafting a contract for a client.

14.5.2   Wording of an undertaking

The SRA's guidance provides that any ambiguity in the wording of the undertaking will be interpreted in favour of its recipient. Accordingly, great care should be taken by the solicitor when drafting undertakings.

14.5.3 Acts outside the solicitor's control

From time to time, a solicitor may be called upon to undertake to perform an action which is outside of his control, such as to forward documents which are not in his possession. The simple fact that the solicitor is unable to perform the undertaking without the cooperation of his client or another third party does not discharge the solicitor's obligation to perform, and the undertaking remains enforceable.

In order to avoid this situation, a solicitor may seek to give an undertaking that, in respect of our example above, he will use his 'reasonable endeavours' to obtain and provide the documents requested. This will impose a lesser obligation upon the solicitor, just as such a 'reasonable endeavours' obligation in contract imposes a lesser obligation on the contracting party. However, it may not give the party who might seek to rely on it the same comfort as an absolute undertaking, and he may therefore choose not to accept it, which may cause delay to the transaction.

14.5.4 Undertakings 'on behalf' of a client

Whilst an undertaking is almost always made for the benefit of the solicitor's client (in order to smooth the transaction as explained above), it is made in the solicitor's name. However, an undertaking may be drafted as being made 'on behalf of' the solicitor's client. This will not prevent the undertaking from being enforceable as against the solicitor, who will remain personally liable.

It is possible for a solicitor to give an undertaking 'on behalf' of a client and exclude personal liability, but in order to do so the SRA's guidance provides that the solicitor must clearly and expressly disclaim personal liability, or make it clear that he is simply informing the other side of his client's intentions.

Therefore an undertaking that seeks to exclude personal liability on behalf of the solicitor is legally possible. However, it is unlikely to be accepted by the proposed recipient, as his ability to enforce it (and therefore rely on it) will be greatly reduced.

14.5.5 Timescale

The SRA's guidance provides that it is important that a timescale is expressed for the performance of an undertaking. In the absence of any such timescale, the SRA will imply certain prescribed terms into an undertaking. For example, where no time frame has been expressly included for the performance of an undertaking, it will be expected that the undertaking will be performed within a 'reasonable time' (Rule 10.05(2)).

14.5.6 Costs

Where an undertaking is given in respect of the payment of costs of another party, the term 'costs' will be implied to mean proper costs unless a specific amount is agreed. Therefore, the SRA's guidance provides that a solicitor is able to request an assessment of the costs by the court.

14.6 Client's authority

As has been made very clear in this chapter, an undertaking is a personal obligation on the solicitor who gave it, and therefore the solicitor will be held liable for it, even if performance would put the solicitor in breach of his duty to his client. A solicitor should therefore ensure that he has clear and express authority from his client before giving any undertakings. When such authority has been received, it may be withdrawn by the client at any time until the solicitor has acted upon it, even if it is expressed to be irrevocable.

14.7   Change of circumstances

An undertaking will remain binding upon the solicitor if the circumstances change so that it is impossible to fulfil it, either wholly or partially. However, the recipient may agree to its variation or discharge.

A solicitor is obliged to keep the recipient of the undertaking informed of any delays in complying with it. Rule 10.05(3) provides that where the undertaking is dependent on a future event, and it becomes clear that the future event will not occur, the solicitor must immediately inform the recipient of the undertaking.

14.8   Enforcement

14.8.1   The courts

The court is able to enforce an undertaking against a solicitor as an officer of the court. Accordingly, where an undertaking has been breached, an aggrieved party may seek compensation for any loss (for example, see *Udall v Capri Lighting Ltd* [1987] 3 All ER 262). Firms are obliged to carry indemnity insurance to cover such claims. However, the value of such claims may well fall within the excess of those policies, leading to personal liability for the solicitor concerned.

As outlined below, a breach of an undertaking is likely to be a breach of professional conduct. However, given the court's jurisdiction over solicitors concerning undertakings, the SRA's guidance to Rule 10.05 provides that the SRA will not investigate a breach of an undertaking given to the court itself, unless the court reports the matter to the SRA.

14.8.2   The SRA and the Solicitors Disciplinary Tribunal

If a solicitor fails to comply with the terms of an undertaking he has given, this will be a breach of professional conduct. The Legal Complaints Service ('LCS'), the SRA and the Solicitors Disciplinary Tribunal have no power to enforce the performance of an undertaking. Neither can these organisations direct that a solicitor pay compensation to an aggrieved party. However, they may investigate the solicitor's conduct and impose disciplinary sanctions (up to and including, in the case of the Solicitors Disciplinary Tribunal, striking the solicitor off the Roll of solicitors).

However, the SRA's guidance provides that where an undertaking has been obtained by fraud or deceit, it is unlikely that any action will be taken against the solicitor who has breached the undertaking.

14.9   Liability of others

It is the responsibility of a sole practitioner or partner in a partnership to ensure that an undertaking given by a member of staff in the course of practice is honoured (Rule 10.05(1)(b)). This includes undertakings given by non-admitted staff, and also undertakings give by anyone held out by the firm as representing the firm. For example, if an undertaking given by an assistant solicitor is not honoured, there will be a breach of professional conduct by the solicitor and also the partners of the firm. Accordingly, many firms have strict procedures in respect of recording undertakings given, and who within the firm is authorised to give undertakings.

14.10 Standard forms of undertaking

Any written undertaking given by a solicitor should be tailored carefully to the circumstances. However, standard forms of wording exist for common undertakings, for example in conveyancing transactions (see the Annex to Rule 3).

14.11 Examples

Example 1

A solicitor is instructed by a landlord regarding the renewal of a lease of a domestic property. The solicitor is told that the landlord is very keen to retain the existing tenant, rather than going to the expense of advertising the property and having it stand empty for possibly weeks whilst a new tenant is found.

The solicitor is told that the tenant will attend the solicitor's office tomorrow (the day the lease is due to expire), to 'tie up a few loose ends' and sign a new tenancy agreement.

The following day the tenant duly arrives at the solicitor's office. However, it soon becomes clear that there are problems to be resolved before the tenant will agree to the new tenancy. The tenant explains that the house is in a shabby state, and the only way that the tenant would be willing to agree to a new tenancy is if the landlord agrees to redecorate the entire house and fit new carpets.

The solicitor tries to negotiate with the tenant that the landlord will look at the matter after the new lease is signed. However, the tenant states that unless the issues are dealt with today, he will terminate the existing lease and rent some other property. The solicitor is unable to contact the landlord and so reluctantly gives an undertaking on behalf of the landlord that the property will be redecorated and the carpets replaced within one month. The tenant happily renews the lease.

The solicitor informs his client of the undertaking the next day. The landlord is outraged, and refuses to carry out the work.

The undertaking was given on behalf of a client, but as the solicitor did not expressly disclaim personal liability, the solicitor will be bound to comply with the undertaking. The tenant can enforce the undertaking by suing the solicitor. If the client maintains his stance and refuses to comply, the solicitor will personally have to pay for the redecoration and carpets. In addition to being sued by the tenant, the solicitor could also be reported to the LCS for a breach of professional conduct.

The solicitor should not have given the undertaking without obtaining his client's authority and consent.

Example 2

A solicitor is acting for a client concerning a large debt. The client owes Berkin Finance £100,000 and is being pressed to pay the debt. The client agrees to sell his holiday cottage by auction in order to pay the debt. The cottage is valued at £120,000 and the client is hopeful that he will receive at least this price at the auction.

Berkin Finance writes to the client stating that unless the debt is paid in full within seven days, it will commence court proceedings. As the auction is to be held in 10 days' time, the solicitor (acting on the instructions of the client) undertakes to Berkin Finance to pay £100,000 from the proceeds of sale of the cottage.

The cottage is sold at auction for £90,000. Berkin Finance demands the full £100,000 from the solicitor. Unfortunately for the solicitor, the SRA's guidance provides that where an undertaking is given to make a payment from the proceeds of sale of an asset, the solicitor must pay the full amount (ie, £100,000), regardless of whether the proceeds of sale are sufficient.

The solicitor should have drafted the undertaking to state clearly that his liability would be limited to the money he received from the sale, or to make it clear that he was disclaiming all personal liability.

14.12 Chapter summary

(1) An undertaking is any statement given by a solicitor (in his capacity as a solicitor) to do or refrain from doing something, given to someone who reasonably places reliance upon it.

(2) A solicitor will be personally bound to honour an undertaking, regardless of whether the undertaking was given orally or in writing.

(3) Any ambiguity in the wording of an undertaking will be construed against the party that gave it.

(4) A solicitor should obtain his client's express authority before giving an undertaking.

(5) An undertaking may be enforced by the court.

(6) The SRA/LCS/Solicitors Disciplinary Tribunal do not have the power to enforce an undertaking. However, any breach of an undertaking may be considered a breach of professional conduct, which may lead to sanctions against the solicitor concerned.

(7) Partners are responsible for ensuring that undertakings given by members of their staff are honoured.

Chapter 15
Money Laundering and the Proceeds of Crime Act 2002

15.1 Introduction

'Money laundering' is the process by which criminals seek to alter or 'launder' their proceeds of crime so that it appears that these funds come from a legitimate source.

Suppose a thief has stolen £1 million. The thief then instructs a number of intermediaries each to invest a relatively small proportion of the money. The investments can later be sold, and the thief then appears to be in possession of the proceeds of a legitimate transaction.

In this particular example the 'audit trail' by which investigators follow the proceeds of crime is not too difficult, but it does not take a great deal of imagination to see how a series of deals using different intermediaries and types of investment could throw the investigators off track.

Solicitors are targets for criminals in their efforts to launder their proceeds of crime. The purpose of regulation in this area is to disrupt serious crime (including terrorism) by inhibiting criminals' ability to reinvest or benefit from the proceeds of crime.

The purpose of this chapter is to introduce some of the issues relating to the Government's anti-money laundering legislation. Further guidance can be sought from the Law Society, which produces detailed advice on this subject.

15.2 The Money Laundering Regulations 2007

15.2.1 Introduction

The Money Laundering Regulations 2007 (SI 2007/2157) came into force on 15 December 2007 and implemented the Third European Money Laundering Directive (2005/60/EC). The Regulations place obligations on 'relevant persons'. This is defined in reg 3, and includes 'independent legal professionals'. This is further defined in reg 3 as including (but not limited to):

> a firm or sole practitioner who by way of business provides legal or notarial services to other persons, when participating in financial or real property transactions . . .

Therefore the vast majority of solicitors firms will be subject to the Regulations. Failure to comply with the Money Laundering Regulations is a criminal offence.

In contrast to the previous regulations, the Money Laundering Regulations 2007 have sought to move away from a 'tick box' approach to a risk-based approach.

Therefore obligations are placed on solicitors to know their clients and understand the transactions they have been instructed upon. On this basis, solicitors are expected to assess the risk that each transaction or client poses, and implement anti-money laundering measures as appropriate.

Firms which are subject to the Regulations must comply with, for example, the matters discussed in **15.2.2** to **15.2.5** below. What follows is simply an overview of the often complex requirements imposed upon solicitors. More guidance can be obtained from www.moneylaundering.lawsociety.org.uk.

15.2.2 Nominated officers and reporting procedures

A firm must have internal procedures in place for the identification and reporting of money laundering (reg 20). Most notably, reg 20 (2)(d)(ii) requires firms to appoint a person within the firm to act as a 'nominated officer', referred to in practice as a 'Money Laundering Reporting Officer' (MLRO).

The nominated officer (who will be a senior member of the firm) will receive reports from within the firm concerning any instances of suspected money laundering, and will then decide whether an external report to the Serious Organised Crime Agency (SOCA) should be made.

15.2.3 Client due diligence (client identification)

15.2.3.1 Introduction

Subject to limited exceptions, firms carrying out relevant business are obliged to obtain verification of the identity of each of their clients (reg 7). The need to verify the client's identity includes the following circumstances:

(a)   if the client and solicitor agree to form a business relationship; or

(b)   occasional transactions, ie a single transaction or linked transactions, which amounts to 15,000 euros or more; or

(c)   where the solicitor suspects money laundering or terrorist financing; or

(d)   where the solicitor doubts the accuracy or adequacy of documents or information supplied to verify the client's identity.

The verification must take place before a business relationship is established and before an occasional transaction can be carried out (reg 9). However, a solicitor may verify the identity of the client during the establishment of a business relationship if:

(a)   there is little risk of any money laundering or terrorist financing occurring;

(b)   it is necessary not to interrupt the normal course of business; and

(c)   the identity is verified as soon as possible.

How the solicitor must verify the identity of the client varies according to the type of client involved and the risk of money laundering.

15.2.3.2 Simplified due diligence

Simplified due diligence will apply where the identity of the client means that the risk of money laundering or terrorist financing is low. The clients which qualify for simplified due diligence are specified in reg 13. These include companies listed on a regulated EEA market subject to specified disclosure obligations (such as a public limited company listed in the United Kingdom on the Stock Exchange), or a public authority within the United Kingdom.

The exact verification required depends on the identity of the client. For example, for a plc listed in the UK, the solicitor must obtain confirmation of the company's listing on the Stock Exchange.

15.2.3.3 Standard due diligence

Standard due diligence will apply to most clients. The solicitor is obliged to verify the identity of the client using 'documentation, data or information obtained from a reliable and independent source' (reg 5) (for example a passport). The solicitor must also identify any 'beneficial owner', where that beneficial owner is not the client (reg 5).

A beneficial owner is defined in reg 6, and the definition varies depending on the nature of the client. For example, a beneficial owner of a limited company is defined by reg 6 as including anybody who owns more than 25% of the shares or voting rights in the company.

15.2.3.4 Enhanced due diligence

Enhanced due diligence applies where:

(a)   the solicitor has not met the client face to face;

(b)   there are higher risk factors in relation to money laundering or terrorist financing; or

(c)   the client is a Politically Exposed Person (PEP) (reg 14).

In these situations, a solicitor will have to apply enhanced due diligence measures. For example, where the client is not present on a face-to-face basis, reg 14(2) suggests that the client's identity is established by additional documents, or by ensuring that the first payment from the client to the solicitor is carried out through a bank account opened in the client's name.

A PEP is anyone who has held, within the last year, a 'prominent public function' for a State (other than within the UK), a Community institution or an international body (reg 14(5)). Where a solicitor is dealing with a PEP, additional obligations are placed on the solicitor, such as having approval from senior management to act for the client, and taking additional measures to identify the source of wealth and source of funds involved in the proposed transaction or business relationship (reg 14(4)).

15.2.3.5 Ongoing monitoring

A solicitor is obliged to undertake ongoing monitoring of business relationships, to ensure that the transactions are consistent with the solicitor's knowledge of the client (reg 8).

15.2.4 Training

Firms are obliged to provide training to their employees in respect of money laundering (reg 21). Employees should be made aware of the law relating to money laundering and terrorism financing (for example, the Proceeds of Crime Act 2002, the Terrorism Act 2000, and the Money Laundering Regulations 2007). The Regulations also specify that employees should be given regular training on how to recognise (and then deal with) transactions that potentially involve money laundering.

The Regulations do not specify how the training should take place. However, guidance provided by The Law Society suggests that appropriate methods of delivery may include face-to-face learning or e-learning. The Law Society's guidance also recommends the use of a staff manual on money laundering issues.

Where no such training is given, this may provide the employee with a defence to some of the offences under the Proceeds of Crime Act 2002 (see **15.3.3.7**).

15.2.5   Record keeping

A firm must keep various records in respect of money laundering. These include evidence supporting client due diligence (reg 19). This can be either a copy of the evidence provided to verify the client's identity (eg a copy of the client's passport, etc) or references to it. These records must be kept for at least five years from when the business relationship ends or the end of the occasional transaction.

The firm must also keep records of a business relationship or occasional transactions for a similar period. The Law Society also recommends that a detailed record is kept of suspicions and disclosures in respect of money laundering.

15.3   The Proceeds of Crime Act 2002

15.3.1   Introduction

The Proceeds of Crime Act 2002 makes it an offence to become involved in money laundering. For example, under s 327, it is an offence to conceal, disguise, convert, transfer or remove criminal property from England and Wales, Scotland or Northern Ireland.

This chapter will focus on the three offences which most concern solicitors in their day-to-day practice.

15.3.2   Arrangements

15.3.2.1   Introduction

> A person commits an offence if he enters into or becomes concerned in an arrangement which he knows or suspects facilitates (by whatever means) the acquisition, retention, use or control of criminal property by or on behalf of another person. (Proceeds of Crime Act 2002, s 328(1))

15.3.2.2   Definitions

Section 328 is drafted very widely. For example, if a solicitor transferred a house to a relative of a client, where the solicitor knew or suspected that the house was purchased with the proceeds of crime, then the solicitor would '[become] concerned in an arrangement' and so would breach s 328(1).

There is no requirement that the funds pass through the hands of the person concerned with the arrangement, ie the solicitor.

'Criminal property' is defined by s 340 of the Act as a person's direct or indirect benefit from criminal conduct (if the offender knows or suspects that the property constitutes or represents such a benefit).

'Criminal conduct' is defined very widely, and includes any offence committed within the United Kingdom. This would include offences ranging from armed robbery to fraudulent receipt of welfare benefits. The definition also includes an international element. For example, if the offence occurred outside of the United Kingdom, it would still constitute criminal conduct if it would be classed as an offence if it had occurred within the United Kingdom. For example, a criminal robs a bank in France. This would still constitute 'criminal conduct' under the Act as robbery is an offence within the United Kingdom. It is irrelevant whether robbery is an offence in France. (However, there are exceptions to this international element – see **15.3.2.6**.)

15.3.2.3   Authorised disclosure

Disclosure prior to the act taking place

A solicitor does not commit an offence under s 328 if he makes an authorised disclosure to the firm's nominated officer as soon as is practically possible prior to the transaction taking place, and the authorisation of the nominated officer or SOCA is obtained to complete the transaction.

However, once the nominated officer has made a report to SOCA, the nominated officer is unable to give consent for the transaction to proceed until one of the following conditions is met:

(a)   the nominated officer, having made a disclosure to SOCA, receives the consent of SOCA;

(b)   the nominated officer, having made a disclosure to SOCA, hears nothing for seven working days (starting with the first working day after the disclosure is made);

(c)   where consent is refused by SOCA, the nominated officer may not give consent for the transaction to proceed unless consent is subsequently granted within 31 days starting on the day refusal is given, or a period of 31 days has expired from the date of refusal. This 31-day period gives the authorities time to take action to seize assets or take other action with respect to the money laundering.

Disclosure during the prohibited act

A solicitor may seek to make an authorised disclosure whilst the prohibited act is ongoing. However, if the solicitor is to avoid breaching s 328 by making the disclosure, he must satisfy the provisions of s 338(2A):

(a)   the disclosure is made whilst the prohibited act is ongoing; and

(b)   when the alleged offender began to do the act, he did not know or suspect that the property constituted or represented a person's benefit from criminal conduct; and

(c)   the disclosure is made as soon as is practicable after the alleged offender first knows or suspects that the property constitutes or represents a person's benefit from criminal conduct, and the disclosure is made on the alleged offender's own initiative.

Take the example of a solicitor conducting a conveyancing transaction on behalf of a client. Until the client exchanges contracts to sell the property, the solicitor has no knowledge or suspicion that the house was bought with the proceeds of crime. Accordingly, there is no breach of s 328, as the solicitor does not possess the requisite knowledge or suspicion. After contracts have been exchanged, the solicitor correctly begins to suspect that the house was bought with the proceeds of crime. Accordingly, he is now concerned in an arrangement which facilitates the acquisition, retention, use or control of criminal property and therefore is in breach of s 328.

In order to seek the protection of making an authorised disclosure, the solicitor must disclose his suspicions to his nominated officer on his own initiative, and must do so as soon as is practicable after his first suspicions arise.

Disclosure after the prohibited act

A solicitor may also seek to make an authorised disclosure after the prohibited act is been completed. However, the solicitor must have a good reason for his failure to disclose prior to his completing the act (s 338(3)). The disclosure must be made as soon as is practicable, and again the solicitor must make the disclosure on his own initiative.

In 2004, the NCIS (SOCA's predecessor) estimated that it would receive approximately 150,000 disclosures during 2004. Consent was forthcoming within 24 hours in approximately 75% of the cases disclosed by lawyers to the NCIS.

15.3.2.4   Reasonable excuse for non-disclosure

A solicitor may have a defence to breaching s 328 where he intended to make an authorised disclosure but has a reasonable excuse for failing to do so. The Law Society's guidance states that a 'reasonable excuse' has not been defined by the courts. However, the guidance advises solicitors to document their reasons for non-disclosure.

15.3.2.5   Litigation proceedings

In *Bowman v Fels* [2005] EWCA Civ 226, the Court of Appeal considered whether taking steps in litigation could be construed as 'arranging' under s 328. The Court concluded that taking steps in litigation (including pre-action steps) and the resolution of issues in a litigious context were excluded from the scope of s 328. Therefore a solicitor would not be obliged to make an authorised disclosure.

> **Example**
>
> A solicitor is acting for Mr Smith in divorce proceedings. Ancillary relief proceedings are issued by Mrs Smith, as she wishes to have the matrimonial home transferred into her sole name. The solicitor becomes aware that the house was purchased by Mr Smith with the proceeds of crime. The solicitor will not breach s 328 by merely conducting the litigation on behalf of Mr Smith.

It was originally thought that transferring the house from Mr Smith to Mrs Smith after the court proceedings would have fallen into the definition of an arrangement. However, the current Law Society guidance provides that dividing assets in accordance with a court judgment would not fall within this definition, therefore no consent would be required. However, the guidance goes on to state that careful consideration should be made of whether the client would be committing an offence by receiving stolen property.

The solicitor would not be able to take advantage of this exclusion if the litigation was a sham created for the purposes of money laundering.

15.3.2.6   'Overseas' defence

Despite the wide definition of 'criminal conduct' (see **15.3.2.2** above), a solicitor will not commit an offence under s 328 where the criminal conduct occurred outside of the United Kingdom and was not unlawful in the country where it happened. However, this defence is not available (subject to certain exceptions) where the offence would carry a sentence of imprisonment for 12 months or more were it to be carried out within the United Kingdom (see the Proceeds of Crime Act 2002 (Money Laundering: Exceptions to Overseas Conduct Defence) Order 2006 (SI 2006/1070)).

15.3.2.7 Penalties

An individual convicted under s 328 may receive a maximum sentence of 14 years' imprisonment.

15.3.3 Failure to disclose

15.3.3.1 Introduction

A person commits an offence under s 330 of the Proceeds of Crime Act 2002 if:

(a)   he knows or suspects, or has reasonable grounds to know or suspect, that a person is engaged in money laundering; and

(b)   the information comes to him in the course of a business in the regulated sector; and

(c)   the information may assist in identifying the money launderer or the location of any laundered property; and

(d)   he does not make an authorised disclosure as soon as is practicable.

15.3.3.2 Objective test

A solicitor will commit this offence even where he genuinely did not know or suspect that a person was engaged in money laundering. The court will consider, based on the information available to the solicitor at the time, whether he *should* have known (or at least suspected) that money laundering was occurring. Accordingly, turning a blind eye to a transaction will not provide the solicitor with a defence.

15.3.3.3 Regulated sector

Firms will be within the 'regulated sector' if they undertake relevant business (see the Proceeds of Crime Act 2002 , Sch 9). Most solicitors firms will fall within the regulated sector.

15.3.3.4 The information

The information obtained by the solicitor must be of some use to the authorities. Accordingly, the solicitor must be able to identify, or believe the information may assist in identifying:

(a)   the money launderer; or

(b)   the location of the laundered property.

If the solicitor is genuinely unable to provide this information, the solicitor will not breach s 330.

The solicitor cannot blindly assume that the information will be of no use to the authorities. When considering whether the solicitor has breached s 330, the court will consider whether it would have been reasonable to expect the solicitor to believe that the information would assist in identifying the offender, or locating the laundered property.

15.3.3.5 Authorised disclosure

A solicitor will be provided with a defence to s 330 if he makes an authorised disclosure to the firm's nominated officer as soon as practically possible. The disclosure on its own will be enough to grant an effective defence under s 330. However, the nominated officer will still consider whether the information should be forwarded to SOCA.

15.3.3.6   Reasonable excuse for non-disclosure

Once again, a solicitor will not commit this offence where he intended to make a disclosure and has a reasonable excuse for not doing so (see **15.3.2.4**).

15.3.3.7   Training

A further defence under s 330 concerns the training provided to an individual. Firms undertaking 'relevant business' are obliged to provide anti-money laundering training to their employees. If an employee does not know or suspect that a client is engaged in money laundering due to a lack of training then the employee may not commit the offence (see **15.2.2**).

15.3.3.8   Confidentiality and privilege

The position concerning a solicitor's duty of confidentiality under Rule 4 of the Solicitors' Code of Conduct 2007 is considered below at **15.4**.

A solicitor is also under a duty at common law to keep confidential certain information given to him from a client. This is referred to as legal professional privilege ('LPP'). Communications will be protected from disclosure if they fall within 'advice privilege' or 'litigation privilege' (see **12.4**). However LPP cannot be relied upon where the communication takes place with the purpose of carrying out an offence.

The Proceeds of Crime Act 2002 mirrors the common law position, in that a solicitor is not obliged under s 330 to disclose any information that comes to him as a professional legal adviser in privileged circumstances, eg in connection with giving or seeking legal advice, or in relation to legal proceedings, whether contemplated or actual. However, this exemption does not apply where the information is communicated with the intention of furthering a criminal purpose (eg, money laundering).

15.3.3.9   'Overseas' defence

A solicitor will not breach s 330 for failing to disclose where he believes that the money laundering is taking place outside of the United Kingdom, and money laundering is not unlawful in that country. The Secretary of State has the power to limit this defence, but at the time of writing has not taken any steps to do so.

15.3.3.10   Penalties

A person convicted of an offence under s 330 may receive a maximum sentence of five years' imprisonment.

15.3.4   Tipping off

15.3.4.1   The offences

There are two aspects of tipping off that must be avoided under s 333A.

Disclosing a suspicious activity report (s 333A(1))

It is an offence to disclose to any person that a suspicious activity report (on money laundering) has been made if that disclosure is likely to prejudice any investigation that follows such a report. For example, this offence would apply where a solicitor informs his client that an authorised disclosure has been made, with the intention of the client taking steps to frustrate any action taken by the law enforcement authorities. This would apply where a disclosure of suspicion is made to a MLRO, the SOCA, the Police, or to Revenue and Customs.

Example

Mr Wilkinson instructs his solicitor to sell his house. The solicitor suspects that the house was purchased with the proceeds of tax evasion and so makes an authorised disclosure under s 328. The transaction cannot be completed until the solicitor obtains the consent of his MLRO or SOCA (see **15.3.2.3**). Mr Wilkinson demands to know why his house sale has not been completed. The solicitor's trainee receives Mr Wilkinson's call and, having checked the file, informs Mr Wilkinson that an authorised disclosure has been made to SOCA. In these circumstances the trainee may breach s 333A unless he can rely on one of the defences (see **15.3.4.2**).

Disclosing an investigation (s 333A(3))

This is a more general offence, and applies regardless of whether or not a suspicious activity report has been made. The offence is committed where a disclosure is made to any person that an investigation into money laundering is being carried out, or is being contemplated, and that disclosure is likely to prejudice the money laundering investigation.

The idea behind both offences is to ensure that information is not leaked to the money launderer or another third party before the authorities have had the opportunity to investigate the matter and consider whether any enforcement action is necessary.

15.3.4.2   Defences

There are a number of defences to tipping off. These include that the person who made the disclosure did not know or suspect that the disclosure would prejudice an investigation into money laundering (s 333D (3) and (4)). Another defence is that the disclosure is made to the client for the purposes of dissuading the client from engaging in the alleged money laundering (s 333D(2)), although this exception should be treated with caution.

15.3.4.3   Penalties

Both the offences set out in **15.3.4.1** above carry a maximum penalty of an unlimited fine, and/or a maximum prison sentence of two years.

15.3.4.4   'Regulated sector'

These sections (ss 333A to 333D) only apply to the regulated sector. However, similar provisions apply to work completed outside of the regulated sector by virtue of s 342.

15.4   Confidentiality

A solicitor is under a duty under Rule 4 of the Solicitors' Code of Conduct 2007 to keep confidential the affairs of clients and former clients. However, when making a disclosure under s 328 or s 330, the legislation expressly provides that such a disclosure will not breach this duty.

The Code recognises that the reporting requirements in respect of money laundering override the duty of confidentiality. Nevertheless, the guidance notes to Rule 4 advise that a solicitor should be mindful of the importance of the duty of confidentiality, and seek advice when uncertain as to whether to report confidential information.

15.5 Chapter summary

(1)   Money laundering is the process whereby the proceeds of crime are changed so that they appear to come from a legitimate source.

(2)   The Government has introduced legislation to disrupt this process.

(3)   Solicitors who undertake relevant business must comply with the Money Laundering Regulations 2007.

(4)   Under the Money Laundering Regulations 2007, firms must appoint a nominated officer, who will receive internal reports concerning money laundering and must consider whether to report the matter to SOCA.

(5)   A person commits an offence under s 328 of the Proceeds of Crime Act 2002 where he becomes concerned in an arrangement involving money laundering.

(6)   Section 328 does not apply to steps taken in litigation.

(7)   A solicitor within the regulated sector is obliged to disclose any suspect money laundering activity to his nominated officer.

(8)   It is an offence to disclose to any person that a disclosure has been made where this may prejudice an investigation.

Chapter 16

Duties Owed to the Court and Third Parties

16.1 Introduction

16.1.1 Duty to the court

A solicitor is under a duty never to deceive or knowingly/recklessly mislead the court (Rule 11.01). Rule 24 defines 'court' as any court, tribunal or enquiry of England and Wales, and also any court within another jurisdiction. The Solicitors Regulation Authority's ('SRA's') guidance provides that Rule 11.01 also prohibits attempting to deceive or mislead the court.

This guidance also provides examples of such behaviour. These include (but are not limited to) the following:

(a) calling a witness whose evidence the solicitor knows to be untrue;

(b) seeking to persuade a witness to change his evidence;

(c) submitting inaccurate information, or allowing another person to do so.

Furthermore, Rule 11.01(3) provides that a solicitor must not 'construct facts supporting your client's case ... containing any contention which you do not consider to be properly arguable'.

Where a solicitor becomes aware that he has inadvertently misled the court, the solicitor (with his client's consent) must inform the court. If the client withholds his consent, the solicitor must stop acting.

Similarly, where a solicitor becomes aware that his client has committed perjury within court proceedings, the solicitor may continue to act in those proceedings only if the client discloses the truth to the court. However, the SRA's guidance states that a solicitor is not obliged to stop acting where the client gives inconsistent evidence – there must be an intention on behalf of the client to submit false evidence.

Rule 11.02 requires that a solicitor must comply with any properly made order of the court requiring him or his firm to take, or refrain from taking, a particular course of action. Furthermore, a solicitor must not become in contempt of court (Rule 11.03). A solicitor must also honour any undertaking given to the court.

Lastly, solicitors appearing before the court should exercise considerable caution when communicating with judges outside of the courtroom. It is advised by the SRA that advocates should communicate with judges in this fashion only when invited to do so and in the presence of the legal representative of the other client.

16.1.2 Witnesses

A solicitor must not make an allegation which is intended only to insult a witness or any other person (Rule 11.05). Neither must a solicitor instruct counsel to do the same.

An advocate should not name a third party in open court where that person's character would be called into question, unless it is necessary for the proper conduct of the case. The character of a witness may not be called into question unless that witness has been given the opportunity to answer the allegations during cross-examination (Rule 11.05).

Should a solicitor wish, or require, in the best interests of his client, to take statements from a witness or potential witness, he may do so at any point in the proceedings. This remains the case whether or not that individual has already been interviewed by another party, or has been called as a witness by another party. However, the SRA's guidance suggests that the witness is interviewed in the presence of their legal representative.

A solicitor may not make (or offer to make) payments to a witness dependent upon the nature of the evidence given, or upon the outcome of the case (Rule 11.07).

16.1.3 Duty to disclose law and facts

16.1.3.1 Prosecutor

A prosecutor has a duty to inform the court of any relevant cases or statutory provisions, even if it would not be in the best interests of his client (ie the Crown) to do so (Rule 11.01(2)).

If a prosecutor obtains evidence which may assist the defence, the prosecutor must supply particulars of this evidence or witnesses to the defence. A prosecutor must also inform the court of any relevant document that has been filed in the proceedings.

16.1.3.2 Defence and civil cases

A solicitor who appears before the court for the defence in a criminal case, or for either party in a civil case, has no duty to inform the court of any evidence or witnesses which would prejudice the solicitor's own client.

However, the solicitor remains under a duty to disclose all relevant cases and statutory provisions, and also to inform the court of any relevant document that has been filed in the proceedings, particularly where failure to draw the court's attention to the contents of the document might result in the court being misled (Rule 11.01(2)).

16.2 Refusing instructions to act

Pursuant to Rule 11.04, a solicitor must not refuse to act as an advocate on the grounds that the:

(a)   nature of the case; or

(b)   conduct, opinions or beliefs of the prospective client,

are objectionable or unacceptable to the solicitor, or to any section of the public.

A solicitor is also prohibited from declining instructions on the basis that the source of any proper financial support which may be given to the prospective client is objectionable to the solicitor.

In addition to complying with Rule 11.04, a solicitor must also apply Rule 6 (avoiding discrimination) when considering whether to refuse to act as an advocate.

16.3 Instructing counsel

A solicitor is obliged to act in the best interests of his client. Accordingly, where the client requires advocacy services, the solicitor must consider, based on the complexity of the case and the solicitor's own experience, whether it would be in the best interests of that client to instruct another solicitor within the firm or counsel to act as the advocate in the proceedings.

16.3.1 Duty to counsel

If it is in the client's best interests to instruct counsel, it remains the solicitor's duty to ensure that adequate instructions are provided to the chosen barrister. As an extension of the solicitor's duty to his client, he should ensure that these instructions, including any relevant supporting statements, information or documents, are provided in good time to allow adequate preparation of the case.

In order to provide such information, it may be necessary, if practicable, to arrange a conference with counsel, either with or without the client, to enable the barrister to discuss directly the nature of the case, obtain instructions or further information, and provide advice in a direct manner. It is a matter for the solicitor to ascertain whether such a conference would be appropriate and in the client's best interests, and if so, to arrange it.

16.3.2 Attending court with counsel

The SRA's guidance provides that a solicitor is under a duty to consider whether, when instructing counsel (or another solicitor) to appear as an advocate, it is in the best interests of the client and the interests of justice for the solicitor or a representative from the firm to attend court. The solicitor must consider the nature and complexity of the matter, and the client's capacity to understand the proceedings.

The guidance further provides a list of circumstances in which a representative should normally attend. These circumstances include (but are not limited to):

(a) where the client is charged with murder, manslaughter or rape;

(b) in cases of complex or serious fraud;

(c) where the client may have difficultly in giving or receiving instructions;

(d) where the client is likely to disrupt proceedings;

(e) where there are a large number of witnesses in the case;

(f) on the day of sentence where the client is likely to receive a custodial sentence.

If a solicitor decides not to send a representative, he should inform the advocate in sufficient time for him to consider whether it would be appropriate for the advocate to attend alone. The client must also be informed of the situation.

16.3.3 Duty to the client when instructing an advocate

Notwithstanding the appointment of counsel and the duties the chosen barrister may owe to a solicitor's client, all the solicitor's duties to his client remain in full force and effect. Instructing counsel does not relieve the solicitor of those duties, particularly the overriding duty to act in the best interests of the client.

The solicitor must therefore exercise care in choosing the appropriate barrister for the case, taking into consideration the experience and seniority of counsel available. The solicitor should also ensure he is are happy with the quality of the advice given, to ensure that there are no obvious errors or inconsistencies. If such errors are apparent, clarification should be requested or a second opinion obtained (see, for example, *Regent Leisuretime v Skerrett* [2005] EWHC 2255).

16.3.4 Counsel's fees

A solicitor is responsible for appointing counsel and (subject to limited exceptions) is therefore responsible personally for the payment of counsel's fees. This applies regardless of whether the solicitor's client has provided the requisite monies. Many solicitors therefore request that their clients provide money on account to cover prospective barristers' fees.

16.3.5 Discrimination – choice of advocate

As noted at **16.3.3** above, a solicitor is under a duty to select an advocate of sufficient seniority and experience to represent his client adequately in court. A solicitor may consult with his client when choosing a barrister. However, a solicitor must not instruct a barrister on the grounds of race, sex, ethnic or nation origin, or any of the other grounds listed in Rule 6.01. If the client's request appears to be based on discriminatory grounds (eg, a male client defending himself in an Employment Tribunal against an allegation of sex discrimination may request to be represented by a female advocate), the SRA's guidance provides that the solicitor must discuss the issue with his client and ask the client to change his instructions. Where the client refuses, the solicitor must cease to act.

16.4 Immunity for advocacy work

In previous years, immunity was granted to advocates against claims of negligence or breach of contract in respect of advocacy work undertaken. However, this was abolished by the House of Lords in *Arthur JS Hall & Co (A Firm) v Simons* [2000] 3 All ER 673.

16.5 Duty to third parties

16.5.1 Not taking an unfair advantage

Rule 10.01 provides that a solicitor must not use his position as a solicitor to take an unfair advantage of anyone. This rule applies to the solicitor acting outside of his practice as well as within his practice, and relates to the protection of the integrity of the profession.

The SRA's guidance notes for Rule 10.01 advise that particular care should be taken when dealing with unrepresented third parties. Usually a solicitor must act in the best interests of his client, but this duty is tempered by a solicitor being required not to take unfair advantage of another person. For example, where it is evident that an unrepresented opponent lacks legal knowledge and skills, the SRA's guidance suggests that the solicitor should advise the individual to seek independent legal advice.

In the event that a solicitor provides some form of help to an unrepresented third party, care should be taken that a retainer does not arise between the solicitor and the third party.

16.5.2   Giving references

Under the general law of negligence, a solicitor will owe a duty of care to the subject of any reference given by that solicitor (see *Spring v Guardian Assurance plc* [1994] 3 All ER 129, HL). Accordingly, great care must be taken when giving any such reference to avoid incurring liability. Many firms have in place policies with regard to the giving of references, covering who may give them and the nature of the content.

Furthermore, giving a false reference would almost certainly breach the Solicitors' Code of Conduct, eg for damaging the public trust in the profession (Rule 1.06).

16.5.3   Offensive letters

A solicitor is under a duty to act with integrity (Rule 1.02). Accordingly, a solicitor must not write to any third party in a manner that could be considered to be offensive.

16.5.4   Third parties and costs

Rule 10.02 provides that when another party is paying the client's costs, a solicitor should provide the third party with sufficient time and information for the costs to be agreed or assessed.

In respect of claiming costs, a solicitor must not claim anything that would not be recoverable by law. For example, a solicitor may be instructed by a client to obtain payment of an outstanding debt from a third party. Where the third party pays the debt in full without the need to issue proceedings, the solicitor must not seek to obtain his costs of acting from the third party.

16.5.5   Beneficiaries

Where a solicitor is instructed to administer a probate estate, the solicitor's client will be the personal representatives of the deceased's estate. However, in certain circumstances a solicitor will also owe a duty of care to the beneficiaries of that estate.

For example, in *Ross v Caunters* [1980] 1 Ch 297 a solicitor failed to warn a testator that the will should not be witnessed by a beneficiary. Accordingly, the beneficiary who witnessed the will was unable to claim her share of the estate. The solicitor was held liable in negligence to the beneficiary. See also *White v Jones* [1995] 1 All ER 891, where a solicitor was instructed to draw up a will. The client died approximately a month later, before the will had been drafted. The solicitor was successfully sued in negligence by the beneficiaries who missed out on their share of the estate as a result of the solicitor's failure to draft the will.

16.5.6   Contacting a represented third party

Where a client instructs a solicitor, it is often because the client lacks legal knowledge and skills, and therefore seeks the assistance of a legal expert. Accordingly, a solicitor must not seek to bypass a party's legal representative by writing directly to the other party where the solicitor knows that party has instructed a legal representative.

Rule 10.04 provides that a solicitor should not communicate directly with a represented third party except:

(a)   to request the name and address of the other party's legal representative;

(b)   with that representative's consent; or

(c)   in exceptional circumstances.

Rule 10.04 also provides that a solicitor may contact a party where the party's legal representative has refused, or failed for no adequate reason, either to pass on messages to his client or to reply to correspondence. However, a warning letter should be sent to the legal representative before contacting the represented third party, giving the legal representative a chance to object.

16.5.7   Dealing with unrepresented parties

The SRA's guidance provides that where a solicitor is dealing with an unrepresented third party, care should be taken that an implied retainer does not arise from the solicitor's dealings with that third party (see **16.5.1**).

Particular care should be taken when a solicitor discovers he is dealing with an unqualified person (see **18.1.1**) who is carrying out work reserved for solicitors, such as preparing papers for a grant of probate. The solicitor is advised to inform the SRA, and seek immediate advice from the Professional Ethics Guideance Team.

16.5.8   Agents' costs

As with counsel's fees, a solicitor is personally responsible for meeting the fees of agents or others he appoints on behalf of his client. This extends only to costs properly incurred. Again, this applies whether or not the solicitor has been put in funds, and therefore the solicitor may ask for monies on account prior to incurring such expenditure. Alternatively, the solicitor and agent may agree that the agent's fee will become payable on receipt by the solicitor of the client's payment.

16.6   Relations with other solicitors

A solicitor must preserve the integrity of the profession (Rule 1.02). Therefore a solicitor must treat other solicitors with due respect in all their communications, whether written or oral.

16.6.1   Agency

As noted at **16.5.8** above, solicitors are personally liable to pay the fees of any agent they instruct on behalf of their clients. This applies even when that agent is another solicitor. Solicitors frequently appoint other solicitors to attend court on their behalf, for example where it is not cost-efficient for the solicitor to travel some distance to attend court. The instructing solicitor therefore remains liable for meeting such costs regardless of whether his client has put him in funds, unless he agrees otherwise with the solicitor-agent.

16.6.2 Other solicitors' clients

A solicitor must not communicate with any party who the solicitor knows has instructed a lawyer (or licensed conveyancer) to represent him, subject to limited exceptions (see **16.5.6**).

16.7 Chapter summary

16.7.1 The solicitor and the court

(1) A solicitor must not mislead or deceive the court. A solicitor must also comply with any order of the court which is lawfully made.

(2) A solicitor must not make an allegation which is purely intended to insult a witness.

(3) In certain circumstances, a solicitor may be under a duty to disclose information to the court (or the other side) which will help the other side's case.

(4) A solicitor cannot refuse to act as an advocate on the grounds that he finds the nature of the case or the opinions/beliefs of the client objectionable.

(5) A solicitor still owes his client a duty to act in the client's best interests even when the solicitor has instructed counsel to act for that client.

16.7.2 Duty to third parties

(1) A solicitor must not take an unfair advantage of any person, either for the solicitor's own benefit or for another person's benefit.

(2) A solicitor cannot demand anything from a third party which is not legally recoverable.

(3) In certain circumstances a solicitor owes a duty of care to third parties, such as beneficiaries.

(4) A solicitor must consider the integrity of the profession when dealing with other solicitors.

Chapter 17

Financial Services

17.1 Introduction

From time to time, solicitors engage in financial services work. To do this, they must be sufficiently competent in that area of practice, and in some cases will need to comply with certain regulations imposed by the Financial Services Authority ('FSA') and/or The Law Society and Solicitors Regulation Authority ('SRA').

Such work could arise:

(a) in conveyancing, if a client needs help in finding a mortgage and a supporting package, which could include a life insurance policy;

(b) in probate, when the executors sell off the deceased's assets;

(c) in litigation, if helping a successful client to invest damages just won;

(d) in company work, in making arrangements for a client to buy or sell shares in a company, and also in arranging corporate finance;

(e) in family work, if arrangements have to be made on a divorce in respect of endowment life policies and/or a family business;

(f) in tax planning or portfolio management, for a private client including trustees.

Under Rule 1 of the Solicitors' Code of Conduct 2007, a solicitor would be in breach of his duty to act in the client's best interests if he did not have sufficient expertise in the area concerned. Therefore, a trainee solicitor should not give investment advice to a client unless the trainee is an expert in that field.

However, many activities in connection with investments are subject to regulation under the Financial Services and Markets Act 2000 (FSMA 2000) and, for example, to give advice on these, or even to make arrangements for clients to acquire or dispose of them, may require the solicitor to be authorised to carry out that activity by the FSA. To do this without authority could involve the commission of a criminal offence. Thus you will, when handling a matter in which investments are involved, even if only peripherally, need to be doubly careful before advising and assisting such clients. You will need to ask yourself two questions:

(a) Have I got the necessary skill and knowledge?

(b) What am I 'permitted' to do under the financial services regulations?

17.2 Source material

The FSMA 2000 gained Royal Assent on 14 June 2000. It contains 433 sections and 22 Schedules. The regulatory regime for financial services came into force at midnight on 30 November 2001. However, the Act provides only a general framework, and the detail is in secondary legislation (eg, Orders in Council made by the Treasury). In order to understand the whole of the regulation, it is necessary to study the FSMA 2000 and the various Orders made by the Treasury, for example:

(a)   Financial Services and Markets Act 2000 (Regulated Activities) Order 2001, SI 2001/544 (RAO 2001);

(b)   Financial Services and Markets Act 2000 (Professions) (Non-Exempt Activities) Order 2001, SI 2001/1227;

(c)   Financial Services and Markets Act 2000 (Financial Promotion) Order 2005, SI 2005/1529 (FPO 2005).

The regulation of financial services is a complex and detailed area. This chapter will serve only as an introduction to the regulatory framework. Further guidance can be sought from the FSA and The Law Society.

The FSA provides guidance on the legislation on its website at www.fsa.gov.uk. A particularly useful publication is *FSA Guidance – August 2001. Professional firms – the need for authorisation under the Financial Services and Markets Act 2000*. Law Society materials on financial services work include:

(a)   the Solicitors' Financial Services (Scope) Rules 2001 (Scope Rules 2001);

(b)   the Solicitors' Financial Services (Conduct of Business) Rules 2001 (COB Rules 2001);

(c)   an information pack containing guidance on 'the basic conditions' and 'avoiding FSA authorisation'.

These can be found on The Law Society's website at www.lawsociety.org.uk.

17.3 The Financial Services Authority

The FSMA 2000 in effect established the FSA. The Authority's areas of responsibility are vast and include the regulation of financial services. Under the FSMA 2000, s 2, the FSA is set the following 'Regulatory Objectives':

(a)   maintaining confidence in the financial system (market confidence);

(b)   promoting public understanding of the financial system (public awareness);

(c)   securing the appropriate degree of protection for consumers (protection of consumers);

(d)   reducing the extent to which it is possible for a business engaged in financial services to be used for financial crime (reduction of financial crime).

The FSA has thus become the single statutory regulator for an enormous number of businesses of varying sizes, including:

(a)   investment firms: stockbrokers, investment and pensions advisers, professional advisers (such as solicitors);

(b)   banks;

(c)   building societies;

(d)   insurance companies.

As far as investment firms are concerned (eg, advisers such as solicitors), one of the principal aims is to ensure that ordinary consumers receive sound advice before making an investment.

17.4 The general framework

Businesses carrying on certain activities, known as 'regulated activities', will need to be authorised by the FSA. The FSMA 2000 contains a special provision for professional firms which do not carry out 'mainstream' investment business but may carry out a regulated activity in the course of carrying out their professional work, such as corporate work. If certain conditions are satisfied, such a firm will be exempt from having to obtain authority from the FSA, provided it is regulated and supervised by a professional body designated by the Treasury (a DPB). The Law Society has been so designated (this role will now be undertaken by the SRA).

17.5 The need for authority

There are two main restrictions of most relevance to solicitors:

(a) carrying out a regulated activity;

(b) making a financial promotion.

Section 19 of the FSMA 2000 provides that: 'No person may carry on a regulated activity in the UK unless authorised or exempt' (the 'General Prohibition'). Authorised persons are persons with permission granted by the FSA under the FSMA 2000. A further offence is that of making an unauthorised financial promotion under s 21. Breach of either of these provisions could result in the commission of a criminal offence and/or any agreement made as a result being unenforceable.

17.6 Regulated activity

17.6.1 The four tests

In order to determine if an activity is regulated there are four tests:

(a) Are you in business?

(b) Is there a specified investment?

(c) Is there a specified investment activity?

(d) Is there an exclusion?

The particular activities and investments are specified by the Treasury in RAO 2001 under the FSMA 2000, s 22. More recently, new investments such as mortgages and general insurance contracts have been specified in the Financial Services and Markets Act 2000 (Regulated Activities) (Amendment) Orders 2003 (SI 2003/1475 and SI 2003/1476 respectively).

17.6.2 Specified investments

These include:

(a) company stocks and shares (but not building society shares);

(b) debentures, loan stock and bonds;

(c) government securities, such as gilts;

(d) unit trusts and open-ended investment companies (OEICs);

(e) insurance contracts;

(f)   mortgages;

(g)   home reversion/home purchase plans.

OEICs are similar to unit trusts, but use the structure of a company rather than a trust.

Investments that will not be relevant include:

(a)   building society share accounts;

(b)   bank and building society deposits (eg, current and deposit accounts);

(c)   certain National Savings products.

17.6.3 Specified activities

These include (but are not limited to):

(a)   dealing as agent;

(b)   arranging;

(c)   managing;

(d)   safeguarding;

(e)   advising;

(f)   lending money on/administering a regulated mortgage contract.

17.6.3.1 Dealing as agent

This involves buying or selling the investments as your client's agent.

17.6.3.2 Arranging

Solicitors will have many clients whose transactions involve investments (eg, endowment policies in conveyancing, unit trusts and shares in probate, etc). The solicitor will very often be involved as the contact between the client and the life company, or the client and the stockbroker. It is in this context that the solicitor may be 'arranging'. Arrangements are excluded where the solicitor merely introduces clients to a person authorised by the FSA (an authorised third person – ATP; see **17.6.4.1**) and the introduction is made with a view to the provision of independent advice to the client. However, this exclusion does not apply where the transaction relates to an insurance contract. If you do something more than just introduce the client in respect of the investment (eg, you help the client to complete an application form), you will be 'arranging'.

17.6.3.3 Managing

Managing requires active participation beyond the mere holding of investments and applies only to 'discretionary management' (ie, involving the exercise of discretion). This investment activity will be most common in firms that undertake probate and trust work, where the solicitor is acting as trustee or personal representative.

17.6.3.4 Safeguarding

This involves safeguarding and administering investments belonging to a client. This is also particularly relevant for firms which undertake probate and trust work.

17.6.3.5 Advising

This involves giving advice to a person in his capacity as an investor on the merits of his buying, selling, subscribing for, or underwriting an investment. Advice must be about a specific investment; generic advice is outside the scope of the FSMA 2000. Thus you can, if you have the knowledge, advise a client to invest in shares rather than gilts, but if you advise the client to buy shares in a particular company, say Tesco, this will be a regulated activity.

17.6.4 Exclusions

There are various exclusions set out in the RAO 2001. If an exclusion applies to a particular activity you are carrying out, you do not need to be authorised for that particular transaction. Those exclusions likely to be relevant to solicitors include:

(a)   introducing (see **17.6.3.2**);

(b)   using an ATP;

(c)   acting for an execution-only client;

(d)   acting as trustee or personal representative;

(e)   the 'necessary' exclusion;

(f)   the 'takeover' exclusion.

17.6.4.1 Authorised third persons – the ATP exclusion

An ATP is some other person authorised by the FSA. Thus if a client wants advice on what shares to buy, you could refer him to an authorised stockbroker. It will be the stockbroker who 'advises' the client under the FSMA 2000. If you do something more than merely 'introduce' the client to the stockbroker, you could be 'arranging' or even ' dealing as the client's agent'. However, these will be excluded under RAO 2001, arts 22 and 29 if the transaction is entered into with or through an ATP on the advice given to the client by the ATP.

You cannot rely on this exclusion if you receive from any person other than the client any pecuniary reward (eg, commission) or other advantage, for which you do not account to your client, arising out of his entering into the transaction.

This exclusion will not apply if the transaction relates to an insurance contract.

17.6.4.2 The execution-only client exclusion

There is a exclusion similar to the ATP exclusion where the client, in his capacity as an investor, is not seeking and has not sought advice from the solicitor as to the merits of the client's entering into the transaction (or, if the client has sought such advice, the solicitor has declined to give it but has recommended that the client seek such advice from an authorised person). There is the same restriction in respect of commissions and contracts of insurance.

17.6.4.3 Trustees or personal representatives

The exclusion applies to arranging, managing, safeguarding and advising fellow trustees and/or beneficiaries. It also applies to lending money on, or administering a regulated mortgage contract.

This exclusion has limitations. It is available to a solicitor acting as a trustee or PR, and not to a solicitor acting *for* a trustee or PR. However, the exclusion does apply if a member of the firm is a trustee or PR but the activity is actually carried out by other members of the firm. Note that the exclusion does not apply if the solicitor is remunerated for what he does 'in addition to any remuneration he receives as trustee or personal representative, and for these purposes a person is not to be regarded as receiving additional remuneration merely because his remuneration is calculated by reference to time spent'. For managing and safeguarding, the exclusion is also not available if the solicitor holds himself out as providing a service comprising managing or safeguarding.

The Law Society's guidance provides that this exemption will not apply to contracts of insurance.

17.6.4.4 Activities carried on in the course of a profession or non-investment business – the 'necessary' exclusion

This applies to advising, arranging, safeguarding and managing. There is an exclusion if the activity is performed in the course of carrying on any profession or business and may reasonably be regarded as a necessary part of other services provided in the course of that profession or business. However, the exclusion does not apply if the activity is remunerated separately from the other services. Examples of where this exclusion may apply include: in matrimonial work, arranging the sale or transfer of a joint endowment insurance; or in probate work, arranging for the sale of *all* the assets to pay IHT.

17.6.4.5 Activities carried on in connection with the sale of a body corporate – the takeover exclusion

This exclusion applies to arranging, advising and dealing as agent. It will apply to a transaction to acquire or dispose of shares in a body corporate (other than an OEIC), or for a transaction entered into for the purposes of such an acquisition or disposal, if:

(a) the shares consist of or include 50% or more of the voting shares in the body corporate; and

(b) the acquisition or disposal is between parties each of whom is a body corporate, a partnership, a single individual or a group of connected individuals.

It is possible to add the number of shares being acquired by a person to those already held by him in order to determine whether the 50% limit has been achieved.

Even if the above criteria are not met, eg the number of shares acquired is less than 50%, but the object of the transaction may nevertheless reasonably be regarded as being the acquisition of day-to-day control of the affairs of the body corporate, the exclusion still applies.

This is an extremely valuable exclusion for the corporate department where a client is seeking to take over, or sell its interest in, a company, whether public or private.

This exclusion does not apply to advising on, arranging, or dealing as an agent in respect of buying or selling contracts of insurance.

17.7 Exemption for professional firms

17.7.1 Introduction

Under s 326 of the FSMA 2000, the Treasury can designate a professional body a designated public body (DPB), and has so designated The Law Society (this role will now be undertaken by the SRA).

Under s 327, the general prohibition in s 19 of the FSMA 2000 will not apply to a regulated activity carried on by a firm of solicitors if the following conditions are met:

(a)   the firm must not receive from a person other than its client any pecuniary or other advantage arising out of the activity for which it does not account to its client;

(b)   the manner of providing 'any service in the course of carrying on the activities must be incidental to the provision' by the firm of professional services, ie services regulated by the SRA.

(c)   the firm must carry out only regulated activities permitted by the DPB, ie the SRA.

(d)   the activities must not be prohibited by an order made by the Treasury, or any direction made by the FSA under s 328 or s 329;

(e)   the firm must not carry on any other regulated activities.

Each of these criteria is discussed further below.

17.7.2   The firm must not receive from a person other than its client any pecuniary or other advantage

Rule 2.06 of the Solicitors' Code of Conduct 2007 provides that firms do not need to account for commissions received of less than £20. However, if the firm wishes to take advantage of the exemption under s 327 then it must account for any such pecuniary advantage to its client.

17.7.3   Incidental

There are two 'incidental' tests: a general test and a specific test. To satisfy the general test of being incidental, the activities carried out by the firm which would otherwise be regulated cannot be a major part of the firm's activities. For example, a firm will be ineligible if its income from investment business is half or more of its total income. Further factors are:

(a)   the scale of regulated activity in proportion to other professional services provided;

(b)   whether and to what extent the exempt regulated activities are held out as separate services; and

(c)   the impression given of how the firm provides those activities, for example through advertising its services.

In addition to the 'general' incidental test, there is also a 'specific' test relating to the particular client concerned. Under the Scope Rules 2001, the relevant regulated activity must arise out of, or be complementary to, the provision of a particular professional service to a particular client. The firm could not, therefore, carry out a regulated activity in isolation for a client; the relevant regulated activity must 'arise out of' or be 'complementary to' some other service being provided by it. This other service must not be a regulated activity but must be a 'professional', ie legal, service (eg, in corporate work, giving legal advice, drafting documents or dealing with a regulatory matter; or in probate work, winding up the estate or giving tax advice). It follows that the professional service being provided to the client should be the primary service, and the regulated activity should be 'incidental' or 'subordinate' to the provision of the professional service. Note also that both the professional service and the regulated activity must be supplied to the same person. Thus, in a probate matter, where the probate client is the executor, advice to a beneficiary under the will not satisfy this test.

17.7.4   The firm must carry out only regulated activities permitted by the DPB

The Law Society is obliged to set out rules concerning the exemption for professional firms (this role has now passed to the SRA). Accordingly, The Law Society has published the Solicitors' Financial Services (Scope) Rules 2001 (see below) and The Law Society Conduct of Business (COB) Rules 2001 for this purpose (see **17.8**). Firms must comply with the requirements prescribed by these rules at all times when seeking to use this exemption.

For example, under the Solicitors' Financial Services (Scope) Rules 2001:

(a)   a solicitor may not recommend, or arrange, for a client to buy or subscribe for a packaged product (ie, financial products which the Government perceives as ones in respect of which ordinary investors require the most protection, such as life policies, unit trusts, and shares in open-ended investment companies). However, a solicitor may advise the client to dispose of a packaged product, or give negative advice (ie, advise the client not to purchase a packaged product). There are also restrictions on advising an individual to acquire certain specified investments (eg, to buy quoted shares), enter into regulated mortgage contracts, or buy/make arrangements to buy/dispose of rights or interests in a personal pension scheme;

(b)   discretionary management is allowed only where the firm, partner or employee is a trustee/PR and an ATP is used when buying an investment. This means that if a solicitor is the trustee of a trust and wishes to acquire some shares, the solicitor will need to be advised by an ATP;

(c)   if a firm wishes to undertake insurance mediation (see **17.9**), it must appoint a compliance officer and be registered on the FSA Register.

17.7.5   The activities must not be prohibited by Treasury order or the FSA

The Treasury has set out, in the FSMA 2000 (Professions) (Non-Exempt Activities) Order 2001, a list of activities which cannot be provided by professional firms under the s 327 exemption. The activities that are most relevant to solicitors are incorporated into The Law Society's Solicitors' Financial Services (Scope) Rules 2001.

17.7.6   The firm must not carry on any other regulated activities.

The exemption for professional firms under s 327 cannot be used by firms which are authorised by the FSA. For example, a firm could be authorised by the FSA concerning defined regulated activities. Such a firm could not use s 327 for any other 'non-mainstream' regulated activities.

17.8   The Solicitors' Financial Services (Conduct of Business) Rules 2001

17.8.1   When do the Rules apply?

The Solicitors' Financial Services (Conduct of Business) Rules 2001 (COB Rules 2001) apply only when the firm is carrying out an exempt regulated activity; they do not apply if the firm is not carrying out a regulated activity at all.

17.8.2 Status disclosure (COB Rules 2001, r 3)

A firm must provide clients with certain information concerning the status of the firm. For example, the firm must confirm to the client that it is not authorised by the FSA, and explain that complaints and redress mechanisms are provided through the SRA and LCS. Any information that is provided under r 3 must be given in a manner that is clear, fair and not misleading.

17.8.3 Best execution (COB Rules 2001, r 4)

A solicitor must act in the best interests of his clients (Code of Conduct, Rule 1.04). Therefore, the firm must carry out transactions for clients as soon as possible and on the best terms available.

17.8.4 Transactions (COB Rules 2001, r 5)

The firm must keep records of:

(a)   instructions from clients to carry out transactions; and

(b)   instructions to third parties to carry them out.

17.8.5 Commissions (COB Rules 2001, r 6)

Under the COB Rules 2001, r 6, the firm must keep records of commissions received in respect of regulated activities and how those commissions were dealt with.

17.8.6 Execution-only clients (COB Rules 2001, r 8)

Where a firm acts for an execution-only client (see **17.6.4.2**) and the investment concerned is a packaged product, it must send a letter to the client confirming that he or she is not relying on the advice of the solicitor, and the firm must keep a copy of this letter.

17.9 Insurance mediation

The Government decided to extend regulation to all general insurance selling and administration in order to comply with the Insurance Mediation Directive (2002/92/EC) approved by the European Parliament on 30 September 2003.

A firm will be carrying out 'insurance mediation' where it carries out (or agrees to carry out) the following activities in relation to contracts of insurance:

(a)   advising;

(b)   arranging;

(c)   acting as agent;

(d)   assisting in the administration and performance of such contracts, in particular in the event of a claim.

'Contracts of insurance' are defined widely, and include life policies, buildings insurance, after-the-event legal insurance, and pension policies.

Thus, whatever the type of insurance policy involved, if a solicitor assists a client to obtain one, even if all he does is to introduce the client to an insurance broker, the solicitor will be carrying out a specified activity. Similarly, if a solicitor is involved in an insurance claim against an insurance company, this will also be caught. All of these activities involve 'insurance mediation'.

Given that the main exclusions will almost certainly not apply to insurance mediation, the firm will have to rely on the exemption for professional firms under s 327 (see **17.7**), seek authorisation from the FSA, or rely on the limited exceptions available for insurance mediation activities (which are beyond the scope of this book).

17.10   Financial promotions

17.10.1   Financial Services and Markets Act 2000, s 21

As a result of the FSMA 2000, s 21, a solicitor who is not authorised by the FSA will be unable to make a financial promotion (ie, 'communicate an invitation or inducement to engage in investment activity') unless its contents are approved by an authorised or exempt person. The structure of the definitions is similar to that for regulated activities, with the Treasury having power by order to specify which investments and activities are 'controlled'. Broadly, the definitions are much the same, although not quite identical.

The result is that you can use almost the same tests as for regulated activities, namely:

(a)   Are you in business?

(b)   Are you making an invitation or inducement?

(c)   In connection with an investment?

(d)   In connection with an investment activity?

Notice, however, that the 'exclusion' test is not applicable. Thus, although you may be carrying out an activity which is not regulated, it may be 'controlled' and subject to the restrictions on financial promotions. The result is that almost anything you may say or write in connection with many transactions could be construed as a financial promotion. Thus if a solicitor advises PRs to sell the deceased's assets, this could be an invitation to deal in investments if, for example, the estate included shares or gilts.

All communications are caught, both real-time and non-real-time. A real-time communication is any communication made in the course of a personal visit, telephone conversation or other interactive dialogue. A non-real-time communication is any other communication, eg, letters e-mails, or brochures. Therefore communications to the other side (eg, letters) and communications to advisers (eg, a fax to a broker) are included just as much as communications to clients.

A real-time communication is 'solicited' where it is made in the course of a personal visit, telephone call or other interactive dialogue, if that call, visit or dialogue:

(a)   was initiated by the recipient (eg, the client) of the communication; or

(b)   takes place in response to an express request from the recipient of the communication (see FPO 2005, art 8).

17.10.2 Exemptions

There are then some exemptions set out in the FPO 2005. Many of these are in terms similar to the exclusions for regulated activities. These include:

(a)   trustees, PRs (FPO 2005, arts 53/54);

(b)   takeover of body corporate (FPO 2005, art 62).

17.10.3 Exemption for exempt professional firms

There are two exemptions designed specifically for firms claiming the special exemption under the FSMA 2000 for exempt regulated activities (see **17.7**). These deal with real-time and non-real-time promotions.

17.10.3.1 Real-time promotions (FPO 2005, art 55)

A solicitor who carries on exempt regulated activities may make a real-time promotion, for example during a meeting or a telephone conversation:

(a)   if made to a client who has, prior to the communication being made, engaged the solicitor to provide professional services; and

(b)   where the controlled activity to which the communication relates is exempt because of the exemption for professional firms, or is excluded from being a regulated activity by the 'necessary' exclusion; and

(c)   where the controlled activity to which the communication relates would be undertaken for the purposes of, and be incidental to, the provision of professional services to or at the request of the client.

The effect is that if the activity is excluded from being a regulated activity by an exclusion other than the 'necessary' exclusion, art 55 does not apply.

17.10.3.2 Non-real time promotions (FPO 2005, art 55A)

This applies to letters, e-mails, brochures, websites, etc, where the solicitor carries on exempt regulated activities, provided the promotion contains certain specific statements.

17.10.4 One-off promotions (FPO 2005, arts 28/28A)

One-off, non-real-time communications and solicited real-time communications are exempt under the FPO 2005, art 28 if certain conditions are satisfied. Basically the communication must be one that is personal to the client.

One-off, unsolicited real-time communications are exempt under art 28A, provided the solicitor believes on reasonable grounds:

(a)   that the client understands the risks associated with engaging in the investment activity to which the financial promotion relates; and

(b)   that, at the time of the communication, the client would expect to be contacted by the solicitor in relation to that investment activity.

17.10.5 Introducers (FPO 2005, art 15)

You may make any real-time communication in order to introduce a client to an ATP, provided:

(a)   you are not connected to (eg, a close relative of) the ATP;

(b)   you do not receive other than from the client any pecuniary reward or other advantage arising out of making the introduction; and

(c)   the client is not seeking and has not sought advice from you as to the merits of his engaging in investment activity (or, if the client has sought such advice, you have declined to give it, but have recommended that the client seeks such advice from an authorised person).

17.11   Chapter summary

17.11.1   Regulated activity

In order to determine if an activity is regulated there are four tests:

(1)   Are you in business?

(2)   Is there a specified investment?

(3)   Is there a specified investment activity?

(4)   Is there an exclusion?

17.11.2   Specified investments

(1)   These include:

    (a)   shares;

    (b)   debentures;

    (c)   gilts;

    (d)   unit trusts and OEICs;

    (e)   contract of insurance;

    (f)   mortgages.

(2)   Investments that will not be relevant include:

    (a)   building society share accounts;

    (b)   bank and building society deposits (eg, current and deposit accounts);

    (c)   National Savings products.

17.11.3   Specified activities

These include:

(1)   dealing as agent;

(2)   arranging;

(3)   managing;

(4)   safeguarding;

(5)   advising.

17.11.4   Exclusions

These include:

(1)   introducing;

(2)   ATP;

(3)   execution-only;

(4)   trustee/PR;

(5)   necessary;

(6)   takeover.

17.11.5   Exempt regulated activities

(1)   A firm not authorised by the FSA should pay attention to:

    (a)   FSMA 2000;

    (b)   RAO 2001;

    (c)   any rules made by the FSA;

    (d)   Scope Rules 2001 passed by The Law Society.

(2)   Conditions set out in the FSMA 2000, the RAO 2001 and the Scope Rules 2001 overlap.

(3) The main conditions for claiming this exemption are:

   (a) the activity must arise out of, or be complementary to, the provision of a particular professional service to a particular client;

   (b) the manner of provision by the firm of any service in the course of carrying out the activities is incidental to the provision by the firm of professional services;

   (c) the firm must account to the client for any reward or other advantage which the firm receives from a third party;

   (d) the Scope Rules do not prohibit the firm using the exemption.

(4) Packaged products. Generally, you are not allowed to recommend or arrange for a client to buy or subscribe for a packaged product, for example:

   (a) endowment life policies;

   (b) unit trusts;

   (c) OEICs.

(5) There are also restrictions on advising an individual to acquire certain specified investments (eg, shares in publicly quoted companies).

17.11.6 Conduct of Business Rules

(1) The COB Rules 2001 apply only when the firm is carrying out an exempt regulated activity; they do not apply if the firm is not carrying out a regulated activity at all.

(2) The COB Rules 2001 cover:

   (a) best execution;

   (b) records of transactions;

   (c) records of commissions;

   (d) letters to execution-only clients.

17.11.7 Financial promotions

(1) There are four questions:

   (a) Are you in business?

   (b) Do you make an invitation or inducement?

   (c) Is there a specified investment?

   (d) Is there a specified investment activity?

(2) There are two special exemptions for professional firms:

   (a) real-time promotions;

   (b) non-real-time promotions.

(3) Other exemptions include:

   (a) one-off promotions;

   (b) introducers;

   (c) trustees, PRs;

   (d) takeover of body corporate.

Chapter 18

Requirements of Practice

18.1 Practising certificates

18.1.1 Requirement to hold a certificate

Section 1 of the Solicitors Act 1974 states:

> No person shall be qualified to act as a solicitor unless—
>
> (a) he has been admitted as a solicitor, and
>
> (b) his name is on the roll, and
>
> (c) he has in force a certificate issued by the Society . . . authorising him to practise as a solicitor (in this Act referred to as a 'practising certificate').

Any person who does not comply with this section will fall within the definition of an 'unqualified person' (Solicitors Act 1974, s 87) and so cannot practise as a solicitor.

Any person who practises as a solicitor without having a practising certificate will commit a criminal offence. Such an individual will also commit a breach of conduct under Rule 20.01.

18.1.2 Persons who need a certificate

The following persons are amongst those who must hold a current practising certificate:

(a) a solicitor who is a partner in a firm;

(b) a solicitor who administers an oath;

(c) all solicitors in private practice;

(d) any person held out, or employed, explicitly or implicitly as a practising solicitor;

(e) any person undertaking work reserved for solicitors in England and Wales;

(f) any person, who is admitted as a solicitor and has his name on the Roll, who is employed by a solicitor (or incorporated practice) in connection with the provision of any legal service (for example as a paralegal);

(g) any person involved in legal practise whose work depends upon him being a solicitor.

18.1.3   Annual enrolment

A solicitor does not have to hold a practising certificate to remain on the Roll of solicitors. Solicitors who wish to remain on the Roll without holding a practising certificate are required to apply annually to the Solicitors Regulation Authority ('SRA') with a fee. At the time of writing this fee is £20.

18.1.4   Issue of certificates

Those who are required to hold a practising certificate must apply to the SRA each year to have their certificates renewed. All practising certificates become due for renewal on 31 October each year. The application is made to the SRA using Form RF1. A fee is payable on renewal of the certificate. At the time of writing the standard fee is £950. However, certain categories of solicitor are entitled to pay a reduced fee. For example, the fee payable by solicitors who work in the Crown Prosecution Service is £630.

A solicitor who has held a practising certificate for three years or more must also pay a set contribution to the SRA's Compensation Fund (see 7.13).

A solicitor is obliged to inform the SRA of any changes to 'relevant information' in respect of the solicitor's practice (see Rule 20.03).

18.1.5   Solicitors Act 1974, s 12

As the issuer of practising certificates, the SRA, pursuant to s 12 of the Solicitors Act 1974, has a certain level of discretion regarding their issue. Where s 12 applies, the SRA may grant or decline to grant the certificate, or may impose conditions on the certificate. Section 12 applies in specific circumstances, including:

(a)   where a solicitor applies for a certificate for the first time;

(b)   where, on the commencement date of the certificate, 12 months have passed since the solicitor last held a certificate;

(c)   where the solicitor has not held a certificate free from conditions since his admission to the profession;

(d)   where the solicitor has been asked by The Law Society/SRA to give an explanation in respect of his conduct, and has either failed to do so or his explanation has been deemed to be unsatisfactory, and he has been informed of this in writing by The Law Society/SRA;

(e)   where the solicitor has been the subject of successful disciplinary proceedings by the Solicitors Disciplinary Tribunal, within which the solicitor has been struck off, suspended, reprimanded, fined, or an order of costs has been made against him;

(f)   where the solicitor is an undischarged bankrupt.

In any of these circumstances, the SRA (amongst others) has the discretion to impose conditions on the issue of a practising certificate. However, s 12(4A) requires that such conditions should be 'conducive to his carrying on an efficient practice as a solicitor', although they may require additional expenditure by the solicitor. In other words, the conditions are not a punishment but are there to improve the performance of the role of the solicitor and service to the client. This may, for example, include additional requirements for filing accountants' reports more frequently than normal if the solicitor in question was found to have been in breach of the Solicitors' Accounts Rules.

18.1.6 Refusal of certificate

Whilst the SRA is granted a discretion with regard to the issue of practising certificates where s 12 applies, measures are in place to ensure that it cannot unreasonably withhold, or impose conditions on, a practising certificate. Applicants who have had an application refused may apply to the High Court or to the Master of the Rolls; and if conditions have been imposed, an appeal may be made to the Master of the Rolls (Solicitors Act 1974, ss 13 and 13A).

With regard to a refusal to issue a certificate, an order may be made 'as may be just', which may include the payment of costs. An appeal against conditions imposed on a certificate must be made within one month of being notified of the conditions, and the Master of the Rolls may make any order he sees fit, including affirming the decision of the SRA, directing the SRA to issue a certificate free of conditions or with only the conditions he sees fit, directing the SRA not to issue a certificate or to suspend an issued certificate.

18.1.7 Suspension of certificate

Where a bankruptcy order is made against a solicitor, his practising certificate is automatically suspended (Solicitors Act 1974, s 15(1)). The SRA may also suspend a current practising certificate if the solicitor is convicted of a crime involving dishonesty or deception, or an indictable offence (Solicitors Act 1974, s 13B).

18.1.8 Post-admission training requirements

All solicitors who are in legal practice in England and Wales and work for more than 32 hours at week are required to undertake Continuing Professional Development (CPD). Solicitors must undertake 16 hours of training each year. The training year runs from 1 November until 31 October.

At least 25% of this training must be completed by participation in courses provided by bodies approved by the SRA.

18.2 Accountants' reports

Under s 34 of the Solicitors Act 1974, all solicitors who hold a practising certificate and client money need to deliver an independent accountant's report each year when they apply for their practising certificate. This is a separate requirement from the requirement to hold a practising certificate, and the report must be submitted within six months after the end of the solicitor's accounting period. A late submission of the report may lead to conditions being placed upon the solicitor's practising certificate (see **18.1.5**).

The purpose of the report is to certify compliance with the Solicitors' Accounts Rules 1998. Any breach of the Rules should be identified by the accountant, who either will decline to issue a certificate or will issue a qualified certificate.

To be independent, the accountant should not be employed by the solicitor's firm or any connected business, and the report must include the name of the individual accountant who has prepared the report.

A partnership may submit one report for the firm.

As outlined in **18.1.5**, the SRA may require a solicitor to submit an accountant's report more frequently as a condition on his practising certificate following disciplinary proceedings.

18.3   Indemnity insurance

18.3.1   Requirement for insurance

The Solicitors' Indemnity Insurance Rules 2007 require that all principals in private practice must carry indemnity insurance, which must meet certain minimum requirements set out in the Rules. The Rules were made by the Council of The Law Society, but now fall under the jurisdiction of the SRA.

The requirement applies to 'principals', meaning all sole practitioners and partners in a law firm. It does not apply to assistant solicitors, trainees, or other individuals employed by a solicitors practice, who will be covered by any insurance taken out by the firm or their principal.

This insurance protects the solicitor against civil claims made against him in the course of his practice; it also protects an injured client by ensuring that solicitors in practice have sufficient monies in place to meet claims made against them.

In previous years, The Law Society ran its own insurance scheme and principals were obliged to obtain their insurance through this scheme. However, principals now obtain insurance from a 'qualified' commercial insurance provider. A list of qualified providers can be obtained from The Law Society. The commercial provider has to comply with certain minimum terms (for example, see **18.3.2**).

Due to poor claims records, some principals may find it impossible, or economically prohibitive, to obtain cover through the commercial market. An 'assigned risks pool', funded by the qualified insurers, is in place which will cover such firms for a limited period. To discourage reliance on this scheme, the cost of being a member of the pool is high, and membership imposes obligations on members to improve their claims record and reduce the risk of claims. Such firms are also subject to additional monitoring by the SRA. They will be allowed to stay in this pool for a maximum of 24 months in every five years.

18.3.2   Amount of cover

All qualified insurers must provide principals with cover of up to £2,000,000 for any one claim, not including defence costs, and principals must ensure that this is the minimum level of cover for their firm. However, this may not be the minimum level of cover they need in order to provide adequate insurance protection for their practice. Principals may therefore take out 'top-up' cover to increase the amount covered under their insurance.

The minimum sum for any one claim for limited liability partnerships (LLPs) and companies is £3,000,000.

18.4   Responsibility of partners

Partners must ensure that their firm complies with the rules of professional conduct. In certain cases, partners will be held to be liable for any breach. For example, where one partner breaches the Solicitors' Accounts Rules, every other partner of the firm will be jointly responsible for this breach and liable to be disciplined. This will be the case even if the other partners had no knowledge of what the 'rogue' partner was doing.

For breaches other than breaches of the Solicitors' Accounts Rules, the SRA has a discretion as to whether to pursue disciplinary action against the other partners.

18.5 Supervision

18.5.1 Qualified to supervise

The Code of Conduct ensures that there is at least one member of every firm of solicitors who is qualified to supervise. This is to ensure the protection of the public. For example, Rule 5.02 provides that at least one partner in a firm, one member of an LLP, one director of a recognised body which is a company and all sole principals must be 'qualified to supervise'.

'Qualified to supervise' is defined by Rule 5.02(2) and requires that the relevant individual:

(a)   must have completed at least 12 hours of training on management skills; and

(b)   must have been entitled to practise as a lawyer for at least 36 months within the last 10 years.

18.5.2 Responsibilities of senior members of firms

Regardless of whether they are 'qualified to supervise' (see above) every partner within a firm, member of an LLP, director of a recognised body which is a company or sole practitioner is obliged to make arrangements for the effective management of his firm.

Rule 5.01 expressly specifies the responsibilities with which the above individuals must comply. These include (but are not limited to):

(a)   their duties (in both law and conduct) to exercise adequate supervision over their staff and ensure adequate supervision of clients' matters;

(b)   the Money Laundering Regulations 2003;

(c)   the firm's obligations concerning client care, costs information and complaints handling;

(d)   the control of undertakings;

(e)   the identification of conflicts of interests;

(f)   Rule 6 concerning equality and diversity.

For example, if an assistant solicitor gives an undertaking which is subsequently breached, the solicitor himself will have committed a breach of professional conduct. However, the partners of the firm may also be disciplined under Rule 5.01 for their failure to monitor the performance of undertakings given by staff.

The Code of Conduct does not specify the steps that must be put in place to satisfy the requirements of Rule 5.01. The SRA's guidance provides that appropriate steps will vary from firm to firm, depending on the size of the firm, the experience of the staff, and the nature of the work undertaken.

18.6 Separate business

A solicitor's ability to set up and run a business which provides legal services of a type normally supplied by solicitors is severely limited by Rule 21.

The object of Rule 21 is very clear. It is important that clients or members of the public understand what activities carried out by a solicitor are subject to the protection of a regulated regime. It is vital that the public is not confused or misled by a solicitor incorporating non-regulated services into his solicitors practice.

Rule 21 prohibits, subject to limited exceptions, certain services being provided through a separate business, such as the provision of legal advice, drafting legal documents (such as wills), or providing advocacy services before a court, tribunal or inquiry. For example, the SRA's guidance provides that a solicitor cannot 'hive off' services (such as wills drafting) from the solicitor's firm to a separate business which is not regulated.

Rule 24 defines 'providing a service through a separate business' as having any active involvement in a separate business. The definition expressly includes:

(a)   any substantial ownership of the business;

(b)   any direct control over the business;

(c)   any indirect control over the business through another person (eg, a spouse); or

(d)   any active participation in the business or the provision of the service to customers.

18.7   Duty to the Solicitors Regulation Authority

18.7.1   Duty to cooperate

Rule 20.03 provides that a solicitor must deal with the SRA and Legal Complaints Service ('LCS') in an open, prompt and cooperative way. For example, a solicitor must provide the SRA with information necessary for it to grant or renew the solicitor's practising certificate.

A solicitor must also deal promptly with any correspondence or communications from the SRA or LCS. For example, a solicitor is obliged to deal promptly with any complaint being dealt with by the LCS on behalf of a client.

A solicitor must also comply with any written notice served by the SRA requesting the production of documents and information. Such a notice may be served where the SRA is investigating whether the solicitor or firm is complying with the rules of professional conduct (Rule 20.06).

Lastly, a solicitor must not make any attempt to hinder or prevent a client reporting the firm for an alleged breach of professional misconduct or an alleged inadequate professional service. Nor must the firm victimise any such complainant (Rule 20.05). However, a firm may make genuine attempts (in respect of an inadequate professional service) to compensate a complainant, or (in respect of all complaints) try to convince the complainant that the complaint is unfounded.

18.7.2   Reporting serious misconduct

A solicitor is obliged, pursuant to Rule 20.04, to report to the SRA any incident of serious misconduct by a solicitor, Registered Foreign Lawyer (RFL) or Registered European Lawyer (REL). This obligation extends to partners in a firm reporting their own employees for serious misconduct.

A solicitor must also report the matter if he has reason to doubt the integrity of a solicitor (or RFL, or REL), or has reason to believe that the individual concerned is in serious financial difficulty.

18.8   Chapter summary

18.8.1   Practising certificates and related matters

(1)   The Solicitors Act 1974, s 1 states:

No person shall be qualified to act as a solicitor unless—

(a)   he has been admitted as a solicitor, and

(b)   his name is on the roll, and

(c)   he has in force a certificate issued by the Society ... authorising him to practise as a solicitor (in this Act referred to as a 'practising certificate').

(2)   Practising certificates are issued annually by the SRA.

(3)   Where s 12 of the Solicitors Act 1974 applies, the SRA may grant or refuse an application for a certificate. The SRA may also grant a certificate subject to specified conditions.

(4)   Solicitors firms are obliged to file an annual accountant's report with the SRA.

18.8.2 Indemnity Insurance

(1)   The Solicitors' Indemnity Insurance Rules 2007 require solicitors to take out compulsory insurance cover against the risks of professional negligence or other civil liability claims.

(2)   Firms can insure with any approved commercial insurer. Firms which are unable to obtain insurance on the open market will be covered temporarily by the assigned risks pool.

(3)   A firm's insurance policy, in most cases, must cover a minimum of £2 million per individual claim. Limited liability partnerships and companies must obtain cover to a minimum to £3 million per individual claim. Voluntary top-up cover may be required.

18.8.3 Supervision

(1)   At least one member of every firm must be 'qualified to supervise'.

(2)   Regardless of whether they are 'qualified to supervise', every partner within a firm is obliged to make arrangements for the effective management of his firm.

Part II Summaries – Professional Conduct

Chapter 6: The Legal Profession

Topic	Summary
Professional conduct	Professional conduct is the term that is used to describe the rules and regulations with which a solicitor must comply. Solicitors are in a position of trust, and so a higher standard of behaviour is expected of them than of members of the public.
Solicitors Regulation Authority ('SRA')	The SRA regulates solicitors in England and Wales. It also controls such matters as training and entry into the profession.
The Law Society	The Law Society is the representative body for solicitors in England and Wales. After admission membership is voluntary, but all solicitors are bound by the rules of professional conduct whether or not they are members of The Law Society.
Different aspects of practice	The legal profession is made up of a number of different types of organisation. Within these organisations, there are a number of roles that a solicitor may fill. However, most solicitors in private practice are employed by partnerships.

Chapter 7: Regulating the Profession

Topic	Summary
Solicitors Regulation Authority ('SRA')	The SRA publishes and enforces rules concerning how solicitors behave and conduct their business. The subject matter of this Part is the Solicitors' Code of Conduct 2007.
Complaints against solicitors	Every firm must have a complaints handling procedure, and must ensure that complaints are handled in a prompt, fair and effective manner in accordance with that procedure (Rule 2.05). If a complaint cannot be resolved by the firm, then the client must be given details of the Legal Complaints Service.
Legal Complaints Service ('LCS')	The LCS exercises some of the SRA's powers in relation to the handling of complaints. The LCS is the sole point of receipt for complaints concerning solicitors. It deals with complaints concerning inadequate professional services, and refers any allegations of breaches of the rules of professional conduct to the SRA.
Inadequate professional services	An inadequate professional service occurs where a solicitor has provided a service to his client which is inadequate, ie not of a standard which is reasonable to expect of a solicitor.
Powers of the LCS	Where the LCS makes a finding of an inadequate professional service, the LCS has the power to order the firm of solicitors to waive its bill, waive the right to recover a fee, or direct that the firm must compensate the client up to the sum of £15,000. The LCS cannot pay compensation to a client itself.
Powers of the SRA – professional misconduct	Where a finding of professional misconduct is made, the SRA may discipline the solicitor by reprimanding him, or referring the matter to the Solicitors Disciplinary Tribunal.
Solicitors Disciplinary Tribunal	The Solicitors Disciplinary Tribunal hears and determines applications relating to allegations of professional misconduct. It is independent of the SRA and The Law Society. It has the power to suspend a solicitor, to fine a solicitor up to the sum of £5,000 per proved allegation and, in the most extreme cases, to strike a solicitor off the Roll – which will effectively end his career.

Topic	Summary
Negligence	In addition to or instead of the actions that the SRA may take against a solicitor, a solicitor may be sued by his client in the tort of negligence. A solicitor owes his client a duty of care. Where this duty is breached, and the client suffers a foreseeable loss as a result of that breach, the solicitor may be sued for negligence. Firms must carry compulsory indemnity insurance against such actions.
The Compensation Fund	The Compensation Fund is maintained by the SRA. Payment may be made from the Fund when a client has suffered loss as a result of a solicitor's dishonesty. No grant may be made from the Fund until the client has exhausted all other remedies.

Chapter 8: The Core Duties

Topic	Summary
The Code of Conduct 2007	The profession is regulated by the Government and by rules of conduct set out by the SRA.
The Core Duties	The Core Duties are contained within Rule 1. They are the 'overarching framework' for the rest of the Rules. They provide guidance to help solicitors deal with situations which are not covered in the detailed rules. They are the fundamental requirements that solicitors must satisfy in practice.
Integrity	The Core Duties include Rule 1.02, which provides that a solicitor must act with integrity, for example towards clients, the courts, lawyers and the public. A solicitor is in a position of trust, and so must behave in an appropriate manner to reflect that position.
Best interests of clients	The Core Duties include Rule 1.04 – the solicitor's duty to act in the best interests of his clients. This places an obligation on the solicitor always to act in good faith, and always to do his best for his clients.
Public confidence	A solicitor must also protect the public trust in the profession (Rule 1.06). Therefore a solicitor must not do anything that would be likely to damage this trust. This obligation extends to both the solicitor's behaviour within practice, and outside of it in his daily life.
Breach of the Core Duties	Where a solicitor breaches the Core Duties, he may well be guilty of professional misconduct. In serious cases, this could also lead to him being 'struck off' the Roll of solicitors, which would effectively end his career.

Chapter 9: Obtaining Instructions

Topic	Summary
General principles	A solicitors' firm must take steps to try to maintain and increase its market share in order to prosper. However, a solicitor must at all times comply with the general law and the Code of Conduct. In particular, no matter what financial pressure he is under, a solicitor should always be independent and impartial when giving advice to a client.
Advertising	Solicitors are free to publicise their practices, provided that they comply with the general law on advertising in force at the time and with Rule 7 of the Code of Conduct 2007.
Rule 7	Rule 7 applies to all forms of publicity. It provides that all publicity issued by, or on behalf of, law firms must not be misleading or inaccurate.
Cold calling	Rule 7.03 provides that a solicitor may not cold call the general public. However, this restriction does not apply to contacting clients or former clients.
Referrals of business	A solicitor may enter into an arrangement with a third party to refer clients to or from that third party. However, such arrangements must comply with Rule 9.
Best interests of the client	Any referral must be made in good faith and in the client's best interests (Rule 9.03).
Solicitors' independence (Rule 9.01)	A solicitor must not place himself in a position whereby his advice to a client is affected due to an attempt not to offend a referrer of work.
Referral fees	A solicitor may pay to or receive referral fees from a third party, but must comply with the provisions of Rule 9.02. For example, the agreement with the introducer of work must be in writing and available for inspection by the SRA, and both the introducer and solicitor must give the client all the relevant information in writing before the referral takes place.
Fee sharing	Subject to limited exceptions, solicitors must not share their professional fees with non-lawyers.

Chapter 10: The Retainer

Topic	Summary
The retainer	The contract between a solicitor and his client is often referred to as a retainer. The contract is governed by the general law, and also the rules of professional conduct.
Acceptance of third party instructions	Where instructions are received from a third party on behalf of a client, the solicitor must not proceed with those instructions until he checks that the client himself agrees with those instructions (Rule 2.01(c)).
Refusal of instructions	A solicitor must not unlawfully discriminate against anyone. Therefore a solicitor must not decline to act for a client based on matters such as the client's sex, race, disability, ethnic origins or nationality.
Where instructions must be refused	A solicitor's freedom to accept instructions is restricted by the Code of Conduct 2007. For example, a solicitor cannot act where to do so would involve the solicitor in a breach of the law or a breach of the rules of professional conduct (Rule 2.01(1)).
Duty to the client during the retainer	A solicitor owes the client a number of duties throughout the retainer. For example, s 13 of the Supply of Goods and Services Act 1982 provides that a supplier of services (such as a solicitor) will carry out those services with reasonable care and skill.
Termination of the retainer	A client may terminate the retainer at any time and for any reason. The solicitor may terminate a retainer only with good reason and on reasonable notice (Rule 2.01(2)).
Responsibilities on termination	A solicitor should confirm to the client in writing that the retainer has been terminated, and take steps to deal with any property of the client that may be held by the solicitor. In certain circumstances a solicitor may exercise a lien over the property until his fees are paid.

Chapter 11: Client Care and Costs

Topic	Summary
Client care	A solicitor must maintain appropriate client care procedures as prescribed by the SRA. The client care information must be given to the client in writing at the start of the matter and be updated throughout.
Client's objective	The solicitor is under a duty to ascertain exactly what the client wishes to achieve by instructing the solicitor. Once this objective has been identified, the solicitor must give the client a clear explanation of the issues involved in achieving the client's goal, and carry out a costs/benefit analysis.
Responsibilities and level of service	The client must be given information relating to various matters, such as the responsibilities of the client and solicitor, who will be dealing with (and supervising) the client's matter, and the level of service that the client may expect from the solicitor.
Obligation to update the client	The solicitor must update the client as to progress throughout the matter.
Costs information	A solicitor is obliged to provide his client with the best possible information as to the likely overall costs of a matter. This information should be given in writing and updated throughout the matter. This information must include details of the basis and terms of the solicitor's charges. The solicitor must also advise the client of any payments to third parties (such as barristers) which the client may have to make.
Accurate estimate not possible	Where it is not possible for a solicitor to provide an accurate estimate of the overall cost, the solicitor should agree a ceiling figure above which the costs cannot go, or alternatively a review date when the parties will revisit the costs position.
Funding options	A solicitor must advise the client as to the availability of public funding or insurance to cover the client's costs.
Costs in litigation	A solicitor must advise the client whether he may be liable to pay the costs of the other party to the matter.

Topic	Summary
Solicitor's fees	A solicitor and client may agree the level of costs that the solicitor may charge. However, this agreement is regulated by statute and the common law. A distinction is made between costs in contentious matters and costs in non-contentious matters.
Solicitor's bill	A solicitor's bill must contain prescribed information in order for the bill to be enforceable.
Client's right to challenge the bill	A client may challenge the costs of a solicitor in both contentious and non-contentious matters. Generally speaking, in both types of matters the client may apply to have the costs assessed by the court. In non-contentious matters the client may, as an alternative to assessment by the courts, apply for a remuneration certificate from the LCS.
Suing on a bill	Generally, a solicitor may not sue to recover his costs from the client until one month has elapsed since the bill was delivered.
Overcharging	A solicitor must act in the best interests of the client and must not take advantage of his client. Therefore a solicitor must not overcharge for work done. Overcharging may well be considered by the SRA as a breach of professional conduct.

Chapter 12: Confidentiality

Topic	Summary
Duty of confidentiality	A solicitor (and his staff) must keep the affairs of his clients and former clients confidential except where disclosure is required or permitted by law or the client (Rule 4.01). This duty applies regardless of the source of the information, and continues until the client waives confidentiality.
Overriding the duty of confidentiality	Information which is the subject of the duty of confidentiality may be disclosed in prescribed circumstances, for example where it is necessary to prevent the client from committing a criminal act which is likely to result in serious bodily harm.
Duty of disclosure	The solicitor also has a duty to disclose to the client all information that is relevant to the client's matter, regardless of the source of that information (Rule 4.02). The duty of confidentiality overrides the duty of disclosure.
Placing confidential information at risk	Where a solicitors' firm holds confidential information for one client, it must not risk breaching confidentiality by acting for (or continuing to act for) another client on a matter where the information might reasonably be expected to be material, and the clients have an adverse interest to one another, unless proper arrangements can be made to protect the confidential information (Rule 4.03). These proper arrangements are specified in Rules 4.04 and 4.05 and include issues such as obtaining informed consent, and erecting information barriers.
Professional embarrassment	Even when a solicitor would be permitted to act for two clients on a matter pursuant to Rule 4, he may still have to refuse instructions on the basis of professional embarrassment.
Privilege	In addition to the duty of confidentiality, a solicitor must also consider legal professional privilege. Where legal professional privilege applies, a solicitor can refuse to disclose communications between himself and a client.

Chapter 13: Conflict of Interests

Topic	Summary
General principles	A solicitor must not act where there is a conflict, or a significant risk of a conflict between the interests of two or more clients (Rule 3.01).
Same or related matters	The conflict of interest must arise in relation to the same matter, or related matters. A matter will be related if it concerns the same asset or liability (Rule 3.01(3)). However, there would need to be some reasonable degree of relationship for a conflict to arise.
Former clients	Due to the definition of a conflict of interest, a conflict cannot arise with a former client. However, the solicitor may still be prevented from acting if he holds confidential information concerning the former client.
Exceptions	Where there is a conflict between two clients, a solicitor may act if he can satisfy the requirements of the common interest exception or the commercial exception.
Conflict between the solicitor's and client's interests	A solicitor must not act where there is a conflict or significant risk of a conflict between the client's interests and the solicitor's interests. There are no exceptions to this rule. (Rule 3.01(2)(b).)
Gifts from clients	A solicitor must not accept a gift from a client where the gift is of a significant amount. Where the client wishes to give the solicitor such a gift, the solicitor must advise the client to seek independent legal advice. If the client refuses, then the solicitor must refuse to act (Rule 3.04).
Public office	A solicitor who holds public office or appointment may be prevented from acting in a matter where there is a conflict, a potential conflict or the public may conclude that the solicitor had used the public office to gain an advantage for his client (Rule 3.05).

Chapter 14: Undertakings

Topic	Summary
Definition	An undertaking is a statement, made by the solicitor or the solicitor's firm to someone who reasonably relies upon it, that the solicitor or his firm will do something or cause something to be done, or refrain from doing something (Rule 24 – 'Interpretation'). Essentially an undertaking is an enforceable promise.
Effect	An undertaking is personally binding on the giver of the undertaking (Rule 10.05(1)). The undertaking does not have to be in writing, and it is not necessary to use the word 'undertake'.
Ambiguity	Any ambiguity in the wording of the undertaking will be construed against the party that gave the undertaking.
Undertakings 'on behalf of a client'	It is possible for a solicitor to give an undertaking on behalf of a client and exclude personal liability. However, the solicitor must clearly and expressly disclaim personal liability or make it clear that he is simply informing the other side of his client's intentions.
Change of circumstances	An undertaking will remain binding upon a solicitor even if the circumstances change so that it is impossible to fulfil the undertaking.
Liability of others	It is the responsibility of a sole practitioner or partner in a partnership to ensure that an undertaking given by a member of staff in the course of practice is honoured.
Breach	Breach of an undertaking is prima facie professional misconduct. The SRA/LCS/Solicitors Disciplinary Tribunal do not have the power to enforce an undertaking. However, any breach may lead to sanctions against the solicitor concerned.
The courts	The court is able to enforce an undertaking against a solicitor as an officer of the court. Accordingly, where an undertaking has been breached, the aggrieved party may sue the solicitor for compensation for any loss.

Chapter 15: Money Laundering and the Proceeds of Crime Act 2002

Topic	Summary
Money laundering	'Money laundering' is the process by which criminals seek to alter or 'launder' their proceeds of crime so that it appears that these funds come from a legitimate source. Solicitors are often targets for criminals in their efforts to launder the proceeds of their crimes. The government has introduced legislation to disrupt this process.
Money Laundering Regulations 2007	Solicitors who undertake 'relevant business' must comply with the Money Laundering Regulations 2007. 'Relevant business' includes the provision of legal services which involves participation in a 'financial or real property transaction', and so the vast majority of solicitors' firms will be subject to the regulations.
Nominated officer	Under the Money Laundering Regulations 2007, firms must appoint a nominated officer, who will receive internal reports concerning money laundering and must consider whether to report the matter to the Serious Organised Crime Agency.
Arrangements	A person commits an offence under s 328 of the Proceeds of Crime Act 2002 where he becomes concerned with an arrangement involving money laundering. However, s 328 does not apply to steps taken in litigation. An individual convicted under s 328 may receive a maximum sentence of 14 years' imprisonment.
Failure to disclose	A solicitor within the regulated sector is obliged to disclose any suspect money laundering activity to his nominated officer (s 330). Failure to do so may result in a maximum sentence of five years' imprisonment.
Tipping off	It is an offence to disclose to any person that a disclosure has been made to a nominated officer or the Serious Organised Crime Agency where this disclosure may prejudice an investigation (s 333), or that an invetigation into money laundering is being carried out or contemplated. An individual convicted under s 333 may receive a maximum penalty of two years' imprisonment.

Chapter 16: Duties Owed to the Court and Third Parties

Topic	Summary	References
Duty to the court	A solicitor is under a duty never to mislead or deceive the court. A solicitor must also comply with any properly made order of the court, and must not become in contempt of court.	Rule 11.01 Rules 11.02 and 11.03
Witnesses	A solicitor must not make an allegation which is purely intended to insult a witness. Equally, a solicitor must not make (or offer to make) payments to witnesses dependent upon the nature of the evidence given, or on the outcome of the case.	Rule 11.05 Rule 11.07
Refusing instructions to act	A solicitor must not refuse to act as an advocate on the grounds that he finds the nature of the case or the opinions/beliefs of the client objectionable.	Rule 11.04
Instructing counsel	A solicitor must act in the best interests of his client. Accordingly, if it is in the client's best interests to instruct counsel, the solicitor must ensure that adequate instructions are provided to the chosen barrister. Instructing counsel does not relieve the solicitor of his duties towards his client, particularly the duty to act in the client's best interests.	
Duty to third parties	A solicitor must not take an unfair advantage of any person, either for the solicitor's own benefit or for another person's benefit (such as the client). Particular care should be taken when dealing with unrepresented third parties.	Rule 10.01
Recovering costs	A solicitor must not demand anything from a third party which is not legally recoverable.	
Represented third parties	Subject to limited exceptions, a solicitor should not communicate directly with third parties where the solicitor knows that the third party has instructed a legal representative.	Rule 10.04

Topic	Summary	References
Beneficiaries	In certain circumstances, a solicitor owes a duty of care to third parties, such as beneficiaries. If this duty is breached, the solicitor may be sued by the third party.	
Dealings with other solicitors	A solicitor must preserve the integrity of the profession. Therefore a solicitor must treat other solicitors with due respect in all their communications.	Rule 1.02

Chapter 17: Financial Services

Topic	Summary
General prohibition	Section 19 of the Financial Services and Markets Act 2000 provides that 'no person may carry on a regulated activity in the UK unless authorised or exempt'.
Regulated activity	A person carries out a regulated activity when, while in business, he carries out a specified investment activity in relation to a specified investment, and cannot take advantage of an exclusion.
Specified investment	Specified investments include company stocks and shares, debentures, unit trusts, insurance contracts and mortgages.
Specified investment activities	Specified investment activities include advising, arranging, dealing as agent, managing and safeguarding.
Exclusions	Numerous exclusions exist, such as the authorised third party exclusion. Each exclusion has different conditions and restrictions. If a solicitor can take advantage of an exclusion, he will not be carrying out a regulated activity.
Exempt regulated activities	As an alternative to using an exclusion, a firm may seek to use the exemption for professional firms to avoid breaching the general prohibition. Once again, a number of conditions must be satisfied. These include that the activity the firm carries out must be incidental to the provision of legal services by the firm. The firm must also comply with the Scope and COB Rules.
Financial promotions	A solicitor who is not authorised by the Financial Services Authority is unable to make a financial promotion unless its contents are approved by an authorised or exempt person (FSMA 2000, s 21). Once again, this prohibition is subject to exclusions.

Chapter 18: Requirements of Practice

Topic	Summary	References
Requirement to hold a practising certificate	No person may act as a solicitor unless he has been admitted as a solicitor, his name is on the Roll of solicitors, and he holds a current practising certificate.	Solicitors Act 1974, s 1
Practising certificates	Practising certificates are issued annually by the SRA, which has a certain level of discretion as to whether to issue a certificate to a particular person. In certain circumstances the SRA may decline to issue a certificate or may impose conditions on the certificate.	
Suspension of practising certificate	A practising certificate is automatically suspended where a bankruptcy order is made against the solicitor concerned. The SRA may also suspend a practising certificate if the solicitor is convicted of a crime involving dishonesty or deception.	
Accountants' reports	All solicitors who hold a practising certificate and also hold client monies must deliver an independent accountant's report each year when they apply for their practising certificate. The purpose of the report is to certify compliance with the Solicitors' Accounts Rules. One report may be submitted for a firm as a whole.	
Indemnity insurance	The Solicitors Indemnity Insurance Rules require solicitors to take out compulsory insurance cover against the risks of professional negligence or other civil liability claims. Firms can insure with any approved commercial insurer. A firm's insurance policy, in most cases, must cover a minimum of £2 million per individual claim. Limited liability partnerships and companies must obtain cover to a minimum of £3 million per individual claim. Voluntary top-up cover may be required.	
Responsibility of partners	Partners must ensure that their firm complies with the rules of professional conduct. In certain cases, partners will be held liable for any breach.	

Topic	Summary	References
Supervision	At least one member of every firm must be 'qualified to supervise'. This means that he must have been entitled to practise as a lawyer for at least 36 months within the last 10 years, and must have completed at least 12 hours of training on management skills.	Rule 5.02
	Regardless of whether he is 'qualified to supervise', every partner within a firm is obliged to make arrangements for the effective management of his firm.	Rule 5.01
Duty to the SRA	A solicitor is under a duty to co-operate with the SRA in a prompt and co-operative manner. This includes dealing promptly with any correspondence from the SRA or LCS.	Rule 20.03
Reporting serious misconduct	A solicitor is obliged to report to the SRA any incident of serious misconduct by a solicitor. A solicitor must also report a matter if he has reason to doubt the integrity of the solicitor, or has reason to believe that the solicitor is in serious financial difficulty.	Rule 20.04

Appendix to Part II

Proceeds of Crime Act 2002

PART 7
MONEY LAUNDERING

OFFENCES

327. **Concealing etc**

   (1)   A person commits an offence if he—

   (a)   conceals criminal property;

   (b)   disguises criminal property;

   (c)   converts criminal property;

   (d)   transfers criminal property;

   (e)   removes criminal property from England and Wales or from Scotland or from Northern Ireland.

   (2)   But a person does not commit such an offence if—

   (a)   he makes an authorised disclosure under section 338 and (if the disclosure is made before he does the act mentioned in subsection (1)) he has the appropriate consent;

   (b)   he intended to make such a disclosure but had a reasonable excuse for not doing so;

   (c)   the act he does is done in carrying out a function he has relating to the enforcement of any provision of this Act or of any other enactment relating to criminal conduct or benefit from criminal conduct.

   (2A)   Nor does a person commit an offence under subsection (1) if—

   (a)   he knows, or believes on reasonable grounds, that the relevant criminal conduct occurred in a particular country or territory outside the United Kingdom, and

   (b)   the relevant criminal conduct—

   (i)   was not, at the time it occurred, unlawful under the criminal law then applying in that country or territory, and

   (ii)   is not of a description prescribed by an order made by the Secretary of State.

   (2B)   In subsection (2A) 'the relevant criminal conduct' is the criminal conduct by reference to which the property concerned is criminal property.

   (2C)   A deposit-taking body that does an act mentioned in paragraph (c) or (d) of subsection (1) does not commit an offence under that subsection if—

   (a)   it does the act in operating an account maintained with it; and

   (b)   the value of the criminal property concerned is less than the threshold amount determined under section 339A for the act.

   (3)   Concealing or disguising criminal property includes concealing or disguising its nature, source, location, disposition, movement or ownership or any rights with respect to it.

328. **Arrangements**

   (1)   A person commits an offence if he enters into or becomes concerned in an arrangement which he knows or suspects facilitates (by whatever means) the

acquisition, retention, use or control of criminal property by or on behalf of another person.

(2)　But a person does not commit such an offence if:

(a)　he makes an authorised disclosure under section 338 and (if the disclosure is made before he does the act mentioned in subsection (1)) he has the appropriate consent;

(b)　he intended to make such a disclosure but had a reasonable excuse for not doing so;

(c)　the act he does is done in carrying out a function he has relating to the enforcement of any provision of this Act or of any other enactment relating to criminal conduct or benefit from criminal conduct.

(3)　Nor does a person commit an offence under subsection (1) if—

(a)　he knows, or believes on reasonable grounds, that the relevant criminal conduct occurred in a particular country or territory outside the United Kingdom, and

(b)　the relevant criminal conduct—

(i)　was not, at the time it occurred, unlawful under the criminal law then applying in that country or territory, and

(ii)　is not of a description prescribed by an order made by the Secretary of State.

(4)　In subsection (3) 'the relevant criminal conduct' is the criminal conduct by reference to which the property concerned is criminal property.

(5)　A deposit-taking body that does an act mentioned in subsection (1) does not commit an offence under that subsection if—

(a)　it does the act in operating an account maintained with it; and

(b)　the arrangement facilitates the acquisition, retention, use or control of criminal property of a value that is less than the threshold amount determined under section 339A for the act.

329.　Acquisition, use and possession

(1)　A person commits an offence if he—

(a)　acquires criminal property;

(b)　uses criminal property;

(c)　has possession of criminal property.

(2)　But a person does not commit such an offence if:

(a)　he makes an authorised disclosure under section 338 and (if the disclosure is made before he does the act mentioned in subsection (1)) he has the appropriate consent;

(b)　he intended to make such a disclosure but had a reasonable excuse for not doing so;

(c)　he acquired or used or had possession of the property for adequate consideration;

(d)　the act he does is done in carrying out a function he has relating to the enforcement of any provision of this Act or of any other enactment relating to criminal conduct or benefit from criminal conduct.

(2A)　Nor does a person commit an offence under subsection (1) if—

(a)　he knows, or believes on reasonable grounds, that the relevant criminal conduct occurred in a particular country or territory outside the United Kingdom, and

(b)   the relevant criminal conduct—

    (i)   was not, at the time it occurred, unlawful under the criminal law then applying in that country or territory, and

    (ii)   is not of a description prescribed by an order made by the Secretary of State.

(2B) In subsection (2A) 'the relevant criminal conduct' is the criminal conduct by reference to which the property concerned is criminal property.

(2C) A deposit-taking body that does an act mentioned in subsection (1) does not commit an offence under that subsection if—

(a)   it does the act in operating an account maintained with it; and

(b)   the value of the criminal property concerned is less than the threshold amount determined under section 339A for the act.

(3)   For the purposes of this section—

(a)   a person acquires property for inadequate consideration if the value of the consideration is significantly less than the value of the property;

(b)   a person uses or has possession of property for inadequate consideration if the value of the consideration is significantly less than the value of the use or possession;

(c)   the provision by a person of goods or services which he knows or suspects may help another to carry out criminal conduct is not consideration.

330.   Failure to disclose: regulated sector

(1)   A person commits an offence if the conditions in subsections (2) to (4) are satisfied:

(2)   The first condition is that he—

(a)   knows or suspects; or

(b)   has reasonable grounds for knowing or suspecting,

that another person is engaged in money laundering.

(3)   The second condition is that the information or other matter—

(a)   on which his knowledge or suspicion is based; or

(b)   which gives reasonable grounds for such knowledge or suspicion,

came to him in the course of a business in the regulated sector.

(3A) The third condition is—

(a)   that he can identify the other person mentioned in subsection (2) or the whereabouts of any of the laundered property; or

(b)   that he believes, or it is reasonable to expect him to believe, that the information or other matter mentioned in subsection (3) will or may assist in identifying the other person or the whereabouts of any of the laundered property.

(4)   The fourth condition is that he does not make the required disclosure to—

(a)   a nominated officer; or

(b)   a person authorised for the purposes of this Part by the Director General of the Serious Organised Crime Agency, as soon as is practicable after the information or other matter mentioned in subsection (3) comes to him.

(5)   The required disclosure is a disclosure of—

(a)   the identity of the other person mentioned in subsection (2), if he knows it;

(b)   the whereabouts of the laundered property, so far as he knows it; and

(c)   the information or other matter mentioned in subsection (3).

(5A)   The laundered property is the property forming the subject-matter of the money laundering that he knows or suspects, or has reasonable grounds for knowing or suspecting, that other person to be engaged in.

(6)   But he does not commit an offence under this section if—

(a)   he has a reasonable excuse for not making the required disclosure;

(b)   he is a professional legal adviser or other relevant professional adviser, and

(i)   if he knows either of the things mentioned in subsection (5)(a) and (b), he knows the thing because of information or other matter that came to him in privileged circumstances, or

(ii)   the information or other matter mentioned in subsection (3) came to him in privileged circumstances, or

(c)   subsection (7) or (7B) applies to him.

(7)   This subsection applies to a person if:

(a)   he does not know or suspect that another person is engaged in money laundering; and

(b)   he has not been provided by his employer with such training as is specified by the Secretary of State by order for the purposes of this section.

(7A)   Nor does a person commit an offence under this section if—

(a)   he knows, or believes on reasonable grounds, that the money laundering is occurring in a particular country or territory outside the United Kingdom, and

(b)   the money laundering—

(i)   is not unlawful under the criminal law applying in that country or territory, and

(ii)   is not of a description prescribed in an order made by the Secretary of State.

(7B)   This subsection applies to a person if—

(a)   he is employed by, or is in partnership with, a professional legal adviser or a relevant professional adviser to provide the adviser with assistance or support,

(b)   the information or other matter mentioned in subsection (3) comes to the person in connection with the provision of such assistance or support, and

(c)   the information or other matter came to the adviser in privileged circumstances.

(8)   In deciding whether a person committed an offence under this section the court must consider whether he followed any relevant guidance which was at the time concerned:

(a)   issued by a supervisory authority or an appropriate body;

(b)   approved by the Treasury; and

(c)   published in a manner it approved as appropriate in its opinion to bring the guidance to the attention of persons likely to be affected by it.

(9)   Disclosure to a nominated officer is a disclosure which—

(a)   is made to a person nominated by the alleged offender's employer to receive disclosures under this section; and

(b)   is made in the course of the alleged offender's employment.

(9A)   But a disclosure which satisfies paragraphs (a) and (b) of subsection (9) is not to be taken as a disclosure to a nominated officer if the person making the disclosure—

(a)   is a professional legal adviser or other relevant professional adviser,

(b)   makes it for the purpose of obtaining advice about making a disclosure under this section, and

(c)   does not intend it to be a disclosure under this section.

(10)   Information or other matter comes to a professional legal adviser or other relevant professional adviser in privileged circumstances if it is communicated or given to him:

(a)   by (or by a representative of) a client of his in connection with the giving by the adviser of legal advice to the client;

(b)   by (or by a representative of) a person seeking legal advice from the adviser; or

(c)   by a person in connection with legal proceedings or contemplated legal proceedings.

(11)   But subsection (10) does not apply to information or other matter which is communicated or given with the intention of furthering a criminal purpose.

(12)   Schedule 9 has effect for the purpose of determining what is—

(a)   a business in the regulated sector;

(b)   a supervisory authority.

(13)   An appropriate body is any body which regulates or is representative of any trade, profession, business or employment carried on by the alleged offender.

(14)   A relevant professional adviser is an accountant, auditor or tax adviser who is a member of a professional body which is established for accountants, auditors or tax advisers (as the case may be) and which makes provision for—

(a)   testing the competence of those seeking admission to membership of such a body as a condition for such admission; and

(b)   imposing and maintaining professional and ethical standards for its members, as well as imposing sanctions for non-compliance with those standards

331.   Failure to disclose: nominated officers in the regulated sector

(1)   A person nominated to receive disclosures under section 330 commits an offence if the conditions in subsections (2) to (4) are satisfied—

(2)   The first condition is that he—

(a)   knows or suspects; or

(b)   has reasonable grounds for knowing or suspecting,

that another person is engaged in money laundering.

(3)   The second condition is that the information or other matter—

(a)   on which his knowledge or suspicion is based; or

(b)   which gives reasonable grounds for such knowledge or suspicion,

came to him in consequence of a disclosure made under section 330.

(3A)   The third condition is—

(a)   that he knows the identity of the other person mentioned in subsection (2), or the whereabouts of any of the laundered property, in consequence of a disclosure made under section 330,

(b)   that that other person, or the whereabouts of any of the laundered property, can be identified from the information or other matter mentioned in subsection (3), or

(c)   that he believes, or it is reasonable to expect him to believe, that the information or other matter will or may assist in identifying that other person or the whereabouts of any of the laundered property.

(4)   The fourth condition is that he does not make the required disclosure to a person authorised for the purposes of this Part by the Director General of the Serious Organised Crime Agency as soon as is practicable after the information or other matter mentioned in subsection (3) comes to him.

(5)   The required disclosure is a disclosure of—

(a)   the identity of the other person mentioned in subsection (2), if disclosed to him under section 330,

(b)   the whereabouts of the laundered property, so far as disclosed to him under section 330, and

(c)   the information or other matter mentioned in subsection (3).

(5A)   The laundered property is the property forming the subject-matter of the money laundering that he knows or suspects, or has reasonable grounds for knowing or suspecting, that other person to be engaged in.

(6)   But he does not commit an offence under this section if he has a reasonable excuse for not making the required disclosure.

(6A)   Nor does a person commit an offence under this section if—

(a)   he knows, or believes on reasonable grounds, that the money laundering is occurring in a particular country or territory outside the United Kingdom, and

(b)   the money laundering—

(i)   is not unlawful under the criminal law applying in that country or territory, and

(ii)   is not of a description prescribed in an order made by the Secretary of State.

(7)   In deciding whether a person committed an offence under this section the court must consider whether he followed any relevant guidance which was at the time concerned:

(a)   issued by a supervisory authority or any other appropriate body;

(b)   approved by the Treasury; and

(c)   published in a manner it approved as appropriate in its opinion to bring the guidance to the attention of the persons likely to be affected by it.

(8)   Schedule 9 has effect for the purpose of determining what is a supervisory authority.

(9)   An appropriate body is a body which regulates or is representative of a trade, profession, business or employment.

332.   Failure to disclose: other nominated officers

(1)   A person nominated to receive disclosures under section 337 or 338 commits an offence if the conditions in subsections (2) to (4) are satisfied.

(2)   The first condition is that he knows or suspects that another person is engaged in money laundering.

(3)   The second condition is that the information or other matter on which his knowledge or suspicion is based came to him in consequence of a disclosure made under the applicable section.

(3A)   The third condition is—

   (a)   that he knows the identity of the other person mentioned in subsection (2), or the whereabouts of any of the laundered property, in consequence of a disclosure made under the applicable section,

   (b)   that that other person, or the whereabouts of any of the laundered property, can be identified from the information or other matter mentioned in subsection (3), or

   (c)   that he believes, or it is reasonable to expect him to believe, that the information or other matter will or may assist in identifying that other person or the whereabouts of any of the laundered property.

(4)   The fourth condition is that he does not make the required disclosure to a person authorised for the purposes of this Part by the Director General of the Serious Organised Crime Agency as soon as is practicable after the information or other mater mentioned in subsection (3) comes to him.

(5)   The required disclosure is a disclosure of—

   (a)   the identity of the other person mentioned in subsection (2), if disclosed to him under the applicable section;

   (b)   the whereabouts of the laundered property, so far as disclosed to him under the applicable section; and

   (c)   the information or other matter mentioned in subsection (3).

(5A)   The laundered property is the property forming the subject-matter of the money laundering that he knows or suspects that other person to be engaged in.

(5B)   The applicable section in section 337 or, as the case may be, section 338.

(6)   But he does not commit an offence under this section if he has a reasonable excuse for not making the required disclosure.

(7)   Nor does a person commit an offence under this section if—

   (a)   he knows, or believes on reasonable grounds, that the money laundering is occurring in a particular country or territory outside the United Kingdom, and

   (b)   the money laundering—

      (i)   is not unlawful under the criminal law applying in that country or territory, and

      (ii) is not of a description prescribed in an order made by the Secretary of State.

333A.   Tipping off: regulated sector

(1)   A person commits an offence if—

   (a)   the person discloses any matter within subsection (2);

   (b)   the disclosure is likely to prejudice any investigation that might be conducted following the disclosure referred to in that subsection; and

   (c)   the information on which the disclosure is based came to the person in the course of a business in the regulated sector.

(2)   The matters are that the person or another person has made a disclosure under this Part—

   (a)   to a constable,

   (b)   to an officer of Revenue and Customs,

(c)   to a nominated officer, or

(d)   to a member of staff of the Serious Organised Crime Agency authorised for the purposes of this Part by the Director General of that Agency, of information that came to that person in the course of a business in the regulated sector.

(3)   A person commits an offence if—

(a)   the person discloses that an investigation into allegations that an offence under this Part has been committed is being contemplated or is being carried out;

(b)   the disclosure is likely to prejudice that investigation; and

(c)   the information on which the disclosure is based came to the person in the course of a business in the regulated sector.

(4)   A person guilty of an offence under this section is liable—

(a)   on summary conviction to imprisonment for a term not exceeding three months, or to a fine not exceeding level 5 on the standard scale, or to both;

(b)   on conviction on indictment to imprisonment for a term not exceeding two years, or to a fine, or to both.

(5)   This section is subject to—

(a)   section 333B (disclosures within an undertaking or group etc),

(b)   section 333C (other permitted disclosures between institutions etc), and

(c)   section 333D (other permitted disclosures etc).

333B.   Disclosures within an undertaking or group etc

(1)   An employee, officer or partner of an undertaking does not commit an offence under section 333A if the disclosure is to an employee, officer or partner of the same undertaking.

(2)   A person does not commit an offence under section 333A in respect of a disclosure by a credit institution or a financial institution if—

(a)   the disclosure is to a credit institution or a financial institution,

(b)   the institution to whom the disclosure is made is situated in an EEA State or in a country or territory imposing equivalent money laundering requirements, and

(c)   both the institution making the disclosure and the institution to whom it is made belong to the same group.

(3)   In subsection (2) 'group' has the same meaning as in Directive 2002/87/EC of the European Parliament and of the Council of 16th December 2002 on the supplementary supervision of credit institutions, insurance undertakings and investment firms in a financial conglomerate.

(4)   A professional legal adviser or a relevant professional adviser does not commit an offence under section 333A if—

(a)   the disclosure is to professional legal adviser or a relevant professional adviser,

(b)   both the person making the disclosure and the person to whom it is made carry on business in an EEA State or in a country or territory imposing equivalent money laundering requirements, and

(c)   those persons perform their professional activities within different undertakings that share common ownership, management or control.

333C. Other permitted disclosures between institutions etc

(1) This section applies to a disclosure—

    (a) by a credit institution to another credit institution,

    (b) by a financial institution to another financial institution,

    (c) by a professional legal adviser to another professional legal adviser, or

    (d) by a relevant professional adviser of a particular kind to another relevant professional adviser of the same kind.

(2) A person does not commit an offence under section 333A in respect of a disclosure to which this section applies if—

    (a) the disclosure relates to—

        (i) a client or former client of the institution or adviser making the disclosure and the institution or adviser to whom it is made,

        (ii) a transaction involving them both, or

        (iii) the provision of a service involving them both;

    (b) the disclosure is for the purpose only of preventing an offence under this Part of this Act;

    (c) the institution or adviser to whom the disclosure is made is situated in an EEA State or in a country or territory imposing equivalent money laundering requirements; and

    (d) the institution or adviser making the disclosure and the institution or adviser to whom it is made are subject to equivalent duties of professional confidentiality and the protection of personal data (within the meaning of section 1 of the Data Protection Act 1998).

333D. Other permitted disclosures etc

(1) A person does not commit an offence under section 333A if the disclosure is—

    (a) to the authority that is the supervisory authority for that person by virtue of the Money Laundering Regulations 2007; or

    (b) for the purpose of—

        (i) the detection, investigation or prosecution of a criminal offence (whether in the United Kingdom or elsewhere),

        (ii) an investigation under this Act, or

        (iii) the enforcement of any order of a court under this Act.

(2) A professional legal adviser or a relevant professional adviser does not commit an offence under section 333A if the disclosure—

    (a) is to the adviser's client, and

    (b) is made for the purpose of dissuading the client from engaging in conduct amounting to an offence.

(3) A person does not commit an offence under section 333A(1) if the person does not know or suspect that the disclosure is likely to have the effect mentioned in section 333A(1)(b).

(4) A person does not commit an offence under section 333A(3) if the person does not know or suspect that the disclosure is likely to have the effect mentioned in section 333A(3)(b).

333E. Interpretation of sections 333A to 333D

(1) For the purposes of sections 333A to 333D, Schedule 9 has effect for determining—

(a)   what is a business in the regulated sector, and

(b)   what is a supervisory authority.

(2)   In those sections—

'credit institution' has the same meaning as in Schedule 9;

'financial institution' means an undertaking that carries on a business in the regulated sector by virtue of any of paragraphs (b) to (i) of paragraph 1(1) of that Schedule.

(3)   References in those sections to a disclosure by or to a credit institution or a financial institution include disclosure by or to an employee, officer or partner of the institution acting on its behalf.

(4)   For the purposes of those sections a country or territory imposes 'equivalent money laundering requirements' if it imposes requirements equivalent to those laid down in Directive 2005/60/EC of the European Parliament and of the Council of 26th October 2005 on the prevention of the use of the financial system for the purpose of money laundering and terrorist financing.

(5)   In those sections 'relevant professional adviser' means an accountant, auditor or tax adviser who is a member of a professional body which is established for accountants, auditors or tax advisers (as the case may be) and which makes provision for—

(a)   testing the competence of those seeking admission to membership of such a body as a condition for such admission; and

(b)   imposing and maintaining professional and ethical standards for its members, as well as imposing sanctions for non-compliance with those standards.

334.   Penalties

(1)   A person guilty of an offence under section 327, 328 or 329 is liable—

(a)   on summary conviction, to imprisonment for a term not exceeding six months or to a fine not exceeding the statutory maximum or to both; or

(b)   on conviction on indictment, to imprisonment for a term not exceeding 14 years or to a fine or to both.

(2)   A person guilty of an offence under section 330, 331 or 332 is liable:

(a)   on summary conviction, to imprisonment for a term not exceeding six months or to a fine not exceeding the statutory maximum or to both; or

(b)   on conviction on indictment, to imprisonment for a term not exceeding five years or to a fine or to both.

(3)   A person guilty of an offence under section 339(1A) is liable on summary conviction to a fine not exceeding level 5 on the standard scale.

CONSENT

335.   Appropriate consent

(1)   The appropriate consent is—

(a)   the consent of a nominated officer to do a prohibited act if an authorised disclosure is made to the nominated officer;

(b)   the consent of a constable to do a prohibited act if an authorised disclosure is made to a constable;

(c)   the consent of a customs officer to do a prohibited act if an authorised disclosure is made to a customs officer.

(2)   A person must be treated as having the appropriate consent if—

(a)   he makes an authorised disclosure to a constable or a customs officer, and

(b)   the condition in subsection (3) or the condition in subsection (4) is satisfied.

(3)   The condition is that before the end of the notice period he does not receive notice from a constable or customs officer that consent to the doing of the act is refused.

(4)   The condition is that—

(a)   before the end of the notice period he receives notice from a constable or customs officer that consent to the doing of the act is refused; and

(b)   the moratorium period has expired.

(5)   The notice period is the period of seven working days starting with the first working day after the person makes the disclosure.

(6)   The moratorium period is the period of 31 days starting with the day on which the person receives notice that consent to the doing of the act is refused.

(7)   A working day is a day other than a Saturday, a Sunday, Christmas Day, Good Friday or a day which is a bank holiday under the Banking and Financial Dealings Act 1971 in the part of the United Kingdom in which the person is when he makes the disclosure.

(8)   References to a prohibited act are to an act mentioned in section 327(1), 328(1) or 329(1) (as the case may be).

(9)   A nominated officer is a person nominated to receive disclosures under section 338.

(10)   Subsections (1) to (4) apply for the purposes of this Part.

336.   Nominated officer: consent

(1)   A nominated officer must not give the appropriate consent to the doing of a prohibited act unless the condition in subsection (2), the condition in subsection (3) or the condition in subsection (4) is satisfied.

(2)   The condition is that—

(a)   he makes a disclosure that property is criminal property to a person authorised for the purposes of this Part by the Director General of the Serious Organised Crime Agency, and

(b)   such a person gives consent to the doing of the act.

(3)   The condition is that—

(a)   he makes a disclosure that property is criminal property to a person authorised for the purposes of this Part by the Director General of the Serious Organised Crime Agency, and

(b)   before the end of the notice period he does not receive notice from such a person that consent to the doing of the act is refused.

(4)   The condition is that—

(a)   he makes a disclosure that property is criminal property to a person authorised for the purposes of this Part by the Director General of the Serious Organised Crime Agency,

(b)   before the end of the notice period he receives notice from such a person that consent to the doing of the act is refused, and

(c) the moratorium period has expired.

(5) A person who is a nominated officer commits an offence if—

    (a) he gives consent to a prohibited act in circumstances where none of the conditions in subsections (2), (3) and (4) is satisfied, and

    (b) he knows or suspects that the act is a prohibited act.

(6) A person guilty of such an offence is liable—

    (a) on summary conviction, to imprisonment for a term not exceeding six months or to a fine not exceeding the statutory maximum or to both, or

    (b) on conviction on indictment, to imprisonment for a term not exceeding five years or to a fine or to both.

(7) The notice period is the period of seven working days starting with the first working day after the nominated officer makes the disclosure.

(8) The moratorium period is the period of 31 days starting with the day on which the nominated officer is given notice that consent to the doing of the act is refused.

(9) A working day is a day other than a Saturday, a Sunday, Christmas Day, Good Friday or a day which is a bank holiday under the Banking and Financial Dealings Act 1971 in the part of the United Kingdom in which the nominated officer is when he gives the appropriate consent.

(10) References to a prohibited act are to an act mentioned in section 327(1), 328(1) or 329(1) (as the case may be).

(11) A nominated officer is a person nominated to receive disclosures under section 338.

DISCLOSURES

337. Protected disclosures

(1) A disclosure which satisfies the following three conditions is not to be taken to breach any restriction on the disclosure of information (however imposed).

(2) The first condition is that the information or other matter disclosed came to the person making the disclosure (the discloser) in the course of his trade, profession, business or employment.

(3) The second condition is that the information or other matter—

    (a) causes the discloser to know or suspect, or

    (b) gives him reasonable grounds for knowing or suspecting,

that another person is engaged in money laundering.

(4) The third condition is that the disclosure is made to a constable, a customs officer or a nominated officer as soon as is practicable after the information or other matter comes to the discloser.

(4A) Where a disclosure consists of a disclosure protected under subsection (1) and a disclosure of either or both of—

    (a) the identity of the other person mentioned in subsection (3), and

    (b) the whereabouts of property forming the subject-matter of the money laundering that the discloser knows or suspects, or has reasonable grounds for knowing or suspecting, that other person to be engaged in,

the disclosure of the thing mentioned in paragraph (a) or (b) (as well as the disclosure protected under subsection (1)) is not to be taken to breach any restriction on the disclosure of information (however imposed).

(5)   A disclosure to a nominated officer is a disclosure which—

    (a)   is made to a person nominated by the discloser's employer to receive disclosures under section 330 or this section, and

    (b)   is made in the course of the discloser's employment.

338.   Authorised disclosures

(1)   For the purposes of this Part a disclosure is authorised if—

    (a)   it is a disclosure to a constable, a customs officer or a nominated officer by the alleged offender that property is criminal property, . . . and

    (c)   the first, second or third condition set out below is satisfied.

(2)   The first condition is that the disclosure is made before the alleged offender does the prohibited act.

(2A)   The second condition is that—

    (a)   the disclosure is made while the alleged offender is doing the prohibited act,

    (b)   he began to do the act at a time when, because he did not then know or suspect that the property constituted or represented a person's benefit from criminal conduct, the act was not a prohibited act, and

    (c)   the disclosure is made on his own initiative and as soon as is practicable after he first knows or suspects that the property constitutes or represents a person's benefit from criminal conduct.

(3)   The third condition is that—

    (a)   the disclosure is made after the alleged offender does the prohibited act,

    (b)   he has a reasonable excuse for his failure to make the disclosure before he did the act, and

    (c)   the disclosure is made on his own initiative and as soon as it is practicable for him to make it.

(4)   An authorised disclosure is not to be taken to breach any restriction on the disclosure of information (however imposed).

(5)   A disclosure to a nominated officer is a disclosure which—

    (a)   is made to a person nominated by the alleged offender's employer to receive authorised disclosures, and

    (b)   is made in the course of the alleged offender's employment.

(6)   References to the prohibited act are to an act mentioned in section 327(1), 328(1) or 329(1) (as the case may be).

339.   Form and manner of disclosures

(1)   The Secretary of State may by order prescribe the form and manner in which a disclosure under section 330, 331, 332 or 338 must be made.

(1A)   A person commits an offence if he makes a disclosure under section 330, 331, 332 or 338 otherwise that in the form prescribed under subsection (1) or otherwise than in the manner so prescribed.

(1B)   But a person does not commit an offence under subsection (1A) if he has a reasonable excuse for making the disclosure otherwise than in the form prescribed under subsection (1) or (as the case may be) otherwise than in the manner so prescribed.

(2)   The power under subsection (1) to prescribe the form in which a disclosure must be made includes power to provide for the form to include a request to

a person making a disclosure that the person provide information specified or described in the form if he has not provided it in making the disclosure.

(3)   Where under subsection (2) a request is included in a form prescribed under subsection (1), the form must—

(a)   state that there is no obligation to comply with the request, and

(b)   explain the protection conferred by subsection (4) on a person who complies with the request.

(4)   A disclosure made in pursuance of a request under subsection (2) is not to be taken to breach any restriction on the disclosure of information (however imposed).

(5)   . . .

(6)   . . .

(7)   Subsection (2) does not apply to a disclosure made to a nominated officer.

339ZA.   Disclosures to SOCA

Where a disclosure is made under this Part to a constable or an officer of Revenue and Customs, the constable or officer of Revenue and Customs must disclose it in full to a person authorised for the purposes of this Part by the Director General of the Serious Organised Crime Agency a soon as practicable after it has been made.

339A.   Threshold amounts

(1)   This section applies for the purposes of sections 327(2C), 328(5) and 329(2C).

(2)   The threshold amount for acts done by a deposit-taking body in operating an account is £250 unless a higher amount is specified under the following provisions of this section (in which event it is that higher amount).

(3)   An officer of Revenue and Customs, or a constable, may specify the threshold amount for acts done by a deposit-taking body in operating an account—

(a)   when he gives consent, or gives notice refusing consent, to the deposit-taking body's doing of an act mentioned in section 327(1), 328(1) or 329(1) in opening, or operating, the account or a related account; or

(b)   on a request from the deposit-taking body.

(4)   Where the threshold amount for acts done in operating an account is specified under subsection (3) or this subsection, an officer of Revenue and Customs, or a constable, may vary the amount (whether on a request from the deposit-taking body or otherwise) by specifying a different amount.

(5)   Different threshold amounts may be specified under subsections (3) and (4) for different acts done in operating the same account.

(6)   The amount specified under subsection (3) and (4) as the threshold amount for acts done in operating an account must, when specified, not be less than the amount specified in subsection (2).

(7)   The Secretary of State may by order vary the amount for the time being specified in subsection (2).

(8)   For the purposes of this section, an account is related to another if each is maintained with the same deposit-taking body and there is a person who, in relation to each account, is the person or one of the persons entitled to instruct the body as respects the operation of the account.

INTERPRETATION

340. **Interpretation**

(1) This section applies for the purposes of this Part.

(2) Criminal conduct is conduct which—

   (a) constitutes an offence in any part of the United Kingdom, or

   (b) would constitute an offence in any part of the United Kingdom if it occurred there.

(3) Property is criminal property if—

   (a) it constitutes a person's benefit from criminal conduct or it represents such a benefit (in whole or part and whether directly or indirectly), and

   (b) the alleged offender knows or suspects that it constitutes or represents such a benefit.

(4) It is immaterial—

   (a) who carried out the conduct;

   (b) who benefited from it;

   (c) whether the conduct occurred before or after the passing of this Act.

(5) A person benefits from conduct if he obtains property as a result of or in connection with the conduct.

(6) If a person obtains a pecuniary advantage as a result of or in connection with conduct, he is to be taken to obtain as a result of or in connection with the conduct a sum of money equal to the value of the pecuniary advantage.

(7) References to property or a pecuniary advantage obtained in connection with conduct include references to property or a pecuniary advantage obtained in both that connection and some other.

(8) If a person benefits from conduct his benefit is the property obtained as a result of or in connection with the conduct.

(9) Property is all property wherever situated and includes—

   (a) money;

   (b) all forms of property, real or personal, heritable or moveable;

   (c) things in action and other intangible or incorporeal property.

(10) The following rules apply in relation to property—

   (a) property is obtained by a person if he obtains an interest in it;

   (b) references to an interest, in relation to land in England and Wales or Northern Ireland, are to any legal estate or equitable interest or power;

   (c) references to an interest, in relation to land in Scotland, are to any estate, interest, servitude or other heritable right in or over land, including a heritable security;

   (d) references to an interest, in relation to property other than land, include references to a right (including a right to possession).

(11) Money laundering is an act which—

   (a) constitutes an offence under section 327, 328 or 329,

   (b) constitutes an attempt, conspiracy or incitement to commit an offence specified in paragraph (a),

   (c) constitutes aiding, abetting, counselling or procuring the commission of an offence specified in paragraph (a), or

   (d) would constitute an offence specified in paragraph (a), (b) or (c) if done in the United Kingdom.

(12) For the purposes of a disclosure to a nominated officer—

(a)   references to a person's employer include any body, association or organisation (including a voluntary organisation) in connection with whose activities the person exercises a function (whether or not for gain or reward), and

(b)   references to employment must be construed accordingly.

(13)   References to a constable include references to a person authorised for the purposes of this Part by the Director General of the Serious Organised Crime Agency.

(14)   'Deposit-taking body' means—

(a)   a business which engages in the activity of accepting deposits; or

(b)   The National Savings Bank.

Part III
EC LAW

Part III

EC LAW

Chapter 19

Sources of EC Law

19.1 Introduction

The time has passed when EC law could be seen as an area for specialists only. Every solicitor now needs to appreciate the potential application of EC law to a wide variety of work.

The Treaty on European Union (the 'Maastricht Treaty') took the EC into a new stage of development, with more ambitious objectives, in order, in the words of the preamble to the Treaty, 'to continue the process of creating an ever closer union among the peoples of Europe'.

The European Union is founded on the European Community and, according to Article 3 (formerly C) of the Maastricht Treaty, the Union is to be served by a single institutional framework which is that of the Community. In so far as legislation is passed by the institutions in relation to their EC responsibilities (ie under the Treaty of Rome ('the EC Treaty'), it is still appropriate to refer to that as EC law. In the following chapters, the term 'EC law' is used throughout, as only EC law has the characteristics of direct effect and supremacy.

Both the EC Treaty and the Maastricht Treaty were amended by the Treaty of Amsterdam. The most obvious change that this Treaty made was the renumbering of the articles of both the EC and Maastricht Treaties. Where the new numbering is used, it is denoted by the suffix 'EC'. When the pre-Amsterdam numbering is used, it is followed by the words 'of the EC Treaty'. There is a full conversion table at **25.5**.

The sources of EC law are:

(a)   the Treaties;

(b)   Regulations;

(c)   Directives;

(d)   the jurisprudence of the European Court of Justice.

The principal treaty is the EC Treaty (as amended by, eg, the Maastricht and Amsterdam Treaties, and intended to be amended by the Treaty of Lisbon). It states in broad outline the objectives of the European Community.

Regulations and Directives are secondary legislation made under Article 249 EC. How these sources of law become part of English law will be discussed in **Chapter 21**.

Article 249 EC also provides for the making of Decisions, Recommendations and Opinions. Of these, only Decisions are legally binding, and they bind only the person (Member State, company or individual) to whom they are addressed.

The European Court of Justice has been highly influential in developing both substantive areas of EC law (eg, the free movement of goods) and general principles of EC law, such as proportionality.

The Treaty of Nice made several institutional changes, including amendments to voting procedures and, in particular, the removal of the power of veto in several areas. These changes were made with enlargement in mind.

The Treaty of Lisbon was signed by the EU leaders on 13 December 2007, and has an intended ratification date of 1 January 2009. Each country chooses its own procedures for ratification, so whilst some countries are holding referenda, others are ratifying it via their national parliaments. The Treaty is intended to amend the existing Treaties to provide the Union with the legal framework and tools necessary to meet future challenges and respond to citizens' demands.

19.2 The Treaties

19.2.1 The Treaty of Rome 1957

The primary aim of the Treaty of Rome ('the EEC Treaty') was to create a European Economic Community, a common market, for the original six signatories: France, West Germany, Italy, The Netherlands, Belgium and Luxembourg. This common market required not only the abolition of customs duties and quotas for goods passing between the six, but also a recognition on the part of the Member States that their populations had a right to share directly in the benefits of the new system. In particular, the Member States had to recognise the right of workers to move freely throughout the Community, and the right of individuals and companies to set up in business or to provide services throughout the Community.

From its very beginning, it was apparent that the Community was more than a mere free trade zone. One of the stated objectives in the preamble to the Treaty was 'to lay the foundations of an ever closer union among the peoples of Europe'. It is also central to an understanding of the Treaty to remember that it created supra-national institutions, not least the European Court of Justice (see **Chapter 20**). The result was, in the words of the European Court itself in *Van Gend en Loos v Nederlandse Belastingadministratie* [1963] ECR 1, a 'new legal order of international law for the benefit of which the States have limited their sovereign rights, albeit within limited fields, and the subjects of which comprise not only Member States but also their nationals' (see **Chapter 21**).

The most important provisions, as far as the achievement of a common market is concerned, are those dealing with free movement, in particular of goods, persons and services, and competition law. These will be considered at **Chapters 23–26**.

19.2.2 The Merger Treaty 1965

Since the Treaty of Paris 1951, there had existed a European Coal and Steel Community (ECSC), created by the original six signatories of the Treaty of Rome. That Treaty had also established supra-national institutions, including a High Authority, the equivalent of the EC Commission.

In 1957, at the same time as the European Economic Community was established, the same signatories created the European Atomic Energy Community (EurAtom). The European Economic Community and EurAtom shared with the ECSC only the Court and the Assembly set up under the Treaty of Paris. In 1965, the institutions of the three Communities were merged. The Merger Treaty is therefore concerned with their integration within a single organisational structure.

19.2.3 The Accession Treaties

In 1973, the UK, the Republic of Ireland and Denmark joined the Community, followed in 1981 by Greece and in 1986 by Spain and Portugal. Sweden, Finland and Austria joined on 1 January 1995. The European Union welcomed 10 new countries in 2004: Cyprus, the Czech Republic, Estonia, Hungary, Latvia, Lithuania, Malta, Poland, Slovakia and Slovenia. Bulgaria and Romania joined on 1 January 2007, bringing the total number of Member States to 27. Croatia and Turkey began membership negotiations in 2005. No date has yet been set for their accession.

19.2.4 The Single European Act 1986

The Single European Act 1986 saw further significant developments in the Community. It formalised as an objective the completion of the single European market envisaged in the EC Treaty, and set a date for its achievement: 31 December 1992. This required enormous legislative activity by the Community in an attempt to overcome remaining barriers to trade, not least the problem of varying trading standards. In order to make this a manageable task, the Single European Act introduced a streamlined legislative process. When single market measures came to the Council for approval, unanimity was not to be required. Instead, only a qualified majority would be needed (see **Chapter 20**). The Single European Act also extended the areas which would be expressly within the Community's competence, including areas such as the environment and the health and safety of workers.

19.2.5 The European Economic Area Treaty 1992

The effect of the European Economic Area Treaty was to create a 'European Economic Area' (EEA) consisting of the Member States of the EC and the European Free Trade Agreement (EFTA) countries (Sweden, Norway, Finland, Austria and Iceland, but not Switzerland which decided in referendum not to ratify the Treaty). Within this area, EC law relating to free movement and to competition law applies, together with all the related Regulations and Directives. The EEA came into effect on 1 January 1994. However, on 1 January 1995, Sweden, Finland and Austria all joined the European Union, leaving just Norway, Iceland and Liechtenstein as members of the EEA but not of the EU. Switzerland remains in EFTA.

19.2.6 The Treaty on European Union 1992 ('the Maastricht Treaty')

The Treaty on European Union (TEU), signed at Maastricht, came into force on 1 November 1993. It officially renamed the 'EEC' the 'EC' and founded, on the base of the European Community, a European Union. It also renamed the Treaty of Rome the EC Treaty. It made a number of important amendments to the Treaty, in particular:

(a)   the EC undertakes to act in any given area only if Community action is a better means of achieving the desired end than action by the individual

Member States (the principle of subsidiarity) (Article 3b of the EC Treaty (now Article 5 EC));

(b)   every EC national becomes a citizen of the European Union (Article 8 of the EC Treaty (now Article 17 EC));

(c)   the EC now specifically assumes responsibility for developing policies in areas such as public health (Article 129 of the EC Treaty (now Article 152 EC)), consumer protection (Article 129b of the EC Treaty (now Article 154 EC)) and education (Article 126 of the EC Treaty (now Article 149 EC)). These had previously been dealt with primarily as issues affecting free movement;

(d)   the European Parliament is given greater powers (Article 189b of the EC Treaty (now Article 251 EC) (co-decision));

(e)   the Council will take decisions on a qualified majority basis on a wider range of matters, such as consumer protection, using the co-decision procedure in Article 189b of the EC Treaty (now Article 251 EC);

(f)   free movement of capital is clarified by directly applicable rights in Articles 73b–73g of the EC Treaty (now Articles 56–60 EC).

The Maastricht Treaty did not just amend the Treaty of Rome. It also set out Union objectives, the most important being the promotion of economic and social progress to be achieved by economic and monetary union. The Union also agreed to develop a common foreign and security policy, and to cooperate in the fields of justice and home affairs. Importantly, the Union also undertook expressly (in TEU, Article 6.2 (F2)) to respect fundamental rights, as guaranteed by the European Convention for the Protection of Human Rights and Fundamental Freedoms 1950. Previous European Court case law had already shown, however, that Member States must respect human rights law when acting on a Community matter.

Despite the Treaty of European Union, it is nevertheless still correct to talk of EC legislation, since it is only in relation to Community matters that the institutions have powers to create rights with direct effect. The TEU is primarily an instrument for inter-governmental cooperation.

19.2.7   The Amsterdam Treaty

The Amsterdam Treaty entered into force at the beginning of May 1999. The Treaty paved the way for EU enlargement. It also provided for greater cooperation in employment matters and for incentive measures to help boost employment. It incorporated into the EC the TEU Social Chapter, which means that all Member States are bound by its provisions. The Treaty also established a new section on freedom, security and justice, which brings some areas into the framework of the EC Treaty from the 'third pillar' (Justice and Home Affairs) of the Maastricht Treaty. It also strengthened provisions relating to environmental protection. There was a strengthening of public health and consumer protection, and the principle of subsidiarity was clarified. Lastly, there was an increase in the number of matters to be decided under qualified majority rules and a substantial increase in the use of the co-decision procedure (see **20.4.2**). In the TEU, there is a revised section on common foreign and security policy.

19.2.8   The Treaty of Nice

The Treaty of Nice came into force on 1 February 2003 and made changes to the Institutions of the Community with a view to accommodating enlargement. In particular it reduced the number of decisions where a power of veto may be used in the Council. This was felt necessary due to its being less likely that unanimous agreement might be reached with an increased number of countries. In addition, a change was made in the weighting of the votes which each country has in Council meetings. The Treaty also made numerical changes to the Parliament and the Commission, with each Member State having only one Commissioner each.

19.2.9 The Treaty of Lisbon

The Treaty of Lisbon (intended ratification date 1 January 2009) brings to an end several years of negotiation about institutional issues. The Treaty of Lisbon amends the current EU and EC Treaties, without replacing them. Its main highlights include:

(a)   a strengthened role for the European Parliament, which will see important new powers emerge over EU legislation, the EU budget and international agreements. In particular, the increase of co-decision procedure in policy-making will ensure the European Parliament is placed on an equal footing with the Council, representing Member States, for the vast bulk of EU legislation;

(b)   effective and efficient decision-making. Qualified majority voting in the Council will be extended to new policy areas to make decision-making faster and more efficient. From 2014 on, the calculation of qualified majority will be based on the double majority of Member States and people, thus representing the dual legitimacy of the Union. A double majority will be achieved when a decision is taken by 55% of the Member States representing at least 65% of the Union's population.

19.3 Regulations

Article 249 EC envisages that secondary legislation is needed to put its broad objectives into effect. It provides that the Council and the Commission 'shall, in accordance with the provisions of this Treaty make Regulations ...'. It goes on to state that a Regulation shall have general application (ie, it will apply throughout the EU in exactly the terms in which it is made). Further, Article 249 EC states that a Regulation shall be directly applicable in all Member States, ie no Member State need pass any implementing measure to make the contents of the Regulation form part of its own national law, except in the unusual situation when the Regulation itself expressly requires the Member State to do so. In fact, according to the European Court in *Variola sPA v Amministrazione Italiana della Finanze* [1973] ECR 981, it would ordinarily be wrong for a Member State to disguise the EC origin of the measure by introducing national legislation to enact it.

Many important EC legal measures have taken the form of Regulations, for example, Regulation 1612/68, which sought to make a reality of the free movement of workers provisions in the Treaty, and the Merger Regulation, Regulation 4064/89, under which big multi-national mergers are vetted by the EC Commission for their effect on competition.

19.4 Directives

Article 249 EC also gives the Council and the Commission power to issue Directives. It is clear from that Article, however, that their legal effect is quite different from that of Regulations. A Directive is stated to be 'binding, as to the result to be achieved, upon each Member State to which it is addressed, but shall leave to the national authorities the choice of form and methods'. Unlike Regulations, Directives therefore do need a response from each Member State.

Unless the national law of the Member State already achieves the objective of the Directive, the Member State must implement it within the specified time-limit. The form of implementing measure may vary from State to State, as may the precise words used to give effect to the Directive. This means that, unlike Regulations, Directives are not of general application throughout the EC in the terms in which they are drafted. Typical UK implementing measures are statutes and statutory instruments.

Directives have been issued across a wide range of areas, for example, Directive 76/207, known as the Equal Treatment Directive, the several Company Law Directives, the Environmental Protection Directive (85/337) and the Product Liability Directive (85/374). In order to bring the Single Market into being, the Commission drafted over 200 separate Directives.

19.5   The jurisprudence of the European Court

The fundamental principles of EC law found in the EC Treaty are set out in outline only, so the European Court has inevitably played a leading role in developing EC law. The Court has not been reluctant to assume this role and has made a major contribution to the evolution of the EC. By interpreting the Treaty and secondary legislation according to the overall purposes of the EC, the Court has often pushed governments further than they might have initially intended to go.

Judgments of the Court are now vital to an understanding of the freedoms upon which the EC is based and to the principles of competition law (another major field of EC activity). In addition, the Court has developed certain general principles of EC law, of which the most important are proportionality (see **Chapter 25**), legal certainty and respect for fundamental rights (see **Chapter 27**). As far as the latter is concerned, the Court's approach can be seen in *Nold (J) KG v EC Commission* [1974] ECR 491, where it stated that fundamental rights, derived from the constitutional traditions common to the Member States and from the international treaties to which they are signatories (in particular, the European Convention on Human Rights), form an integral part of the general principles of EC law.

In applying 'legal certainty' the Court has sometimes ruled that its more surprising interpretations of the Treaty should be non-retrospective, for example in *Defrenne (Gabrielle) v SABENA* [1976] ECR 455 and *Barber v Guardian Royal Exchange Assurance Group* [1991] 1 QB 344 (see **21.3.1**) where direct claims for equal pay and equal pensions were allowed under Article 141 EC. To have held otherwise would have had serious financial consequences in the Member States. Ordinarily, Court judgments are retrospective, ie they go back to the date of the original legislation that the Court is interpreting.

19.6   Other EC measures

Apart from the measures already indicated, there exist two other EC measures which have only limited legal effect under Article 249 EC.

Decisions are binding only on the parties to whom the Decisions are addressed (Article 249 EC). The best examples are Commission Decisions under the competition rules in Articles 81 EC and 82 EC. Their Decisions that an agreement or conduct infringes Article 81 EC or 82 EC, that an exemption should be given under Article 81(3) EC, or that fines be imposed are all subject to review by the Court of First Instance (CFI). Subject to this, they bind the parties and must be given effect by national courts. Thus, a Decision that an agreement is exempt will (subject to review) validate the agreement before a national court.

The least effective measure of all is a Council Recommendation. This is certainly not legally binding and cannot create any Community rights, but is still worth referring to as 'persuasive opinion' on a particular issue. A good example is the Code of Practice on Sexual Harassment set out at [1992] OJ L49/1. This can be referred to for guidance to determine whether employers who have allowed such conduct are guilty of sex discrimination under the Sex Discrimination Act 1975 (see *Wadman v Carpenter Farrer Partnership* [1993] 3 CMLR 93 (EAT)).

19.7 Conclusion

If a client has a problem which has an EC dimension, this could be because it clearly raises questions of substantive EC law, perhaps in relation to one of the freedoms such as free movement of goods or workers. In this case, a solicitor must, of course, pay careful attention to the EC Treaty itself. It will often be necessary to look at the secondary legislation which supplements that particular area of the Treaty, as well as at decided cases on the subject.

On the other hand, a client's problem may have an EC aspect because of the ever-increasing pervasiveness of EC law: for example, a business client may be concerned about the significance of the recent Directives on workplace safety. In this case, a detailed consideration of the relevant legislation will be vital, including an appreciation of how it can interact with relevant domestic law (see further **Chapter 21**).

For information as to how to research a problem of EC law and how to use the possible sources, see Chapter 7 of *Skills for Lawyers*.

19.8 Overview of the EC Treaty

(1)   To create the common (single) market, it guarantees four freedoms:
  (a)   free movement of goods (Articles 28–30 EC);
  (b)   free movement of services (Article 49 EC);
  (c)   free movement of persons, ie workers (Article 39 EC) and firms (Article 43 EC – right of establishment);
  (d)   free movement of capital (Article 56–60 EC).

(2)   To create the customs union, it imposes a common external tariff and prohibits internal custom duties (Article 25 EC).

(3)   To prevent distortion in the market, it:
  (a)   prohibits anti-competitive practices by undertakings (Articles 81 EC, 82 EC);
  (b)   prohibits discrimination against EC nationals, both generally (Article 12 EC) and under particular Articles (eg, on free movement), or through indirect taxes (Article 90 EC);
  (c)   guarantees equal pay between men and women (Article 141 EC).

(4)   To provide a framework for future integration, it enables the Council of Ministers to make legislation (ie, Directives or Regulations).

(5)   Most legislation is passed by qualified majority vote, for example:
  (a)   single market measures;
  (b)   health and safety at work measures (Article 138 EC).

(6)   Some legislation needs unanimity (ie, can be vetoed), for example:

(a)   some aspects of social security and employment measures (Article 137(3) EC);

(b)   tax measures (Article 95(2) EC);

(c)   some aspects of immigration measures (Article 95(2) EC).

Chapter 20

The Institutions

20.1 Introduction

The Treaty of Rome established the following institutions of the Community:

(a)   the Council (Articles 145–154 of the EC Treaty (now Articles 202–210 EC));

(b)   the Commission (Articles 155–163 of the EC Treaty (now Articles 211–219 EC));

(c)   the Parliament (originally known as the 'Assembly') (Articles 137–144 of the EC Treaty (now Articles 189–201 EC));

(d)   the Court (Articles 164–188 of the EC Treaty (now Articles 220–245)).

The Single European Act renamed the Assembly the European Parliament and created the Court of First Instance. The Treaty on European Union made the already existing Court of Auditors into a fifth institution. Although they do not have the status of institutions, mention will be made below of the Committee of Permanent Representatives (COREPER), the Economic and Social Council and the Committee of the Regions (see **20.8–20.10**). There will also be a brief explanation of how EC law is made.

20.2 The Council

20.2.1 What is its membership?

The Council consists of one government representative from each Member State. The representative need not be the same person at every Council meeting: it depends on the matters on the agenda at that particular meeting. If, for example, the Council were discussing the environment, the representatives would be the ministers responsible for the environment. When the representative is the Head of State or government, the Council is referred to as the 'European Council'.

Each Member State takes it in turn to be the President of the Council; the Presidency rotates every six months. The European Council is required to meet at least twice a year.

20.2.2   What is its role?

The Treaty of Rome gave the Council responsibility for ensuring that the Treaty's objectives were attained. The Council ensures the co-ordination of policies and, above all, takes decisions within the Community. This means that it is the Council rather than the Commission which is responsible for the final decision as to whether a Regulation should be made or a Directive should be issued, although the Commission does have some decision-making powers (see **20.3**).

20.2.3   How does it take decisions?

Although the Treaty of Rome envisaged that the Council would normally take decisions on a simple or qualified majority basis, it became clear that, in practice, unanimity would be required. This practice, though, was modified by the Single European Act. In order to facilitate the establishment of the Single Market, the Act provided that, on most matters relating to the internal market, a qualified majority of votes would suffice to pass a particular measure. The Treaty of Nice has extended qualified majority voting to 30 areas which previously required unanimity. Under this voting system, each Member State is allocated a certain number of votes, dependent on its size. In order to pass a qualified majority vote, 255 votes out of 345 (73.9%) are needed (thus 91 are required to block). In addition, in order to pass a qualified majority vote, a Member State may ask for confirmation that 62% of the population of the EU lives in Member States voting in favour. Under this new system, Germany, the UK, France and Italy each have 29 votes, Spain 27, The Netherlands 13, Belgium, Portugal and Greece 12, Sweden and Austria 10, Denmark, Ireland and Finland 7, and Luxembourg 4. New Member States have: Poland 27, Romania 14, Czech Republic and Hungary 12, Bulgaria 10, Slovakia and Lithuania 7, Slovenia, Latvia, Estonia and Cyprus 4, and Malta 3.

20.3   The Commission

20.3.1   What is its membership?

There are 27 EC Commissioners, one from each Member State, each of whom is responsible for a particular area of Community competence. The Commission is divided into 23 Directorates-General which are responsible for such matters as the environment (Directorate-General XI) and competition law (Directorate-General IV). The Commissioners are appointed by the Member States, but once appointed they must be independent of national loyalties. They cannot be recalled by their appointing State. They hold office for a fixed term of five years, although this is subject to renewal. Each Commissioner's appointment must be approved by all Member States and, since Amsterdam, by the President and by the European Parliament. The President of the Commission is appointed by the Member States after consultation with the European Parliament. The appointment is for a fixed term of two years, although this also is renewable. The Commission is based in Brussels.

20.3.2   What is its role?

The Treaty of Rome required the Commission to pursue infringements of EC law. It can, for example, take action before the European Court against Member States who breach EC law. It is also responsible for enforcing EC competition policy and has the power to exact fines for any breach. Above all, however, the Commission is responsible for initiating EC policy and legislation. It has some delegated powers of law making, particularly in the field of competition law, where (under the authority of an enabling Council Regulation 19/65) it has issued Block Exemption Regulations under Article 81(3) EC (see **Chapter 26**).

20.3.3 How does it reach its decisions?

Within the Commission, decisions are taken on a simple majority basis.

20.4 The Parliament

20.4.1 What is its membership?

There are 785 members of the European Parliament (MEPs), all of whom are directly elected, although the voting systems throughout the Community are not uniform. The number of MEPs which each State has depends on its size; for example, Germany has 99, the UK has 78, The Netherlands has 27 and Luxembourg has 6. The MEPs sit in the Parliament according to their political sympathies (political groups) rather than according to national origin. MEPs are elected for a five-year term. The Parliament holds plenary sessions in Strasbourg for one week per month. Much of its work is, however, done in committees (and plenary sessions) in Brussels. It is organised by an Executive (including a President, ie Speaker) based in Luxembourg.

20.4.2 What is its role?

The Parliament's role was traditionally a consultative one. In a number of areas, the Treaty of Rome provided that once the Commission had initiated a proposal for legislation and the Council had given its preliminary approval to it, the Parliament had to be given an opportunity to comment. It had to respond to the proposal within a reasonable time and the Council had to take its responses into account, although it was not bound by them.

The Single European Act developed the role of the Parliament by introducing a co-operation procedure in certain areas, for example single market legislation. This meant that if the Council did not wish to accept the Parliament's comments, the Parliament had to be given a second opportunity to respond. If it continued to object to the Council's version of the measure, the Council could adopt it in its original form only if it did so unanimously within three months. The Single European Act also increased the number of matters on which the Parliament had to be consulted so as to include most matters relating to the Single Market.

The Treaty on European Union further increased the role of the Parliament. In certain limited areas there is a 'co-decision' procedure (Article 251 EC) which involves the Parliament further in the legislative process. If the Parliament proposes amendments to draft legislation and these amendments are not accepted by the Council, the Parliament can veto the legislation. This procedure applies to measures intended to develop the Single Market.

The Amsterdam and Nice Treaties have greatly extended the areas in which the co-decision procedure is used. They have also streamlined this procedure.

The Parliament has the right to ask questions of the Commission and, in the last resort, it has the power to remove the whole Commission, though not individual Commissioners. (This almost happened at the beginning of 1999. The Commission actually resigned around four weeks after the threat of censure.) The Council, too, must report to the Parliament.

20.5 The Court

20.5.1 What is its membership?

There are currently 27 judges of the European Court (one from each Member State), each of whom must be eligible for appointment to the highest judicial office in the country from which he or she comes. There must be at least one judge from each Member State. Each judge is appointed for six years at a time. Their appointments are staggered, so they do not all retire at once. There is no retirement age for a judge, nor can one be recalled by the Member State which made the appointment. He or she can be removed only by the unanimous resolution of the other judges and Advocates-General. The judges elect one of their number to be President of the Court for a three-year term.

In addition to the judges, there are also eight Advocates-General. Their task is to assist the judges in reaching their decisions. One Advocate-General will be assigned to each case and will hear the evidence and read the papers available to the Court. He will then prepare a reasoned opinion indicating the conclusion to which he would come in that case. The Court is not bound to follow that opinion. When the case is reported, the Advocate-General's opinion is reported, together with the decision of the Court. The Court sits in Luxembourg.

20.5.2 What is its role?

The Treaty of Rome required the Court to ensure that EC law is observed throughout the Community. The three usual ways in which a case may come before it are:

(a)   as a result of a reference by a national court under the Article 234 EC procedure (see **21.7**);

(b)   as a result of an action brought by the Commission against a Member State pursuant to its powers under Article 226 EC;

(c)   as a result of an action brought by one Member State against another under Article 227 EC.

If a Member State fails to comply with a judgment of the European Court, the Treaty on European Union now allows the Court to impose a fine on that Member State.

20.5.3 How are such cases heard?

The European Court usually sits in chambers and consists of three, five or seven judges. In particularly important cases, 13 judges will hear the case. In very rare situations, they can sit as a full court. The procedure is largely by means of written submissions, following a typical civil law (as distinct from common law) pattern. There is very limited scope for oral argument. Barristers and solicitors have a right of audience before the European Court, although if a solicitor wishes to appear in the European Court following an Article 234 EC reference (see **21.7**) he may do so only if he had a right of audience before the court or tribunal which made the reference.

The working language of the court during deliberations is French, although, at hearings, the parties present their arguments in their own language (with simultaneous translation). Each case will have its own official language. One judge (*le juge rapporteur*) puts together a draft judgment synthesising judicial opinions on which the judges then vote.

When the Court has reached a decision, it delivers a single, succinct judgment. No dissenting judgments are delivered.

20.5.4 The nature of EC legal reasoning

The Treaty of Rome was drafted by States which shared a civil law heritage. The original judges of the European Court had been trained in civil law systems which, although they might diverge significantly in their substantive provisions, shared a similar approach to legal reasoning. In particular, such judges were familiar with legislation which provided a framework of principles and which was not intended to be interpreted in an exclusively literal way. They were therefore accustomed to drawing inspiration from the spirit behind legislation. This approach was particularly necessary when interpreting the Treaty of Rome, which is very much a framework treaty. In addition, the early judges of the Court were conscious of the role entrusted to them by the Treaty and the accompanying responsibility to ensure that EC law was a uniform body of legal principles which took effect in the same way throughout the entire Community.

Thus, from a very early stage, it is possible to recognise the purposive (or 'teleological') approach adopted by the European Court. This entailed the Court interpreting the Treaty of Rome, and later subordinate legislation, in accordance with the ethos of the Treaty of Rome. In doing so it had to bear in mind the fundamental freedoms upon which the Community was expressly stated to be based and, in particular, Article 12 EC, which prohibits discrimination on the grounds of nationality.

20.5.5 Precedent

In accordance with the civil law tradition, there is no use of precedent as such in the European Court. However, although the Court is not bound by its own previous decisions, it has tended to develop a body of consistent case law. The European Court may cite earlier cases in its judgment, and the Advocate-General is likely to discuss earlier decisions in his opinion.

Decisions of the European Court are reported in an official set of reports, the *European Court Reports* (ECR). There is also a commercial series of reports called the *Common Market Law Reports* (CMLR). The All England Reports also produce their own EC series cited as [*year*] All ER (EC).

20.6 The Court of First Instance

The Court of First Instance (CFI) was established by the Single European Act because of the heavy work-load faced by the European Court. Many of the cases before the European Court concerned disputes between Community institutions and their employees. These staff cases were assigned to the CFI, as were competition law cases (ie, appeals from Commission decisions banning agreements, imposing fines, etc). As a result of provisions in the Treaty on European Union, the Council has now transferred to the CFI all of the European Court's jurisdiction apart from most Article 234 EC references and cases involving infringement proceedings against Member States. Appeals on points of law lie to the European Court itself. The Treaty of Nice contains provisions for the CFI to share more of the ECJ's workload.

20.7 The Court of Auditors

The Court of Auditors is responsible for auditing the accounts of the Community and its institutions. It has 25 members appointed by the Council.

20.8 The Committee of Permanent Representatives (COREPER)

The Committee of Permanent Representatives (COREPER) was created by the Merger Treaty. It comprises ambassadors of the Member States. They undertake much of the detailed analysis of Commission proposals on behalf of the Council. If COREPER can agree a response to such a proposal, that response will be automatically approved by the Council. Only if there is disagreement at COREPER level will a matter be actively discussed in the Council.

20.9 The Economic and Social Committee (ESC)

The Economic and Social Committee (ESC) is a body which comprises representatives of different sectional interests throughout the Community. There are 344 representatives, for example, of business, of the trade unions and of consumers. The ESC's role is purely consultative.

20.10 The Committee of the Regions

The role of this Committee is purely advisory. It consists of 344 members appointed by the Council.

20.11 EC legislative process

The EC legislative process (somewhat simplified) may be illustrated as follows.

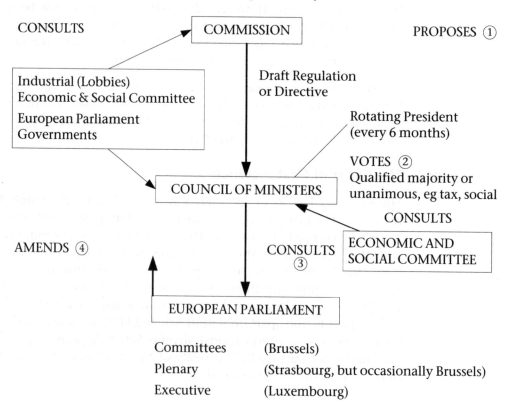

(Matters requiring a qualified majority vote under the co-decision procedure of Article 251 EC may involve amendment or rejection of the 'common position' taken by the Council, by Parliament voting by majority.)

20.12 Overview of the roles of the Commission and Court

20.12.1 Commission's policing role

(a) Ensures Member States' conformity with Treaty rules and implementation of Directives:

    (i)   proceedings to enforce before European Court (Article 226 EC).

(b) Ensures firms' conformity with competition rules (Articles 81, 82 EC):

    (i)   Directorate-General IV investigates;

    (ii)   can by decision ban agreements or practices (or grant exemption);

    (iii)   can fine up to 10% of worldwide turnover.

(c) Ensures that Member States do not distort competition by giving State aids to nationalised industries and other favoured firms. State aids must be notified in advance and approved by the Commission on certain objective criteria (Article 87 EC). Unapproved State aids must be repaid by firms following a Commission decision.

(d) Negotiates trade agreements on behalf of the Community, for example GATT, and investigates firms (eg in the Far East) which 'dump' their products on the EC market at less than the price at home.

20.12.2 European Court of Justice (ECJ Luxembourg)

(a) Hears Commission's complaints against Member States under Article 226 EC.

(b) Hears Member States' complaints against other Member States under Article 227 EC.

(c) Can fine governments which disobey its rulings.

(d) Can hear references under Article 234 EC from national courts asking for a preliminary ruling on interpretation of EC law (eg, Treaty, Regulations, Directives).

(e) Provides no direct access for individual citizens, except in relation to actions against EC institutions under Articles 230 and 288 EC. Most such cases now go to the CFI (see **20.12.3**).

(f) All rulings preceded by opinion of the Advocate-General (usually a guide to how the Court will decide).

(g) Hears appeals from CFI on points of law only.

20.12.3 Court of First Instance (CFI Luxembourg)

(a) Hears judicial review actions under Article 230 EC from decisions of the Commission in competition matters (ie, bans and fines on individual firms).

(b) Hears judicial review actions under Article 230 EC from decisions imposing anti-dumping duties, ie, extra Customs duty imposed on products from outside the EC by a Council Regulation following investigation by the Commission (see **20.12.1**).

20.13 Chapter summary

The four main institutions have the following primary responsibilities:

(1) the Commission develops policy and proposes legislation;

(2)   the Parliament has an advisory role, subject to the limited ability to veto legislation;

(3)   the Council is the decision-making body;

(4)   the Court ensures that the law which emerges from these three institutions is interpreted correctly and consistently.

Chapter 21

The Relationship Between EC Law and National Law

21.1 Introduction

The primary source of EC law is the EC Treaty (as amended). Under English law, international treaties are not automatically part of national law, so, when the UK joined the EC, the Treaty of Rome (as it was then known) had to be incorporated into English law. This was done by the European Communities Act 1972.

However, the interrelationship between the EC and the national legal system is not entirely the product of national statute. If it were, there might be a diversity of approach to EC law in the various Member States. The European Court has instead developed two key concepts:

(a) that EC law can, in certain circumstances, be relied on directly in national proceedings; and

(b) that, when it is utilised, it takes priority over any conflicting national law.

Taken together, these two concepts can give a client a right of action and a remedy which otherwise might not be available under national law.

21.2 EC law and the EC citizen

EC law, as incorporated into English law by the European Communities Act 1972 (ECA 1972), can have two possible effects on the citizen. First, it can have 'direct effect' (see **21.3**), ie it can create rights which can be relied on in national courts directly against the State or another legal person. Secondly, EC law (in particular, Directives) may have 'indirect effect' (see **21.5**) in that courts should comply with EC law when interpreting national legislation.

21.3 The concept of direct effect

In *Van Gend en Loos v Nederlandse Belastingadministratie* [1963] ECR 1 (see **22.2.1**), the European Court recognised the existence of the Community as a 'new legal order'. In that case, an importer of goods from Germany into The Netherlands argued that Article 12 of the EC Treaty (now Article 25 EC), which prohibited any increase in customs tariffs for goods passing from one Member State to another, meant that a reclassification of his products into a higher tariff was unlawful. Consequently, he sought to rely on Article 12 of the EC Treaty (now Article 25 EC) to claim back from the Dutch customs authorities, which had extracted the increased tariff, the money he had paid. The question for the Court was whether the Treaty could be used in that way by an individual citizen of the Community rather than a Member State or the Commission. The European Court held that it could if the provision in question met certain conditions: it would have to be clear, precise and unconditional; and it would have to leave the Member State with no discretion as to how it should be implemented. In other words, if the provision in question is sufficiently clear, precise and unconditional to create an 'enforceable Community right' for the client, as did Article 12 of the EC Treaty (now Article 25 EC), that right can be enforced through the national courts in preference to national law. In *Van Gend en Loos* itself, the Court found that an individual could rely on Article 12 of the EC Treaty directly to recover the extra tax from the government.

21.3.1 Direct effect and the provisions of the EC Treaty

It has now been established that, applying the criteria set out in *Van Gend en Loos*, all the fundamental Treaty provisions have direct effect, in particular:

(a)   Article 30 of the EC Treaty (now Article 28 EC) on free movement of goods (*Ianelli and Volpi sPA v Meroni* [1977] ECR 557);

(b)   Article 48 of the EC Treaty (now Article 39 EC) on free movement of workers (*Van Duyn v Home Office* [1974] ECR 1337);

(c)   Article 52 of the EC Treaty (now Article 43 EC) on freedom of establishment (*Reyners v The Belgian State* [1974] ECR 631);

(d)   Article 59 of the EC Treaty (now Article 49 EC) on freedom to provide services (*Van Binsbergen (JHM) v Bestuur van de Bedrijfsvereniging voor de Metaalnijverheid* [1974] ECR 1299);

(e)   Article 85 of the EC Treaty (now Article 81 EC) on anti-competitive agreements (*Belgische Radio en Televisie v SV SABAM* [1974] ECR 313);

(f)   Article 86 of the EC Treaty (now Article 82 EC) on abuse of a dominant position (*Garden Cottage Foods v Milk Marketing Board* [1984] AC 130); and

(g)   Article 119 of the EC Treaty (now Article 141 EC) on equal pay (*Defrenne (Gabrielle) v SABENA* [1976] ECR 455).

In addition, Articles 6 of the EC Treaty (now Article 12 EC) (discrimination), 73b–73g of the EC Treaty (now Articles 56–60 EC) (capital), 92 of the EC Treaty (now Article 87 EC) (State aids) and 95 of the EC Treaty (now Article 91 EC) (discriminatory indirect taxes on goods) are considered to have direct effect.

21.3.2 Direct effect and Regulations

Regulations are said by Article 249 EC to be 'directly applicable', ie they are part of national law and do not need implementing legislation. They are binding in the form in which they are made. However, they still have to be sufficiently 'clear, precise and unconditional' to create directly effective rights.

21.3.3 Direct effect and Directives

Directives are not of general application throughout the Community but require implementing measures, which are likely to vary from one Member State to another. Despite this, the European Court has held, for example in *Van Duyn v Home Office* (see **21.3.1**), that in appropriate circumstances even Directives may be directly effective. The reason for this is that Article 189 of the EC Treaty (now Article 249 EC) expressly states that a Directive is to be legally binding on the State to which it is addressed; this would be meaningless unless there was some possibility that Directives themselves could be relied on where the Member State failed to implement them. However, in the case of Directives, any rights they contain can have direct effect only after the time-limit for implementing the Directive has elapsed (see, eg, *Pubblico Ministero v Ratti* [1979] ECR 1629). Thereafter, again provided that the rights in the Directive are sufficiently clear, precise and unconditional, they can be relied on *against the State*, even though not implemented in national law.

21.3.4 'Horizontal' direct effect

In the early cases on direct effect, the defending party was always the State or some State agency, such as the customs authorities in *Van Gend en Loos* ('vertical' direct effect). Subsequent cases have shown that a party may rely on a Treaty provision, or even a Regulation (but not a Directive), where the other party is not a State body ('horizontal' direct effect). So, for example, in *Defrenne v SABENA* (see **20.3.1**) the plaintiff relied on Article 119 of the EC Treaty (now Article 141 EC) against a private employer.

Again, Directives are different. A Directive can be used only against a Member State or an 'emanation of the State'. This is clear from *Marshall v Southampton and South West Hampshire Area Health Authority (Teaching)* [1986] ECR 723. The rationale here is that allowing the use of a Directive against a Member State that is in delay encourages it to implement that Directive. A non-State body, on the other hand, has no power to influence the implementation of a Directive. If it is clear that the defendant is the State or a State body, it is also apparent from *Marshall* that it makes no difference whether or not the State is fulfilling a public function in the circumstances which gave rise to the case. In *Marshall*, the defendant health authority had dismissed the female plaintiff because she had reached the age of 62, although a male employee would not have been dismissed until the age of 65. The plaintiff argued that this breached the Equal Treatment Directive. The defendant conceded that it was a State body but argued that, as it was acting purely as an employer of the plaintiff, the Directive could not be relied upon against it. This argument failed before the European Court.

From cases following *Marshall*, it appears that other emanations of the State for this purpose include a police force (*Johnston v Chief Constable of the RUC* [1986] ECR 1651) and a local authority (*Re London Boroughs* [1990] 3 CMLR 495 and *East Riding of Yorkshire County Council v Gibson* [2000] 3 CMLR 329).

The European Court has subsequently given guidance on the meaning of the term 'emanation of the State'. According to *Foster v British Gas* [1990] ECR I-3133, it must be some body (whatever its legal form) which is carrying out a public service under the control of the State, or which has for that purpose special powers. In *Foster*, the English court applied that definition to find that British Gas prior to privatisation was an emanation of the State. On the other hand, it has since been held by the Court of Appeal in *Doughty v Rolls Royce plc* [1992] IRLR 126 that Rolls Royce was not an emanation of the State when it was in public ownership because it was not providing a public service. By contrast, the High Court has recently ruled that even the privatised water boards are sufficiently controlled by State regulators to satisfy the criteria in *Foster* (see *Griffin v South West Water Services Ltd* [1995] IRLR 15). Clearly even the privatised British Gas or British Telecom could be regarded as State bodies if this case is correct.

This distinction between public and non-public bodies inevitably means that some individuals will be protected by the provisions of a Directive while others will not. This is especially evident in the employment field, where employees of the State or State bodies will have an advantage over employees of a private employer. The European Court in *Marshall* pointed out that such unfairness is easily countered by the Member State: it can implement the Directive.

Lastly, it should be remembered that even though enforceable only against the State, a Directive may still have indirect consequences for private persons. In *R v Durham, ex p Huddleston* [2000] 1 WLR 1484, a developer obtained from a planning authority permission to develop a site. An objector argued that the development had not been subjected to an environmental impact assessment as required by Directive 85/337. This had direct effect against the local planning authority (an emanation of the State) which was compelled to reconsider the permission. The effect was financially disastrous for the developer.

21.4 The supremacy of EC law

The European Court, in the seminal case of *Amministrazione delle Finanze dello Stato v Simmenthal* [1978] ECR 629, held that it was fundamental to EC law that EC law should be supreme over the domestic law of the Member States. In this way, EC law would apply uniformly throughout the EC. According to *Simmenthal*, 'every national court must ... accordingly set aside any provision of national law which may conflict with' EC law. The European Court has reinforced that message on numerous occasions. The courts of individual Member States have, from time to time, found the concept of supremacy difficult to accept. After the European Communities Act 1972, the English courts tended to rely upon interpreting English law to comply with EC law as far as possible. In recent years, however, the courts have been increasingly prepared to give effect to the *Simmenthal* doctrine. This can be seen in the case of *R v Secretary of State for Transport, ex p Factortame (No 2)* [1990] 3 WLR 818, in which some Spanish fishermen challenged the Merchant Shipping Act 1988 as being incompatible with EC law. The House of Lords referred the matter to the European Court under the procedure under Article 177 of the EC Treaty (now Article 234 EC) (see **21.7**). In the meantime, the fishermen sought interim relief to suspend the operation of the Act until the European Court replied to the reference. They argued that if the Act continued to operate, their livelihoods would be so seriously affected that the ruling of the European Court might prove to be academic. The House of Lords refused relief, partly because it had no power to suspend the effect of an Act of Parliament, and partly because under English law an interim injunction could not be granted against the Crown. The House of Lords did, however, refer to the European Court a second question: was it right to refuse relief? The European Court responded that, where an individual seeks to rely on EC law, a rule of national procedure cannot be invoked in the national courts which would effectively deny the individual that right. The English court then granted the interim relief (see further **22.4**).

21.5 The concept of indirect effect

It would therefore seem clear that when a national court is confronted by national legislation and directly effective EC legislation which conflict, the court should, under the principle of the supremacy of EC law, apply EC law to the dispute. However, there may be situations in which EC legislation does not have direct effect and a staightforward preference for it cannot be made. This might be the case where a Directive lacks the qualities necessary to give direct effect, as where it is being used against a non-State body.

In such cases, it may be possible to argue that the Directive has indirect effect. The national court is not asked to apply the Directive instead of the national legislation, but is asked to *interpret* the national legislation in the light of the EC Directive.

Accordingly, in *Litster v Forth Dry Dock & Engineering Co Ltd* [1990] 1 AC 546, the House of Lords interpreted the Transfer of Undertakings (Protection of Employment) Regulations 1981 (SI 1981/1794), in the light of Directive 77/187, which the Regulations purported to implement, even though that interpretation was contrary to the meaning on the face of the Regulations. In *Marleasing SA v La Comercial Internacional de Alimentacion SA* [1990] ECR I-4135, the European Court took the concept of 'indirect effect' a stage further by ruling that national law should be interpreted, as far as possible, to give effect to an EC Directive, whether or not the Directive predates the national law. The European Court expressly based the latter decision on Article 5 of the EC Treaty (now Article 10 EC), which requires Member States to take all necessary steps to ensure the fulfilment of their Community obligations. Contrary to its earlier ruling in *Duke v GEC Reliance Ltd (formerly Reliance Systems)* [1988] AC 618, the House of Lords has now conceded that, in interpreting the Sex Discrimination Act 1975, it must take account of the Equal Treatment Directive 76/207 and Court rulings on its interpretation. See *Webb v EMO Air Cargo (UK)* [1994] IRLR 482, where the House of Lords accepted that (from 1978 onwards) they were obliged to interpret the Act in line with the later Directive, even though, in their view, the result was not what Parliament had intended when passing the Act.

21.6 Action against a State for failure to implement a Directive

The European Commission has the responsibility of monitoring the implementation rates of Member States, and it has the power to bring a State in default before the European Court. An individual cannot take this action. However, following *Francovich* and *Bonifacti v Italy* [1992] IRLR 84, an individual can, in appropriate circumstances, sue a State for damages for failure to implement a particular Directive. In that case, Italy had failed to implement Directive 80/987 which would have established a fund available to employees dismissed by insolvent businesses which could not pay them their arrears of salary. Although the Directive was sufficiently precise in the rights it set out to create, these rights were conditional on there being a relevant fund. They were thus not directly effective. However, the European Court gave a right of action against the State itself for non-implementation, relying on Article 5 of the EC Treaty (now Article 10 EC), which requires Member States to take all appropriate measures to ensure the fulfilment of their obligations. The European Court said that a right of action arises where three conditions are met:

(a) the Directive confers rights on individuals;

(b) the content of the rights is identifiable from the Directive;

(c) there is a causal link between the failure to implement and the damage.

This is clearly what we would call in English law a claim in tort.

The action itself would be brought before the relevant national court in accordance with the appropriate national procedure (in England, this would be a High Court action against the Attorney-General). That procedure would have to ensure an effective remedy for the plaintiff.

In *R v Secretary of State for Transport, ex p Factortame (No 4)* [1996] 2 WLR 506, the Court ruled on whether the Spanish fishermen could recover damages for breach of Article 52 of the EC Treaty (now Article 43 EC) for being denied the right to form UK fishing companies (see **22.4–22.5**). The Court introduced a further condition for State liability in this type of case, ie damages are recoverable only where the breach of the Treaty is sufficiently serious, that is where the State manifestly and gravely disregards the limits on its own powers. This extra condition has also been applied in a case of an incorrectly implemented Directive. In *R v HM Treasury, ex p British Telecommunications plc* [1996] All ER (EC) 411, it was held that no damages are recoverable against the State if it has made a reasonable mistake in interpreting the Directive when drafting its implementing legislation. This is a very important case for governments, because the broad principles of EC law do provide plenty of scope for innocent, non-negligent interpretation. This will not, however, excuse governments which rely on negligent advice from their lawyers, as happened in the *Factortame* case. The British Government was eventually required to pay damages; the House of Lords accepting that the law on establishment and discrimination being clear, there was a sufficiently serious breach (*R v Secretary of State for Transport, ex p Factortame (No 5)* [1999] 4 All ER 906, HL).

However, note that the non-implementation of a Directive will still be assessed under the original *Francovich* test, since non-implementation is a sufficiently serious breach in itself (see *Dillenkofer and Others v Germany* [1996] 3 CMLR 469).

21.7　Article 234 EC reference procedure

21.7.1　What is the purpose of this procedure?

The Article 234 EC reference procedure enables the European Court to give a preliminary ruling to a national court principally on the interpretation of the EC Treaty, although it can also rule on the validity of acts of Community institutions. This means that the European Court will not, as such, rule on the compatibility of national law with EC law, or on the application of EC law to particular facts. This is the national court's responsibility. Thus, in *Foster v British Gas* [1990] ECR I-3133 (see **21.3.4**) the European Court explained how an emanation of the State could be recognised, and the English court then applied the definition to British Gas. It may be, however, that in stating the principle, the European Court, in effect, indicates how it must apply to the facts before the national court. The advantage of Article 234 EC is that it provides a mechanism which enables the European Court to ensure that EC law develops along parallel lines throughout the Community.

21.7.2　How does the procedure work?

Article 234 EC distinguishes two situations.

21.7.2.1　Where the case is being heard before a court from which there is no judicial remedy

In this case, the national court must make a reference if it believes that a clarification of the EC point is necessary in order to decide the case. It may not be necessary where the point of EC law is irrelevant to the case, where there is an existing ECJ judgment on the matter, or where the court believes the correct interpretation to be obvious (see *CILFIT Srl v Ministro della Sanitro* [1982] ECR 3415).

A particularly striking example of this is the case involving part-timers (*Equal Opportunities Commission v Secretary of State for Employment* [1994] 1 All ER 910 (HL)). This is another illustration of the point that discrimination, here in relation to pay between men and women (Article 141 EC), always includes unjustifiable indirect discrimination. In this context, paying part-timers less than full-timers means indirectly paying women less than men because most part-timers are women. Thus, the House of Lords ruled that legislation requiring part-timers to work for five years before qualifying for redundancy payments/unfair dismissal compensation (whereas full-timers qualified after two years) was unlawful because it was a breach of equal pay under Article 141 EC. There was no objective reason for the discrimination. The House emphatically rejected Government arguments that it would create new jobs by reducing the burdens on business, saying that there was no evidence that this was the case. No reference was made to the European Court because the position in EC law was clear. The provisions of the Employment Protection (Consolidation) Act 1978, which had stood for 13 years, were declared unlawful without the need for a reference. The Act has since been amended. In the light of subsequent cases (notably *R v Secretary of State for Employment, ex p Seymour-Smith* [1999] 3 WLR 460), it is suggested that the House of Lords should have made a reference.

21.7.2.2 Where the case is being heard before any other court or a tribunal that is exercising a judicial function

In this case, the court or tribunal has a discretion whether to make a reference. Again, the European Court's opinion must be necessary in order for a decision to be reached. Throughout the Community, a wide range of lower courts and tribunals have made references under Article 234 EC, including UK magistrates' courts and social security appeal tribunals.

In either case, the question whether a reference should be made is one for the court rather than the parties to the case. Once the court has decided that a reference should be made, it should then draft the questions to which it requires a reply. In certain cases, the European Court has reformulated these questions so that they more accurately reflect the issue that needs to be addressed. Although the European Court has no discretion, as such, as to whether it replies to a reference, it has refused to respond where there is no genuine dispute between the parties and where the reference was made in order to raise wider political issues (*Foglia v Novello* [1980] ECR 745).

21.8 Chapter summary

If a client seeks advice on a problem where there could be an EC dimension, remember:

(1) EC law can also be used in its own right if it meets the criteria for direct effect (see **21.3**);

(2) if there is EC legislation which has direct effect, an English court or tribunal must prefer it to conflicting domestic law (see **21.4**);

(3) EC legislation can affect the interpretation of domestic law (see *Marleasing SA v La Comercial Internacional de Alimentacion SA* [1990] ECR I-4135 at **21.5**);

(4) in case of doubt as to the meaning of EC law, consider a reference to the Court under Article 234 EC (see **21.7**).

Chapter 22

Seeking a Remedy in National Courts

22.1 Introduction

This chapter is an attempt to consolidate the rules and think more practically about how they can be applied in English courts when acting for a client. It serves as a warning to English solicitors who believe that they can advise their clients on English law alone. Ignoring relevant EC law is undoubtedly solicitor's negligence. Although there have been no reported cases in England, lawyers have been successfully sued in other States for ignoring the competition rules (and thus putting their client at risk of a fine or void agreements), or for ignoring the Brussels Convention on Civil Jurisdiction and Enforcement of Judgments 1968 (and thus losing their client's case by suing in the wrong jurisdiction). A lawyer who advises on English law alone will thus often give wrong advice on English law, because English law by definition includes Community law – lock, stock and barrel.

22.2 EC law as a defence

As Community law overrides conflicting national law, directly effective EC law can always be used as a defence to any civil claim, prosecution or tax claim that is based on that national law. Thus, for example, since Article 81(2) EC makes restrictive agreements void, a defendant can plead Article 81 EC when sued in a civil claim for breach of the agreement. Likewise, if Articles 28, 49, 39 and 43 EC make measures restricting free movement of goods, services and working persons unlawful, a client prosecuted under such national measures can plead the Articles of the Treaty as a defence. In tax claims, a client can plead the VAT Directive (77/388) or the Treaty provisions on non-discrimination (Article 90 EC). Thus, where an exemption from VAT exists in the Directive but not in the UK tax legislation, a taxpayer can plead the Directive as defence to a demand for tax. VAT is very much an EC tax and cannot be collected in circumstances not allowed for under the Directive.

22.3 Effective remedies

In relation to more active remedies, the European Court has made it plain in cases like *R v Secretary of State for Transport, ex p Factortame (No 2)* [1990] 3 WLR 818, that national courts must provide a sufficient remedy to protect EC rights. In general, this would be the nearest equivalent national remedy. Where no adequate remedy is available under national law, the court must provide one to protect the EC right in question (as it did in *Factortame*). Thus, a client may be better protected by asserting an EC right than he is under national law (examples being *Marshall v Southampton Area Health Authority (No 2)* [1993] 3 CMLR 293, discussed below at **22.9**, and *R v Secretary of State for Transport, ex p Factortame (No 4)* [1996] 2 WLR 506).

It should also be noted that administrative decisions affecting EC law must be reasoned, 'proportional' and subject to review by a higher tribunal. Neither the duty to give reasons nor 'proportionality' are well established under English administrative law, so that once again the client asserting an EC right may be better protected when dealing with administrative institutions.

22.4 Injunctions/interim injunctions

If one thinks of actual remedies available to protect EC rights, probably the first thing one would think of would be an injunction. This is certainly available to be used against a private person to restrain a breach of Articles 85 or 86 of the EC Treaty (now Articles 81 or 82 EC) (see *Garden Cottage Foods v Milk Marketing Board* [1984] AC 130). Thus, a client who feels he is being excluded from a particular market because of a restrictive agreement breaching Article 81 EC, or an abuse of a dominant position breaching Article 82 EC, can get an injunction to restrain such unlawful behaviour, and get back into the market.

However, the remedy of injunction or interim injunction is also available against the Government to restrain a breach of EC rules, despite the fact that under English law interim injunctive relief is not normally available to suspend statutes or statutory instruments (see *R v Secretary of State for Transport, ex p Factortame (No 2)* [1990] 3 WLR 818).

In *Factortame*, some Spanish fishermen had set up a UK company to operate UK trawlers with the intention of exploiting the UK fishing quota in the North Sea. The Merchant Shipping Act 1988 provided that, in order to qualify as a UK company for this purpose, the company must itself be owned at least 75% by UK nationals who were UK residents. Not surprisingly, the Spanish fishermen who found themselves excluded by this rule complained that the Act was contrary to the Treaty in that it denied their right of establishment as a UK company (Article 52 of the EC Treaty (now Article 43 EC)) and discriminated against them as EC nationals (Article 6 of the EC Treaty (now Article 12 EC)). Faced with this issue, the House of Lords felt obliged to make a reference to the European Court, but the question then arose as to whether the House of Lords would be bound to grant interim relief protecting the fishermen's rights until the European Court could rule on the main issue. This issue, too, was referred to the European Court, which replied, somewhat more promptly than normal, that the national court must grant an interim injunction to suspend the Act of Parliament where this was necessary to protect the EC rights pending the ruling from the European Court. Eventually, the ruling came back (*R v Secretary of State for Transport, ex p Factortame (No 3)* [1991] 3 All ER 769) that the 1988 Act did contravene the Treaty and therefore, in relation to EC nationals, the provisions concerned had to be suspended indefinitely.

It should be noted that *Factortame* involved an urgent case where the fishermen's livelihood was being threatened in circumstances where damages (at the time uncertain) would not have been an adequate remedy. The ruling does not mean that in EC cases the court need not follow the normal balance of convenience test when deciding when to grant an interim injunction, nor that the court need not take into account other factors, for example public policy, when exercising its discretion. In two other cases, a reference was made but an interim injunction was refused in the meantime. These cases are *R v HM Treasury, ex p British Telecommunications plc* [1994] 1 CMLR 621 and *R v Heritage Secretary, ex p Continental TV (Red Hot TV)* [1993] 2 CMLR 333. Both cases rested on the 'balance of convenience', with the adequacy of damages being a particular fact in the first case and public policy (protecting sensitive viewers from pornographic television) being a factor in the second.

22.5   Damages for breach of EC rights

Again, there seems little doubt that damages are available against private persons for breach of their statutory duty, for example for anti-competitive behaviour under Articles 85 or 86 of the EC Treaty (now Articles 81 and 82 EC). Although there have been no reported court decisions of damages being awarded, the House of Lords in *Garden Cottage Foods v Milk Marketing Board* [1984] AC 130 was certainly of the opinion that damages could be recovered. A large number of cases have been settled on the basis that this is the case. It would seem, however, in the light of *Factortame (No 4)*, that a purely innocent, non-negligent infringement of the competition rules would attract no damages from the national courts just as it would attract no fine from the Commission (see below). Ignorance of the law, however, is no excuse!

Where the defendant concerned is the Government, the claim for tort damages under English public law is a little more complicated. According to the Court of Appeal in *Bourgoin SA v Ministry of Agriculture, Fisheries and Food* [1985] 3 WLR 1027, the Government cannot be liable for damages for exercising its powers unlawfully unless it is guilty of deliberate abuse of power ('misfeasance in public office'). This may be a true reflection of English public law, but the decision in *Bourgoin* itself (where the court refused to award damages for what was a flagrant breach of Article 30 of the EC Treaty (now Article 28 EC), a ban on importing French turkeys) is now clearly contrary to the European Court rulings in *Factortame* and *Francovich*. The House of Lords suggested as much (obiter) in *Kirklees MBC v Wickes Building Supplies Ltd* [1992] 3 All ER 717, where their Lordships suggested that the Government would have had to compensate Sunday traders if the Shops Act 1950 was found to be in breach of Article 30 of the EC Treaty (now Article 28 EC), ie the traders would have been entitled to issue writs against the Attorney-General for damages for all the loss sustained through breach of the statutory duty under Article 30 of the EC Treaty (now Article 28 EC). Clarification of the position in regard to damages was given finally by the European Court in *Factortame (No 4)* [1996] 2 WLR 506, where the question was whether the Spanish fishermen were entitled to damages against the Government for the period in which they were prevented from operating their trawlers before they got their interim injunction. The European Court having given its ruling on EC law that damages can be awarded where the breach is sufficiently serious (see **21.4**), the English courts then had to determine whether this was such a case. The House of Lords finally awarded damages to the fishermen, thus bringing the long saga to an end (*Factortame (No 5)* [1999] 4 All ER 906). The Court gave a similar ruling in *R v Ministry of Agriculture, Fisheries and Food, ex p Hedley Lomas* [1996] All ER (EC) 493. An Irish company which was refused a British export licence to export live animals to Spain (in breach of Article 34 of the EC Treaty (now Article 29 EC)) received damages for its loss.

See also **21.6**.

22.6   Repayment of discriminatory tax/VAT

Again, if the tax has been unlawfully collected in breach of Article 95 of the EC Treaty (now Article 90 EC) or in breach of the VAT Directives, the requirement that an adequate remedy be given means that this tax must be repaid in full with interest (see the Court's ruling in *Amministrazione delle Finanze dello Stato v Spa San Giorgio* [1983] ECR 359). For reasons which will be explained at **22.8**, it may be that the normal time-limit for reclaiming tax under national tax law cannot run to protect the Government until such time as the Government brings its own tax law into line with EC law. This case does recognise a principle of 'unjust enrichment'. Thus, tax should not be repaid where it has been passed on to a customer who cannot himself be traced.

22.7   Statutory remedies

Initially when asserting an EC right, one starts by looking at the nearest equivalent national remedy. Thus, the client who asserts EC rights in the context of employment law, for example equal pay under Article 141 EC, or sex discrimination under the Equal Treatment Directive (76/207), is effectively asserting statutory employment rights and therefore must take his claim to an employment tribunal where the remedies and procedures he will be seeking will be equivalent to those under the Equal Pay Act 1970 and the Sex Discrimination Act 1975. In two respects, however, time-limits and limits on compensation, the remedies provided for breach of these EC rights may be better than those for the equivalent rights under national law.

22.8   Time-limits

Although initially the national time-limits will apply to the claim, the European Court has made it clear that these cannot be used to protect the Government where the claim is based on a Directive which the Government has failed to implement. In other words, the claimant cannot be deprived of a right by the Government delaying implementation for so long that he is out of time. In such circumstances the Government is estopped from relying on its own wrong, and therefore the time-limit begins to run only when it has righted that wrong by introducing national legislation that complies with the Directive (see *Emmott v Minister for Social Welfare and Attorney-General* [1991] IRLR 387). The Court seems to have reduced the effectiveness of this ruling in *Johnson v Chief Adjudication Officer (No 2)* [1995] IRLR 187, where it indicates that a time-limit which limits back-payments of social security may be enforceable even where the Government is in breach of a Directive. The same rule applies to tax (see now *Edilizia Industriale v Ministero delle Finanze* [1999] 2 CMLR 995. The normal national time-limits will of course be available to protect a private person, for example an employer faced with a claim for equal pay under Article 141 EC. But even these may not start to run until the employee is aware of his rights under Article 141 EC (see *Cannon v Barnsley Metropolitan Borough Council* [1992] IRLR 474). The Court has made it clear in the case of *Fischer* [1994] IRLR 662, that the time-limit must not make it impossible to exercise the EC rights which national courts and governments are obliged to protect. There are thus two basic rules that national time-limits must satisfy (see *Comet BV v Produktschap voor Siergewassen* [1997] ECR 2043). First, they must still leave the applicant with an effective remedy and not make recovery virtually impossible. Secondly, they must be equivalent to time-limits in similar national claims. This second principle of non-discrimination is well-illustrated by the case of *Levez v TH Jennings (Harlow Pools) Ltd* [1999] IRLR 764, where the two-year time-limit on back pay in equal pay cases was held to be unlawful as in other similar claims for race and disability discrimination there was no such limit. The EAT's ruling followed guidance from the European Court in *Levez v TH Jennings (Harlow Pools) Ltd* [1999] All ER (EC) 1. The time-limits for making these claims are not, however, discriminatory. In *Biggs v Somerset County Council* [1996] ICR 364, the Court of Appeal refused to allow a claim brought by a part-time employee for unfair dismissal compensation as equal pay under Article 119 of the EC Treaty (now Article 141 EC), when it was brought 18 years after the dismissal but within three months of the House of Lords ruling in *Equal Opportunities Commission v Secretary of State for Employment* [1994] 1 All ER 910 (see **21.7.2**).

22.9 Limits on compensation

As indicated above, EC rules like those protecting against sex discrimination under the Equal Treatment Directive do require an adequate remedy. Thus, the European Court has ruled that the national limits on compensation under the Sex Discrimination Act 1975 (the maximum until November 1993 was £11,000) cannot be used to protect a State employer in a claim based on an EC Directive. This is the now famous case of *Marshall v Southampton Area Health Authority (No 2)* [1993] 3 CMLR 293. Mrs Marshall, who established her right to compensation for breach of the EC Directive in *Marshall v Southampton and West Hampshire Area Health Authority (Teaching)*, then went back to an industrial tribunal where her compensation was assessed at over £20,000. This figure included an assessment of interest. However, both the EAT and the Court of Appeal ruled that the compensation had to be restricted to the limit set by the Sex Discrimination Act 1975, which not only restricted compensation (at the time to £6,000) but also denied the award of interest. On a reference from the House of Lords, the Court ruled that compensation must be awarded without limit and that in assessing compensation the tribunal must, to give an adequate remedy, award interest. The Government reacted promptly and commendably to this ruling by removing both the upper limit and the restriction on interest for all discrimination and equal pay claims with effect from November 1993 (see Sex Discrimination and Equal Pay (Remedies) Regulations 1993, SI 1993/2798). It should be noted that in relation to rights under English law which do not implement EC rights, it is perfectly lawful for the law to provide an inadequate remedy. Thus, 'unfair dismissal' compensation is still limited by statute

Chapter 23

Free Movement of Workers

23.1 Introduction

The EC Treaty gave the right of free movement within the Community to people who wished to take up offers of employment made from outside their home State. This fundamental Treaty right has been buttressed by a considerable amount of secondary legislation. Further, EC law has developed to the stage where the rights of individuals to move within the EC are not necessarily dependent on the desire to take up employment. Indeed, as a consequence of the Single European Act, from 1 January 1993, internal barriers to movement within the EC should have been removed. Further, Article 17 EC now states that every EC national shall be a citizen of the European Union. Under Article 18 EC, the Union citizen has the right to move and reside freely within the territory of the Member States, subject to the limitations and conditions in the EC Treaty and in other legislation.

23.2 What does the EC Treaty provide?

Free movement of workers is guaranteed by Article 39 EC, which gives the EC worker the right of entry and residence for the purpose of taking up employment. According to Article 39(2) EC, Member States must abolish

> ... any discrimination based on nationality between workers of the Member States as regards employment, remuneration and other conditions of work and employment.

'Work and employment' has been interpreted very widely to include sportspeople. Hence, in *Union Royale Belge des Sociétés de Football Association ASBL v Bosman* [1996] All ER (EC) 97, the European Court made it plain that restrictions on the number of EC nationals in football teams imposed by UEFA and requirements for large transfer fees in cross-border transfers were both illegal.

23.2.1 How is nationality interpreted?

Nationality is entirely a matter for the domestic law of each Member State, which means that, inevitably, rules vary. In particular, not all Member States permit their nationals to hold dual nationality. One result of this was seen in *Micheletti v Delegacion del Gobierno en Cantabria* [1992] ECR I-4238. The case concerned a dual national of Argentina and Italy who sought entry into Spain. Entry was refused because under Spanish law only the nationality of the State in which the person had last been habitually resident was recognised, and in this case that was Argentina. The European Court found, however, that, as he was an Italian national under Italian law, he was an EC migrant worker protected by Article 48 of the EC Treaty (now Article 39 EC), so that entry into Spain could not be denied.

23.2.2   What rights of residence does the EC national obtain under Article 39 EC?

The EC national has an absolute right of residence so long as he remains in work. If the worker becomes involuntarily unemployed, Directive 2004/38 will continue to guarantee him a right to reside in the host State. However, if he becomes voluntarily unemployed his position is changed as (in accordance with most social security systems) he would be disqualified from social security benefits. Under Directive 2004/38, he has a right of residence simply by being a citizen of another Member State as long as he has sufficient resources not to be a burden on the host State. If a worker becomes permanently disabled or reaches retirement age, his right of permanent residence continues under this Directive as well.

An individual can claim the rights of a worker as long as he is genuinely employed, even if his work is part time and obtained so that EC rights can be asserted, and even if the salary paid is below a minimum wage limit (*Levin v Secretary of State for Justice* [1982] 1 ECR 1035).

A period of five years' residence gives the worker and/or his family (see **23.4**) a right of permanent residence.

23.2.3   What terms of employment is an EC national entitled to expect?

An EC national can claim the same terms as those offered to a national of the host State. Article 39(2) EC expressly refers to the right not to be discriminated against as regards conditions of work. So, in the case of *Allué (Pilar) and Coonan (Mary Carmel) v Università degli Studi di Venezia* [1991] 1 CMLR 283, an Italian law which provided that non-Italians who accepted jobs in Italy to teach a language could only enter into fixed-term contracts for one year was contrary to Article 48(2) of the EC Treaty (now Article 39(2) EC). In addition, Regulation 1612/68, Article 7, and Directive 2004/38, Article 24 prohibit discrimination in relation to conditions of employment, dismissal, social and tax advantages, training and union membership.

23.2.4   What about his social security rights?

Social security rights are governed by Regulation 1408/71, which basically guarantees to EC nationals the social security benefits of the host State. However, where the benefits are dependent on contributions, a worker's entitlement will take into account contributions to the equivalent benefit in his home State or other Member States in which he has worked. The Regulation does not provide for harmonisation of benefits or of levels of benefits throughout the Community.

23.2.5   Does an EC national have a right of entry to look for work?

Article 39 EC has been interpreted to mean that an EC national has a right of entry to look for work and a reasonable period of residence to find it. This is confirmed in Directive 2004/38, which grants a three-month right of residence without qualifying as a worker. In the UK, the immigration rules used to allow such a person to be deported if he did not succeed in finding work after six months. The European Court held this rule to be consistent with EC law in *R v Immigration Appeals Tribunal, ex p Antonissen* [1991] 2 CMLR 373, although it stressed that the job seeker might still have a right of residence if he had reasonable prospects of finding work. (There is no longer a fixed time-limit for finding work in the UK.) An EC national has a right to remain in the host State as an ordinary citizen if his resources are adequate and he is covered by health insurance by virtue of Directive 2004/38 on the right to residence for EU citizens.

23.3 When does the EC Treaty allow Member States to deny entry?

Article 39(3) EC permits derogations on grounds of public policy, public security and public health. Because these are derogations from one of the fundamental freedoms of the Community, the European Court has interpreted them strictly. Further, Directive 2004/38 has made it clear that only personal conduct can be taken into account. Even prior criminal convictions will not necessarily entitle the Member State to deny entry. They will do so only where they indicate that the individual represents a current threat to public security. For example, in *Astrid Proll v Entry Clearance Officer* [1988] 2 CMLR 387, the former Baader Meinhoff terrorist was allowed entry into the UK because she did not represent a present threat.

Article 39(4) EC provides that the rights granted earlier in the Article do not apply to employment in the public service. This has been interpreted strictly by the European Court in *Commission of European Communities v Belgium; Re Public Employees (No 1)* [1980] ECR 3881 to mean only 'posts involving the exercise of official authority and functions related to safeguarding the general interests of the State'.

23.4 Can the worker bring his family with him?

Because a worker might be deterred from moving to another Member State if he could not take his family with him, Directive 2004/38 enables him to do so. It does, however, limit the family members who are entitled to entry to the spouse, registered partner, children under 21 and dependent relatives of the worker or spouse/partner. Member States do, however, have an obligation to 'facilitate entry and residence' of any other family members who are dependants or members of the household. It is not necessary for family members to be EC nationals. The host State can refuse entry to family members only in those circumstances which allow it to refuse entry to the worker himself (see **23.3** above). The rights of a spouse are not dependent on his or her residing with the worker, and thus can terminate only if the worker leaves the host State permanently (*Diatta v Land Berlin* [1985] ECR 567). Prior to Directive 2004/38 there was no clear European authority as to whether deportation could follow divorce, but in *Baumbast v Secretary of State for the Home Department* [2002] ECR I-7091 the mother of children was entitled to remain having been awarded custody. Directive 2004/38 provides for the spouse (or unmarried cohabitee) to remain in the country if he or she has resided for three years, or if they have been awarded custody or access to children, or alternatively if the court feels that allowing them to remain is warranted in the circumstances.

Directive 2004/38 lays down formal requirements for entry (including visa) and for obtaining residence documents. Thereafter, the family have the same rights as the worker himself to jobs, social security and education.

23.5 Chapter summary

If an EC national or a family member is refused entry or residence rights by UK immigration authorities, he will be allowed to invoke his EC rights before the appropriate immigration authority or Appeal Tribunal, or as a defence in criminal proceedings where deportation is being considered.

If an EC national believes that he has been discriminated against in relation to employment, he should, as usual, follow the appropriate national procedure in the host State to obtain a suitable remedy. In England, this would mean commencing proceedings before an employment tribunal under the Race Relations Act 1976. It is important to remember that, to comply with EC law, such national procedure must not discriminate, even indirectly, against the EC national and must give an effective remedy for breach of EC law (see **22.9**).

Chapter 24

Freedom of Establishment and Provision of Services

24.1 Introduction

The freedom of establishment is the right to base one's business in another Member State permanently. This right is guaranteed by the EC Treaty, with the important qualification that it cannot give the establishing business greater rights than those enjoyed by businesses operated by nationals of the host Member State. Thus a French business wishing to establish itself in England would have to comply with laws affecting an English business relating, for example, to employment, health and safety, and taxes and social security (except to the extent that these might discriminate directly or indirectly against the foreign firm). The governing Article in the EC Treaty is Article 43 EC.

The freedom to provide services guarantees that a business can provide a service across a Community frontier even if that business does not want to be permanently based outside its home State. As with the right of establishment, the right to provide services is granted on the basis that the services will be provided subject to the same conditions as apply to nationals of the State in which the service is supplied (again subject to these rules constituting indirect discrimination). The governing Article in the EC Treaty is Article 49 EC.

Although under both Articles the firm concerned must comply with the same conditions which apply to local nationals, those conditions are likely to be tighter for establishment. In *Gebhard v Consiglio dell'Ordine degli Avvocati e Procuratori di Milano* [1996] All ER (EC) 139 it was held that a German lawyer giving advice on German law in Italy was prima facie 'established' there by virtue of his permanent office and his adoption of the title Avvocato. Had he merely been providing services, he could have relied on his home title as a German lawyer and the earlier Directive on free movement of legal services. However, by establishing himself in Italy, he had to requalify as an Italian lawyer.

In the cases taken to the European Court under Articles 43 EC and 49 EC, emphasis has often successfully been placed on Article 12 EC which prohibits discrimination on the ground of nationality, wherever the matter is covered by the Treaty.

Article 12 EC has direct effect, so that provisions of UK statutes can be disapplied by UK courts in so far as they directly or indirectly discriminate against other EU nationals. Residence requirements are a good example of indirect discrimination.

24.2   The right of establishment: Article 43 EC

Article 43 EC provides that restrictions on the freedom of establishment by nationals of a Member State in the territory of another Member State must be abolished. This freedom is stated to include the right to take up and pursue activities as self-employed persons and to set up and manage undertakings, in particular companies or firms, under the conditions laid down for its own nationals by the law of the country where the establishment is effected.

24.2.1   What is the implication of this Article?

Article 43 EC means that no Member State can, through its legislation or administrative practices, impose a nationality barrier to businesses which wish to be based permanently in another Member State. In *R v Secretary of State for Transport, ex p Factortame (No 3)* [1991] 3 All ER 769, Article 52 of the EC Treaty (now Article 43 EC) was invoked by Spanish fishermen who operated British-registered fishing boats but who were prevented from fishing the British quota because the Merchant Shipping Act 1988 laid down nationality and residence requirements for the owners of shares in companies operating such boats. The European Court held that such legislation was contrary to Article 52 of the EC Treaty (see **22.4**).

24.2.2   Are there any limitations on the kind of undertaking which can benefit from Article 43 EC?

Article 43 EC refers in particular to companies and firms. This phrase is defined in Article 48 EC to mean 'companies or firms constituted under civil or commercial law including co-operative societies'. The meaning of company or firm is really a matter for the law of the home State. A French company wishing to set up a branch or subsidiary in England can do so provided it meets the requirements under French law for being a company. It must not hold itself out as having been incorporated under English law. The only qualification here is that EC law requires that an undertaking wishing to rely on Article 52 EC must be a profit-making body.

It is particularly important to realise, however, that an entrepreneur wishing to set up a company can choose the State with the least regulatory company regime and then establish a branch back in the State he wishes to trade in. In *Centros Ltd v Erhvervsog Selskabsstyrelsen* [1999] 2 CMLR 551, the European Court recognised that it was legitimate to set up a company in the UK and trade through a branch in Denmark, even though the purpose was to avoid the Danish requirements for a minimum paid-up share capital.

24.3   The right to provide services: Article 49 EC

According to Article 49 EC, restrictions on the freedom to provide services within the Community must be abolished in respect of nationals of Member States who are established in a State of the Community other than that of the person for whom the services are intended. Services for this purpose, according to Article 50 EC, are services normally provided for remuneration. In *Commission of European Communities v France* [1991] ECR I-659, for example, it was held that a French law which required tourist guides to hold a licence dependent on the passing of an examination in France was contrary to Article 59 of the EC Treaty (now Article 49 EC) as being unnecessary and discriminatory. There are many similar cases. This Article also means that a business providing services in another Member State had the right to bring its own employees into the host State to enable it to perform those services, even where they would not have been entitled to claim rights under Article 48 of the EC Treaty (now Article 39 EC) (eg, because of transitional rules for nationals of new EU Member States or because the workforce includes immigrants from outside the EU) (*Rush Portuguesa v Office National d'Immigration* [1990] ECR I-1417, *Van der Elst* [1994] ECR I-3803). The workers would, of course, need to be lawfully employed in the State where the employer is established and might need visas to enter the host country; they would not need fresh work permits. The European Court of Justice, however, stresses that the host State can impose its own mandatory rules for workers' protection. Since statutory protection for workers in some countries (eg, the UK) is less than in other countries (eg, Germany), this might enable British firms to provide services to Germany using their British workforce at cheaper rates than German firms which have to pay their employees a higher minimum wage. A Directive on Posted Workers (96/71) was adopted in September 1996 and implemented in the UK by the Equal Opportunities (Employment Legislation) (Territorial Limits) Regulations 1999 (SI 1999/3163). Under the Regulations, a UK company posting its workers in another EU State (eg, whilst working on a building contract) will have to comply with local employment laws where the posting is longer (usually) than one month. The employees can enforce these rights in their UK employment tribunal (as well as in local courts).

24.4 Constraints under Articles 43 EC and 49 EC

The in-coming business is subject to the laws that would apply to a business operated by nationals of that State. This can create barriers to the business wishing to operate across a frontier. The host State may require, perhaps, that all such businesses obtain the authority of the State before they can start to operate. Professional people may be required to conform to rules of professional conduct, professional qualifications or to the rules of a professional body within the host State.

Article 57 of the EC Treaty (now Article 47 EC) envisaged that a series of Directives would be issued dealing with mutual recognition and harmonisation of professional regulations. In the light of this, the European Commission, recognising the public interest in maintaining standards while wishing to minimise unnecessary barriers to cross-border enterprise, tried to develop uniform codes in certain sectors which would apply throughout the Community. These 'sectoral' Directives apply to medical professions such as doctors, nurses, dentists and vets, but the development of harmonised professional training and qualifications in all professions would have taken many years. So after the European Court held that Articles 52 and 59 of the EC Treaty (now Articles 43 EC and 49 EC) were directly effective (see *Reyners v The Belgian State* [1974] ECR 631 and *Van Binsbergen (JHM) v Bestuur van de Bedrijfsvereniging voor de Metaalnijverheid* [1974] ECR 1299 at **21.3.1**), the Commission changed its approach to one of encouraging mutual recognition of standards. Thus a professional qualified in one State must, in principle, be recognised in another State to the extent that his qualification is equivalent.

A particularly important Directive in this respect is Directive 89/48 on recognition of higher education qualifications. The effect of the Directive is that where entry into a particular profession depends upon the candidate having obtained a 'diploma' which proves that he has completed at least three years' professional education and training, a non-national cannot be denied entry to that profession if he holds the equivalent 'diploma' which would entitle him to enter the profession in his home State. However, if there are substantial differences in the content of the course leading to the diploma in the home State, the Directive allows the host State to require the candidate to follow an adaptation period of no more than three years. As an alternative, the candidate could choose to take an aptitude test. The Directive makes special provision regarding entry to the legal profession. It allows a State to specify whether a candidate must take an aptitude test or follow a period of adaptation. Thus, in England and Wales, qualified lawyers from other EC States must pass the Law Society's Qualified Lawyers Transfer Test (QLTT) before they can be admitted as solicitors. Solicitors from Ireland are, however, admitted without a test, as their qualification is equivalent. The more recent establishment Directive of 1998 (98/5) provides for automatic requalification after a period of practice as a foreign lawyer.

The principle behind Directive 89/48 has been extended to cover diplomas awarded after one year's post-secondary education by Directive 92/51.

In *Van Binsbergen (JHM) v Bestuur van de Bedrijfsvereniging voor de Metaalnijverheid* [1974] ECR 1299, the European Court held that professional rules of conduct regulating the legal profession would not be in breach of Community law provided they did not discriminate against the non-national, they were objectively justifiable and they were not disproportionate to the aim to be achieved. Hence, a lawyer established in France had the right to provide services by representing clients before Belgian tribunals. He could not be forced to establish himself in Belgium. Simply having an address for service in Belgium would be proportional to any need for supervision of his activities. (An EC Directive has now adopted the *Van Binsbergen* line and allows qualified EU lawyers to represent their clients before foreign tribunals within the EU (see Directive 77/249).) A similar approach can be seen in the more recent case of *Commission of European Communities v Germany* [1988] ECR 5427, which was concerned with the regulation of the German insurance sector. In that case, the Court held that restrictions on the right of an insurance company to provide services in Germany would be acceptable only if they were objectively justified, in the general public good and if they applied to all undertakings so far as they were not regulated in their home State.

Lastly, it would seem that if there is only a tenuous link between the services being provided and a particular restrictive provision, the latter will not be in breach of EC law (see *Society for the Protection of the Unborn Child (Ireland) v Grogan (Stephen)* [1991] 3 CMLR 849). That case concerned Irish legislation prohibiting the supply of information on abortion facilities provided outside Ireland. The European Court acknowledged that the overseas clinics provided services within the meaning of Article 59 of the EC Treaty (now Article 49 EC), but went on to hold that since the information in question was being made available by student unions rather than by the clinics themselves, there was an insufficient link between the restriction and the provision of the services. Had the clinics been advertising directly themselves (or through an advertising agency), the position would have been different. (The ban on these leaflets may raise questions of freedom of speech under Article 10 of the European Convention on Human Rights – see **Chapter 27**.)

24.5 Can the self-employed person bring his family with him to the host State?

Directive 2004/38 (as mentioned in **Chapter 23**) applies to freedom of establishment as it does to workers (see **23.4**).

24.6   Derogations from Articles 43 EC and 49 EC

It is possible to derogate from Articles 43 EC and 49 EC on grounds of public health, public security and public policy (Articles 46 EC and 55 EC). The interpretation of these terms is the same as that under Article 39(3) EC and Directive 2004/38 (see **23.3**). Moreover, the right of establishment does not apply to activities involving, even occasionally, 'the exercise of official authority' (Article 45 EC). Thus a number of 'legal professions', for example judges, magistrates, court registrars and notaries (but not lawyers), can be reserved to home nationals.

24.7   Rights of potential recipients of services under EC law

In *Luisi and Carbone v Ministero del Tesoro* [1984] ECR 377, the European Court interpreted Article 59 of the EC Treaty (now Article 49 EC) to mean that potential recipients of services had the right to go to another Member State to receive those services and that tourists qualified as potential recipients of services. This approach was further developed in *Cowan v Le Trésor Public (The Treasury)* [1989] ECR 195, which concerned a British tourist who was the victim of a criminal assault while in France. His claim for compensation from the French Criminal Injuries Compensation Board was denied because he was not a French national. On an Article 234 EC reference, the European Court held that compensation could not be denied to a recipient of compensation services on grounds of nationality.

In a number of cases, the European Court has considered whether this approach entitles a national of a Member State to take advantage of education services elsewhere in the Community. Strictly speaking, State education cannot constitute 'services' because, under Article 50 EC, services must normally be paid for. In cases such as *Gravier v City of Liège* [1985] ECR 593, however, it was held that students cannot be asked to pay an additional fee for educational courses because they are non-nationals, provided the course represents vocational training, ie it facilitates access to a particular trade or profession. Even if the courses are normally free (ie not 'services') they still relate to a Treaty matter (training), and therefore any discrimination is unlawful under Article 12 EC (see **24.1**).

24.8   Summary and conclusion

24.8.1   Distinguish between establishment and services

Establishment (Article 43 EC) implies permanence; services (Article 49 EC) are more temporary. Hence, the presence of a permanent office implies establishment under Article 43 EC (see *Gebhard v Consiglio dell'Ordine degli Avvocati e Procuratori di Milano* [1996] All ER (EC) 139 at **24.1**).

24.8.2   Restriction on free movement

Where services are involved, for Article 49 EC to apply there must be a restriction on free movement. However, services may move in four different ways.

(a)   The provider of services moves to another Member State to provide services on a temporary basis (the normal case).

(b)   The recipient of services moves to receive services (eg, as a tourist – see *Cowan v Le Trésor Public* [1989] ECR 195 at **24.7**).

(c)   The provider moves to another Member State to provide services to nationals of his own State (eg, a British interpreter/guide/ski instructor who accompanies a party of British tourists abroad).

(d)   Neither provider nor recipient moves, but services are provided by post, fax, telephone, broadcast, etc.

This last situation arose in the instructive case of *Alpine Investments BV v Minister Van Financien* [1995] All ER (EC) 543, which concerned Dutch financial services laws banning the cold-calling of customers at home or abroad. The Dutch company prosecuted in this case argued that the law banning the cold-calling of foreign clients infringed Article 59 of the EC Treaty (now Article 49 EC). Clearly, the law in question did not discriminate against foreign service providers, but it still restricted the export of services because it directly affected access to the market in other States. Nevertheless, the restriction could be objectively justified in the general interest on grounds of consumer protection or the good reputation of the industry. Moreover, the restriction was proportional (the fact that other countries had no (or less strict) controls on cold-calling was considered irrelevant). It should be noted that, as in the *Cassis de Dijon* case (see **25.2.2**), restrictions like this, which apply without distinction to all service providers, could be justified on a wider range of grounds than those which appear in Article 46 EC (public policy, public security and public health).

24.8.3   Need to satisfy local conditions

Whether seeking establishment or providing services, the foreign national who tries to work abroad must satisfy local conditions for pursuit of the activity in question. However (according to *Gebhard*; see **24.8.1**), these conditions:

(a)   must be non-discriminatory;

(b)   must be justified by imperative requirements in the general interest;

(c)   must be suitable for securing the attainment of the objective which they pursue; and

(d)   must not go beyond what is necessary to achieve it.

24.8.4   General approach to free movement under EU law

The approach of the European Court in *Gebhard* is very similar to that already established by the Court in relation to goods (see the key case of *Cassis de Dijon* at **25.2.2**). It has been stressed that the approach is common to all cases of free movement. It thus applies in relation to workers under Article 48 of the EC Treaty (now Article 39 EC) (see *Bosman* at **23.2**), to establishment under Article 52 of the EC Treaty (now Article 43 EC) (*Gebhard*), and to services under Article 59 of the EC Treaty (now Article 49 EC) (*Alpine Investments* at **24.8.2**).

Chapter 25

Free Movement of Goods

25.1 Introduction

The free movement of goods is one of the fundamental freedoms on which the EC is based. One of the most important aims of the EC Treaty was to create a single market in goods throughout all the Member States of the Community. Following amendments to the Treaty by the Single European Act 1986, this aim was intended to be achieved by 31 December 1992. Because of the importance of this freedom, the European Court has consistently interpreted the relevant Treaty provisions in such a way as to give maximum effect to this basic objective.

25.2 What does the EC Treaty provide?

The principal Treaty provision is Article 28 EC, which states that:

> Quantitative restrictions on imports and all measures having equivalent effect shall be prohibited between Member States.

Article 29 EC makes similar provision in relation to exports, ie the requirement for or refusal of an export licence.

25.2.1 What is meant by 'quantitative restrictions'?

Quantitative restrictions are limitations on the import of goods fixed by reference to quantitative criteria, ie amount or value ('quotas'). A complete ban on the import of a particular type of goods is also such a restriction (see *Commission of European Communities v Italy* [1961] ECR 317).

25.2.2 What is meant by a 'measure having equivalent effect'?

The phrase 'a measure having equivalent effect' (MEQR) is not defined in the EC Treaty itself but was defined by the European Court in *Dassonville* [1974] ECR 837. In that case, the phrase was said to extend to 'all trading rules enacted by Member States that are capable of hindering, directly or indirectly, actually or potentially, intra-Community trade'.

It is important to note the following about this definition.

(a) A measure having equivalent effect does not have to have an immediate or substantial effect on intra-Community trade. In particular, it is clear from *Re Prantl (Karl)* [1984] ECR 1299 that the European Court will not apply a de minimis principle here. This means that any legislation which is capable of affecting trade between Member States, even indirectly, because it is not the primary aim of the legislation, can infringe Article 28 EC. However, the case of *Criminal Proceedings Against Keck and Mithouard* [1995] 1 CMLR 101 shows that for 'selling arrangements' the measure must have the effect of putting the imported goods at a disadvantage before it can be said to restrict imports. Contrary to the view expressed earlier in cases involving Sunday trading laws (*Torfaen Borough Council v B&Q plc* [1989] ECR 765), a restriction on volume of imports (ie, the argument that with shops shut there will be fewer sales and therefore fewer imports) is not enough if domestic goods are at the same disadvantage.

(b)   A measure having equivalent effect must be taken by an 'organ of the State'. Actions by private individuals, companies or other undertakings cannot fall within this definition. However, this requirement will be satisfied even if the Member State acts through another undertaking. In *Commission of European Communities v Ireland; Re 'Buy Irish' Campaign* [1982] ECR 4005, the Irish Government initiated a campaign to encourage Irish consumers to buy home-produced goods. The campaign was launched by an Irish Government Minister and was funded by the Government, but was actually managed by a guarantee company set up for the purpose. The fact that it was not the Irish Government which was directly running the campaign did not prevent it being a measure having effect equivalent to a quantitative restriction. Likewise, other State bodies, for example local authorities, licensing authorities or courts, may see their 'measures' (eg, injunctions) controlled in the same way.

(c)   A measure having equivalent effect need not affect imported products alone, that is, be 'distinctly applicable' to imports. It could be a measure applying to all goods, domestic and imported, without distinction ('indistinctly applicable'), for example national technical standards. The difference is that whereas the latter can be justified under the 'rule of reason' and so do not infringe Article 28 EC at all (see *Cassis de Dijon* below), the former are justifiable only under Article 30 EC. The following cases involved distinctly applicable measures. In *International Fruit Co NV v Produktschap voor Groenten en Fruit (No 3)* [1971] ECR 1107, a requirement that a licence be obtained before apples could be imported into France was struck down by the European Court as an infringement of Article 30 of the EC Treaty (now Article 28 EC). Similarly, in *Rewe-Zentralfinanz e GmbH v Landwirtschaftskammer* [1975] ECR 843, a requirement that apples had to be inspected before they could be imported into Germany was also held to breach Article 30 of the EC Treaty. Although these types of measure do not completely prevent the marketing of the product, they do result in delay and inconvenience for the importer, which may lead to fewer such products being imported. In both these cases, the measures could not be justified under Article 36 of the EC Treaty (now Article 30 EC) which is restrictively interpreted.

Increasingly, the European Court has found measures to be within the *Dassonville* definition, and therefore caught by Article 28 EC, where the domestic product is also affected by the measure in question. The leading case is *Rewe Zentral v Bundesmonopolverwaltung fur Branntwein (Cassis de Dijon)* [1979] ECR 649. A German law required that spirits such as Cassis de Dijon should be of a stipulated alcoholic strength. Cassis was significantly less strong and therefore could not be sold on the German market. The European Court held that the German law fell within the *Dassonville* definition and was in breach of Article 30 of the EC Treaty (now Article 28 EC). The case is considered vital to the development of a single market in that it shows that imported products do not have to be changed to meet national technical standards unless the need to do so is justified. The case is considered further in **25.3.1**.

25.3 Are there circumstances in which Article 28 EC will not apply?

25.3.1 The 'rule of reason'

Although it is no answer to an Article 28 EC complaint to say that the measure in question affects the equivalent domestic product as well as the imported one, it is important to know whether or not this is the case. This is because only such a measure can benefit from the 'rule of reason' approach of the European Court in *Cassis de Dijon* referred to above. The Court recognised in that case that if goods were lawfully manufactured in a particular way in a given Member State, they should ordinarily be entitled to move throughout the rest of the Community. However, where the EC itself had not imposed Community-wide standards, disparities between Member States' legislation could be acceptable. In the words of the Court:

> obstacles to movement within the Community resulting from disparities between the national laws relating to the marketing of products must be accepted in so far as those provisions are necessary in order to satisfy mandatory requirements relating in particular to the effectiveness of fiscal supervision, the protection of public health, the fairness of commercial transactions and the defence of the consumer.

The list of mandatory requirements is not closed. The Court has since added to them the protection of the environment (see *Commission of European Communities v Denmark; sub nom Re Disposable Beer Cans* [1989] 1 CMLR 619), the protection of culture (eg, the cinema from the threat of video cassettes in *Cinethèque v Federation Nationale des Cinemas Français* [1986] 1 CMLR B65) and employment in the Sunday trading cases. The list inevitably includes (but is much wider than) the list of justifications in Article 30 EC.

In order for a measure to be 'necessary' to satisfy a mandatory requirement, the aim of the measure in question must be justifiable in EC law and the measure taken must be *proportionate* to that aim. Therefore, if the aim could be achieved by a measure which was less restrictive of the free movement of goods, the measure taken will be held to be disproportionate. In *Cassis de Dijon*, the German Government successfully argued that the law in question was for the defence of the consumer, but the Court found that it was nevertheless disproportionate to its objective: the same aim could have been achieved by a law requiring that such spirits should be clearly labelled with their alcoholic strength.

25.3.2 The EC Treaty

Where a government measure is distinctly applicable (ie, provides different conditions for imported goods), it can only be justified under the terms of the Treaty, ie Article 30 EC.

Article 30 EC provides a number of important exceptions to Article 28 EC. It states that:

> The provisions of Articles 28 to 29 shall not preclude prohibitions or restrictions on imports, exports or goods in transit justified on grounds of public morality, public policy or public security; the protection of health and life of humans, animals or plants; the protection of national treasures possessing artistic, historical or archaeological value; or the protection of industrial or commercial property. Such prohibitions or restrictions shall not, however, constitute a means of arbitrary discrimination or a disguised restriction on trade between Member States.

As this Article derogates from a fundamental principle of the EC, the Court construes it strictly; in particular, no further justifiable restrictions can be read into the list given above. Further, the burden of establishing that a measure does come within Article 30 EC will fall on the relevant Member State.

The following points should be borne in mind when considering the exceptions in Article 30 EC.

25.3.2.1 Public morality

The European Court will not seek to impose its own standards of morality; what is required in this area will be a matter for each Member State (see *DPP v Darby; DPP v Henn* [1979] ECR 3795). It is important to appreciate the significance of the final sentence of Article 30 EC, ie the measure taken by the Member State must not amount to arbitrary discrimination against the imported product, or to a disguised restriction on trade. In *Darby and Henn*, the seizure of imported pornography by UK customs was not in breach of Article 30 of the EC Treaty (now Article 28 EC) as that type of pornography could not be lawfully sold in the UK. On the other hand, in *Conegate v Customs and Excise Commissioners* [1986] ECR 1007, the import of rubber dolls into the UK could not be prevented because if they had been produced in this country they could lawfully have been sold here.

25.3.2.2 Public policy

A Member State cannot invoke public policy whenever it is convenient to do so to avoid falling foul of Article 28 EC. The European Court has made it clear that this exception can be used only where there is a serious threat to a fundamental interest of society. See, for example, *R v Thompson (Brian Ernest)* [1978] ECR 2247, where it was applied to the right to mint coinage. Economic reasons, for example protection of industry from competition, are never, however, acceptable.

25.3.2.3 Public security

Similarly, public security cannot be readily called upon in defence of a breach of Article 28 EC. It seems clear only that it extends to the need to safeguard essential public services. Note *Campus Oil Ltd v The Minister for Industry and Energy* [1984] ECR 2727, where the Irish Government required importers of petrol to buy a percentage of their needs from an Irish refinery to ensure that the refinery remained viable. It seems that it can relate to the State's internal as well as external security (*Minister of Finance v Richardt* [1992] 1 CMLR 61).

25.3.2.4 Public health

In the absence of EC standards, Member States are entitled to decide what is appropriate for their own citizens in the field of public health. In the case of *Aragonesa de Publicidad v Departmamento de Sanidad y Seguridad Social de la Generalitat de Cataluna* [1991] OJ C220/8, the European Court upheld on public health grounds Spanish legislation which prohibited roadside advertisements for strong spirits. Despite the later case of *Keck and Mithouard* (see **25.4.1**), this case may still involve a measure equivalent to quantitative restriction (MEQR) as it may be indirectly discriminatory against imported spirits not known to the Spanish public. It is, however, clearly justified.

Again, it is essential to pay close attention to the last sentence of Article 30 EC. For example, in *Commission of European Communities v United Kingdom; sub nom Re Imports of Poultry Meat* [1982] ECR 2793, where the UK Government prohibited the import of French poultry into the UK, ostensibly in order to avoid the spread of

Newcastle Disease, the evidence indicated that the prohibition was unnecessarily restrictive and in reality was intended to protect the English poultry industry. It should be noted that in most areas there are now Directives laying down the minimum requirements for health or animal welfare. For example, EC Directives lay down minimum rules for the carriage of live animals and their stunning before slaughter. It is not a sufficient justification for the refusal of an export licence for live animals that these rules may be ignored in the importing State (see *R v Ministry of Agriculture, Fisheries and Food, ex p Hedley Lomas (Ireland) Ltd* [1996] All ER (EC) 493). The refusal will breach Article 29 EC.

25.3.2.5 The protection of national treasures and intellectual property rights

The exception for the protection of national treasures, although not yet used, is likely to be of value where a Member State wishes to impose an export ban on items representing part of its national heritage, ie in breach of Article 29 EC.

Intellectual property rights have posed difficulties for the European Court. In the absence of Community-wide regimes, such rights are granted by individual Member States and relate only to the territory of the State in question. This offers enterprises an opportunity to divide up the market on national lines. This is clearly contrary to the spirit of the Community. Because of this the European Court has been careful not to over-extend the protection given to intellectual property rights in Article 30 EC. Accordingly, the Court has distinguished between the existence and the exercise of intellectual property rights. Thus, measures (eg, court injunctions keeping out imports of goods infringing a patent) are not caught by Article 28 EC even if their effect is to restrict imports (because of Article 30 EC).

In order to protect the existence of intellectual property rights, however, the Court has had to decide what the existence of each right amounts to. It has done this by developing the concept of the 'specific subject matter' of a right. Thus, for example, the specific subject matter of a patent is the exclusive right to use an invention for the manufacture of products and to be the first to market them (*Centrafarm BV and De Peijper v Sterling Drug Inc* [1974] ECR 1147). This means that once a company has marketed (or consented to the marketing of) a drug in, say, France, it cannot thereafter purport to use its patent rights in, say, the UK to prevent the import of the patented product. The products marketed in France could therefore be re-imported into the UK and the patent holder or UK court could not interfere with their free movement. The company's rights over that particular product were 'exhausted' when it consented to its marketing in France. The European Court has adopted a similar approach to trade mark rights and copyright. This protection of 'parallel imports' through exhaustion of rights applies only where the goods are marketed within the EU. The European Court has ruled in *Silhouette International Schmied GmbH & Co KG v Hartlauer Handelsgesellschaft mbH* [1998] 3 WLR 1218 that following the harmonisation of trade mark rights through the 1994 Directive, Member States' laws can no longer recognise a wider principle of world-wide exhaustion (ie, through marketing outside the EU). Thus manufacturers can use their national trade marks to keep out goods which they authorised for sale only in countries outside the EU.

25.4 Summary of the position regarding trading measures

The problem can be tackled by asking a series of questions.

25.4.1   Is the measure an MEQR (*Dassonville* test)?

To be an MEQR, the rule in question must affect the product itself, ie require some change, before it can be sold in the territory. In general, rules about *selling arrangements* (ie, the arrangements for selling the product once it is imported), for example Sunday trading, licensing hours, and prohibitions on selling at a loss (*Keck and Mithouard*), do not come within the *Dassonville* formula and thus (in the absence of discrimination) need no justification. Although they may restrict the volume of imports (if you sell less, you import less), these measures do not put imports at a disadvantage and thus cannot count as MEQRs.

Advertising restrictions, for example bans on leaflets (*GB-INNO-BM v Confédération du Commerce Luxembourgeoise Asbl* [1991] 2 CMLR 801) or comparative advertising (*Unwesen in den Wirtschaft eV v Yves Rocher GmbH* (1994) *Financial Times*, 9 June), may well put the imported product at a disadvantage because advertising is the most effective way for new imported products to penetrate a market. The rival domestic products may well be better known. It would, however, seem that restrictions on retailers advertising their sales (eg, *Hünermund v Landespothekerkammer Baden-Württemberg* [1993] ECR I-6787, where German pharmacists were prohibited from advertising off the premises, or *Leclerc v TFI Publicité* [1995] ECR I-179, where French retailers could not advertise at all on French television and thus were restricted in advertising their cheap foreign fuel) are to be treated as selling arrangements under *Keck and Mithouard*. By contrast, a blanket ban on advertising a particular product, for example alcoholic products or toys, would be seen, it is felt, as either a restriction to be justified under the 'rule of reason' in *Cassis de Dijon* or a case of indirect discrimination against imports which would have to be justified on similar objective criteria (see *Konsumentombudsmannen (KO) v De Agostini (Svenska) Forlag AB; Konsumentombudsmannen (KO) v TV-Shop I Sverige AB (De Agostini)* [1997] All ER (EC) 687).

25.4.2   If it is an MEQR, does it apply only to imports (ie distinctly applicable measures) or directly discriminate (as selling arrangements)?

The best example of this is the French ban on British beef. This could only be justified under Article 30 EC (eg, protection of public health) but the French failed to prove a sufficient health risk. It therefore was a distinctly applicable breach which the French had failed to justify.

Likewise, an injunction prohibiting the imports of goods said to infringe a national patent could only be justified under Article 30 EC (protection of intellectual property rights).

25.4.3   Does the measure apply to all products (ie indistinctly applicable measures) or (if a selling arrangement) indirectly discriminate?

Measures which apply to all goods (domestic and imported) without distinction will be caught by Article 28 EC only if they put the imported goods at a disadvantage compared with domestic goods. Thus, where the imported product has to be adapted before it can be sold on the domestic market it is prima facie at a disadvantage compared with domestic products which are made to domestic specifications. Here, because we are dealing with indirect discrimination, the measure infringes Article 28 EC unless it can be shown to be justified by a public interest objective (eg, consumer protection, health, environment, etc – the list given in *Cassis de Dijon* is not exhaustive) which is proportional and takes precedence over the free movement of goods. If so justified, there is no Article 28 EC infringement. Measures falling into this category would be German measures on purity of spirits (*Cassis de Dijon*), sausages, beer, etc; packaging rules (eg, Danish or German rules on recyclable bottles or containers – these may be justified on environmental protection grounds (see *Commission of European Communities v Kingdom of Denmark; sub nom Re Disposable Beer Cans* [1989] 1 CMLR 619)), rules on labelling, weight, trade marks, etc. In *Verband Sozialer Wettbewerb eV v Clinique Laboratories SNC and Estée Lauder Cosmetics* (Case C-315/92) [1994] ECR I-317, the cosmetic 'Clinique' could not be marketed under that mark in Germany because it was considered to suggest therapeutic properties which it did not have. Since the cosmetic had to be repackaged for sale in Germany, there was clearly an indirect restriction on imports which could not be justified on the basis of protecting consumers from confusion.

Since the effect of *Cassis de Dijon* is that Member States must mutually recognise different product standards which give equivalent protective effect, modern product standard Directives under the '1992' campaign (and after) have merely set a minimum level of protection ('the essential requirements') which different national products can satisfy. The obligatory Euro standard is a thing of the past, except for hazardous products like drugs and motor cars where full harmonisation of the specification requirements may be needed. In other areas, Euro standards are considered optional.

25.5 How to use Article 28 EC

Article 28 EC is directly effective; this means it can be relied upon before national courts and tribunals. It can therefore be used defensively, for example in response to a criminal prosecution for breach of trading standards in another Member State, or offensively, for example to challenge a 'buy national' campaign. In the latter case, the challenger must follow the most appropriate national procedure and claim the most effective national remedy. The European Court has made it clear that a Member State is under an obligation to provide an effective remedy for infringement of EC rights. Thus, a challenge to a Government-sponsored 'buy national' campaign in the UK would be made by judicial review proceedings for a declaration that the Government was acting ultra vires, accompanied by a claim for an injunction (see *R v Secretary of State for Transport, ex p Factortame (No 2)* (Case C-213/89) [1990] 3 WLR 818) or possibly damages (see *R v Secretary of State for Transport, ex p Factortame (No 4)* [1996] 2 WLR 506). The case of *Brasserie du Pêcheur*, decided with *Factortame (No 4)*, concerned a damages claim under Article 30 of the EC Treaty (now Article 28 EC) by beer importers who fell foul of Germany's purity laws. Since the particular restrictions (relating to a ban on additives) were not manifestly unlawful at the time, no damages were payable.

It should be noted that all new national rules on product standards have to be notified to Brussels under Directive 83/189. The failure to do so will invalidate the national law because Directive 83/189 has direct effect. (See *CIA Security International SA v Signalson SA* [1996] 2 CMLR 781.) This, too, can be used as a defence.

Chapter 26

Competition Law

26.1 Introduction

The regulation of competition between businesses is as important to the Community as the attainment of the freedoms discussed in the previous chapters. It is of little use to provide that goods can move freely throughout the Community unless at the same time businesses are able to trade across frontiers without facing improper competition. Improper competition, particularly where it has the effect of dividing up markets along national lines, must be controlled. Thus, Article 3(1)(g) EC states that one of the activities of the Community is the institution of a system ensuring that competition in the common market is not distorted. This system is principally established in two Articles of the Treaty: Articles 81 and 82 EC. Article 81 EC controls anti-competitive agreements, while Article 82 EC regulates an abuse of a dominant position. It should be remembered that the object of any competition law is greater customer choice, either of manufacturers (different brands) or of dealers supplying the same brand. More competition equals more choice; this in turn compels competing manufacturers (or dealers) to cut costs and improve quality of goods or services.

26.2 Anti-competitive agreements: Article 81 EC

26.2.1 What does Article 81 EC provide?

Article 81 EC provides that:

> The following shall be prohibited as incompatible with the common market: all agreements between undertakings, decisions by associations of undertakings and concerted practices which may affect trade between Member States and which have as their object or effect the prevention, restriction or distortion of competition within the common market ...

It then gives examples of the types of conduct which would be caught by this definition, such as fixing prices, controlling production and sharing markets. To discover what other practices may be within Article 81 EC, it is necessary to look at the Article in detail.

26.2.1.1 Agreements between undertakings

The term 'undertaking' is not defined in the Treaty but is taken to include any business enterprise, whatever legal form it may take. In particular, under English law it will include a company or a partnership, a sole trader or a trade association. A parent and a subsidiary company are usually taken to amount to a single undertaking for this purpose. Likewise, agreements between a company and its employees or agents are unlikely to be agreements 'between undertakings' as they lack the necessary independence.

Not only written agreements between two or more such undertakings but also less formal arrangements, such as a mere understanding or 'gentlemen's agreement', may breach Article 81 EC (see the *Quinine Cartel* case, *Boehringer Mannheim GmbH v Commission of the European Communities* [1970] ECR 661). It was originally thought that Article 85 of the EC Treaty (now Article 81 EC) applied only to agreements between potential competitors, ie 'horizontal agreements' between undertakings at the same level of the production process, for example the traditional cartel where manufacturers meet in secret to carve up markets or fix prices. The agreement may, however, be a 'vertical' one, that is between undertakings involved at different stages of the manufacturing or trading process, for example an agreement between a wholesaler and a retailer. Even if the manufacturer is not involved in distribution itself, restrictions, eg on prices or exports, can affect competition between distributors (see, for example, *Consten SA and Grundig-Verkaufs-GmbH (Etablissements) v EEC Commission* [1996] CMLR 418).

26.2.1.2 Decisions by associations of undertakings

The phrase 'decisions by associations of undertakings' would include, for example, decisions taken by a trade association, whether or not they were legally binding.

26.2.1.3 Concerted practices

An enterprise may breach Article 81 EC if it deliberately co-ordinates its behaviour with another business in the same market, for example if they agree to raise prices at the same time and by the same amount. It is not necessary to be able to prove an agreement that they should do so; the fact of synchronised activity may be enough, so that, in the words of the European Court in *Dyestuffs* [1972] ECR 619, 'the parties have substituted practical co-operation for the risks of competition'. It is important to appreciate that a business is entitled to respond to market conditions, including the behaviour of its competitors. This may well mean that enterprises operating within the same market do show similar behaviour without there being a 'concerted practice'.

26.2.1.4 How much of an effect does there have to be on trade between Member States?

Article 81 EC states that it is necessary that the agreement, etc 'may' have an effect on trade. According to the European Court in *STM v Maschinenbau Ulm* [1966] ECR 235:

> it must be possible to foresee with a sufficient degree of probability on the basis of a set of objective factors of law or fact that the agreement in question may have an influence, direct or indirect, actual or potential, on the pattern of trade between Member States.

Such an effect may result even where the parties to the agreement or concerted practice are based within one Member State if the effect is to distort competition elsewhere in the EC, for example because a company based in another Member State is unable to break into that market (see *Vereeniging van Cementhandelaren v Commission of the European Communities (No 2)* (Case 8/72) [1972] ECR 977 (the *Dutch Cement* case)).

It can even occur where the parties are based outside the EC, provided the agreement or practice is implemented within it (*Re Wood Pulp Cartel* [1988] ECR 5193).

It has been held by the European Court of Justice that Article 81 EC can apply to exclusive distribution agreements in countries outside the EU (here Russia, the Ukraine and Slovenia), which contain restrictions on exporting into the EU. Here, the distribution agreements for Yves St Laurent Perfumes were subject to French law and jurisdiction. The French courts therefore would be entitled to rule that the agreements were invalid under Article 81(2) EC (see *Javico v Yves St Laurent* (1998) *Financial Times*, 13 May).

This part of Article 81 EC therefore determines the jurisdiction of the EC competition authorities. But it also sets out clearly the policy of EC competition law, which is partly to create a single market. Agreements which have the effect of partitioning the single market (eg, exclusive territories for dealers) are prima facie likely to infringe Article 81 EC.

26.2.1.5 '... which have as their object or effect'

If, objectively, the parties intend the agreement or the practice to prevent, restrict or distort competition, there is no need to consider further what the effect of the agreement might be. On the other hand, if that is not the object, but it would be its effect, then Article 81 EC will still be breached.

26.2.1.6 'the prevention, restriction or distortion of competition'

The words 'the prevention, restriction or distortion of competition' are given their ordinary meaning. However, if the effect is likely to be minimal, Article 81(1) EC will not be breached (*Volk v Verwaecke* [1969] ECR 295). See further the Commission's Notice on Agreements of Minor Importance in **26.2.4**.

It should be remembered that even if the agreement has no effect on competition between the parties, it may still be prohibited by Article 81 EC if its effect is to restrict competition with third parties. This is the case with vertical agreements such as the exclusive distribution agreement which may restrict intra-brand competition between the different dealers.

26.2.2 Can an undertaking apply for clearance that its arrangements are outside Article 81 EC?

This possibility was removed as from 1 May 2004 except that the Commission does have the power 'to adopt a decision of a declaratory nature finding that the prohibition in Article 81 [or Article 82] of the Treaty does not apply'. Indications are that this power will be used sparingly. Parties must generally now 'self-assess', ie decide for themselves whether their arrangement is permitted by Article 81(3) EC. Their decision may be challenged by national competition authorities, the Commission, or by national courts, should it be relevant in court proceedings.

26.2.3 What is the result if there is a breach of Article 81 EC?

According to Article 81(2) EC, any agreement or decision prohibited by Article 81(1) EC is automatically void. This means that any agreement is unenforcable. It may be possible to sever offending clauses from the agreement and leave the rest of it standing. Whether this is possible depends on the domestic law to which the agreement is subject. Thus, under English law, such clauses can be severed if the remaining agreement still reflects accurately the agreement reached by the parties

(*Chemidus Wavin v Société pour la Transformation et l'Exploitation des Resines Industrielles SA* [1978] 3 CMLR 514). Because Article 81(1) EC has been held to be directly effective, it seems that a party whose business interests are being or have been harmed by the anti-competitive agreement may seek an injunction to restrain operation of the agreement and may be able to claim damages (*Garden Cottage Foods v Milk Marketing Board* [1983] 3 WLR 143). In addition, the Commission and national competition authorities have the power to levy fines upon the parties to an anti-competitive agreement, the size of the fine (up to a maximum of 10% of turnover) being dependent on the degree of fault. A recent fine for Microsoft was in the sum of £335 million.

26.2.4 Are there any ways out for a business which seems to be at risk of breaching this Article?

There are primarily three ways in which a business may avoid breaching Article 81 EC.

26.2.4.1 The Notice on Agreements of Minor Importance

The Commission, which is responsible for implementing the Community's competition policy, has issued a Notice on Agreements of Minor Importance. According to this Notice, only agreements which have an appreciable effect on trade between Member States should be taken as breaching Article 81. It goes on to provide that this will be assumed not to be the case where the parties to the agreement have only a limited market share, or if they are small or medium-sized enterprises (SMEs) (fewer than 250 employees and either an annual turnover not exceeding €40 million, or an annual balance sheet total not exceeding €27 million). If the parties are at the same level (horizontal agreement), the joint market share must not be more than 10%. If the parties are at different levels, for example distribution or franchising (vertical agreements), they may each have a market share of up to 15%. The relevant market here is determined in the same way as under Article 82 EC by looking at all the goods and services which the customer would take in substitution for those under the agreement. The more generous treatment of vertical agreements reflects the Commission's growing awareness that restrictions on intra-brand competition may be compensated by more inter-brand competition (see also the vertical restraints block exemption (at **26.2.4.3**)).

The Notice does not give complete legal protection because:

(a) the market may be a very specialised one where even small companies (especially with patent protection) may have more than the relevant percentage; and

(b) account is to be taken of market share of other companies within the same group, or within the same distribution network and the fact that the share may increase; and

(c) account has to be taken of the overall effect of a network of similar agreements. For example, beer ties with smallish breweries may be caught by Article 81 EC since they are part of a network of similar ties with a substantial effect on competition (see *Delimitis v Henninger Braü* [1991] ECR 1-935); and

(d) in any event, the Notice states that 'hardcore' clauses which would be prohibited by the vertical restraints block exemption (eg, price fixing and total export bans – see **26.2.5**) are not permitted even if the parties are within the market share figures.

26.2.4.2 Article 81(3)

It may be possible to avoid the effects of Article 81(2) EC for a particular agreement because of the operation of Article 81(3) EC. This provides for exemption for any agreement which:

(a) contributes to improving the production or distribution of goods, or to promoting technical or economic progress; and

(b) allows consumers a fair share of the resulting benefit; and

(c) does not impose on the undertakings concerned restrictions which are not indispensable to the attainment of these objectives; and

(d) does not afford such undertakings the possibility of eliminating competition in respect of a substantial part of the products in question.

Thus, to satisfy Article 81(3) EC, the agreement must bring with it certain benefits while at the same time not including excessive restriction of competition.

As mentioned at **26.2.2** above, parties must decide for themselves whether they fit within Article 81(3) – the previous notification system (individual exemption) has been largely removed as from 1 May 2004.

26.2.4.3 Using a block exemption

The Commission in the early years of the Community was inundated with individual notifications, and it was not unusual for years to go by without a reply being received from the Commission. To try to deal with this volume of agreements, the Commission began to introduce block exemptions (as Article 81(3) EC allows them) for particular categories of agreement which fulfil the conditions for an exemption. Several Regulations have now been issued by the Commission to deal with a range of different types of agreement. An important step took place in June 2000 when the vertical restraints block exemption (Regulation 2790/1999) came into effect, which covers all types of vertical agreement. Examples of block exemptions are:

(a) Regulation 2790/99 on Vertical Restraints;

(b) Regulation 417/85 on Specialisation Agreements;

(c) Regulation 418/85 on Research and Development Agreements.

Note that since the Commission alone can give an exemption, severance by national courts is not possible as the parties must stick to the terms of the block exemption before it can apply (see *Delimitis v Henninger Braü* [1991] ECR 1-935). Thus, firms which wish to have the certainty of a valid agreement must take particular care to draft their agreements to fit the relevant block exemption. If they include restrictions which are not allowed by the block exemption, the block exemption cannot apply and the national court cannot sever restrictions before applying the block exemption.

The only exception is the vertical restraints block exemption (Regulation 2790/99, Article 5) which allows for the severance of (inter alia) non-compete clauses including post-term restrictive covenants. If not within the block exemption, the agreement may be exempted by national courts under Article 81(3) EC, but there is no real chance of justifying an agreement with prohibited clauses.

26.2.5 Using the Vertical Restraints Regulation 2790/1999

This Regulation is a significant improvement on the previous regulations for exclusive distribution, exclusive purchasing (eg, beer ties) and franchising. It now exempts in Article 2(1) all vertical agreements (ie, between two or more parties at different levels of the production or distribution chain). There are basically four things to check.

26.2.5.1   Is it vertical?

Under the exemption in Article 2(1), the parties to the agreement must be at different levels, but this would take in a number of different agreements involving goods or services, such as exclusive distribution, selective distribution, franchises and exclusive purchasing. Exemptions would also cover exclusive supply agreements (eg, where a large retailer persuades a supplier of parts to supply only him). Unlike previous block exemptions, it is no longer necessary to identify which type of vertical agreement one is dealing with.

The exemption can apply to multi-party agreements provided they are still vertical. Thus Article 2(2) specifically refers to agreements between a supplier and a trade association of small retailers. There is no reason why a British manufacturer wishing to distribute his product in France should not agree to supply the various retailers in such a trade association and achieve national retail coverage that way rather than supply an individual distributor.

It can also apply even though the chosen distributor is another manufacturer and thus a potential competitor. There is a danger here of the arrangements operating as a horizontal cartel, but provided the arrangements are not reciprocal and the distributor's turnover is limited the exemption will still apply (Article 2(4)).

The exemption does not apply to agreements which are primarily concerned with licensing intellectual property (IP) rights, for example patent, trade mark, copyright or software licences (Article 2(3)). Licensing of 'technology' (patents, software copyright, know-how) is covered by a new Technology Transfer Block Exemption (Regulation 772/2004).

26.2.5.2   Prohibited list

Assuming that the agreement is vertical then the exemption under Article 2(1) applies to all vertical restraints otherwise prohibited by Art 81 EC, unless the agreement contains prohibited clauses. So, the second stage is to check the prohibited list in Article 4. Some of the prohibited clauses are directed to particular types of agreement, so it may be helpful to see how this applies to exclusive distribution and selective distribution.

If it is *exclusive distribution* the clauses to avoid are as follows:

(a)   Article 4(a) – price fixing. This includes minimum prices (which effectively prevent discounts) as well as fixed prices. It does not include maximum or recommended prices unless the price has become in practice fixed through pressure from the supplier. It may be worth considering why prices would be recommended – this may be more justified in selective distribution or franchising than in exclusive distribution.

(b)   Article 4(b) – Restrictions on the buyer's resales to customers or into other territories. It should be noticed that only restrictions on the buyer (the distributor) are prohibited; the block exemption would certainly cover restrictions on the supplier selling into the buyer's territory (the essence, of course, of exclusive distribution).

As far as restrictions on the buyer are concerned, it is permissible to prohibit the distributor from *actively* marketing the goods in territories reserved to the supplier or allocated to other distributors. Passive sales (where the customer approaches the dealer unsolicited) can never be restricted. The enterprising customer must always be allowed to shop around the network to get the cheapest deal. With new methods of marketing over the Internet, which knows no frontiers, the distinction between active and passive sales into other territories becomes a fine one. Fortunately, the Commission's guidelines make it clear that having a website is not actively selling outside the territory. A UK customer can thus check the websites of the dealers in, say, France, Germany and Italy, and order from the cheapest. That is a passive sale and the agreement cannot prohibit the dealer from meeting that order without imperiling the validity of the agreement itself.

Although the agreement can stop the distributor from actively selling to a reserved territory or customer group, it cannot stop him from selling to a customer who would resell to such customers (see Article 4(b), first indent). This is the parallel importer (or exporter), the enterprising dealer who buys from the distributor with the cheapest prices with a view to reselling in those territories where prices are highest. Any restrictions on such sales would lose the block exemption.

If it is *selective distribution* the supplier must again avoid price fixing, but he is even more restricted in the limitations he can put on dealers' customers. The definition of 'selective distribution' appears in Article 1(d). The dealers must be selected on the basis of specified criteria. These might be their qualifications to handle the product (eg, computers or other hi-tech products), or to give the right ambience to accord with the image of the brand (eg, perfumes). The dealers in the network undertake, therefore, not to sell to unauthorised dealers, but other restrictions on sales are all black-listed. Thus dealers must be permitted to supply other selected dealers (Article 4(d)) and selected retailers cannot be prevented from supplying end-users, whether actively or passively (Article 4(c)). Thus, it is not possible to give selected dealers any territorial protection at all from other dealers, who will all compete, whether actively or passively, for the customers of each other.

26.2.5.3 Market share

Once it is clear there are no prohibited clauses, the agreement (and all its restrictions) is covered by the exemption, but it is still necessary to check whether the supplier has more than 30% of the relevant market. If he has, the block exemption cannot apply (Article 3). The rationale for this is that the Commission needs to be satisfied that the agreement does not substantially eliminate competition. Equally, the bigger the market share, the closer the firm comes to being dominant on that market, at which point many of the restrictions permitted under the block exemption would be seen as abuses under Article 82 EC. Thirty per cent has always been taken as the bottom line for dominance. So, even though most cases would be well over 40%, the Commission would still want to vet these agreements individually to be sure. Under the new rules on notifications, however, this can be done when the dispute arises. Article 9 of Regulation 2790/99 gives a definition of the relevant market, but this is entirely in accordance with the tests applied under Article 82 EC (*United Brands* [1978] (Case 27/76) ECR 207– see **26.3.2**).

26.2.5.4 Severable restrictions

This leaves one final step, which is to check through Article 5 to see whether there are any severable restrictions in the agreement. These restrictions, which all concern non-compete obligations, do not destroy the exemption given to other vertical restraints. The national court is permitted to sever them from the agreement (assuming this is possible under its own national rules). The restrictions are:

(a) *Non-compete obligations (including exclusive purchase).* These must be for a fixed term under five years, although, for beer ties with tenanted pubs, the duration could be the length of the lease. Any indefinite exclusive purchase obligation will thus be void but severable. Article 1(b) defines such clauses to include those where the buyer has to take more than 80% of his purchases from the supplier. Thus, in beer ties, the pub may well be taking a guest beer. If guest beers make up less than 20% of the beer supply, the supplier needs to be wary of Article 5.

(b) *Post-term restrictive covenants.* As under English law, these are void if unjustified. But, under Article 5(b), they benefit from the exemption only if they are confined to the same premises, the same goods and a maximum duration of one year. Moreover, and most importantly, they can be justified only if they are there to protect trade secrets ('know-how'). It is unlikely that such covenants could ever be justified in exclusive distribution. There will, however, be trade secrets to protect in franchises, and possibly in selective distribution.

(c) Lastly, selective distribution dealers can never be prevented from selling competing goods, but such clauses are severable.

26.2.6 Agency agreements

The Commission has stated in its Guidance Note to the Vertical Restraints Regulation that such agreements will be outside Article 81 provided the agent accepts no financial risks and the principal is responsible for setting prices and terms. The point here is that such an agent is integrated into the principal's business and thus is not an independent undertaking. The Commission has now put the Notice in its new guidelines on vertical agreements.

26.2.7 Mergers

In principle, when two companies merge (eg, one takes over the other) they cease to be independent undertakings and thus the agreement between them cannot be caught by Article 81 EC.

26.3 Abuse of a dominant position: Article 82 EC

26.3.1 What is the general effect of Article 82 EC?

Article 82 EC renders unlawful any behaviour which amounts to an abuse of its position by an undertaking which is dominant in its particular market. It will therefore be crucially important, when faced with a potential breach of Article 82 EC, to identify the relevant market; it will be seen that undertakings with quite small shares of one market can be dominant in a section of that market and so be at risk from Article 82 EC. It will also be seen that a distinction has to be drawn between an undertaking legitimately taking advantage of what may be a hard-won dominant position and an undertaking which illegitimately abuses that position.

26.3.2 What does Article 82 EC provide?

According to Article 82 EC:

> Any abuse by one or more undertakings of a dominant position within the common market or in a substantial part of it shall be prohibited as incompatible with the common market in so far as it may affect trade between Member States.

The Article then goes on to give a non-exclusive list of the types of behaviour which might amount to such an abuse, for example an undertaking imposing unfair trading conditions, such as unfair prices.

26.3.2.1 What is a dominant position within the common market?

It is by no means essential for an undertaking to be in a monopoly position throughout the EC. The guiding principle here is that an undertaking is likely to be dominant where its economic strength allows it to behave independently of other operators within the market (*United Brands Co (New Jersey, USA) and United Brands Continentaal B (Rotterdam, The Netherlands) v EC Commission* [1978] ECR 207). An example of the principle is where a manufacturing company can set prices or conditions of supply to retailers of its product without regard to the prices or conditions imposed by its competitors. This is more likely to be the case where the undertaking has a larger market share. (In *Hilti v Commission of the European Communities* [1992] 4 CMLR 16, for example, an undertaking was held to be dominant with a 70–80% share of its market.) However, a relatively low market share does not necessarily mean that the undertaking is not dominant. In *United Brands*, dominance was established although the company had a market share of only 40–45%. A particularly important factor to take into account here is whether there are barriers to entry for other undertakings who might wish to enter the market. Does the allegedly dominant undertaking, for example, possess intellectual property rights which would create such a barrier? Whether or not an undertaking is dominant can be considered only in relation to a particular market. In order to identify the relevant market it is important to look at two things: the product market and the geographic market.

How is the product market recognised?

The key question in recognising the product market is 'what other product, if any, can be substituted for the product in question, given the nature of it, its price and its intended use?'. If a number of products are interchangeable, from the point of view of the user, it is arguable that they are all part of one market. On the other hand, if there is no acceptable alternative to the product in question then it can form a market on its own. In *United Brands*, the European Court found that bananas represented a single market because, in certain respects, bananas could not easily be replaced by another fruit. In particular, children and the elderly or the infirm might find it easier to digest bananas than any other fruit.

Similarly, in *Hugin Kassareregister AB and Hugin Cash Registers v EC Commission* [1979] ECR 1869, the European Court found that spare parts for Hugin cash registers represented a separate market in their own right because, once a customer had bought a Hugin machine, no other spare parts could be used. Clearly, if the product market is drawn so narrowly, an undertaking may find itself dominant even if its share of, say, the fruit market or the market for spare parts for cash registers generally is very small.

How is the geographic market recognised?

It is important to look at the geographic area within which the undertaking markets the product where the conditions of competition are the same. Here, too, the definition of the geographical scope of the market is based on substitutability; how far will customers look for their substitute product if the firm's product is unobtainable or too pricey. In many cases, this will be the whole of the single market, but factors such as cultural preferences, the personal nature of services contracts and the costs of transporting heavier goods may restrict the market to a particular region or country.

Article 82 EC applies where an undertaking is dominant in the common market or a substantial part of it. Dominance within a single Member State is likely to be within a substantial part of the common market.

26.3.2.2   What amounts to an abuse of a dominant position?

There are broadly two types of abusive behaviour: one affects competitors or potential competitors in the field; the other affects consumers. Abuse affecting competitors would include pricing the undertaking's products so low that those competitors are forced out of the market, or requiring purchasers of one type of product to buy other products produced by the same undertaking in order to tie them in to a single supplier. Examples of abuses affecting consumers would be setting prices extortionately high, or requiring the product to be sold in certain outlets only.

26.3.3   Are there any exceptions to Article 82 EC?

There is no equivalent in Article 82 EC of Article 81(3) EC (see **25.2.4**); the Commission cannot grant an individual exemption from Article 82 EC, nor are there block exemptions. Even if an undertaking is entitled to claim the benefit of a block exemption under Article 81(3) EC for its activities, that does not necessarily mean that such activities do not amount to an abuse of a dominant position (*Tetra Pak Rausing SA v Commission of the European Communities* [1991] FSR 654). The Commission will, in theory, give guidance letters on whether an action represents a breach, but it is thought that such guidance letters will be few and far between.

26.3.4   What are the sanctions for breach of Article 82 EC?

The Commission and national competition authorities have the power to fine undertakings for breaches of Article 82 EC. As there is no possibility of exemption, there is no equivalent of Article 81(3). Behaviour in breach of Article 82 EC may also give rise to civil liability. It seems that under English law, an injunction can be granted to restrain breaches of Article 82 EC, and it is arguable that damages could also be sought (see *Garden Cottage Foods* at **26.2.3**).

26.4   Chapter summary

Article 82 EC cases are likely to be rare for most solicitors. Article 81 EC, however, is likely to be of much greater relevance.

In drafting commercial agreements, such as licensing agreements for intellectual property rights, distribution agreements, joint ventures (or other arrangements with potential competitors), franchise agreements and exclusive purchasing arrangements (eg, beer ties with public houses or solus agreements for petrol stations), the practitioner has to take Article 81 EC into account. He should consider in turn:

(1)   whether the restrictive agreement might affect trade between Member States, but remember that many agreements between UK parties have such potential;

(2)   whether it is covered by the Notice on Agreements of Minor Importance (but this is only limited security as market share may change). The determination of the relevant market is as critical here as under Article 82 EC;

(3)   for full certainty that the agreement is valid; however, the parties must draft their agreement to fit the relevant block exemption Regulation;

(4)   if the parties wish to include clauses which are not permitted by a block exemption, the agreement is likely to be void under Article 81(2) EC and thus (subject to severance) unenforceable in the national courts, unless the parties show that the agreement fits within the exemption contained in Article 81(3).

The following is an illustration of how Article 81 EC might apply to an exclusive distribution agreement (based on *Consten SA and Grundig-Verkaufs-GmbH v EEC Commission* [1996] CMLR 418).

Example

Widgets Ltd, a UK manufacturer with 15% of the EU widgets market, has a network of exclusive distributors at the wholesale level in France, UK and Germany (see diagram below). It sells to its distributors at £5 per widget and they then mark the price up when selling on to retailers. The UK distributor (a wholly-owned subsidiary) charges £10, whereas the German distributor charges only £6. To protect its position in the UK, therefore, Widgets Ltd imposes clauses on the German wholesaler which prevent it selling to customers outside its territory (export bars) and from selling to dealers in Germany who could resell outside (ie sales to parallel importers). It is hoped that it would thus have absolute territorial protection from competition on prices with its other EU distributors.

Such protection is, however, contrary to Article 81 EC and will attract fines, potential tort claims and void agreements. The block exemption on vertical agreements (Regulation 2790/99) allows territorial exclusivity and a ban on active sales (advertising, etc) outside the territory, but not a ban on passive sales (ie to unsolicited customers who place orders on their own initiative), nor a ban on sales to parallel exporters (see Article 4(b), first indent). Retailers across the EU are perfectly entitled to buy from the cheapest wholesaler in the network.

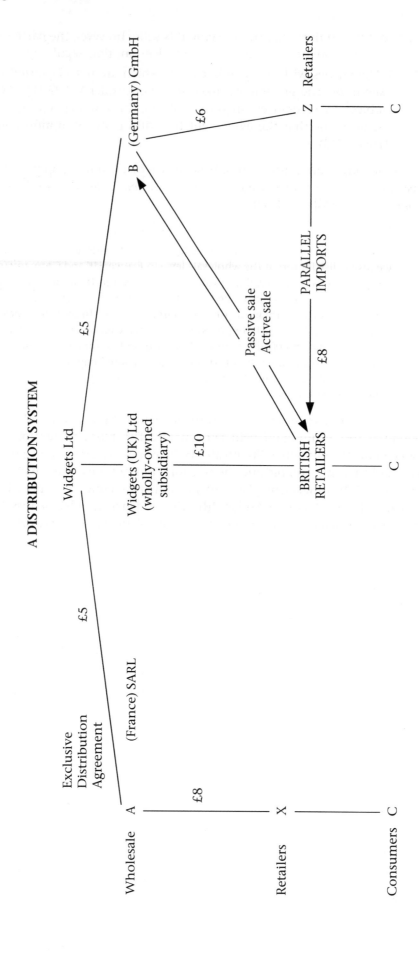

A DISTRIBUTION SYSTEM

26.5 Conversion table for the EC Treaty as amended by the Treaty of Amsterdam

The old numbers will still be relevant when consulting European Court judgments and other sources.

Post-Amsterdam	Pre-Amsterdam	Post-Amsterdam	Pre-Amsterdam
Article 1	Article 1	Article 47	Article 57
Article 2	Article 2	Article 48	Article 58
Article 3	Article 3	Article 49	Article 59
Article 4	Article 3a	Article 50	Article 60
Article 5	Article 3b	Article 51	Article 61
Article 6	Article 3c	Article 52	Article 63
Article 7	Article 4	Article 53	Article 64
Article 8	Article 4a	Article 54	Article 65
Article 9	Article 4b	Article 55	Article 66
Article 10	Article 5	Article 56	Article 73b
Article 11	Article 5a	Article 57	Article 73c
Article 12	Article 6	Article 58	Article 73d
Article 13	Article 6a	Article 59	Article 73f
Article 14	Article 7a	Article 60	Article 73g
Article 15	Article 7c	Article 61	Article 73i
Article 16	Article 7d	Article 62	Article 73j
Article 17	Article 8	Article 63	Article 73k
Article 18	Article 8a	Article 64	Article 73l
Article 19	Article 8b	Article 65	Article 73m
Article 20	Article 8c	Article 66	Article 73n
Article 21	Article 8d	Article 67	Article 73o
Article 22	Article 8e	Article 68	Article 73p
Article 23	Article 9	Article 69	Article 73q
Article 24	Article 10	Article 70	Article 74
Article 25	Article 12	Article 71	Article 75
Article 26	Article 28	Article 72	Article 76
Article 27	Article 29	Article 73	Article 77
Article 28	Article 30	Article 74	Article 78
Article 29	Article 34	Article 75	Article 79
Article 30	Article 36	Article 76	Article 80
Article 31	Article 37	Article 77	Article 81
Article 32	Article 38	Article 78	Article 82
Article 33	Article 39	Article 79	Article 83
Article 34	Article 40	Article 80	Article 84
Article 35	Article 41	Article 81	Article 85
Article 36	Article 42	Article 82	Article 86
Article 37	Article 43	Article 83	Article 87
Article 38	Article 46	Article 84	Article 88
Article 39	Article 48	Article 85	Article 89
Article 40	Article 49	Article 86	Article 90
Article 41	Article 50	Article 87	Article 92
Article 42	Article 51	Article 88	Article 93
Article 43	Article 52	Article 89	Article 94
Article 44	Article 54	Article 90	Article 95
Article 45	Article 55	Article 91	Article 96
Article 46	Article 56	Article 92	Article 98

Post-Amsterdam	Pre-Amsterdam	Post-Amsterdam	Pre-Amsterdam
Article 93	Article 99	Article 145	Article 122
Article 94	Article 100	Article 146	Article 123
Article 95	Article 100a	Article 147	Article 124
Article 96	Article 101	Article 148	Article 125
Article 97	Article 102	Article 149	Article 126
Article 98	Article 102a	Article 150	Article 127
Article 99	Article 103	Article 151	Article 128
Article 100	Article 103a	Article 152	Article 129
Article 101	Article 104	Article 153	Article 129a
Article 102	Article 104a	Article 154	Article 129b
Article 103	Article 104b	Article 155	Article 129c
Article 104	Article 104c	Article 156	Article 129d
Article 105	Article 105	Article 157	Article 130
Article 106	Article 105a	Article 158	Article 130a
Article 107	Article 106	Article 159	Article 130b
Article 108	Article 107	Article 160	Article 130c
Article 109	Article 108	Article 161	Article 130d
Article 110	Article 108a	Article 162	Article 130e
Article 111	Article 109	Article 163	Article 130f
Article 112	Article 109a	Article 164	Article 130g
Article 113	Article 109b	Article 165	Article 130h
Article 114	Article 109c	Article 166	Article 130i
Article 115	Article 109d	Article 167	Article 130j
Article 116	Article 109e	Article 168	Article 130k
Article 117	Article 109f	Article 169	Article 130l
Article 118	Article 109g	Article 170	Article 130m
Article 119	Article 109h	Article 171	Article 130n
Article 120	Article 109i	Article 172	Article 130o
Article 121	Article 109j	Article 173	Article 130p
Article 122	Article 109k	Article 174	Article 130r
Article 123	Article 109l	Article 175	Article 130s
Article 124	Article 109m	Article 176	Article 130t
Article 125	Article 109n	Article 177	Article 130u
Article 126	Article 109o	Article 178	Article 130v
Article 127	Article 109p	Article 179	Article 130w
Article 128	Article 109q	Article 180	Article 130x
Article 129	Article 109r	Article 181	Article 130y
Article 130	Article 109s	Article 182	Article 131
Article 131	Article 110	Article 183	Article 132
Article 132	Article 112	Article 184	Article 133
Article 133	Article 113	Article 185	Article 134
Article 134	Article 115	Article 186	Article 135
Article 135	Article 116	Article 187	Article 136
Article 136	Article 117	Article 188	Article 136a
Article 137	Article 118	Article 189	Article 137
Article 138	Article 118a	Article 190	Article 138
Article 139	Article 118b	Article 191	Article 138a
Article 140	Article 118c	Article 192	Article 138b
Article 141	Article 119	Article 193	Article 138c
Article 142	Article 119a	Article 194	Article 138d
Article 143	Article 120	Article 195	Article 138e
Article 144	Article 121	Article 196	Article 139

Post-Amsterdam	Pre-Amsterdam	Post-Amsterdam	Pre-Amsterdam
Article 197	Article 140	Article 249	Article 189
Article 198	Article 141	Article 250	Article 189a
Article 199	Article 142	Article 251	Article 189b
Article 200	Article 143	Article 252	Article 189c
Article 201	Article 144	Article 253	Article 190
Article 202	Article 145	Article 254	Article 191
Article 203	Article 146	Article 255	Article 191a
Article 204	Article 147	Article 256	Article 192
Article 205	Article 148	Article 257	Article 193
Article 206	Article 150	Article 258	Article 194
Article 207	Article 151	Article 259	Article 195
Article 208	Article 152	Article 260	Article 196
Article 209	Article 153	Article 261	Article 197
Article 210	Article 154	Article 262	Article 198
Article 211	Article 155	Article 263	Article 198a
Article 212	Article 156	Article 264	Article 198b
Article 213	Article 157	Article 265	Article 198c
Article 214	Article 158	Article 266	Article 198d
Article 215	Article 159	Article 267	Article 198e
Article 216	Article 160	Article 268	Article 1992y
Article 217	Article 161	Article 269	Article 2001
Article 218	Article 162	Article 270	Article 201a
Article 219	Article 163	Article 271	Article 202
Article 220	Article 164	Article 272	Article 203
Article 221	Article 165	Article 273	Article 204
Article 222	Article 166	Article 274	Article 205
Article 223	Article 167	Article 275	Article 205a
Article 224	Article 168	Article 276	Article 206
Article 225	Article 168a	Article 277	Article 207
Article 226	Article 169	Article 278	Article 208
Article 227	Article 170	Article 279	Article 209
Article 228	Article 171	Article 280	Article 209a
Article 229	Article 172	Article 281	Article 210
Article 230	Article 173	Article 282	Article 211
Article 231	Article 174	Article 283	Article 212
Article 232	Article 175	Article 284	Article 213
Article 233	Article 176	Article 285	Article 213a
Article 234	Article 177	Article 286	Article 213b
Article 235	Article 178	Article 287	Article 214
Article 236	Article 179	Article 288	Article 215
Article 237	Article 180	Article 289	Article 216
Article 238	Article 181	Article 290	Article 217
Article 239	Article 182	Article 291	Article 218
Article 240	Article 183	Article 292	Article 219
Article 241	Article 184	Article 293	Article 220
Article 242	Article 185	Article 294	Article 221
Article 243	Article 186	Article 295	Article 222
Article 244	Article 187	Article 296	Article 223
Article 245	Article 188	Article 297	Article 224
Article 246	Article 188a	Article 298	Article 225
Article 247	Article 188b	Article 299	Article 227
Article 248	Article 188c	Article 300	Article 228

Post-Amsterdam	Pre-Amsterdam	Post-Amsterdam	Pre-Amsterdam
Article 301	Article 228a	Article 308	Article 235
Article 302	Article 229	Article 309	Article 236
Article 303	Article 230	Article 310	Article 238
Article 304	Article 231	Article 311	Article 239
Article 305	Article 232	Article 312	Article 240
Article 306	Article 233	Article 313	Article 247
Article 307	Article 234	Article 314	Article 248

Part IV
HUMAN RIGHTS

Chapter 27

The European Convention on Human Rights

27.1 Introduction to human rights

Since the Human Rights Act 1998 (HRA 1998) came into force, the subject of human rights has been treated as a pervasive topic on the Legal Practice Course. Perhaps more than any other pervasive topic, its reach is long, and it has begun to make its presence felt in almost every area of law and practice.

This part of this book is intended to provide a brief introduction to human rights. This chapter introduces you to the European Convention and some of the most important Convention rights. **Chapter 28** deals with the mechanism by which the HRA 1998 makes those rights enforceable in the UK.

27.2 Introduction to the Convention

The UK was instrumental in drafting the European Convention for the Protection of Human Rights and Fundamental Freedoms 1950 (European Convention on Human Rights) (ECHR). The Convention was drafted by members of the Council of Europe (a body unrelated to the European Community) in the aftermath of the Second World War and the human rights abuses which took place during it. The UK was one of the original signatories on 4 November 1950. The Convention came into force on 3 September 1953. However, unlike many of the other signatories, the UK did not incorporate the Convention into its own legal system. The Government believed that incorporation was unnecessary because the rights contained in the Convention already flowed from British common law.

The original ECHR contained the civil and political rights to be found in classical liberal thought, such as freedom of expression, freedom of religion and freedom from interference with privacy. A series of protocols, some of which have been ratified by the UK, deal with certain matters including the right to education and the right to peaceful enjoyment of private property (First Protocol) and the prohibition of the death penalty (Sixth Protocol).

The most imaginative feature of the ECHR was that it imposed an international judicial system for the protection of human rights on Europe. It is the most developed of regional systems for the protection of human rights.

27.3 The relationship between the ECHR and English law

The HRA 1998 (which came into force in October 2000) has bridged the gap between the domestic and international planes so far as the Convention is concerned. Domestic English courts are now empowered to enforce Convention rights. Exactly how they may do so will be discussed in **Chapter 28**.

27.4   The relationship between the ECHR and the EC

While there is a close relationship between the EC and the ECHR, the two are distinct and should not be confused. In particular, bear in mind the following differences.

(a)   Far more countries are signatories to the ECHR than are members of the EC.

(b)   The EC's concern with human rights has traditionally been limited. Some rights are protected. Article 141 EC, for example, deals with sex discrimination.

(c)   The ECHR confers rights on everyone within the jurisdiction of a State which is party to the Convention, and not just those who are nationals of the State in question. This is important for asylum seekers, for example. EC law is usually concerned only with the rights of nationals of Member States.

(d)   The ECHR has its own institutions and procedures, in particular the European Court of Human Rights (ECtHR) which sits in Strasbourg, not Luxembourg or Brussels.

There have been suggestions since 1977 that the EC might become a party to the ECHR. So far, this has not happened, and indeed the European Court of Justice (ECJ) has ruled that the Council has no power to accede to the ECHR under the Treaty as currently drafted (see *Opinion No 2/94* [1996] ECR I-1759, 28 March 1996). But the ECJ has said that EC law will draw upon the jurisprudence of the ECHR because it represents the common traditions of the EC Member States in the field of human rights. In the context of the European Union, the Maastricht Treaty makes an express reference to human rights and in particular to the ECHR: see the Recitals and TEU, Article 6.

27.5   The substantive law of the ECHR

27.5.1   The Convention rights

These are the main rights protected by the Convention:

(a)   right to life (Article 2);

(b)   prohibition of torture (Article 3);

(c)   prohibition of slavery and forced labour (Article 4);

(d)   right to liberty and security (Article 5);

(e)   right to a fair trial (Article 6);

(f)   no punishment without lawful authority (Article 7);

(g)   right to respect for family and private life (Article 8);

(h)   right to freedom of thought, conscience and religion (Article 9);

(i)   right to freedom of expression (Article 10);

(j)   right to freedom of assembly and association (Article 11);

(k)   right to marry (Article 12);

(l)   prohibition of discrimination (Article 14);

(m)   right to peaceful enjoyment of possessions (First Protocol, Article 1);

(n)   right to education and right of parents to educate children in accordance with religious and philosophical convictions (First Protocol, Article 2).

The most important of these rights are described below (**27.5.3–27.5.9**).

27.5.2 Some general considerations when dealing with Convention rights

27.5.2.1 Drafting

The Convention is drafted in quite a different way from a United Kingdom statute. In the UK, legislative drafting tends to be very tight and exhaustive. The rights in the Convention are deliberately left open-ended, and the Strasbourg organs do not interpret the Convention in the same way as English judges interpret domestic legislation. Lawyers in the UK must appreciate this different way of working.

27.5.2.2 Absolute and limited rights

Some of the Convention rights are absolute. For example, the right to freedom from torture: the Convention allows no circumstances in which torture could be legitimate. But most of the rights are subject to limitations and qualifications. For example, the right to freedom of expression may be interfered with where the matters being expressed are defamatory or harmful to national security. Much of the argument in Convention cases turns not on whether there has been an interference with Convention rights, but on whether that interference is justifiable. In considering the interference, the ECtHR has invented a number of tools with which UK lawyers need to be familiar.

27.5.2.3 Judicial method

Once it has been established that a Convention right has been interfered with, the court must consider whether the interference is justified (unless the right is one which is absolute, in which case no interference is allowed).

There are four key concepts which the ECtHR uses.

The rule of law

No matter how desirable the end to be achieved, any interference with a Convention right must be based on some ascertainable law, and not on an arbitrary executive decision. Without detailed authorisation by law, any interference, however justified, will violate the Convention. For example, telephone tapping by the police in the 1970s was regulated by nothing more than an internal police guidance note which was not available to the public. The interference with the right to respect for correspondence (Article 8) was not therefore justified by law and was contrary to the Convention (*Malone v United Kingdom* (1984) 7 EHRR 14).

Legitimate aims

The defendant must say why the right is being interfered with, and the reason must be a legitimate one. Many of the Articles (eg, Articles 8, 9, 10 and 11) set out what sorts of aims are legitimate, for example the interests of public safety, national security or the protection of the rights and freedoms of others. For example, if a prisoner's correspondence is being read by the prison authorities then the prevention of disorder or crime within the prison would be a legitimate reason for the interference with Article 8 if there was a genuine belief that there was a risk. But the routine reading of mail would not be legitimate (*Campbell v United Kingdom* (1992) 15 EHRR 137).

Proportionality

The cliché usually used to describe the doctrine of proportionality is that the State cannot use a sledgehammer to crack a nut. In the more formal language of the court, any restriction on a right must be 'necessary in a democratic society' or based on some 'pressing social need'. For example, in the domestic UK case of *Lindsay v Customs & Excise Commissioners* [2002] EWCA Civ 267, [2002] STC 588, the defendant had been caught by customs officers driving his Ford Focus car into the UK containing 18,400 cigarettes, 10 kilos of handrolling tobacco, 31 litres of beer and 3 litres of spirits. The goods were for members of his family, for which he had received payment. This was unlawful. As well as seizing the goods, the customs officers seized his car and refused to return it to him. The Court of Appeal held that the interference with the defendant's right to peaceful enjoyment of his possessions by the forfeiture of his car, although within the legal powers of the customs officers, was disproportionate for small-scale smuggling of this nature.

Margin of appreciation

This is the Strasbourg equivalent of what in Brussels is called subsidiarity. It means that the States which are party to the Convention are allowed a degree of leeway out of sensitivity to their own political and cultural traditions. For example, the case of *Handyside v United Kingdom* (1976) 1 EHRR 737 concerned the publication in England in 1971 of *The Little Red School Book*, a children's book including a section on sex. The publisher had been convicted under the Obscene Publications Act 1959. The ECtHR had to consider the UK Government's argument that the interference with the publisher's right to freedom of expression was necessary for the purpose of the 'protection of morals'. The Court accepted that such a matter was within the competence of national authorities and a standard could not be imposed by an international body:

> By reason of their direct and continuous contact with the vital forces of their countries, state authorities are in principle in a better position than the international judge to give an opinion. (para 48)

The majority of commentators agree that, by its nature, the doctrine of the margin of appreciation will not be relevant to cases decided under the HRA 1998 by UK courts. The doctrine exists to take account of the geographical and cultural gaps between an international court and the various countries it supervises. Within a unitary domestic legal system it will serve no purpose.

27.5.3 Article 5: The right to liberty and security

1.   Everyone has the right to liberty and security of person. No one shall be deprived of his liberty save in the following cases and in accordance with a procedure prescribed by law:

   (a)   the lawful detention of a person after conviction by a competent court;

   (b)   the lawful arrest or detention of a person for non-compliance with the lawful order of a court or in order to secure the fulfilment of any obligation prescribed by law;

   (c)   the lawful arrest or detention of a person effected for the purpose of bringing him before the competent legal authority on reasonable suspicion of having committed an offence or when it is reasonably considered necessary to prevent his committing an offence or fleeing after having done so;

   (d)   the detention of a minor by lawful order for the purpose of educational supervision or his lawful detention for the purpose of bringing him before the competent legal authority;

(e)   the lawful detention of persons for the prevention of the spreading of infectious diseases, of persons of unsound mind, alcoholics or drug addicts or vagrants;

(f)   the lawful arrest or detention of a person to prevent his effecting an unauthorised entry into the country or of a person against whom action is being taken with a view to deportation or extradition.

2.   Everyone who is arrested shall be informed promptly, in a language which he understands, of the reasons for his arrest and of any charge against him.

3.   Everyone arrested or detained in accordance with the provisions of paragraph 1(c) of this Article shall be brought promptly before a judge or other officer authorised by law to exercise judicial power and shall be entitled to trial within a reasonable time or to release pending trial. Release may be conditioned by guarantees to appear for trial.

4.   Everyone who is deprived of his liberty by arrest or detention shall be entitled to take proceedings by which the lawfulness of his detention shall be decided speedily by a court and his release ordered if the detention is not lawful.

5.   Everyone who has been the victim of arrest or detention in contravention of the provisions of this Article shall have an enforceable right to compensation.

Article 5 is the most lengthy of the Convention rights. It is of particular importance to criminal litigation practitioners, especially in challenging arrests and detentions. Its overall purpose is to ensure that no one is deprived of his or her liberty in an arbitrary fashion (*Engel v Netherlands* (1979–80) 1 EHRR 647, para 58).

The Article has two distinct limbs. Paragraph 1 prohibits interference with liberty or security of person except in certain, well-defined circumstances. No distinction tends to be made in Strasbourg jurisprudence between the two concepts of liberty and security of person. Paragraphs 2–5 provide a set of procedural rights for detainees.

27.5.3.1 Lawful detention

Paragraph 1 insists in particular that any detention must be 'lawful' (the word is used in each of subparas (a)–(f)). This requires that the domestic law upon which a detention is based must be accessible and precise. The paragraph also requires that the detention be 'in accordance with a procedure prescribed by law'. This calls for a consideration of how the detainer has gone about detaining the individual rather than why. Where there is no procedure prescribed by domestic law, or where the detainer has failed to follow it, Article 5 will have been breached.

27.5.3.2 Reasons

Paragraph 2 provides a right for those placed under arrest to be given reasons. These do not need to be in writing, and formal notification is not necessary if the reasons are made clear during the arrest (*X v Netherlands* 5 YB 224, at 228).

27.5.3.3 Judicial supervision

Paragraph 3 requires that the person under arrest be brought promptly before a judge (usually a magistrate in the UK). The paragraph also provides for trial within a reasonable time, or release pending trial (ie bail). There is a presumption that bail will be granted unless there are good reasons not to grant it (for example, because there is a risk that the accused will fail to appear at the trial: *Stögmüller v Austria* (1969) 1 EHRR 155).

27.5.3.4 Challenge and review

Paragraph 4 requires that a speedy procedure must be available by which detention can be challenged. The habeas corpus procedure in the UK fulfils this requirement, so long as it concludes swiftly. The ECtHR has also held that where the circumstances of detention vary over time a regular reviewing procedure must exist.

27.5.3.5 Compensation

Paragraph 5 provides a right to compensation for any interference with Article 5 rights. In practice, this is unlikely to add anything to the availability of damages (and possibly exemplary damages) in tort for wrongful arrest or unlawful detention.

27.5.4 Article 6: The right to a fair trial

1. In the determination of his civil rights and obligations or of any criminal charge against him, everyone is entitled to a fair and public hearing within a reasonable time by an independent and impartial tribunal established by law. Judgment shall be pronounced publicly but the press and public may be excluded from all or part of the trial in the interest of morals, public order or national security in a democratic society, where the interests of juveniles or the protection of the private life of the parties so require, or to the extent strictly necessary in the opinion of the court in special circumstances where publicity would prejudice the interests of justice.

2. Everyone charged with a criminal offence shall be presumed innocent until proved guilty according to law.

3. Everyone charged with a criminal offence has the following minimum rights:

    (a) to be informed promptly, in a language which he understands and in detail, of the nature and cause of the accusation against him;

    (b) to have adequate time and facilities for the preparation of his defence;

    (c) to defend himself in person or through legal assistance of his own choosing or, if he has not sufficient means to pay for legal assistance, to be given it free when the interests of justice so require;

    (d) to examine or have examined witnesses against him and to obtain the attendance and examination of witnesses on his behalf under the same conditions as witnesses against him;

    (e) to have the free assistance of an interpreter if he cannot understand or speak the language used in court.

Article 6 is arguably the most important, and certainly the most utilised, of all the Convention rights. It provides for a right to fair criminal and civil trials, and lays down certain procedural standards. It is of direct importance to all litigators, and therefore indirectly to all lawyers.

27.5.4.1 Determination of civil rights or a criminal charge

Paragraph 1 lays down the basic 'due process' standards for the determination of civil and criminal matters. The phrase 'in the determination of his civil rights' needs some explanation. It does not simply cover any issue which might be the subject of a trial in civil law as an English lawyer would understand that expression. The Strasbourg case law on this is complex. All proceedings between private individuals and private bodies are included. Not all proceedings involving public authorities are, and here further research may be necessary. Broadly, a distinction is made between those decisions of public bodies which affect private law rights (which are within the scope of the Article) and those affecting public law rights (which are not). For example, planning decisions affect property rights and are included. Actions to sue public authorities for compensation will be included, because private law rights in tort or contract are involved. But decisions of public authorities affecting education involve public law, not private law rights, and are not subject to Article 6 requirements (*Simpson v United Kingdom* (1989) 64 DR 188). For the same reason decisions on the categorisation of prisoners for security purposes are not covered (*Brady v United Kingdom* (1979) 3 EHRR 297).

What is a criminal charge for the purposes of Article 6? To determine this, three questions must be answered. How is the offence classified in domestic law? What is the nature of the offence? What is the nature and purpose of the penalty; how severe is it? See *Engel v Netherlands* (1979–80) 1 EHRR 647.

27.5.4.2   A fair trial

Paragraph 1 sets out the minimum requirements for a fair trial. They are:

(a)   a fair and public hearing;

(b)   an independent and impartial tribunal;

(c)   trial within a reasonable period;

(d)   public judgment (with some exceptions); and

(e)   a reasoned decision.

As the most litigated Article, a great deal of case law has grown up around these requirements. The approach of the ECtHR in interpreting and applying Article 6(1) is generous to applicants, and the Court reaches its decisions 'bearing in mind the prominent place which the right to a fair trial holds in a democratic society' (*Delcourt v Belgium* (1979–80) 1 EHRR 355). Not only have these decisions built on the requirements expressly contained in the paragraph set out above, they have read other rights into the paragraph. These include:

(a)   the right of access to a court (eg, *Osman v United Kingdom* (2000) 29 EHRR 245: police immunity a denial of the right of access to a court);

(b)   equality of arms (*Dombo Beheer BV v Netherlands* (1994) 18 EHRR 213); and

(c)   the right to participate effectively in proceedings (*Stanford v United Kingdom* (Case A/282) (1994) *The Times*, 8 March: poor court room acoustics).

Should a fugitive from justice be denied these Convention rights? In *Conde Nast Publications Ltd v UK* (2008) Application No 00029746/05, LTL 29 February, the applicant publishers had been sued successfully for defamation. The claimant had left America and moved to France before being sentenced for an offence in respect of which he had pleaded guilty. The High Court had allowed the claimant to give his evidence by video link from a Paris hotel. The House of Lords had upheld that decision. The applicants argued that the principle of equality of arms was broken and so the proceedings were unfair. The ECtHR held that the UK Government could not be condemned under Article 6 for providing the claimant with facilities that were available to other litigants simply because of his status as a fugitive from justice. Why? Because the deprivation of such facilities would run counter to the Convention guarantee of equal treatment that is inherent in the principle of equality of arms.

Furthermore, in civil litigation, paragraph 1 has been held to require a right to legal aid should the circumstances of the case demand it, especially 'by reason of the complexity of the procedure of the case' (*Airey v Ireland* (Case A/32) (1979) 2 EHRR 305; see also *Steel and Morris v United Kingdom* [2005] ECHR 68416/01 (the so-called 'McDonald's libel case'). (Article 6(3)(c) expressly requires legal aid in criminal litigation.)

27.5.4.3 Presumption of innocence

Paragraph 2 provides for the presumption of innocence in criminal trials. 'Reverse onus' provisions, which place the burden of proof upon a defendant to demonstrate his innocence, have been held not necessarily to violate Article 6(2) (*Lingens v Austria* (1981) 26 DR 171, also *R v Director of Public Prosecutions, ex p Kebilene* [2000] 2 AC 326, the first HRA 1998 case to reach the House of Lords). In *Murray v United Kingdom (Right to Silence)* (1996) 22 EHRR 29, the ECtHR ruled that the drawing of adverse inferences from the exercise by the accused of his right to silence did not violate the Article either. However, in *Saunders v United Kingdom* (1996) 23 EHRR 313, the use of statements obtained by compulsion by inspectors exercising statutory powers under the Companies Act 1985 was held to be a violation of Article 6(2).

Since the HRA 1998 came into force the issue of reverse onus provisions has been raised in domestic UK litigation in several motoring cases. For example, in *R v Drummond* [2002] EWCA Crim 527, [2002] 2 Cr App R 25, the defendant was accused of causing death by dangerous driving and driving with excess alcohol. He tried to rely on the 'hip flask' defence, that he had drunk the alcohol after the accident and before the arrival of the police to steady his nerves. The legislation placed the burden upon him to prove that this was the case rather than requiring the prosecution to show that he had drunk the alcohol before the accident. The Court of Appeal held that the imposition of this burden on the defendant was justified and he lost his appeal against conviction.

In *R v Keogh* [2007] EWCA Civ 528, the Court of Appeal held that the reverse burdens of proof contained in s 2(3) and s 3(4) of the Official Secrets Act 1989 were incompatible with Article 6. Why? Because the Act can operate effectively without the imposition of those reverse burdens. The Court held that it was not necessary to impose them and to do so would be disproportionate and unjustifiable.

27.5.4.4 Procedural safeguards in criminal trials

Because of the serious nature of criminal litigation, paragraph 3 provides specific procedural rights in this context. These are rights for the defendant:

(a)   to be informed promptly of the accusation against him;

(b)   to have adequate time and facilities to prepare his defence;

(c)   to choose his legal representative and to receive legal aid if necessary;

(d)   to call witnesses and to cross-examine witnesses against him; and

(e)   to have free access to an interpreter if necessary.

Again, these rights have caused a great deal of litigation. Reference to the case law or to a specialist work is needed to understand them fully.

27.5.5 Article 8: The right to respect for private and family life

1.   Everyone has the right to respect for his private and family life, his home and his correspondence.

2.   There shall be no interference by a public authority with the exercise of this right except such as is in accordance with the law and is necessary in a democratic society in the interests of national security, public safety or the economic wellbeing of the country, for the prevention of disorder or crime, for the protection of health or morals, or for the protection of the rights and freedoms of others.

Article 8 has been used creatively by lawyers and judges. Its essential object is to protect the individual against arbitrary action by public authorities (*Kroon v Netherlands* (1994) 19 EHRR 263). It has been used in cases where it might seem quite at home, such as those involving phone tapping, or interference with prisoners' mail. But it has also been used in contexts which might come as a surprise to those who drafted it, such as the rights of transsexuals to have official records amended to recognise their status, the right to an environment unpolluted by noise and chemicals, and the right to practise one's sexuality freely.

Paragraph 1 protects four distinct rights.

27.5.5.1   Private life

This encompasses:

(a)   noise pollution issues (*Rayner v United Kingdom* (1986) 47 DR 5);

(b)   pollution by waste (*López Ostra v Spain* (1994) 20 EHRR 277);

(c)   sexual orientation (*Smith and Grady v United Kingdom* (2000) 29 EHRR 548);

(d)   the unauthorised disclosure of confidential data to third parties (*MS v Sweden* (1999) 28 EHRR 313);

(e)   covert police surveillance (*Wood v United Kingdom* [2004] ECHR 23414/02);

(f)   the monitoring by an employer of office telephone calls without warning (*Halford v United Kingdom* (1997) 24 EHRR 523);

(g)   the opening and censoring of prisoner's confidential correspondence with a court (*Klyakhin v Russia* [2004] ECHR 46082/99);

(h)   administration of medication against wishes (*Glass v United Kingdom* [2004] ECHR 61827/00);

(i)   a State's obligation to make adequate and effective efforts to assist a person in his attempt to have his child returned to him with a view to exercising his parental rights (*Monory v Romania* [2005] ECHR 71099/01); and

(j)   unauthorised publication of wedding photographs (*Douglas v Hello!* [2003] 3 All ER 996).

27.5.5.2   Family life

It is disruption of the family unit which is most likely to offend against this aspect of Article 8. This might include, for example, a situation in which the State wishes to take a child into care. It is also an extremely important issue for immigration lawyers, as immigration controls may often result in families being broken up.

'Family' clearly includes those with blood and marital links, but has also been extended by the ECtHR to include other emotional ties. In *K v United Kingdom* (1986) 50 DR 199, the ECtHR said 'the question of the existence or non-existence of "family life" is essentially a question of fact depending upon the real existence in practice of close personal ties'.

Does a private or family life include such interests as an individual's social life; a person's life being centred, or work being dependent on, a particular activity; family involvement in a particular activity; the social and economic impact on a local community of the loss of a particular activity; cultural heritage; loss of job or loss of business? In *R (on the application of the Countryside Alliance and Others) v AG* [2007] UKHL 52, the claimants put forward these interests as part of their case that the ban on hunting wild mammals with dogs under the Hunting Act 2004 engaged Article 8. However, the House of Lords observed that these arguments stretched the ambit of Article 8 far wider than had ever been recognised in Strasbourg jurisprudence and the House held that Article 8 was not engaged.

27.5.5.3   Home

Clearly, there is some overlap between private life, family life and home life. This element of Article 8(1) specifically protects the right to occupy one's home without harassment or interference. Noise nuisance can violate this right (*Arrondelle v United Kingdom* (1982) 26 DR 5). So can entry by the police to search or for other purposes. In *McLeod v United Kingdom* (1999) 27 EHRR 493, the police accompanied an estranged husband into the former matrimonial home. As there was little risk of disorder the ECtHR held that this was a disproportionate interference with the applicant's right to home life.

In the context of housing law, the Article does not extend to the right to have a home (*Buckley v United Kingdom* (1996) 23 EHRR 101). But can it constitute a defence to possession proceedings? Yes, but the court will proceed on the rebuttable assumption that domestic law strikes a fair balance and that it is compatible with the requirements of Article 8 (and also Article 1 of the First Protocol): see *Kay v London Borough of Lambeth*; *Leeds City Council v Price* [2006] UKHL 10.

27.5.5.4   Correspondence

It was under this provision that *Malone v United Kingdom* (1984) 7 EHRR 14 was brought, successfully challenging telephone tapping by the police without statutory authority. This resulted in the enactment of the Interception of Communications Act 1985 to grant the police statutory powers. Similar issues were raised in the *Halford* case (see **27.5.5.1**). The Regulation of Investigatory Powers Act 2000 is an important piece of legislation in this area which now, amongst other things, governs interference with communications by employers. As for interference with written correspondence, most of the case law concerns prisoners' rights. Broadly they may correspond freely with their lawyers, but prison authorities may interfere with other correspondence so long as this is justified (*Golder v United Kingdom* (1975) 1 EHRR 524; *Silver v United Kingdom* (1983) 5 EHRR 347).

27.5.5.5   Justification for interference

Article 8 is not absolute. Paragraph 2 sets out reasons which may justify interference with para 1 rights. The principle of proportionality requires that the interference must be the minimum necessary to achieve the legitimate aim (for example, see the *McLeod* case, at **27.5.5.3** above).

27.5.6   Article 10: The right to freedom of expression

1. Everyone has the right to freedom of expression. This right shall include freedom to hold opinions and to receive and impart information and ideas without interference by public authority and regardless of frontiers. This Article shall not prevent States from requiring the licensing of broadcasting, television or cinema enterprises.

2. The exercise of these freedoms, since it carries with it duties and responsibilities, may be subject to such formalities, conditions, restrictions or penalties as are prescribed by law and are necessary in a democratic society, in the interests of national security, territorial integrity or public safety, for the prevention of disorder or crime, for the protection of health or morals, for the protection of the reputation or rights of others, for preventing the disclosure of

information received in confidence, or for maintaining the authority and impartiality of the judiciary.

The ECtHR has described this right as 'one of the essential foundations of a democratic society and one of the conditions of its progress' (*Handyside v United Kingdom* (1976) 1 EHRR 737). It is particularly useful to the press and broadcast media, as well as other publishers and political organisations. The right extends to receiving as well as imparting information. However, this does not oblige public authorities to disclose information against their will (*The Gaskin Case* [1990] 1 FLR 167, no right of access to fostering records held by a local authority). It merely prohibits restrictions on the receipt of information, for example information about abortion in Ireland (*Open Door Dublin Well Women v Ireland* (1992) 15 EHRR 244).

Where there is an interference with Article 10 rights, it will be incompatible with the Convention unless:

(a)   it is prescribed by law;

(b)   it pursues a legitimate aim (see para 2);

(c)   it is necessary in a democratic society; and

(d)   it is proportionate.

27.5.6.1   Defamation

The ECtHR recognises that individuals have a right to have their reputations protected. But defamation claims are an interference with Article 10 rights and so must be justified using the criteria listed above on a case-by-case basis. In *Tolstoy Miloslavsky v United Kingdom*; *Lord Aldington v Watts* (1995) 20 EHRR 442, for example, the ECtHR found that a damages award of £1.5 million was disproportionate.

The ECtHR has also recognised, however, that criticism of public figures, especially politicians, is more easily justifed under Article 10. In *Lingens v Austria* (1986) 8 EHRR 407 it said:

> The limits of acceptable criticism are ... wider as regards a politician as such than as regards a private individual. Unlike the latter, the former inevitably and knowingly lays himself open to close scrutiny of every word and deed by both journalists and the public at large, and he must consequently display a greater degree of tolerance. (para 42)

What about pressure groups? In *Steel and Morris v United Kingdom* [2005] ECHR 68416/01 (the so-called 'McDonald's libel case') the ECtHR stated that:

> the Court considers, however, that in a democratic society even small and informal campaign groups ... must be able to carry on their activities effectively and that there exists a strong public interest in enabling such groups and individuals outside the mainstream to contribute to the public debate by disseminating information and ideas on matters of general public interest such as health and the environment ... If, however, a State decides to provide such a remedy [defamation] to a corporate body, it is essential, in order to safeguard the countervailing interests in free expression and open debate that a measure of procedural fairness and equality of arms is provided for.

27.5.6.2   Prior restraint

The use of injunctions to prevent publication of material in advance is viewed with suspicion by the ECtHR. In the *Spycatcher* case (*Guardian Newspapers v United Kingdom* (1992) 14 EHRR 153) it said:

the dangers inherent in prior restraint are such that they call for the most careful scrutiny ... News is a perishable commodity and to delay its publication, even for a short period, may well deprive it of all its value and interest. (para 60)

The concern which the Strasbourg Court has is reflected in s 12 of the HRA 1998 (see **Appendix to Part IV**).

27.5.7   Article 11: The right to freedom of assembly and association

1.   Everyone has the right to freedom of peaceful assembly and to freedom of association with others, including the right to form and to join trade unions for the protection of his interests.

2.   No restrictions shall be placed on the exercise of these rights other than such as are prescribed by law and are necessary in a democratic society in the interests of national security or public safety, for the prevention of disorder or crime, for the protection of health or morals or for the protection of the rights and freedoms of others. This Article shall not prevent the imposition of lawful restrictions on the exercise of these rights by members of the armed forces, of the police or of the administration of the State.

This Article contains two distinct rights: freedom of peaceful assembly and freedom of association.

27.5.7.1   Freedom of peaceful assembly

This extends to anyone who intends to organise a peaceful march or static assembly. The possibility of violence arising because of the intentions of counter-demonstrators or extremist infiltrators does not affect the right (*Christians Against Racism and Fascism v United Kingdom* (1980) 21 DR 138).

The sorts of restrictions which para 2 envisages include limitations on the location of a demonstration or the route of a march.

27.5.7.2   Freedom of association

This covers the right of individuals to join together, especially in organisations like political parties and trade unions. It also extends to the right not to join such organisations. For example, compulsory membership of a union (a 'closed shop') will usually be contrary to the Convention (*Young, James and Webster v United Kingdom* (1982) 4 EHRR 38).

The right does not extend to a right to negotiate with employers via collective bargaining (*Swedish Engine Drivers' Union v Sweden* (1976) 1 EHRR 617). Nor does it include a right to strike (*Schmidt and Dahlstrom v Sweden* (1979–80) 1 EHRR 632).

27.5.8   Article 14: The prohibition on discrimination

The enjoyment of the rights and freedoms set forth in this Convention shall be secured without discrimination on any ground such as sex, race, colour, language, religion, political or other opinion, national or social origin, association with a national minority, property, birth or other status.

Article 14 is not as important as it may at first appear. It is vital to realise that the right not to be discriminated against cannot be relied upon on its own. It may only be invoked in conjunction with another Convention right.

As the Court has consistently held, Article 14 of the Convention complements the other substantive provisions of the Convention and the Protocols. It has no independent existence since it has effect solely in relation to 'the enjoyment of the rights and freedoms' safeguarded by those provisions. Although the application of Article 14 does not presuppose a breach of those provisions – and to this extent it is autonomous – there can be no room for its application unless the facts at issue fall within the ambit of one or more of the latter. (*Van Raalte v Netherlands* (1997) 24 EHRR 503 at para 33)

A claimant relying on Article 14 must first establish that a substantive Convention right is in issue. There need not necessarily have been a breach of that right. It must only be shown that the facts fall within the ambit of that provision. The next step is to ask whether there is a difference in treatment between different sorts of people. Lastly, one must examine whether that difference has a legitimate aim.

An example is the case of *Abdulaziz v United Kingdom*; *Cabales v United Kingdom*; *Balkandali v United Kingdom* (1985) 7 EHRR 471, an immigration case. The exclusion of spouses of new entrants from the UK in certain circumstances was held not to breach Article 8. However, the admission of the spouses of male entrants but the exclusion of spouses of female entrants breached Article 14.

You will have noted that Article 14 ends with the words 'other status'. Who might fall within that category? The ECtHR has interpreted this as meaning a personal characteristic (see *Kjeldsen, Busk Madsen and Pedersen v Denmark* (1976) 1 EHRR 711, para 56). It is therefore necessary to examine whether the ground for different treatment in a case amounts to a status in the sense of a personal characteristic (see *R (on the application of S) v Chief Constable of South Yorkshire* [2004] UKHL 39). This led the Court of Appeal, for example, in *R (on the application of RJM) v Secretary of State for Work and Pensions* [2007] EWCA Civ 614, to hold that a person who chooses to be homeless or sleep rough does not fall within this provision.

27.5.9 Protocol 1, Article 1: The right to peaceful enjoyment of possessions

Every natural or legal person is entitled to the peaceful enjoyment of his possessions.

No one shall be deprived of his possessions except in the public interest and subject to the conditions provided for by law and by the general principles of international law.

The preceding provisions shall not, however, in any way impair the right of a State to enforce such laws as it deems necessary to control the use of property in accordance with the general interest or to secure the payment of taxes or other contributions or penalties.

'Possessions' in this Article has a wide meaning. It includes, amongst other things, land, money, shares and goodwill.

The Article contains two distinct rights:

(a) the right not to be deprived of possessions, subject to certain conditions; and

(b) the right not to have the State control possessions, subject to certain conditions.

Deprivation covers situations in which title is transferred or extinguished, for example the creation of a presumption of title in land in favour of the State (*Holy Monasteries v Greece* (1994) 20 EHRR 1). Control covers situations falling short of this, for example limiting the amount of rent which a landlord may charge, placing restrictions upon developing property and rules restricting rights of inheritance.

In both cases interference with the right is permissible in the public interest or the general interest (a distinction which is of little importance). The guiding principle is one of fair balance between individual and community interests. In striking this balance regard must always be had to the principle of proportionality (see **27.5.2**).

27.5.10 Identifying and addressing Convention rights

27.5.10.1 Has there been an interference with a Convention right?

Do the facts complained of disclose an interference with the enjoyment of any particular right or rights?

Example 1

Assume that you are a solicitor and a court has made a wasted costs order against you. What rights might be relevant? Is the order a determination of your civil rights such that Article 6 is engaged? Or is it a criminal charge for the purposes of that Article? Otherwise, is it an interference with your possessions for the purposes of the First Protocol, Article 1? In fact the ECtHR has already answered all these questions in the negative (see, eg, *Tormala v Finland* (2004) 41528/98).

Example 2

Assume that you are protesting peacefully against an arms fair being held in London. You are stopped by two police officers and searched. You are handed a copy of Stop/ Search Form 5090 which records that you were stopped and searched under s 44 of the Terrorism Act 2000. The search was said to be for 'articles concerned in terrorism'. The whole incident lasts about 20 minutes. What rights might be engaged? Have you been deprived of your liberty under Article 5? Has there been a lack of respect for your private life such that Article 8 is engaged? Have your rights to free expression and free assembly protected by Articles 10 and 11 been infringed? The House of Lords have answered all of these questions in the negative (or otherwise felt that the measures were justified): see *R (on the application of Gillan and Another) v Commissioner of Police for the Metropolis and Another* [2006] UKHL 12. However, for a similar case where the House held that Articles 10 and 11 were infringed, see *R (on the application of Laporte) v Chief Constable of Gloucestershire* [2006] UKHL 55.

How are you going to be able to identify relevant rights in the future? You need to have in mind the structure of the Articles. A breakdown of the key Articles by way of a checklist appears at **Appendix 2 to Part IV**.

Once any particular qualified right has been identified, the following questions need to be answered. The detail can be found at **27.5.2.3** above:

(a)   Is the interference prescribed by law?

(b)   Does the interference have a legitimate aim under the relevant Article?

(c)   Is the interference proportionate?

(d)   Is the interference within any appropriate margin of appreciation?

27.5.10.2 Worked example

In *Connors v UK* (2004) 66746/01, the applicant, a gypsy, complained that he and his family had been evicted by a local authority from its gypsy caravan site in breach of Article 8.

The parties were agreed that Article 8 was engaged as the eviction of the applicant from the site on which he had lived with his family in his caravan disclosed an interference with his right to respect for his private life, family life and home. The parties were also agreed, in the context of the second paragraph of Article 8, that the interference was in accordance with the law and pursued a legitimate aim, namely, the protection of the rights of other occupiers of the site by the local authority which owned and managed the site. The question for the Court was whether the interference was 'necessary in a democratic society' in pursuit of that aim, ie if there was a 'pressing social need' and, in particular, if it was proportionate to the legitimate aim pursued. As to the scope of the margin of appreciation, the Court indicated that this depends on the context of the case, with particular significance attaching to the extent of the intrusion into the personal sphere of the applicant. The procedural safeguards available to the individual are especially material in determining whether the respondent State has, when fixing the regulatory framework, remained within its margin of appreciation. In particular, the court must examine whether the decision-making process leading to measures of interference was fair and such as to afford due respect to the interests safeguarded to the individual by Article 8.

The Court found that the eviction of the applicant and his family from the local authority site was not attended by the requisite procedural safeguards, namely the requirement to establish proper justification for the serious interference with his rights. Consequently it could not be regarded as justified by a 'pressing social need' or proportionate to the legitimate aim being pursued. There had, accordingly, been a violation of Article 8 of the Convention.

27.6   Petitioning the Court in Strasbourg

27.6.1   Introduction

Despite the HRA 1998, there will be situations where an individual is denied a remedy under UK law, for example because primary legislation is clearly incompatible with the Convention, or because there is some gap in the legislation which cannot be filled by the common law and in either case the Government will not make amends. In such cases, the individual can petition the ECtHR in Strasbourg. This, however, will be the last resort as the Convention requires the applicant to exhaust domestic remedies (including the HRA 1998) before going to Strasbourg.

27.6.2   Procedural law of the ECHR

A complaint will be addressed to the Secretary of the Court of Human Rights. The initial complaint does not need to be on a special form, although one would have to be completed eventually. Under the rules made under the Eleventh Protocol, a chamber of the court will determine admissibility. Around 90% of complaints are ruled inadmissible, usually because of failure to exhaust domestic remedies, or because they are 'manifestly ill-founded' or because they fail to meet the time-limit of six months from the exhaustion of the final domestic remedy. The initial decision on admissibility will be taken by a committee of three.

Once the committee has judged a complaint admissible, the ECtHR will try to reach a friendly settlement with the government concerned, which must include the reform of any offending rules. Failing a settlement, there will be further submissions, including an oral hearing at which, as well as the parties, relevant organisations like Liberty or Justice may be represented. The ECtHR (usually a chamber of seven, but exceptionally a grand chamber of 17) may award compensation as part of its judgment, but the judgment itself does not change the law in the UK. That is a matter for the UK Government. There is also a right of appeal to the Grand Chamber on issues of general importance (subject to the leave of the first chamber). This is a little like obtaining leave to appeal to the House of Lords. The Rules of Court were published in March 2005 and can be found on the ECtHR website.

22.6 Petitioning the Court in Strasbourg

22.6.1 Introduction

22.6.2 Procedure/law of the ECtHR

Chapter 28

The Human Rights Act 1998

28.1 Introduction

> It is clear that the 1998 Act must be given its full import and that long or well entrenched ideas may have to be put aside, sacred cows culled. (per Lord Slynn in *R v Lambert* [2001] UKHL 37 at para 6)

In brief, the effect of the HRA 1998 is to make it possible for litigants in the UK to rely on Convention rights in our own domestic courts without the delay and expense incurred by taking the case to the ECtHR in Strasbourg. The constitutional issues which are raised by this are potentially momentous. Giving the judiciary a yardstick against which they can measure UK legislation and find it to be wanting has obvious impacts on the traditional conception of parliamentary supremacy. The HRA 1998 attempts to defuse this by the device of the declaration of incompatibility (see **28.3.3**). It also shifts power towards the judiciary, giving them greater scope to determine difficult, perhaps emotive and politically charged questions. This raises questions about the accountability of our judges.

There are five central planks of the HRA 1998. First, all legislation, whether primary or subordinate must, if possible, be interpreted so as to be compatible with the ECHR. Secondly, where it is not possible to interpret primary legislation so as to be compatible with the ECHR, certain courts can make a declaration of incompatibility. Thirdly, where it is not possible to interpret subordinate legislation so as to be compatible with the Convention, the courts have power to disapply it. Fourthly, all public authorities, including courts and tribunals, must, if possible, act in a way that is compatible with the ECHR. Finally, individuals who believe that their ECHR rights have been infringed by a public authority can rely on the ECHR to take proceedings in English courts rather than having to apply to Strasbourg.

All lawyers in the UK must bear Convention rights in mind. These rights have much more impact in some areas of law than others. For example, criminal law and immigration practitioners need to have regard to the HRA 1998 on a day-to-day basis. However, the HRA 1998 requires that all legislation be read in accordance with Convention rights and that all public authorities make their decisions in accordance with them: any lawyer who makes use of legislation or who has dealings with organs of the State does so against the backdrop of the HRA 1998.

28.2 Convention rights

The concept of Convention rights is central to the HRA 1998. There are certain rights from the ECtHR which are listed in Sch 1 to the HRA 1998. The most important are those discussed in **Chapter 27**.

Section 2 requires that any court or tribunal determining a Convention right must take into account any decision of the Strasbourg institutions, in particular judgments of the ECtHR. Notice that these decisions are not binding in the same way that decisions of higher courts within the UK are, or even decisions of the ECJ in the context of EC law. They must only be taken into account. Clearly, they will be highly persuasive, but, should a UK court feel the need to decide the matter differently (perhaps because public opinion on the point has changed with time), then it is free to do so.

Decisions on the meaning to be given to Convention rights may involve UK courts and lawyers looking further afield than Strasbourg. The House of Lords has accepted that it is appropriate to look to case law from other jurisdictions in determining such matters (*R v Khan* [1997] AC 558). Most other countries have an established constitutional human rights document with a well-developed jurisprudence, especially those from common law jurisdictions such as New Zealand and Canada.

28.3   The mechanisms of the Act

28.3.1   Introduction

The HRA 1998 seeks to give Convention rights effect in UK law through two pathways. Whenever legislation is relevant lawyers are able to rely on a rule of statutory interpretation that legislation should be read in line with Convention rights. Even where there is no legislation in issue, all public authorities have an obligation to act in accordance with Convention rights.

28.3.2   The interpretative obligation

Section 3(1) reads:

> So far as it is possible to do so, primary legislation and subordinate legislation must be read and given effect in a way which is compatible with the Convention rights.

This interpretative obligation applies whether the legislation in question was passed before or after the HRA 1998. All legislation must be read in such a way as to be compatible with Convention rights, even if it is unambiguous, so long as the wording will bear such an interpretation. Our judges are certainly becoming accustomed to the purposive approach to statutory construction which is required by EC law. For example, in *Litster v Forth Dry Dock & Engineering Co Ltd* [1990] 1 AC 546, the House of Lords was prepared to read delegated legislation as if it contained words which were not there in order to make it comply with an EC Directive. Section 3 extends the purposive approach beyond those pieces of legislation which implement EC law to all legislation.

Notice that this principle applies whether the other party is public or private. So long as a litigant can find a piece of legislation to which the Convention right can be pinned, the nature of their opponent does not matter. For example, *R (on the application of Sacker) v HM Coroner for the County of West Yorkshire* [2004] UKHL 11 involved an inquest into a prisoner's death. The House of Lords had to rule on the interpretation of the word 'how' in s 11(5) of the Coroners Act 1988, in the context of 'how' the prisoner had died. In order to protect Article 2 rights, the House of Lords held that it was not simply to be interpreted as meaning 'by what means', but rather 'by what means in and in what circumstances'.

Section 19 gives judges an extra spur to find a construction which is compatible with Convention rights. It provides that all Bills introduced into Parliament must be accompanied by a statement from the sponsoring Minister on the compatibility or otherwise of the Bill with Convention rights. Clearly, Ministers will almost invariably make statements of compatibility: were a Minister to stand up and state that a Bill did not comply with Convention rights, some very good reasons why it should be enacted in spite of this would have to be provided. The doctrine in *Pepper v Hart* [1993] AC 59 allows the courts to look to such ministerial statements in *Hansard* as evidence of parliamentary intention. Equipped with such evidence, courts may feel especially justified in straining legislative wording where necessary to give it a meaning compatible with Convention rights.

28.3.3 Declarations of incompatibility

Section 4 applies to higher courts (the High Court, Crown Courts, the Employment Appeals Tribunal and above). It empowers them to make declarations of incompatibility. This provides a fallback for situations in which a court recognises that legislation does not comply with Convention rights but, because of the clear words used by the legislator, does not feel that it is possible to give it a purposive interpretation.

Any declaration must be 'necessary'. In *R v HM Attorney General, ex p Rusbridger* [2003] UKHL 38, [2003] 3 All ER 784, a newspaper sought a declaration as to the proper construction of s 3 of the Treason Felony Act 1848 (which made it an offence punishable by imprisonment for life or any shorter period to 'compass by publication to deprive or depose the Queen from the Crown'). No prosecution had been brought under the section since 1883. The newspaper wished to publish a series of articles urging abolition of the monarchy and asked the Attorney-General to clarify the legal position under s 3. He refused. The House of Lords held that it was not appropriate to bring proceedings against the part of s 3 of the 1848 Act that appeared to criminalise the advocacy of republicanism since it was a relic of a bygone age. The idea that it could survive scrutiny under the HRA 1998 was unreal. It was clear that no one who advocated the abolition of the monarchy by peaceful and constitutional means was at any risk of prosecution or conviction. The litigation was therefore unnecessary and the application was dismissed.

In *Lancashire County Council v Taylor* [2005] EWCA Civ 284, the Court of Appeal had to determine if a litigant can obtain a declaration of incompatibility on a ground from which he cannot benefit. The Court stated that the primary objective of the ECHR is to secure for individuals the rights and freedoms set out in the Convention. The HRA 1998 and the Convention also play an educative role by promoting the observance of human rights and thus the Convention. One way in which this objective is achieved is by requiring a Minister to make a statement of compatibility with regard to any new legislation in accordance with s 9 of the HRA 1998. But it is not the intention of the HRA 1998 or the Convention that members of the public should use these provisions if they are not adversely affected by them to change legislation because they consider that the legislation is incompatible with the Convention.

These declarations are a compromise between the need to provide a remedy in such cases and the attachment of the UK to the doctrine of parliamentary supremacy which prevents courts from striking down Acts of Parliament. They flag up the incompatibility but provide no further redress. They do not affect the continuing operation of the offending legislation (s 4(6)).

Clearing up the aftermath of such a declaration is left to the politically accountable organs of State: the Government and Parliament. Section 10 and Sch 2 allow Ministers to amend an incompatible Act by a 'fast track' procedure rather than having to put amending legislation through the full process in both Houses of Parliament. Broadly speaking, this allows Ministers to lay before Parliament a 'remedial order' amending the offending legislation. The order will take effect after 120 days, so long as no objections are made by either House. In emergencies the remedial order can take effect immediately, but will automatically cease to have effect if not given positive approval by both Houses within 120 days.

However, remedial action is optional. The HRA 1998 places no obligation on Ministers to do anything after a declaration of incompatibility is made. Even if they decide to take action, they do not have to do so via the fast track. Remember, though, that the road to Strasbourg is not closed. If a UK court declares legislation to be incompatible with Convention rights and the UK Government does not take adequate steps to put matters right, then a judgment could be sought in the ECtHR. The Government would then have an obligation in international law to act.

Declarations of incompatibility are reserved in the main for primary legislation, that is Acts of Parliament. Delegated or subordinate legislation (usually made by Ministers under an enabling power in an Act of Parliament) is more easily attacked. Striking out such subordinate legislation does not offend against the principle of parliamentary supremacy. In fact by ensuring that Ministers only use enabling powers in an appropriate way it reinforces the will of Parliament. Because of this, courts have never shied away from ruling subordinate legislation to be ultra vires and therefore inoperative. They will continue to do so in circumstances in which subordinate legislation is incompatible with Convention rights and it is not possible to place a purposive interpretation upon it in accordance with s 3.

Worked example

In *Westminster City Council and The First Secretary of State v Morris; R (on the application of Badu) v London Borough of Lambeth and The First Secretary of State* [2005] EWCA Civ 1184, the Court of Appeal declared s 185 of the Housing Act 1996 incompatible. The Court arrived at its decision by taking the following steps.

(a) The provision made by s 185(4) of the Housing Act 1996 precluding a British parent from establishing a priority need for housing assistance where the claim is based on a resident dependent child who is ineligible for UK citizenship and, therefore, subject to immigration control, was within the ambit of Article 8 of the ECHR.

(b) The effect of s 185(4), when read with Article 8, was plainly discriminatory within the meaning of Article 14 of the Convention because the differential treatment for which it provides turns on national origin, or on a combination of one or more of the following forms or aspects of status: nationality, immigration control, settled residence and social welfare.

(c) Regardless of the precise basis of the differential treatment, it could only be justified, particularly under Article 8, if there were 'very weighty' or 'solid' grounds for it, or if it could be shown that it is a proportionate and reasonable response to a perceived need to discourage 'benefit tourism' by British citizens or the 'overstaying' of any of their dependent children subject to immigration control.

(d) The justification advanced in the proceedings on behalf of the Secretary of State was neither 'very weighty' nor 'solid', nor did it amount to a proportionate and reasonable response by him to his concerns.

(e) It was not apparent that the Executive in proposing, or Parliament in enacting, s 185(4) gave consideration to its potential discriminatory impact in any of the respects proscribed by Article 14 or to the justification, if any, for it; but even if they did, the enactment of such a provision, with such effect, could not have fallen within even the very wide ambit of discretion allowed to the Government and Parliament in such matters.

(f) On the issue of compatibility and whether a court should, in the exercise of its discretion under s 4(2) of the HRA 1998, make a declaration of incompatibility, it is immaterial that there may be other forms of statutory protection, and the Court should grant a declaration.

28.3.4 Public authorities

Public authorities may find themselves challenged because the statutory framework within which they operate gives rise to the indirect application of Convention rights via the interpretative obligation as described in **28.3.2**. However, in addition, the Convention can be applied directly to their activities: it is not necessary for a litigant first to find a legislative provision to interpret purposively. Section 6(1) provides simply:

> It is unlawful for a public authority to act in a way which is incompatible with a Convention right.

Section 6 does not fully define public authority, but does say that it includes 'any person certain of whose functions are functions of a public nature'. The dividing line between public and private bodies is a difficult one to draw. The question has exercised the minds of judicial review lawyers for some time because only public bodies are susceptible to judicial review (eg, *R v Panel on Takeovers and Mergers, ex p Datafin plc* [1987] QB 815). It has also been an issue for EC lawyers because of the important distinction between the horizontal and vertical effect in EC law (eg, *Foster v British Gas* Case (C-188/89) [1990] ECR I-3133). For the purposes of the HRA 1998 there is no doubt that the departments of central government are public authorities, nor that local government is. Large companies which exercise quasi-public regulatory authorities are likely to be regarded as public authorities when exercising their public functions. But there are many grey areas which will doubtless be a fertile ground for litigation. See further *Parochial Church Council of Aston Cantlow & Wilmcote with Billesley, Warwickshire v Wallbank* [2003] UKHL 37 and *Cameron v Network Rail Infrastructure Ltd* [2006] EWHC 1133 (QB).

So, for example, the BBC is to be regarded as a public authority under the HRA 1998. When it takes a decision not to broadcast certain matter it must have regard to Article 10, the right to freedom of expression (*R (on the application of ProLife Alliance) v British Broadcasting Corporation* [2002] EWCA Civ 297, [2002] 2 All ER 756). Similarly, the police, when they exercise their powers at common law to arrest to prevent a breach of the peace, must have regard to Article 5, the right to liberty and security of the person. However, a large and flourishing private-sector provider of residential care homes was not a public authority, and did not have to act in accordance with Convention rights when deciding to close a care home, despite the applicant having lived there for 17 years (*R (on the application of Heather and Others) v Leonard Cheshire Foundation* [2002] EWCA Civ 366). See also *YL (by her litigation friend) v Birmingham City Council* [2007] UKHL 27.

Sometimes a public authority will attempt to argue that it had no choice but to act in the way it did because it was merely obeying obligations imposed by an Act of Parliament. In such cases there are two possibilities. The court may use the interpretative obligation in s 3 to read the offending legislation in such a way that the public authority was not restricted as it thought; in such a case, the public authority will be regarded as having made an error of law and an appropriate remedy will be awarded against it. Alternatively, the court may agree with the public authority's reading of the legislation, which may be so clear that it cannot be purposively interpreted in line with Convention rights. In this case, the public authority will have the defence that as a result of the legislation in question it could not have acted differently (s 6(2)) and the other party will have to content themselves with a declaration of incompatibility against the legislation.

What is the territorial scope of s 6? Does it apply to a public authority that acts both within and outside the UK? In *R (on the application of Al-Skeini) v Secretary of State for Defence* [2007] UKHL 26, the claimants were relatives of Iraqi citizens who, it was claimed, had been unlawfully killed by members of British armed forces in southern Iraq in 2003. The Secretary of State argued that the 1998 Act did not apply outside the territory of the UK and that the deceased had not been within the jurisdiction of the UK for the purposes of Article 1 of the Convention when they were killed. The House of Lords rejected these arguments. It held that s 6 should be interpreted as applying not only when a public authority acted within the UK, but also when it acted within the jurisdiction of the UK for the purposes of Article 1 of the Convention but outside the territory of the UK. Why? The House stated that the purpose of the 1998 Act was to provide remedies in domestic law to those whose human rights had been violated by a UK public authority. Making such remedies available for acts of a UK authority in the territory of another State is not offensive to the sovereignty of the other State.

28.3.5   Direct effect in cases not involving public authorities

There is a significant gap in the way in which the HRA 1998 allows Convention rights to be enforced. It would appear from s 6 that Convention rights can only be applied directly against public authorities. Experience from the domain of EC law has shown that this can lead to unfairness. For example, employees of public authorities may enjoy more rights than employees of private authorities. Such an interpretation of s 6 would not prevent claimants against private defendants from relying on the interpretative obligation in s 3. But, to take advantage of the interpretative obligation, they would have to be litigating a point which was dealt with by UK legislation which itself was capable of a Convention-compatible interpretation. Claimants against public authorities would have a simpler solution by applying Convention rights directly under s 6.

However, it would seem that a doctrine of direct effect in cases involving private bodies is being developed by the courts. For example, *Venables and Thompson v News Group Newspapers Ltd and Others* [2001] 2 WLR 1038 involved an application to the court by the two boys convicted of murdering Jamie Bulger. After their release from prison, they wanted an injunction preventing the press from revealing their new identities. Their application was based partly on Article 2 because they feared for their lives should their identities become public. It was argued on their behalf that, because the court is a public authority (the HRA 1998 says so in s 6(3)), the court has a duty under s 6(1) to ensure that Convention rights are protected even when it decides cases involving private litigants. This was accepted by Dame Elizabeth Butler-Sloss. She said (para 24):

> It is clear that, although operating in the public domain and fulfilling a public service, the defendant newspapers cannot sensibly be said to come within the definition of public authority in s 6(1) of the 1998 Act. Consequently, Convention rights are not directly enforceable against the defendants ... That is not, however, the end of the matter, since the court is a public authority, see s 6(3), and must itself act in a way compatible with the Convention, see s 6(1), and have regard to European jurisprudence ...

The injunction was granted.

28.4 Procedure for using the Act

> One principal achievement of the Act is to enable the Convention rights to be directly invoked in the domestic courts. In that respect the Act is important as a procedural measure which has opened a further means of access to justice for the citizen, more immediate and more familiar than a recourse to the Court in Strasbourg. (per Lord Clyde in *R v Lambert* [2001] UKHL 37 at para 135)

The s 3 interpretative obligation (see **28.3.2**) may be raised in any court or tribunal hearing in which the meaning of a legislative provision needs to be construed.

Many HRA points are raised in criminal proceedings by defendants. This may be on the basis that an Act upon which the prosecution seeks to rely does not bear the meaning which the prosecution attributes to it when s 3 is applied. Alternatively, it may be that the defence wish to raise a 'freestanding' HRA point, not linked to any legislation, that the police or the Crown Prosecution Service have acted contrary to Convention rights and therefore have broken s 6.

The other procedure which is commonly used to raise Convention rights against public authorities is judicial review under CPR, Part 54. Under this procedure, the Divisional Court is well accustomed to scrutinising the decisions of public authorities and measuring them against a variety of standards of legality and procedural fairness. The HRA 1998 adds another string to the bow of judicial review lawyers.

The HRA 1998 introduces some special procedural rules for s 6 challenges to public authorities. Section 7(1) introduces a locus standi test for such challenges. The claimant must be a 'victim' of the unlawful act. Existing Strasbourg case law on this expression says that to qualify a person must be actually and directly affected by the act or omission which is the subject of the complaint. This is a narrower gateway than the usual judicial review test of 'sufficient interest'.

Section 6 challenges are also subject to a one-year limitation period from the date on which the offending act took place (s 7(5)). This may be extended if the court thinks it equitable to do so. However, it is also subject to any stricter time-limit imposed by the particular procedure being used. If judicial review is used, an application must usually be made 'promptly and in any event within three months' (CPR, Part 54).

The s 3 interpretative obligation is not subject to these special provisions for locus standi or limitation period. The usual rules will apply for whatever procedure is chosen.

Section 8 provides for remedies in s 6 challenges to public authorities. It empowers a court to award such remedies within its powers as it considers just and appropriate. This will include injunctions to restrain breaches of Convention rights and damages. In awarding damages under this provision, UK courts must take account of the principles applied by the ECtHR in awarding compensation under Article 41. The main guiding principle applied by the ECtHR is that an award of damages should seek to return the applicant to the position that he would have been in had there not been a breach of Convention rights. So, for example, in *Smith v UK* [2000] ECHR 33985/86, gay men and lesbians who had been discharged from military service were awarded £19,000 each for their emotional suffering, loss of career and loss of privacy. See further the House of Lords decision in *R (on the application of Greenfield) v Secretary of State for Home Department* [2005] UKHL 14, [2005] 1 WLR 673 and the Court of Appeal judgments in *Re C (a child)* [2007] EWCA Civ 2 and *Colle v Chief Constable of Hertfordshire* [2007] EWCA Civ 325.

Claims which introduce Convention rights indirectly via the interpretative obligation are not subject to s 8. If they are civil claims, they will have available whatever remedies are available for the cause of action being used (eg, tort).

28.5 The Commission for Equality and Human Rights

The Commission for Equality and Human Rights (CEHR) is a non-departmental public body that is intended to act as a central point of advice and guidance on all equality and human rights issues in Great Britain. Its remit is to promote awareness and understanding of human rights and encourage good practice by public authorities in meeting their obligations under the HRA 1998. The CEHR has powers to take human rights cases on behalf of minorities who suffer discrimination. The Commission's web address is www.cehr.org.uk.

Appendix to Part IV

Human Rights Act 1998

Introduction

1. The Convention Rights

(1) In this Act 'the Convention rights' means the rights and fundamental freedoms set out in—

    (a)   Articles 2 to 12 and 14 of the Convention,

    (b)   Articles 1 to 3 of the First Protocol, and

    (c)   Article 1 of the Thirteenth Protocol,

    as read with Articles 16 to 18 of the Convention.

(2) Those Articles are to have effect for the purposes of this Act subject to any designated derogation or reservation (as to which see sections 14 and 15).

(3) The Articles are set out in Schedule 1.

(4) The Secretary of State may by order make such amendments to this Act as he considers appropriate to reflect the effect, in relation to the United Kingdom, of a protocol.

(5) In subsection (4) 'protocol' means a protocol to the Convention—

    (a)   which the United Kingdom has ratified; or

    (b)   which the United Kingdom has signed with a view to ratification.

(6) No amendment may be made by an order under subsection (4) so as to come into force before the protocol concerned is in force in relation to the United Kingdom.

2. Interpretation of Convention rights

(1) A court or tribunal determining a question which has arisen in connection with a Convention right must take into account any—

    (a)   judgment, decision, declaration or advisory opinion of the European Court of Human Rights,

    (b)   opinion of the Commission given in a report adopted under Article 31 of the Convention,

    (c)   decision of the Commission in connection with Article 26 or 27(2) of the Convention, or

    (d)   decision of the Committee of Ministers taken under Article 46 of the Convention,

whenever made or given, so far as, in the opinion of the court or tribunal, it is relevant to the proceedings in which that question has arisen.

(2) Evidence of any judgment, decision, declaration or opinion of which account may have to be taken under this section is to be given in proceedings before any court or tribunal in such manner as may be provided by rules.

(3) In this section 'rules' means rules of court or, in the case of proceedings before a tribunal, rules made for the purposes of this section—

    (a)   by the Lord Chancellor or the Secretary of State, in relation to any proceedings outside Scotland;

    (b)   by the Secretary of State, in relation to proceedings in Scotland; or

    (c)   by a Northern Ireland department, in relation to proceedings before a tribunal in Northern Ireland—

(i)   which deals with transferred matters; and

(ii)   for which no rules made under paragraph (a) are in force.

Legislation

3. Interpretation of legislation

(1)   So far as it is possible to do so, primary legislation and subordinate legislation must be read and given effect in a way which is compatible with the Convention rights.

(2)   This section—

(a)   applies to primary legislation and subordinate legislation whenever enacted;

(b)   does not affect the validity, continuing operation or enforcement of any incompatible primary legislation; and

(c)   does not affect the validity, continuing operation or enforcement of any incompatible subordinate legislation if (disregarding any possibility of revocation) primary legislation prevents removal of the incompatibility.

4. Declaration of incompatibility

(1)   Subsection (2) applies in any proceedings in which a court determines whether a provision of primary legislation is compatible with a Convention right.

(2)   If the court is satisfied that the provision is incompatible with a Convention right, it may make a declaration of that incompatibility.

(3)   Subsection (4) applies in any proceedings in which a court determines whether a provision of subordinate legislation, made in the exercise of a power conferred by primary legislation, is compatible with a Convention right.

(4)   If the court is satisfied—

(a)   that the provision is incompatible with a Convention right, and

(b)   that (disregarding any possibility of revocation) the primary legislation concerned prevents removal of the incompatibility,

it may make a declaration of that incompatibility.

(5)   In this section 'court' means—

(a)   the House of Lords;

(b)   the Judicial Committee of the Privy Council;

(c)   the Courts-Martial Appeal Court;

(d)   in Scotland, the High Court of Justiciary sitting otherwise than as a trial court or the Court of Session;

(e)   in England and Wales or Northern Ireland, the High Court or the Court of Appeal;

(f)   the Court of Protection, in any matter dealt with by the President of the Family Division, the Vice-Chancellor or a puisne judge of the High Court.

(6)   A declaration under this section ('a declaration of incompatibility')—

(a)   does not affect the validity, continuing operation or enforcement of the provision in respect of which it is given; and

(b)   is not binding on the parties to the proceedings in which it is made.

5. Right of Crown to intervene

(1) Where a court is considering whether to make a declaration of incompatibility, the Crown is entitled to notice in accordance with rules of court.

(2) In any case to which subsection (1) applies—

(a) a Minister of the Crown (or a person nominated by him),

(b) a member of the Scottish Executive,

(c) a Northern Ireland Minister,

(d) a Northern Ireland department,

is entitled, on giving notice in accordance with rules of court, to be joined as a party to the proceedings.

(3) Notice under subsection (2) may be given at any time during the proceedings.

(4) A person who has been made a party to criminal proceedings (other than in Scotland) as the result of a notice under subsection (2) may, with leave, appeal to the House of Lords against any declaration of incompatibility made in the proceedings.

(5) In subsection (4)—

'criminal proceedings' includes all proceedings before the Courts-Martial Appeal Court; and

'leave' means leave granted by the court making the declaration of incompatibility or by the House of Lords.

Public Authorities

6. Acts of public authorities

(1) It is unlawful for a public authority to act in a way which is incompatible with a Convention right.

(2) Subsection (1) does not apply to an act if—

(a) as the result of one or more provisions of primary legislation, the authority could not have acted differently; or

(b) in the case of one or more provisions of, or made under, primary legislation which cannot be read or given effect in a way which is compatible with the Convention rights, the authority was acting so as to give effect to or enforce those provisions.

(3) In this section 'public authority' includes—

(a) a court or tribunal, and

(b) any person certain of whose functions are functions of a public nature,

but does not include either House of Parliament or a person exercising functions in connection with proceedings in Parliament.

(4) In subsection (3) 'Parliament' does not include the House of Lords in its judicial capacity.

(5) In relation to a particular act, a person is not a public authority by virtue only of subsection (3)(b) if the nature of the act is private.

(6) 'An act' includes a failure to act but does not include a failure to—

(a) introduce in, or lay before, Parliament a proposal for legislation; or

(b) make any primary legislation or remedial order.

7. Proceedings

(1)   A person who claims that a public authority has acted (or proposes to act) in a way which is made unlawful by section 6(1) may—

    (a)   bring proceedings against the authority under this Act in the appropriate court or tribunal, or

    (b)   rely on the Convention right or rights concerned in any legal proceedings, but only if he is (or would be) a victim of the unlawful act.

(2)   In subsection (1)(a) 'appropriate court or tribunal' means such court or tribunal as may be determined in accordance with rules; and proceedings against an authority include a counterclaim or similar proceeding.

(3)   If the proceedings are brought on an application for judicial review, the applicant is to be taken to have a sufficient interest in relation to the unlawful act only if he is, or would be, a victim of that act.

(4)   If the proceedings are made by way of a petition for judicial review in Scotland, the applicant shall be taken to have title and interest to sue in relation to the unlawful act only if he is, or would be, a victim of that act.

(5)   Proceedings under subsection (1)(a) must be brought before the end of—

    (a)   the period of one year beginning with the date on which the act complained of took place; or

    (b)   such longer period as the court or tribunal considers equitable having regard to all the circumstances,

but that is subject to any rule imposing a stricter time limit in relation to the procedure in question.

(6)   In subsection (1)(b) 'legal proceedings' includes—

    (a)   proceedings brought by or at the instigation of a public authority; and

    (b)   an appeal against the decision of a court or tribunal.

(7)   For the purposes of this section, a person is a victim of an unlawful act only if he would be a victim for the purposes of Article 34 of the Convention if proceedings were brought in the European Court of Human Rights in respect of that act.

(8)   Nothing in this Act creates a criminal offence.

(9)   In this section 'rules' means—

    (a)   in relation to proceedings before a court or tribunal outside Scotland, rules made by the Secretary of State for the purposes of this section or rules of court,

    (b)   in relation to proceedings before a court or tribunal in Scotland, rules made by the Secretary of State for those purposes,

    (c)   in relation to proceedings before a tribunal in Northern Ireland—

        (i)   which deals with transferred matters; and

        (ii)   for which no rules made under paragraph (a) are in force,

    rules made by a Northern Ireland department for those purposes,

and includes provision made by order under section 1 of the Courts and Legal Services Act 1990.

(10)   In making rules, regard must be had to section 9.

(11)   The Minister who has power to make rules in relation to a particular tribunal may, to the extent he considers it necessary to ensure that the tribunal can provide an appropriate remedy in relation to an act (or proposed act) of a public authority which is (or would be) unlawful as a result of section 6(1), by order add to—

(a)   the relief or remedies which the tribunal may grant; or

(b)   the grounds on which it may grant any of them.

(12) An order made under subsection (11) may contain such incidental, supplemental, consequential or transitional provision as the Minister making it considers appropriate.

(13) 'The Minister' includes the Northern Ireland department concerned.

8. Judicial remedies

(1)   In relation to any act (or proposed act) of a public authority which the court finds is (or would be) unlawful, it may grant such relief or remedy, or make such order, within its powers as it considers just and appropriate.

(2)   But damages may be awarded only by a court which has power to award damages, or to order the payment of compensation, in civil proceedings.

(3)   No award of damages is to be made unless, taking account of all the circumstances of the case, including—

(a)   any other relief or remedy granted, or order made, in relation to the act in question (by that or any other court), and

(b)   the consequences of any decision (of that or any other court) in respect of that act, the court is satisfied that the award is necessary to afford just satisfaction to the person in whose favour it is made.

(4)   In determining—

(a)   whether to award damages, or

(b)   the amount of an award,

the court must take into account the principles applied by the European Court of Human Rights in relation to the award of compensation under Article 41 of the Convention.

(5)   A public authority against which damages are awarded is to be treated—

(a)   in Scotland, for the purposes of section 3 of the Law Reform (Miscellaneous Provisions) (Scotland) Act 1940 as if the award were made in an action of damages in which the authority has been found liable in respect of loss or damage to the person to whom the award is made;

(b)   for the purposes of the Civil Liability (Contribution) Act 1978 as liable in respect of damage suffered by the person to whom the award is made.

(6)   In this section—

'court' includes a tribunal;

'damages' means damages for an unlawful act of a public authority; and

'unlawful' means unlawful under section 6(1).

9. Judicial acts

(1)   Proceedings under section 7(1)(a) in respect of a judicial act may be brought only—

(a)   by exercising a right of appeal;

(b)   on an application (in Scotland a petition) for judicial review; or

(c)   in such other forum as may be prescribed by rules.

(2)   That does not affect any rule of law which prevents a court from being the subject of judicial review.

(3)   In proceedings under this Act in respect of a judicial act done in good faith, damages may not be awarded otherwise than to compensate a person to the extent required by Article 5(5) of the Convention.

(4)   An award of damages permitted by subsection (3) is to be made against the Crown; but no award may be made unless the appropriate person, if not a party to the proceedings, is joined.

(5)   In this section—

'appropriate person' means the Minister responsible for the court concerned, or a person or government department nominated by him;

'court' includes a tribunal;

'judge' includes a member of a tribunal, a justice of the peace (or, in Northern Ireland, a lay magistrate) and a clerk or other officer entitled to exercise the jurisdiction of a court;

'judicial act' means a judicial act of a court and includes an act done on the instructions, or on behalf, of a judge; and

'rules' has the same meaning as in section 7(9).

Remedial Action

10. Power to take remedial action

(1)   This section applies if—

(a)   a provision of legislation has been declared under section 4 to be incompatible with a Convention right and, if an appeal lies—

(i)   all persons who may appeal have stated in writing that they do not intend to do so;

(ii)   the time for bringing an appeal has expired and no appeal has been brought within that time; or

(iii)   an appeal brought within that time has been determined or abandoned; or

(b)   it appears to a Minister of the Crown or Her Majesty in Council that, having regard to a finding of the European Court of Human Rights made after the coming into force of this section in proceedings against the United Kingdom, a provision of legislation is incompatible with an obligation of the United Kingdom arising from the Convention.

(2)   If a Minister of the Crown considers that there are compelling reasons for proceeding under this section, he may by order make such amendments to the legislation as he considers necessary to remove the incompatibility.

(3)   If, in the case of subordinate legislation, a Minister of the Crown considers—

(a)   that it is necessary to amend the primary legislation under which the subordinate legislation in question was made, in order to enable the incompatibility to be removed, and

(b)   that there are compelling reasons for proceeding under this section,

he may by order make such amendments to the primary legislation as he considers necessary.

(4)   This section also applies where the provision in question is in subordinate legislation and has been quashed, or declared invalid, by reason of incompatibility with a Convention right and the Minister proposes to proceed under paragraph 2(b) of Schedule 2.

(5)   If the legislation is an Order in Council, the power conferred by subsection (2) or (3) is exercisable by Her Majesty in Council.

(6)   In this section 'legislation' does not include a Measure of the Church Assembly or of the General Synod of the Church of England.

(7)   Schedule 2 makes further provision about remedial orders.

Other Rights and Proceedings

11. Safeguard for existing human rights

A person's reliance on a Convention right does not restrict—

(a)   any other right or freedom conferred on him by or under any law having effect in any part of the United Kingdom; or

(b)   his right to make any claim or bring any proceedings which he could make or bring apart from sections 7 to 9.

12. Freedom of expression

(1)   This section applies if a court is considering whether to grant any relief which, if granted, might affect the exercise of the Convention right to freedom of expression.

(2)   If the person against whom the application for relief is made ('the respondent') is neither present nor represented, no such relief is to be granted unless the court is satisfied—

    (a)   that the applicant has taken all practicable steps to notify the respondent; or

    (b)   that there are compelling reasons why the respondent should not be notified.

(3)   No such relief is to be granted so as to restrain publication before trial unless the court is satisfied that the applicant is likely to establish that publication should not be allowed.

(4)   The court must have particular regard to the importance of the Convention right to freedom of expression and, where the proceedings relate to material which the respondent claims, or which appears to the court, to be journalistic, literary or artistic material (or to conduct connected with such material), to—

    (a)   the extent to which—

        (i)   the material has, or is about to, become available to the public; or

        (ii)   it is, or would be, in the public interest for the material to be published;

    (b)   any relevant privacy code.

(5)   In this section—

'court' includes a tribunal; and

'relief' includes any remedy or order (other than in criminal proceedings).

13. Freedom of thought, conscience and religion

(1)   If a court's determination of any question arising under this Act might affect the exercise by a religious organisation (itself or its members collectively) of the Convention right to freedom of thought, conscience and religion, it must have particular regard to the importance of that right.

(2)   In this section 'court' includes a tribunal.

...

21. Interpretation, etc

(1)   In this Act—

'amend' includes repeal and apply (with or without modifications);

'the appropriate Minister' means the Minister of the Crown having charge of the appropriate authorised government department (within the meaning of the Crown Proceedings Act 1947);

'the Commission' means the European Commission of Human Rights;

'the Convention' means the Convention for the Protection of Human Rights and Fundamental Freedoms, agreed by the Council of Europe at Rome on 4th November 1950 as it has effect for the time being in relation to the United Kingdom;

'declaration of incompatibility' means a declaration under section 4;

'Minister of the Crown' has the same meaning as in the Ministers of the Crown Act 1975;

'Northern Ireland Minister' includes the First Minister and the deputy First Minister in Northern Ireland;

'primary legislation' means any—

(a)   public general Act;

(b)   local and personal Act;

(c)   private Act;

(d)   Measure of the Church Assembly;

(e)   Measure of the General Synod of the Church of England;

(f)   Order in Council—

(i)   made in exercise of Her Majesty's Royal Prerogative;

(ii)   made under section 38(1)(a) of the Northern Ireland Constitution Act 1973 or the corresponding provision of the Northern Ireland Act 1998; or

(iii)   amending an Act of a kind mentioned in paragraph (a), (b) or (c);

and includes an order or other instrument made under primary legislation (otherwise than by the Welsh Ministers, the First Minister for Wales, the Counsel General to the Welsh Assembly Government, a member of the Scottish Executive, a Northern Ireland Minister or a Northern Ireland department) to the extent to which it operates to bring one or more provisions of that legislation into force or amends any primary legislation;

'the First Protocol' means the protocol to the Convention agreed at Paris on 20th March 1952;

'the Eleventh Protocol' means the protocol to the Convention (restructuring the control machinery established by the Convention) agreed at Strasbourg on 11th May 1994;

'the Thirteenth Protocol' means the protocol to the Convention (concerning the abolition of the death penalty in all circumstances) agreed at Vilnius on 3rd May 2002;

'remedial order' means an order under section 10;

'subordinate legislation' means any—

(a)   Order in Council other than one—

(i)   made in exercise of Her Majesty's Royal Prerogative;

(ii)   made under section 38(1)(a) of the Northern Ireland Constitution Act 1973 or the corresponding provision of the Northern Ireland Act 1998;

        (iii) or amending an Act of a kind mentioned in the definition of primary legislation;

(b)   Act of the Scottish Parliament;

(ba)   Measure of the National Assembly for Wales;

(bb)   Act of the National Assembly for Wales;

(c)   Act of the Parliament of Northern Ireland;

(d)   Measure of the Assembly established under section 1 of the Northern Ireland Assembly Act 1973;

(e)   Act of the Northern Ireland Assembly;

(f)   order, rules, regulations, scheme, warrant, byelaw or other instrument made under primary legislation (except to the extent to which it operates to bring one or more provisions of that legislation into force or amends any primary legislation);

(g)   order, rules, regulations, scheme, warrant, byelaw or other instrument made under legislation mentioned in paragraph (b), (c), (d) or (e) or made under an Order in Council applying only to Northern Ireland;

(h)   order, rules, regulations, scheme, warrant, byelaw or other instrument made by a member of the Scottish Executive, Welsh Ministers, the First Minister for Wales, the Counsel General to the Welsh Assembly Government, a Northern Ireland Minister or a Northern Ireland department in exercise of prerogative or other executive functions of Her Majesty which are exercisable by such a person on behalf of Her Majesty;

'transferred matters' has the same meaning as in the Northern Ireland Act 1998; and

'tribunal' means any tribunal in which legal proceedings may be brought.

(2)   The references in paragraphs (b) and (c) of section 2(1) to Articles are to Articles of the Convention as they had effect immediately before the coming into force of the Eleventh Protocol.

(3)   The reference in paragraph (d) of section 2(1) to Article 46 includes a reference to Articles 32 and 54 of the Convention as they had effect immediately before the coming into force of the Eleventh Protocol.

(4)   The references in section 2(1) to a report or decision of the Commission or a decision of the Committee of Ministers include references to a report or decision made as provided by paragraphs 3, 4 and 6 of Article 5 of the Eleventh Protocol (transitional provisions).

(5)   Any liability under the Army Act 1955, the Air Force Act 1955 or the Naval Discipline Act 1957 to suffer death for an offence is replaced by a liability to imprisonment for life or any less punishment authorised by those Acts; and those Acts shall accordingly have effect with the necessary modifications.

22. Short title, commencement, application and extent

(1)   This Act may be cited as the Human Rights Act 1998.

(2)   Sections 18, 20 and 21(5) and this section come into force on the passing of this Act.

(3)   The other provisions of this Act come into force on such day as the Secretary of State may by order appoint; and different days may be appointed for different purposes.

(4)   Paragraph (b) of subsection (1) of section 7 applies to proceedings brought by or at the instigation of a public authority whenever the act in question took

place; but otherwise that subsection does not apply to an act taking place before the coming into force of that section.

(5)   This Act binds the Crown.

(6)   This Act extends to Northern Ireland.

(7)   Section 21(5), so far as it relates to any provision contained in the Army Act 1955, the Air Force Act 1955 or the Naval Discipline Act 1957, extends to any place to which that provision extends.

SCHEDULE 1

The Convention Rights

Article 2
Right to life

1.   Everyone's right to life shall be protected by law. No one shall be deprived of his life intentionally save in the execution of a sentence of a court following his conviction of a crime for which this penalty is provided by law.

2.   Deprivation of life shall not be regarded as inflicted in contravention of this Article when it results from the use of force which is no more than absolutely necessary:

    (a)   in defence of any person from unlawful violence;

    (b)   in order to effect a lawful arrest or to prevent the escape of a person lawfully detained;

    (c)   in action lawfully taken for the purpose of quelling a riot or insurrection.

Article 3
Prohibition of Torture

No one shall be subjected to torture or to inhuman or degrading treatment or punishment.

Article 4
Prohibition of Slavery and Forced Labour

1.   No one shall be held in slavery or servitude.

2.   No one shall be required to perform forced or compulsory labour.

3.   For the purpose of this Article the term 'forced or compulsory labour' shall not include:

    (a)   any work required to be done in the ordinary course of detention imposed according to the provisions of Article 5 of this Convention or during conditional release from such detention;

    (b)   any service of a military character or, in case of conscientious objectors in countries where they are recognised, service exacted instead of compulsory military service;

    (c)   any service exacted in case of an emergency or calamity threatening the life or well-being of the community;

    (d)   any work or service which forms part of normal civic obligations.

Article 5
Right to Liberty and Security

1. Everyone has the right to liberty and security of person. No one shall be deprived of his liberty save in the following cases and in accordance with a procedure prescribed by law:

    (a) the lawful detention of a person after conviction by a competent court;

    (b) the lawful arrest or detention of a person for non-compliance with the lawful order of a court or in order to secure the fulfilment of any obligation prescribed by law;

    (c) the lawful arrest or detention of a person effected for the purpose of bringing him before the competent legal authority on reasonable suspicion of having committed an offence or when it is reasonably considered necessary to prevent his committing an offence or fleeing after having done so;

    (d) the detention of a minor by lawful order for the purpose of educational supervision or his lawful detention for the purpose of bringing him before the competent legal authority;

    (e) the lawful detention of persons for the prevention of the spreading of infectious diseases, of persons of unsound mind, alcoholics or drug addicts or vagrants;

    (f) the lawful arrest or detention of a person to prevent his effecting an unauthorised entry into the country or of a person against whom action is being taken with a view to deportation or extradition.

2. Everyone who is arrested shall be informed promptly, in a language which he understands, of the reasons for his arrest and of any charge against him.

3. Everyone arrested or detained in accordance with the provisions of paragraph 1(c) of this Article shall be brought promptly before a judge or other officer authorised by law to exercise judicial power and shall be entitled to trial within a reasonable time or to release pending trial. Release may be conditioned by guarantees to appear for trial.

4. Everyone who is deprived of his liberty by arrest or detention shall be entitled to take proceedings by which the lawfulness of his detention shall be decided speedily by a court and his release ordered if the detention is not lawful.

5. Everyone who has been the victim of arrest or detention in contravention of the provisions of this Article shall have an enforceable right to compensation.

Article 6
Right to a Fair Trial

1. In the determination of his civil rights and obligations or of any criminal charge against him, everyone is entitled to a fair and public hearing within a reasonable time by an independent and impartial tribunal established by law. Judgment shall be pronounced publicly but the press and public may be excluded from all or part of the trial in the interest of morals, public order or national security in a democratic society, where the interests of juveniles or the protection of the private life of the parties so require, or to the extent strictly necessary in the opinion of the court in special circumstances where publicity would prejudice the interests of justice.

2.   Everyone charged with a criminal offence shall be presumed innocent until proved guilty according to law.

3.   Everyone charged with a criminal offence has the following minimum rights:

(a)   to be informed promptly, in a language which he understands and in detail, of the nature and cause of the accusation against him;

(b)   to have adequate time and facilities for the preparation of his defence;

(c)   to defend himself in person or through legal assistance of his own choosing or, if he has not sufficient means to pay for legal assistance, to be given it free when the interests of justice so require;

(d)   to examine or have examined witnesses against him and to obtain the attendance and examination of witnesses on his behalf under the same conditions as witnesses against him;

(e)   to have the free assistance of an interpreter if he cannot understand or speak the language used in court.

Article 7
No Punishment Without Law

1.   No one shall be held guilty of any criminal offence on account of any act or omission which did not constitute a criminal offence under national or international law at the time when it was committed. Nor shall a heavier penalty be imposed than the one that was applicable at the time the criminal offence was committed.

2.   This Article shall not prejudice the trial and punishment of any person for any act or omission which, at the time when it was committed, was criminal according to the general principles of law recognised by civilised nations.

Article 8
Right to Respect for Private and Family Life

1.   Everyone has the right to respect for his private and family life, his home and his correspondence.

2.   There shall be no interference by a public authority with the exercise of this right except such as is in accordance with the law and is necessary in a democratic society in the interests of national security, public safety or the economic well-being of the country, for the prevention of disorder or crime, for the protection of health or morals, or for the protection of the rights and freedoms of others.

Article 9
Freedom of Thought, Conscience and Religion

1.   Everyone has the right to freedom of thought, conscience and religion; this right includes freedom to change his religion or belief and freedom, either alone or in community with others and in public or private, to manifest his religion or belief, in worship, teaching, practice and observance.

2.   Freedom to manifest one's religion or beliefs shall be subject only to such limitations as are prescribed by law and are necessary in a democratic society in the interests of public safety, for the protection of public order, health or morals, or for the protection of the rights and freedoms of others.

Article 10
Freedom of Expression

1. Everyone has the right to freedom of expression. This right shall include freedom to hold opinions and to receive and impart information and ideas without interference by public authority and regardless of frontiers. This Article shall not prevent States from requiring the licensing of broadcasting, television or cinema enterprises.

2. The exercise of these freedoms, since it carries with it duties and responsibilities, may be subject to such formalities, conditions, restrictions or penalties as are prescribed by law and are necessary in a democratic society, in the interests of national security, territorial integrity or public safety, for the prevention of disorder or crime, for the protection of health or morals, for the protection of the reputation or rights of others, for preventing the disclosure of information received in confidence, or for maintaining the authority and impartiality of the judiciary.

Article 11
Freedom of Assembly and Association

1. Everyone has the right to freedom of peaceful assembly and to freedom of association with others, including the right to form and to join trade unions for the protection of his interests.

2. No restrictions shall be placed on the exercise of these rights other than such as are prescribed by law and are necessary in a democratic society in the interests of national security or public safety, for the prevention of disorder or crime, for the protection of health or morals or for the protection of the rights and freedoms of others. This Article shall not prevent the imposition of lawful restrictions on the exercise of these rights by members of the armed forces, of the police or of the administration of the State.

Article 12
Right to Marry

Men and women of marriageable age have the right to marry and to found a family, according to the national laws governing the exercise of this right.

Article 14
Prohibition of Discrimination

The enjoyment of the rights and freedoms set forth in this Convention shall be secured without discrimination on any ground such as sex, race, colour, language, religion, political or other opinion, national or social origin, association with a national minority, property, birth or other status.

Article 16
Restrictions on Political Activity of Aliens

Nothing in Articles 10, 11 and 14 shall be regarded as preventing the High Contracting Parties from imposing restrictions on the political activity of aliens.

Article 17
Prohibition of Abuse of Rights

Nothing in this Convention may be interpreted as implying for any State, group or person any right to engage in any activity or perform any act aimed at the destruction of any of the rights and freedoms set forth herein or at their limitation to a greater extent than is provided for in the Convention.

Article 18
Limitation on Use of Restrictions on Rights

The restrictions permitted under this Convention to the said rights and freedoms shall not be applied for any purpose other than those for which they have been prescribed.

The First Protocol

Article 1
Protection of Property

Every natural or legal person is entitled to the peaceful enjoyment of his possessions. No one shall be deprived of his possessions except in the public interest and subject to the conditions provided for by law and by the general principles of international law.

The preceding provisions shall not, however, in any way impair the right of a State to enforce such laws as it deems necessary to control the use of property in accordance with the general interest or to secure the payment of taxes or other contributions or penalties.

Article 2
Right to Education

No person shall be denied the right to education. In the exercise of any functions which it assumes in relation to education and to teaching, the State shall respect the right of parents to ensure such education and teaching in conformity with their own religious and philosophical convictions.

Identifying and Addressing Convention Rights: a Checklist

Article 2

- Was there an intentional deprivation of life?
- Was it in execution of a court sentence following conviction of a crime for which the sentence is the death penalty?
- Was it for a ground permitted under para 2?
- Did it comply with the conditions set out in para 2?

Article 3

- Was there torture or inhuman or degrading treatment or punishment?

Article 4

- Was there slavery or servitude (para 1)?
- Was there forced or compulsory labour (para 2) save as excluded by para 3?

Article 5 (para 1)

- Was there a deprivation of liberty?
- Was it in accordance with a procedure prescribed by law?
- Was it for any of the grounds permitted by paras (a) to (f)?

Article 6, civil matters

- Was a civil right or obligation determined?
- Were the rights under para 1 met?

Article 6, criminal matters

- Did the proceedings concern a criminal charge?
- Were the rights under para 1 met?

Article 7

- Did the act or omission constitute a criminal offence at the time it was committed?

Article 8

- Was there an interference with a person's private or family life, home or correspondence?
- Was any interference lawful (para 2)?
- Was any interference necessary pursuant to the reasons set out in para 2?

Article 9

- Was there an interference with a person's freedom of thought or conscience?
- Was there an interference with a person's religion? If so, was it lawful and necessary (para 2)?

Article 10

- Was there an interference with a person's right to freedom of expression?
- Was any interference lawful (para 2)?

- Was any interference necessary pursuant to the reasons set out in para 2?

Article 11

- Was there an interference with a person's freedom of peaceful assembly or association?
- Was any interference lawful (para 2)?
- Was any interference necessary pursuant to the reasons set out in para 2?

Article 12

- Was the person of marriageable age?
- Did the person comply with national laws?
- Was there an interference with a person's right to marry or found a family?

First Protocol, Article 1

- Was there an interference with a person's peaceful enjoyment of his possessions?
- Was any interference lawful?
- Was any interference necessary pursuant to any of the specified grounds?

First Protocol, Article 2

- Was there a denial of the right to education?
- Was there a lack of respect of parents' religious or philosophical views?

Article 14

- Is another ECHR right or freedom in issue?
- Has there been discrimination on any of the specified grounds?

Part V

PROBATE AND ADMINISTRATION

Chapter 29

Succession to Property on Death:
The Background Law

Note

The Civil Partnership Act received the Royal Assent in November 2004 and came into force on 5 December 2005. It provides that *same sex* couples can register a civil partnership. Once a partnership has been registered, the partners will be treated as spouses for the purposes of statutes dealing with property and succession.

The Gender Recognition Act 2004 came into force on 4 April 2005. The purpose of the Act is to provide transsexuals with legal recognition in their acquired gender. Legal recognition follows the issue of a full gender recognition certificate by a Gender Recognition Panel.

29.1 What property passes by the will or the intestacy rules?

When an individual dies, he may have provided for the disposition of his property on death by leaving a valid will. A will can operate to dispose of most types of property which an individual may own on death. A gift in a valid will of 'all my estate to my son, John' would include property held in the sole name of the testator at the time of his death in a variety of different forms, such as cash, money in bank and building society accounts, stocks and shares and other investments, land and chattels.

If an individual does not dispose of such property by will, it passes on his death according to the intestacy rules.

However, there are some important types of property which pass on death independently of the terms of the will or the intestacy rules.

29.1.1 Joint property

Where property is held by more than one person as joint tenants in equity, on the death of one joint tenant his interest passes by survivorship to the surviving joint tenant(s).

Example

George makes a will leaving all his estate to a charity. He and his brother Harry have a joint bank account and own a house as joint tenants in equity. On George's death his interests in the house and the bank account pass automatically to Harry, not to the charity under the terms of George's will.

The doctrine of survivorship does not apply to land held on a tenancy in common. The share of each tenant in common passes on his death under his will (or under the intestacy rules).

29.1.2 Nominated property

There are statutory provisions allowing individuals to 'nominate' what is to happen to certain types of funds after the nominator's death. The statutory provisions apply to deposits not exceeding £5,000 in certain trustee savings banks, friendly societies and industrial and provident societies.

A nomination is a direction to the institution to pay the money in the account, on the death of the investor, to a chosen ('nominated') third party.

If an individual has an account to which these provisions apply and has made a nomination, on his death the property passes to the chosen nominee regardless of the terms of the will (if any) or intestacy rules. If no nomination has been made, the money in the account will pass under the will or intestacy in the usual way.

There are very few statutes which allow new nominations to be made although those already made will continue to be valid unless and until revoked.

29.1.3 Insurance policies

Where a person takes out a simple policy of life assurance, the benefit of that policy belongs to him. On his death, the policy matures and the insurance company will pay the proceeds to his representatives who will distribute the money according to the terms of his will or the intestacy rules.

However, a person may take out a life assurance policy for the benefit of specified individuals. This is effectively a gift to those individuals. It may be done in two ways.

(a)   Under the terms of the Married Women's Property Act 1882, s 11. Under this section, a person taking out a life assurance policy on his own life may express the policy to be for the benefit of his spouse and/or children. This creates a trust in favour of the named beneficiaries.

(b)   Alternatively, a policy may be expressly written in trust for or assigned to named beneficiaries.

In either case, once given away, the benefit of the policy does not belong to the policy holder. On death, the policy matures and the insurance company will pay the proceeds to the named beneficiaries (or to trustees for them) regardless of the terms of the deceased's will.

29.1.4 Pension benefits

Many pension schemes provide for the payment of benefits if an employee dies 'in service'. Commonly, a lump sum calculated on the basis of the employee's salary at the time of his death is paid by the trustees of the pension fund to members of the family or dependants chosen at their discretion. Such a scheme usually allows the employee to leave a letter of wishes for the trustees indicating which people he would like to benefit. The employee's choice is not binding on the pension fund trustees, but they will normally abide by his wishes.

Such pension benefits do not belong to the employee during his lifetime and pass on death independently of the terms of any will.

29.2 Is there a valid will?

In order to create a valid will, a testator must have the necessary capacity and intention and must observe the formalities for execution of wills laid down in the

Wills Act 1837. Once the will is made, it can be revoked by subsequent marriage or the formation of a civil partnership , by destruction or by later will.

29.2.1 Capacity

In order to make a valid will, an individual must be aged 18 or over (with certain limited exceptions) and must have the requisite mental capacity. This testamentary capacity was defined in *Banks v Goodfellow* (1870) LR 5 QB 549 as 'soundness of mind, memory and understanding'. The testator must understand:

(a)   the nature of his act and its broad effects;

(b)   the extent of his property (although not necessarily recollecting every individual item); and

(c)   the moral claims he ought to consider (even if he decides to reject such claims and dispose of his property to other beneficiaries).

29.2.1.1 Proof and presumptions

Normally the person who puts forward a will has to prove that all the necessary elements are present. However, in relation to the mental capacity required for a valid will, the Mental Capacity Act 2005 appears to have changed the burden of proof. Section 1(2) provides that 'a person must be assumed to have capacity unless it is established that he lacks capacity'. Therefore, a person who alleges that a testator lacked capacity to make a valid will has to prove it.

29.2.2 Intention

When the will is signed, the testator must have both general and specific intention. This means that the testator must intend to make a will (as opposed to any other sort of document), and must also intend to make the particular will now being executed (ie the testator must know and approve its contents).

29.2.2.1 Proof and presumptions

The burden of proving the testator's knowledge and approval falls on the propounder of the will, but there is one presumption which will usually assist.

A testator who has capacity and has executed his will, having read it, is presumed to have the requisite knowledge and approval. However, this presumption does not apply in the situations listed below.

Testator blind/illiterate/not signing personally

The presumption that the testator knew and approved the contents of his will does not apply if the testator was blind or illiterate, or another person signed the will on the testator's behalf (eg, because he had an injured hand).

In these cases, the probate registrar will require evidence to prove knowledge and approval. It is usual to include a statement at the end of the will stating that the will was read over to the testator, or read by the testator who knew and approved the contents.

Suspicious circumstances

Similarly, the presumption of knowledge and approval does not apply if there are suspicious circumstances surrounding the drafting and/or execution of the will (eg, the will has been prepared by someone who is to be a major beneficiary under its terms or who is a close relative of a major beneficiary).

In such cases, because the presumption does not apply, the propounder of the will must remove the suspicion by proving that the testator did actually know and approve the will's contents.

Note: Conduct issues for solicitors

Rule 3.04 of the Law Society's Code of Conduct 2004 provides that where a client wishes to make a gift (lifetime or by will) to:

(a)   the solicitor; or

(b)   the solicitor's partner; or

(c)   a member of staff; or

(d)   the families of any of them,

and the gift is of a significant amount, either in itself or in relation to the size of the client's estate and the reasonable expectations of the prospective beneficiaries, the solicitor must advise the client to obtain independent advice and must refuse to act if the client declines. There is an exception if the client is a member of the beneficiary's family. However, the guidance to Rule 3.04 states at para 57 that the solicitor should 'exercise caution' when giving advice in such cases.

29.2.2.2   Undue influence and mistake

Where a testator with capacity appears to have known and approved the contents of the will, any person who wishes to challenge the will (or any part of it) must prove one or more of the following to prevent some or all of the will from being admitted to probate. (There are no presumptions, so the person claiming invalidity on one of these grounds must prove it.)

Force, fear, fraud or undue influence

The testator made his will (or part of it) as a result of force or fear (through actual or threatened injury); or fraud (eg, after being misled by some pretence); or undue influence (where the testator's freedom of choice was overcome by intolerable pressure, even though his judgement remained unconvinced).

Notice that it is necessary to *prove* undue influence in relation to a will. This is different from the position in relation to a lifetime gift. If a donor makes a lifetime gift which requires explanation (for example, because it is large in relation to the donor's other assets) to a person who is in a position of trust and confidence, there is a presumption of undue influence. The donee will be able to keep the gift only if he can provide the court with a satisfactory explanation.

Mistake

All or part of the will was included by mistake. Any words included without the knowledge and approval of the testator will be omitted from probate. In this respect, it is important to distinguish between actual mistake (ie absence of knowledge and approval) and misunderstanding as to the true legal meaning of words used in the will. The latter will not invalidate the will.

29.2.3   Formalities for execution

Section 9 of the Wills Act 1837 (as substituted by Administration of Justice Act 1982, s 17) provides:

> No will shall be valid unless—

(a)   it is in writing, and signed by the testator, or by some other person in his presence and by his direction; and

(b)   it appears that the testator intended by his signature to give effect to the will; and

(c)   the signature is made or acknowledged by the testator in the presence of two or more witnesses present at the same time; and

(d)   each witness either—

    (i)   attests and signs the will; or

    (ii)   acknowledges his signature,

    in the presence of the testator (but not necessarily in the presence of any other witness),

but no form of attestation shall be necessary.

29.2.3.1   Proof and presumptions

If the will includes a clause which recites that the s 9 formalities were observed, a presumption of due execution is raised. The will is valid unless there is proof that the formalities were not observed. Such a clause is called an attestation clause.

An example of an attestation clause is:

Signed by the testator in our joint presence and then by us in his/hers.

If the will does not contain an attestation clause, the district judge (or registrar) must require an affidavit of due execution from a witness or any other person who was present during the execution, or, failing that, an affidavit of handwriting evidence to identify the testator's signature, or refer the case to a judge (all of which involve time and expense).

29.2.3.2   Witnesses

There are no formal requirements relating to the capacity of witnesses, although they must be capable of understanding the significance of being the witness to a signature.

If either of the witnesses is a beneficiary under the will or is the spouse or a civil partner of a beneficiary, the will remains valid but the gift to the witness or to the witness's spouse fails (Wills Act 1837, s 15; see **29.3.3**).

It is important for solicitors preparing wills to give clear instructions to their clients explaining how to sign and witness the will, and warning that beneficiaries and those married to beneficiaries should not be witnesses.

If the will is returned to the solicitor for storage, the solicitor is under a duty to check the signatures to see whether ss 9 and 15 appear to have been complied with.

29.2.4   Revocation

Testators can always revoke a will during their lifetime provided they have testamentary capacity. There are three ways of revoking a will.

29.2.4.1   By a later will or codicil

Under the Wills Act 1837, s 20, a will can be revoked in whole or in part by a later will or codicil. Normally, a will contains an express clause revoking all earlier wills and codicils.

If a will does not contain an express revocation clause, it operates to revoke any earlier will or codicil by implication to the extent that the two are inconsistent.

Exceptionally, the court may decide that a testator's intention to revoke an earlier will by an express revocation clause was conditional upon a particular event (eg, the effectiveness of a gift in the new will). If that condition is not satisfied, the revocation may be held to be invalid so that the earlier will remains effective (the doctrine of 'dependent relative revocation').

29.2.4.2   By marriage or civil partnership

If the testator marries or forms a civil partnership after executing a will, the will is automatically revoked (Wills Act 1837, s 18, as substituted by the Administration of Justice Act 1982). The rule does not apply where a testator makes a will prior to and in expectation of a forthcoming marriage or civil partnership if it appears from the will that the testator does not intend the will to be revoked (s 18(3)).

If the testator makes a will and is later divorced or if the civil partnership is dissolved (or the marriage or civil partnership is annulled or declared void) then, under the Wills Act 1837, s 18A (amended by the Law Reform (Succession) Act 1995 with effect from 1 January 1996):

(a)   provisions of the will appointing the former spouse or civil partner as executor or trustee take effect as if the former spouse or civil partner had died on the date on which the marriage or civil partnership is dissolved or annulled; and

(b)   any property, or interest in property, which is devised or bequeathed to the former spouse or civil partner passes as if the former spouse or civil partner had died on that date.

This means that substitutional provisions in the will which are expressed to take effect if the testator's spouse predeceases him will also take effect if the marriage is dissolved or annulled.

29.2.4.3   By destruction

A will can be revoked by 'burning, tearing or otherwise destroying the same by the testator or by some person in his presence and by his direction with the intention of revoking the same' (Wills Act 1837, s 20). Physical destruction without the intention to revoke is insufficient; a will destroyed accidentally or by mistake is not revoked. If its contents can be reconstructed (eg, from a copy) an order may be obtained allowing its admission to probate as a valid will.

Physical destruction is required: symbolic destruction (eg, simply crossing out wording or endorsing 'revoked' across the will) is not sufficient, although if a vital part (eg, the signature) is destroyed, this partial destruction may be held to revoke the entire will. If the part destroyed is less substantial or important, then the partial destruction may revoke only that part which was actually destroyed.

Occasionally, the court may apply the doctrine of dependent relative revocation to save a will, on the basis that the testator's intention to revoke his will by destruction was conditional upon some future event (eg, upon the later execution of a new will). If that event did not in fact take place, the original will may be valid even though it was destroyed. The contents of the original will may be reconstructed from a copy or draft.

29.2.5 Alterations

If a will has been altered, the basic rule is that the alterations are invalid unless it can be proved that they were made before the will was executed, or unless the alterations are executed like a will (the initials of the testator and witnesses in the margin beside the alteration are sufficient).

If a will includes invalid alterations, the original wording will stand if the original words are 'apparent', ie can still be read. If the original words have been obliterated in such a way that they can no longer be read, those words have effectively been revoked by destruction. The rest of the will remains valid, and takes effect with the omission of the obliterated words.

Again, the court may decide that the testator's intention to revoke the obliterated words was conditional only. This inference is most likely where the testator attempted to replace the obliterated words with a substitution. The implied condition is that the testator intended to revoke the original words only if the substitution was effective. As it is not, the original words remain valid, and if they can be reconstructed (eg, from a copy or draft) they will take effect.

29.3 What is the effect of the will?

When a testator dies, the people dealing with the estate must decide (usually with the help of a solicitor) the effect of the will in the light of the circumstances at the date of the testator's death. They will need to consider what property the testator owned when he died and which of the people named in the will have survived the testator in order to decide the effect of the gifts.

The people dealing with the estate will be called executors, if they were appointed by the will, and administrators, if there was no appointment in the will. There are statutory rules as to who is able to act as an administrator (see **Chapter 30**). Both executors and administrators can be referred to as 'personal representatives' (PRs).

29.3.1 What property passes under the gifts in the will?

As seen in **29.1** above, certain types of property pass independently of the will either because they have their own rules of succession (eg, joint property), or because the testator did not own them beneficially at death (eg, life assurance policies written in trust).

When the PRs have decided what property is capable of passing under the will, they must apply the terms of the will to the property.

29.3.1.1 Basic rule

The basic rule is stated in the Wills Act 1837, s 24 which provides:

> ... every will shall be construed, with reference to the real estate and personal estate comprised in it, to speak and take effect as if it had been executed immediately before the death of the testator, unless a contrary intention shall appear by the will.

This means that a gift of 'all my estate' or 'all the rest of my estate' takes effect to dispose of all property the testator owned when he died, whether or not the testator owned it at the time the will was made.

29.3.1.2 Ademption

A specific legacy, ie a gift of a particular item or group of items of property, will fail if the testator no longer owns that property at death. The gift is said to be 'adeemed'. Ademption usually occurs because the property has been sold, given away or destroyed during the testator's lifetime.

Example

In her will Ellen gives 'my diamond bracelet' to her sister Grace and the rest of her estate to her husband Harry. Ellen no longer owns the bracelet when she dies. Grace receives nothing: her legacy is adeemed. All Ellen's estate passes to Harry under the residuary gift.

Problems may arise where the asset has been retained but has changed its nature since the will was made. For example, where the will includes a specific gift of company shares, the company may have been taken over since the will was made so that the testator's shareholding has been changed into a holding in the new company. In such a case, the question is whether the asset is substantially the same, having changed merely in name or form, or whether it has changed in substance. Only if there has been a change in substance will the gift be adeemed.

Another area of potential difficulty occurs where the testator disposes of the property described in a specific gift but before his death acquires a different item of property which answers the same description; for example a gift of 'my car' or 'my piano' where the original car or piano has been replaced since the will was made. It has been held that the presumption in such a case is that the testator meant only to dispose of the particular asset he owned at the date of the will so that the gift is adeemed. By referring to 'my' car or piano, the testator is taken to have shown a contrary intention to s 24. It has been suggested that this construction may vary according to the circumstances and that the respective values of the original and substituted assets may be taken into account.

If the property given is capable of increase or decrease (eg, 'my shares', 'my jewelry'), the testator will normally be taken to have made a gift of any items satisfying the description at death.

29.3.2   Has the beneficiary survived the testator?

29.3.2.1   Basic rule

A gift in a will fails or 'lapses' if the beneficiary dies before the testator. If a legacy lapses, the property falls into residue. If a gift of residue lapses, the property passes under the intestacy rules, unless the testator has provided for the possibility of lapse by including a substitutional gift in the will. Where no conditions to the contrary are imposed in the will, a gift vests on the testator's death. This means that provided the beneficiary survives the testator, for however short a time, the gift takes effect. If the beneficiary dies soon *after* the testator the property passes into the beneficiary's estate.

29.3.2.2   Law of Property Act 1925, s 184

The principle outlined above means that if the deaths of the testator and beneficiary occur very close together, it is vital to establish who died first. The law of succession does not accept the possibility that two people might die at the same instant. If the order of their deaths cannot be proved, s 184 provides that the elder of the two is deemed to have died first. If the testator was older than the beneficiary, the gift takes effect and the property passes as part of the beneficiary's estate.

29.3.2.3   Survivorship clauses

Commonly, gifts in wills are made conditional upon the survival of the beneficiaries for a specific period of time, such as 28 days. These survivorship provisions prevent a gift from taking effect where the beneficiary survives the testator for only a relatively short time or is deemed to have survived by s 184. As with any other contingent gift, if the beneficiary fails to satisfy the contingency the gift fails.

29.3.2.4 Lapse of gifts to more than one person

A gift by will to two or more people as joint tenants will not lapse unless all the donees die before the testator. If a gift is made 'to A and B jointly' and A dies before the testator, the whole gift passes to B.

If the gift contains words of severance, for example 'to A and B in equal shares', this principle does not apply. If A dies before the testator, A's share lapses and B takes only one share. The lapsed share will pass under the intestacy rules unless the testator included a substitutional gift to take effect if one of the original beneficiaries predeceased.

If the gift is a class gift (eg, 'to my children in equal shares'), there is no lapse unless all the members of the class predecease the testator.

29.3.2.5 Wills Act 1837, s 33: gifts to children and remoter issue

This section applies to all gifts by will to the testator's children or remoter issue unless a contrary intention is shown in the will and its effect is to incorporate an implied substitution provision into such gifts. It provides that, where a will contains a gift to the testator's child or remoter descendant and that beneficiary dies before the testator, leaving issue of his own who survive the testator, the gift shall not lapse but shall pass instead to the beneficiary's issue. The issue of a deceased beneficiary take the gift their parent would have taken in equal shares.

Example

Tom's will includes a gift of £40,000 to his daughter, Caroline. Caroline and her daughter Sarah both die before Tom, but Caroline's son, James, and Sarah's children, Emma and Daniel, all survive him. Under s 33, the legacy is saved from lapse. James takes half the gift (£20,000) while Sarah's half passes to her own children equally. Thus, Emma and Daniel take £10,000 each.

Section 33 does not apply if the will shows a contrary intention. This is usually shown by including an express substitution clause.

29.3.3 Does the gift fail for any other reason?

29.3.3.1 Divorce or dissolution of a civil partnership

Under the Wills Act 1837, s 18A (as substituted by the Law Reform (Succession) Act 1995), where after the date of the will the testator's marriage or civil partnership is dissolved or annulled or declared void, 'any property which, or an interest in which, is devised or bequeathed to the former spouse or civil partner shall pass as if the former spouse or civil partner had died' on the date of the dissolution or annulment of the marriage or civil partnership.

Example

Fiona makes a will in which she leaves all her estate to her husband, Simon, with a substitutional provision that, if Simon dies before her, the property should pass to her children equally. Fiona and Simon are later divorced but Fiona does not change her will. She dies, survived by Simon and the children. Under s 18A, the gift to Simon fails. Even though Simon in fact survived Fiona, the substitutional gift takes effect and Fiona's estate passes to the children.

29.3.3.2   Beneficiary witnesses will

Under the Wills Act 1837, s 15, a gift by will fails if the beneficiary, his spouse or civil partner witnesses the will.

29.3.3.3   Disclaimer

A beneficiary need not accept a gift given to him by will. He can disclaim the gift, which will then fall into residue or, in the case of disclaimer of a gift of residue, pass on intestacy.

However, a beneficiary who has received a benefit from a gift (eg, a payment of income) is taken to have accepted the gift and may no longer disclaim.

29.4   Intestacy

The intestacy rules contained in the Administration of Estates Act 1925 (AEA 1925) apply to decide who is entitled to an individual's property when he dies without disposing of it by will.

This may occur because the deceased has died intestate (ie, without a valid will), or because his will failed to dispose of all his estate (partial intestacy).

The intestacy rules only apply to property which is capable of being left by will (see **29.1**).

Example

Laura dies intestate, survived by her husband, Michael, and their two children. Laura and Michael own their house as beneficial joint tenants. Laura has taken out a life assurance policy for £100,000 which is written in trust for the children and she owns investments worth £150,000. The intestacy rules do not affect Laura's share of the house (which passes to Michael by survivorship) or the life policy (which passes to the children under the terms of the trust). Only the investments pass under the intestacy rules.

29.4.1   Statutory trust for payment of debts, etc

The intestacy rules impose a trust over all the property (real and personal) in respect of which a person dies intestate (AEA 1925, s 33). This trust is similar to the usual express trust found in a will and includes a power of sale: it provides that the PRs must pay the funeral, testamentary and administration expenses and any debts of the deceased. The balance remaining (after setting aside a fund to meet any pecuniary legacies left by the deceased in the will) is the 'residuary estate' to be shared among the family under the rules of distribution set out in s 46 of the AEA 1925. The PRs have power under s 41 to appropriate assets in or towards satisfaction of a beneficiary's share (with the beneficiary's consent).

29.4.2   Spouse or civil partner and issue

29.4.2.1   Definition

Under the intestacy rules, a spouse is the person to whom the deceased was married at his death, whether or not they were living together. A divorced spouse is excluded. A cohabitee has no rights under the intestacy rules.

Civil partners are treated in the same way as spouses.

The term 'issue' includes all direct descendants of the deceased: ie, children, grandchildren, great grandchildren, etc. Adopted children (and remoter descendants) are included, as are those whose parents were not married at the time of their birth.

29.4.2.2   Entitlements

Where the intestate is survived by both spouse or civil partner and issue, the 'residuary estate' (as defined in **29.4.1**) is distributed as follows:

(a)   The spouse or civil partner receives the personal chattels absolutely. 'Personal chattels' are defined in s 55(x) of the AEA 1925:

"Personal chattels" mean carriages, horses, stable furniture and effects (not used for business purposes), motor cars and accessories (not used for business purposes), garden effects, domestic animals, plate, plated articles, linen, china, glass, books, pictures, prints, furniture, jewellery, articles of household or personal use or ornament, musical and scientific instruments and apparatus, wines, liquors and consumable stores, but do not include any chattels used at the death of the intestate for business purposes nor money or securities for money.

(b)   In addition, the spouse or civil partner receives a 'statutory legacy' of £125,000 free of tax and costs plus interest from death until payment. The rate of interest payable is determined from time to time by statutory instrument, and is currently 6%. If the residuary estate, apart from the personal chattels, is worth less than £125,000, the spouse or civil partner receives it all (and the issue receive nothing).

(c)   The rest of the residuary estate (if any) is divided into two equal funds. One fund is held on trust for the spouse or civil partner for life with remainder to the issue on the statutory trusts. The other fund is held for the issue on the statutory trusts.

For deaths after 1 January 1996, the entitlement of the intestate's spouse or civil partner is conditional upon the spouse or civil partner surviving the intestate for 28 days. Under the Law Reform (Succession) Act 1995, where the intestate's spouse or civil partner dies within 28 days of the intestate, the estate is distributed as if the spouse or civil partner has not survived the intestate.

29.4.2.3   Applying the statutory trusts

The statutory trusts determine membership of the class of beneficiaries, and the terms on which they take, as follows.

(a)   The primary beneficiaries are the children of the intestate who are living at the intestate's death. Remoter issue are not included, unless a child has died before the intestate.

(b)   The interests of the children are contingent upon attaining the age of 18 or marrying or forming a civil partnership under that age. Any child who fulfils the contingency at the intestate's death takes a vested interest. If a child dies after the intestate but without attaining a vested interest, the child's interest fails and the estate is redistributed.

(c)   If any child of the intestate predeceased the intestate, any children of the deceased child (grandchildren of the deceased) who are living at the intestate's death take their deceased parent's share equally between them, contingently upon attaining 18 or earlier marriage or formation of a civil partnership. Great grandchildren would be included only if their parent had also predeceased the intestate. This form of substitution and division is known as a 'per stirpes' distribution.

Example

Joanne dies intestate survived by her husband, Kenneth, and their children, Mark (who has a son, Quentin) and Nina. Their daughter, Lisa, died last year. Lisa's two children, Oliver and Paul, are living at Joanne's death.

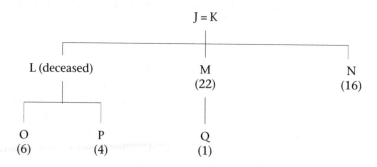

Joanne's estate consists of her share in the house, held as joint tenants with Kenneth, and other property worth £440,000 after payment of debts, funeral and testamentary expenses. This figure includes personal chattels worth £15,000.

DISTRIBUTION

Joanne's share in the house passes to Kenneth by survivorship. The rest of her estate passes on intestacy.

£	
15,000	personal chattels to Kenneth
125,000	statutory legacy to Kenneth
150,000	(Fund A) on trust for Kenneth for life remainder to the issue on the statutory trusts
150,000	(Fund B) for issue on the statutory trusts
440,000	

The statutory trusts apply to both funds of £150,000 to determine the distribution between Joanne's issue.

Mark and Nina, Joanne's children, are living at her death and take one share each. The share Lisa would have taken had she survived is held for her children, Oliver and Paul in equal shares. The interests of Nina, Oliver and Paul are contingent upon attaining 18 or earlier marriage.

Thus, Mark has a vested interest in one-third of each fund. He is entitled to £50,000 on Joanne's death, and to one-third of Fund A when Kenneth dies. If Mark should die shortly after Joanne, his share in both funds would form part of his estate on death. Quentin has no entitlement under Joanne's intestacy.

Nina has a contingent interest in one-third of each fund, which will vest when she is 18 or if she marries or forms a civil partnership before 18. If Nina should die under the age of 18 and without marrying or forming a civil partnership, her interest would fail. One half of Nina's share would pass to Mark and the other half would be held for Oliver and Paul equally. This result would follow even if Nina had a child who survived her. The substitution of grandchildren applies only where a child of the intestate dies before him, whereas Nina was alive at the date of Joanne's death.

Oliver and Paul have contingent interests in one-sixth of each fund, which will vest at 18 or earlier marriage or formation of a civil partnership. If Oliver should die under the age of 18 and without marrying or forming a civil partnership, his share would pass to Paul (and vice versa). If both Oliver and Paul were to die under the age of 18 and without marrying or forming a civil partnership, their shares would be divided equally between Mark and Nina.

29.4.2.4 Right of spouse or civil partner to redeem the life interest

Under s 47 of the AEA 1925, the surviving spouse or civil partner may elect to take a lump sum in place of the life interest.

This means that the half of the residue which would, under the provisions outlined above, be held on trust for the spouse or civil partner for life with remainder to issue will instead be divided between the spouse or civil partner and issue. The spouse or civil partner receives the capital value of the life interest immediately and the balance is held for the issue on the statutory trusts.

The spouse or civil partner must give written notice of his or her election to the PRs within 12 months of the grant of representation.

29.4.2.5 Right of spouse or civil partner to require appropriation of the matrimonial home

If the matrimonial home forms part of the estate passing on intestacy, the surviving spouse or civil partner can require the PRs to appropriate the matrimonial home in full or partial satisfaction of any absolute interest in the estate (including the capitalised value of the life interest in residue) (Intestates' Estates Act 1952, s 5).

If the property is worth more than the entitlement of the spouse or civil partner, the spouse or civil partner may still require appropriation provided he or she pays the difference, 'equality money', to the estate.

The election must be made in writing to the PRs within 12 months of the grant of representation.

29.4.3 Spouse or civil partner and parents, brothers or sisters or their issue

Where the intestate leaves a surviving spouse or civil partner but no issue, the distribution of the estate depends on whether any other close relatives survive. If the intestate is survived by either or both parents, by brothers or sisters of the whole blood, or by issue of deceased brothers and sisters, the following rules apply.

29.4.3.1 Entitlement of spouse or civil partner

From the 'residuary estate' (as defined in **29.4.1**) the spouse or civil partner receives:

(a)   the personal chattels absolutely (as in **29.4.2**);

(b)   a statutory legacy of £200,000 free of tax and costs plus interest from the date of death until payment. If the residuary estate apart from the personal chattels is worth less than £200,000, the spouse or civil partner receives it all (and the parents receive nothing);

(c)   half the rest of the residuary estate absolutely (ie no life interest arises in this case).

For deaths on or after 1 January 1996, the entitlement of the spouse or civil partner is conditional upon surviving the intestate for 28 days. If the spouse or civil partner dies within 28 days of the intestate, the intestate's estate is distributed as if the spouse or civil partner had not survived him.

29.4.3.2   Distribution of remainder

If the intestate is survived by either parent, that parent receives the rest of the estate absolutely. If both parents survive, the rest of the estate is shared equally between them. If both parents have predeceased the intestate, the rest of the estate is divided between the intestate's brothers and sisters of the whole blood on the statutory trusts. The terms of the statutory trusts are the same as those for issue (see **29.4.2**). The substitution provision means that if a brother or sister of the intestate has predeceased him leaving issue, such issue (nephews and nieces of the intestate) take their parent's share.

Example

Irene dies intestate. Her estate passing on intestacy is worth £350,000 (including personal chattels of £10,000). She is survived by her husband, Henry, and brother Brian and sister Susan. She has no issue and both her parents are dead.

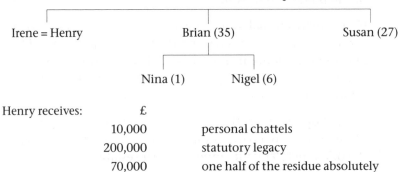

| Irene = Henry | Brian (35) | Susan (27) |

Nina (1)   Nigel (6)

Henry receives: £

	10,000	personal chattels
	200,000	statutory legacy
	70,000	one half of the residue absolutely

(If Irene dies on or after 1 January 1996, Henry will be entitled as above only if he survives Irene for 28 days.)

The remaining £70,000 is held for the brothers and sisters on statutory trusts. This means that it is divided equally between Brian and Susan, who both have vested interests because they are over 18.

If Brian had predeceased Irene, his share (£35,000) would be held for his children, Nina and Nigel, equally, contingently upon attaining the age of 18 or earlier marriage.

29.4.3.3   Right of spouse or civil partner to require appropriation of the matrimonial home

As described in **29.4.2.5**, the surviving spouse or civil partner may elect to take the matrimonial home in full or partial satisfaction of his interest in the estate.

29.4.4   Intestate survived by spouse or civil partner and no other close relatives

Where the intestate leaves a surviving spouse or civil partner but no issue, parent, brother or sister of the whole blood, or issue of a deceased brother or sister, the whole estate, however large, passes to the spouse or civil partner absolutely. More distant relatives, such as half brothers and sisters, grandparents and cousins, are not entitled.

If the intestate died on or after 1 January 1996, the entitlement of the spouse or civil partner is conditional upon surviving the intestate for 28 days. If the spouse or civil partner died within that period, the estate is distributed as if the spouse or civil partner had not survived the intestate.

29.4.5   Distribution where there is no surviving spouse or civil partner

Where there is no surviving spouse or civil partner (or, for deaths after 1 January 1996, where the spouse or civil partner dies within 28 days of the intestate), the 'residuary estate' is divided between the relatives in the highest category in the list below:

(a)   issue on the 'statutory trusts' (see **29.4.2**), but if none,

(b)   parents, equally if both alive, but if none,

(c)   brothers and sisters of the whole blood on the 'statutory trusts', but if none,

(d)   brothers and sisters of the half blood on the 'statutory trusts', but if none,

(e)   grandparents, equally if more than one, but if none,

(f)   uncles and aunts of the whole blood on the 'statutory trusts', but if none,

(g)   uncles and aunts of the half blood on the 'statutory trusts', but if none,

(h)   the Crown, Duchy of Lancaster, or Duke of Cornwall (bona vacantia).

29.4.5.1   The statutory trusts

Each category other than parents and grandparents takes 'on the statutory trusts'. This means that members of the specified class share the estate equally (children under 18 take their interest contingently upon attaining 18 or marrying earlier), and that issue of a deceased relative may take that relative's share. This means that relatives not mentioned in s 46 (eg, nephews, nieces and cousins) may inherit on intestacy if their parents died before the intestate.

Example 1

Tom dies intestate. He was not married to his partner, Penny, although the couple have a son, Simon, aged 13, Tom's only child. Tom's parents predeceased him but he is survived by his only sibling, his brother Bob, aged 40.

Tom's estate is held on trust for Simon, contingently upon attaining 18 or marrying earlier. If Simon dies before the contingency is fulfilled, Tom's estate passes to Bob absolutely.

Example 2

Vera, a widow aged 80, is cared for by her step-daughter, Carol (the child of her deceased husband's first marriage). Her only living blood relatives are cousins, the children of her mother's brothers and sisters. Vera dies intestate. Her estate is divided 'per stirpes' between her cousins (and the children of any cousins who predeceased her). Carol receives nothing from Vera's estate.

29.4.5.2   Adopted and illegitimate children

Adopted children are treated for intestacy purposes as the children of their adoptive parents and not of their natural parents. If a person who was adopted dies intestate without spouse or issue, his estate will be distributed between the closest relatives in the adoptive family. An adopted child may also inherit on the intestacy of any member of his adoptive family.

Similarly, the intestacy rules are applied regardless of whether or not a particular individual's parents were married to each other. However, on the intestacy of an individual whose parents were not married to each other, it is presumed that the individual has not been survived by his father or by any person related to him through his father unless the contrary is shown (Family Law Reform Act 1987, s 18(2)). This presumption avoids any necessity for the PRs to make awkward enquiries where the identity or whereabouts of the father is unknown.

Example

Jessica, whose parents did not marry, dies intestate. Her only known relative is a half brother, the child of her mother's later marriage. Nothing is known of Jessica's father or any other children he may have had. Jessica's PRs may distribute her estate to her half brother, relying on the presumption in s 18(2).

29.4.5.3 Bona vacantia

Where an estate passes bona vacantia, the Crown, Duchy of Lancaster or Duke of Cornwall has a discretion to provide for dependants of the intestate, or for other persons for whom the intestate might reasonably have been expected to make provision.

Genealogists say that it is rare for an estate to be truly bona vacantia. They can usually trace some relatives (provided the estate is large enough to meet their fees).

29.5 The Inheritance (Provision for Family and Dependants) Act 1975

The Inheritance (Provision for Family and Dependants) Act 1975 (I(PFD)A 1975) allows certain categories of people who may be aggrieved because they have been left out of a will, or are not inheriting on an intestacy, to apply for a benefit from the estate following the testator's or intestate's death. The I(PFD)A 1975 can also be used by a person who has received some benefit under the will or intestacy but is dissatisfied with the amount of the inheritance.

The I(PFD)A 1975 applies only where the deceased died domiciled in England and Wales. It does not apply where a person originally domiciled in England and Wales has acquired a domicile of choice elsewhere.

Section numbers below refer to the I(PFD)A 1975 unless otherwise stated.

29.5.1 When should a claim be made?

An application must be brought within six months of the date of issue of the grant of representation to the deceased's estate (s 4). However, the court has a discretion to extend this time-limit.

29.5.2 Who can make a claim?

The following persons can make a claim (s 1(1)):

(a)   the spouse or civil partner of the deceased;

(b)   a former spouse or civil partner of the deceased who has not remarried (except where, on the granting of the decree of dissolution or nullity, the court made an order barring the former spouse or civil partner from making a claim);

(c)   a child of the deceased (whatever the child's age);

(d)   any person treated by the deceased as a child of the family in relation to any marriage of the deceased (eg, a step-child);

(e)   any person who, immediately before the death of the deceased, was being maintained by him either wholly or in part. A person is 'maintained' if 'the deceased, otherwise than for full valuable consideration, was making a substantial contribution in money or money's worth towards the reasonable needs of that person' (s 1(3));

(f)   any person who, during the whole of the period of two years ending immediately before the date when the deceased died, was living:

  (i)   in the same household as the deceased, and

  (ii)   as the husband or wife of the deceased (this category was added by the Law Reform (Succession) Act 1995);

(g)   any person who, during the whole of the period of two years ending immediately before the date when the deceased died, was living:

  (i)   in the same household as the deceased, and

(ii)   as the civil partner of the deceased.

29.5.3   What must the applicant prove?

The only ground for a claim is that 'the disposition of the deceased's estate effected by his will or the law relating to intestacy, or a combination of his will and that law, is not such as to make reasonable financial provision for the applicant'. Section 1(2) sets out two standards for judging 'reasonable financial provision':

(a)   'the surviving spouse standard', which allows a surviving spouse or civil partner such financial provision as is reasonable in all the circumstances 'whether or not that provision is required for his or her maintenance' (s 1(2)(a)); and

(b)   'the ordinary standard', which applies to all other categories of applicant and allows 'such financial provision as it would be reasonable in all the circumstances ... for the applicant to receive for his maintenance' (s 1(2)(b)).

29.5.4   What factors does the court take into account?

Section 3 contains guidelines to assist the court in determining whether the will and/or intestacy does make reasonable financial provision for the applicant. Some matters should be considered for every claimant (ie, the common guidelines). There are also special guidelines for each category of applicant.

The common guidelines in s 3(1) are:

(a)   the financial resources and needs of the applicant, other applicants and beneficiaries of the estate now and in the foreseeable future;

(b)   the deceased's moral obligations towards any applicant or beneficiary;

(c)   the size and nature of the estate;

(d)   the physical or mental disability of any applicant or beneficiary;

(e)   anything else which may be relevant, such as the conduct of the applicant.

The special guidelines vary with the category of applicant. For example, where the applicant is the surviving spouse or civil partner, the court takes into account the applicant's age and contribution to the welfare of the family, the duration of the marriage or civil partnership and the likely financial settlement if the marriage or civil partnership had ended in divorce or dissolution rather than death. On an application by a child of the deceased the applicant's education or training requirements are considered. (The courts have shown a reluctance to award financial provision to adult, able-bodied children unless there is a particular need.)

When considering the common and special guidelines, the court takes into account:

(a)   the facts at the date of the hearing (s 3(5)); and

(b)   with regard to the financial resources and needs of the applicant:

(i)   his earning capacity; and

(ii)   his financial obligations and responsibilities (s 3(6)).

29.5.5   What orders can the court make?

The court has wide powers to make orders against the 'net estate' of the deceased, including orders for periodical payments, lump sum payments or the transfer of specific property to the applicant.

The 'net estate' against which an order can be made includes not only property which the deceased has, or could have, disposed of by will or nomination, but also the deceased's share of joint property passing by survivorship if the court so orders. However, the court can make an order against the deceased's share of joint property only where the application is made within six months of the grant. If the court extends the time-limit, the share of the joint property is unavailable. This limitation is to provide certainty for the surviving joint tenant.

In making an order, the court will declare how the burden of the order is to be borne, ie which beneficiary is to lose part or all of the property he would otherwise have taken.

For IHT purposes, the altered disposition of the estate is treated as taking effect from death.

If the order alters the amount passing to the deceased's spouse, the amount of any IHT payable on the estate will be affected.

29.5.6   Protecting the PRs

Personal representatives should be advised not to distribute the estate until six months have elapsed from the issue of the grant. In any event, they must not distribute once they have notice of a possible claim. If PRs do distribute within the six-month period and an applicant subsequently brings a successful claim, the PRs will be personally liable to satisfy the claim if insufficient assets remain in the estate. Where a court permits an application out of time, the PRs will not be liable personally if they have distributed the estate, but the claimant may be able to recover property from the beneficiaries.

Chapter 30

Probate Practice and Procedure

30.1 Introduction

This chapter considers the events immediately following death. The deceased may have been the client of the solicitor. Whether or not that is the case, the solicitor's clients at this stage are the deceased's personal representatives (PRs). The solicitor (or partners in the firm) may be acting as PR (or one of several PRs). The practice and procedure will be substantially the same whether the solicitor is a PR, or is merely acting for the PRs.

30.2 Who are the PRs?

The PRs will be either the deceased's executors, or intended administrators.

30.2.1 The executors

If the will is valid and contains an effective appointment of executors of whom one or more is willing and able to prove the deceased's will, a grant of probate will be issued to the executor(s) willing to act (see **30.9**).

30.2.2 Administrators with the will annexed

If there is a valid will but there are no persons willing or able to act as executors, then the next persons entitled to act are administrators with the will annexed, who should be appointed in accordance with the Non-Contentious Probate Rules 1987, r 20 (NCPR 1987) (SI 1987/2024) (see **30.10**).

30.2.3 Administrators (simple administration)

If a deceased left no will, or no valid will, the estate will be administered in accordance with the law of intestacy by administrators appointed by the application of NCPR 1987, r 22 (see **30.11**).

30.2.4   Number of PRs required

One executor may obtain a grant and act alone. This is so, even if the estate contains land which may be sold during the administration, because a receipt for the proceeds of sale from one executor is sufficient for the purchaser. This is in contrast to the position of trustees where, if a good receipt for the proceeds of sale of land is to be given to a purchaser, it must be given by at least two trustees (or a trust corporation).

In the case of administrators (with or without the will), it will often be sufficient for one to act in the administration of the estate. However, where the will or intestacy creates a life or minority interest, two administrators are normally required.

30.2.5   Authority of PRs before the grant

An executor derives authority to act in the administration of an estate from the will. The grant of probate confirms that authority. Although the executor has full power to act from the time of the deceased's death, the executor will be unable to undertake certain transactions (eg, sale of land) without producing the grant as proof of authority.

An administrator (with or without the will) has very limited powers before a grant is made. His authority stems from the grant which is not retrospective to the date of death.

30.3   First steps after receiving instructions

Following a person's death, a number of matters will require the immediate attention of the solicitor who is to act for the PRs, including those set out below.

30.3.1   The deceased's will

Ascertain whether the deceased made a will. If so, ensure the executors named in the will receive copies of it.

30.3.2   Directions as to cremation, etc

Give immediate consideration to the terms of the will to ascertain any special directions by the deceased as to cremation, or the use of his body for medical research or other purposes.

30.3.3   Details of assets and liabilities

Obtain details of the deceased's property and of any debts outstanding at the date of death, by asking the PRs for building society passbooks, share certificates and details of bank accounts, etc. Ask the deceased's bank manager as to whether the bank holds in safe custody any share certificates or other property owned by the deceased (the bank manager will require sight of the death certificate before giving such information).

From these details, the solicitor will be able to begin to evaluate the size of the deceased's estate, and the amount of any liability to IHT.

30.3.4   Details of the beneficiaries

From the deceased's will (if any), the solicitor must establish the identity of the beneficiaries, and the nature and extent of their entitlement (eg, whether as legatee or as residuary beneficiary). If specific legacies have been given, it is important to ascertain whether the property given by those specific gifts is part of the estate (if not the gift(s) will have adeemed) (see **29.3.1**). If the deceased has died intestate, it is necessary to establish which members of the family have survived so that the basis of distribution of the estate may be established in accordance with the rules discussed at **29.4**.

30.3.5 Missing and/or unknown creditors and beneficiaries

Personal representatives are responsible for administering the estate correctly. This means that they have to collect in all the assets, pay all the debts and transfer the remaining funds and assets to those entitled under the will or intestacy.

They may have two problems.

(a)   There may be creditors of whom they are unaware or unknown relatives (eg, children born outside marriage whose existence has been kept secret).

(b)   They may not know the whereabouts of some beneficiaries who may have lost contact with the deceased's family.

If the PRs fail to pay someone who is entitled either as a creditor or as a beneficiary, they will be personally liable to that person.

They can protect themselves against *unknown* claims by advertising for claimants under the Trustee Act 1925, s 27. Provided they wait for the time period specified in the section (at least two months) the PRs will be protected from liability if an unknown claimant later appears. However, the claimant will have the right to claim back assets from the beneficiaries who received them.

The following procedure should be adopted.

30.3.5.1 Early advertisement

In view of the minimum notice period of two months, PRs should advertise as early as possible in the administration. If they are executors, they may advertise at any time after the death; if they are administrators, they have power to advertise at any time after obtaining their grant.

30.3.5.2 Placing the advertisement

The PR should give notice of the intended distribution of the estate, requiring any person interested to send in particulars of his claim, whether as a creditor or as a beneficiary, by:

(a)   advertisement in the *London Gazette*;

(b)   advertisement in a newspaper circulating in the district in which land owned by the deceased is situated; and

(c)   'such other like notices, including notices elsewhere than in England and Wales, as would, in any special case, have been directed by a court of competent jurisdiction in an action for administration'.

A court would normally order the placing of advertisements as are appropriate in the particular circumstances of the case. Printed forms for the advertisements can be obtained from law stationers.

30.3.5.3 Time for claims

Each notice must require any person interested to send in particulars of his claim within the time specified in the notice, which must not be less than two months from the date of the notice.

30.3.5.4 Searches in case of land

The PRs should also make searches which the prudent purchaser of land would make in Land Registry, the Land Charges Register and the Local Land Charges Registry, as appropriate. The purpose of these searches is to reveal the existence of any liability in relation to the deceased's ownership of an interest in land, for example a second mortgage.

30.3.5.5 Distribution after notices

When the time-limit in the notice has expired, the PRs may distribute the deceased's estate, taking into account only those claims of which they have actual knowledge, or which they discover as a result of the advertisements. The PRs are not personally liable for any other claim, but a claimant may pursue the claim by following the assets into the hands of the beneficiaries who have received them from the PRs.

The Trustee Act 1925, s 27 will not give any protection to PRs who knows that there is a person with a claim but cannot find him. It protects only against unknown claims.

Where PRs cannot trace a beneficiary, they must consider one of the following:

(a)   Keeping back assets in case the claimant appears. This is unpopular with the other beneficiaries.

(b)   Taking an indemnity from the beneficiaries that they will meet any claims if the claimant reappears. This is dangerous for the PR as the beneficiaries may have no assets when the claimant appears.

(c)   Taking out insurance to provide funds. This can be expensive and, as the claimant may be entitled to interest, it is difficult to know what sum to insure.

(d)   Applying to the court for an order authorising the PRs to distribute the estate on the basis that the claimant is dead. This is referred to as a *Benjamin* order after the case in which it was first ordered (*Re Benjamin* [1902] 1 Ch 723). This protects the PRs from liability, although the claimant retains the right to recover the assets from the beneficiaries. Applying to court is an expensive process, but it is the only solution that offers the PR full protection.

30.4 Necessity for a grant of representation

A grant enables the PRs to prove their authority to deal with the deceased's assets which passes under the will or the intestacy rules. However, it is not always necessary to obtain a grant of representation to deal with assets. The ability to access assets without a grant is particularly useful where the deceased's family needs funds immediately for paying IHT or other purposes.

A grant may not be required in the three situations which follow.

30.4.1 Assets which may pass to the PRs without a grant

30.4.1.1 Administration of Estates (Small Payments) Act 1965

Orders made under this Act permit payments to be made under various statutes and statutory instruments to persons appearing to be beneficially entitled to the assets without formal proof of title. This facility is restricted, in that it is not available if the value of the asset exceeds £5,000; in addition, as the payments are made at the discretion of the institutions concerned, it is not possible for PRs to insist that payments should be made. Payment is often refused where the estate is of substantial overall value, leaving the PRs in a position where they must obtain a grant before the asset can be collected. Subject to these points, payments can be made in respect of, for example:

(a) money in the National Savings Bank and Trustee Savings Bank (but not in other bank accounts);

(b) National Savings Certificates and Premium Bonds; and

(c) money in building societies and friendly societies.

30.4.1.2 Chattels

Movable personal property such as furniture, clothing, jewellery and cars can normally be sold without the PRs having to prove formally to the buyer that they are entitled to sell such items.

30.4.1.3 Cash

Normally, the PRs do not require a grant when taking custody of any cash found in the deceased's possession (ie found in the home of the deceased as opposed to deposited in a bank or other account).

30.4.2 Assets not passing through the PRs' hands

30.4.2.1 Joint property

On death, any interest in property held by the deceased as joint tenant in equity with another (whether it is an interest in land or personalty, eg a bank account) passes by survivorship to the surviving joint tenant. As it does not pass via the PRs, any grant is irrelevant. The survivor has access to the property and can prove title to the whole of it merely by producing the deceased's death certificate. Since it is common for married couples and civil partners to own property jointly, there are many occasions where a grant is not required for this reason.

(Conversely, if the property is held by persons as beneficial tenants in common, the share of each tenant in common passes on his death to his PRs for distribution, and a grant will be required.)

30.4.3 Property not forming part of the deceased person's estate

The deceased may have insured his/her own life, but in such a way that the policy and its proceeds are held in trust for others. This trust may be established by writing the policy under the Married Women's Property Act 1882, s 11 ('a Married Women's Property Act policy') for the spouse or children of the deceased, or by making a separate declaration of trust for those or other beneficiaries. On death, the policy money is payable to the trustees of the policy on production of the death certificate. A grant is not required since the money does not form part of the estate. As the deceased had no beneficial interest in the policy or its proceeds (because of the trust) no IHT will be payable on the proceeds. Such a policy is particularly advantageous, as the proceeds make tax-free provision for dependants of the deceased and can be collected in immediately following the death.

30.4.3.1 Pension benefits

Death in service benefits under a pension scheme are often payable to persons to be selected at the discretion of the pension fund trustees. Payments are made to the beneficiaries on production of the death certificate. A grant is not required, since the pension benefits do not form part of the deceased's estate. This is another method of making tax-free provision for dependants, and such provision can also be collected in immediately following the death.

30.5 Application for grant

Where a grant is required, it is necessary to apply to the Principal Registry of the Family Division or to a district probate registry. The application is made by lodging such of the following documents as are appropriate to the particular case:

(a)   receipted HM Revenue & Customs (HMRC) Form D18 confirming payment of any IHT or Form IHT 205 if the estate is 'excepted' (see **30.7**);

(b)   Form IHT 216, claiming the transfer of any unused proportion of the nil rate band of a spouse or civil partner who died before the deceased without fully using his or her nil rate band;

(c)   the deceased's will and codicil, if any, marked (ie, signed for identification purposes) by the executors (or administrators if there are no proving executors) and the solicitor before whom the supporting oath is sworn or affirmed;

(d)   the oath, sworn or affirmed by the executors or administrators;*

(e)   any affidavit evidence which may be required (see **30.5.2**);

(f)   probate court fees (an administration fee based on the value of the net estate passing under the grant).

* There is a proposal to replace swearing/affirming with a statement of truth.

30.5.1 Admissibility of will to probate

The solicitor must check the will carefully to make sure that it is valid and admissible to probate. If it is not, application will be made instead for a grant of simple administration.

To ensure that the will is admissible, the solicitor should check the following:

(a)   the will is the last will of the testator;

(b)   that it has not been validly revoked;

(c)   that it is executed in accordance with the Wills Act 1837, s 9; and

(d)   that it contains an attestation clause which indicates that the will was executed in accordance with the requirements of the Wills Act 1837 and raises a presumption of 'due execution'.

30.5.2 The registrar's additional requirements

If the application is in order, the registrar will issue the original grant, sealed with the court seal and signed by him. In some cases, before issuing the grant, the registrar may require further evidence. At present evidence to the probate registry is presented in the form of oaths and affidavits, which are sworn statements. These are due to be replaced by Statements of Truth but at the time of writing there is no date for the change.

30.5.2.1 Affidavit of due execution

If there is no attestation clause, if the clause is in some respect defective, or if there are doubtful circumstances about the execution of the will, the registrar will require affidavit evidence, usually by an attesting witness, to establish that the will has been properly executed. The evidence is provided by means of an affidavit of due execution. If there is doubt about the mental capacity of the testator to make the will, the affidavit of a doctor may be necessary. In such cases, the doctor should have been asked to examine the testator to ascertain whether he had sufficient capacity at the time the will was made.

30.5.2.2   Affidavit as to knowledge and approval

It may appear to the registrar that there is doubt as to whether the testator was aware of the contents of the will when he executed it. This may arise through blindness, illiteracy or frailty of the testator, or because of suspicious circumstances, for example where the person who prepared the will for the testator benefits substantially by its terms.

In any of these circumstances, the attestation clause should be suitably adapted, ideally by indicating that the will was read over to the testator or was independently explained to him. In the absence of this, the registrar will require to be satisfied that the testator had knowledge and approval of the contents of the will. The evidence is provided by means of an affidavit of knowledge and approval of contents made by someone who can speak as to the facts. Normally, this will be one of the attesting witnesses, but it could be an independent person who explained the provisions of the will to the testator.

30.5.2.3   Affidavit of plight and condition

If the state of the will suggests that it has been interfered with in some way since execution, the registrar will require further evidence by way of explanation. This may arise:

(a)   where the will has been altered since its execution;

(b)   where there is some obvious mark on it indicating a document may have been attached to it (eg, the marks of a paper clip, raising a suggestion that some other testamentary document may have been attached); or

(c)   where it gives the appearance of attempted revocation.

Generally, the explanation required will take the form of an affidavit of plight and condition made by some person having knowledge of the facts.

30.5.2.4   Lost will

A will which was known to have been in the testator's possession but which cannot be found following the death is presumed to have been destroyed by the testator with the intention of revoking it.

However, if the will has been lost or accidentally destroyed, probate may be obtained of a copy of the will, such as a copy kept in the solicitor's file, or a reconstruction. In such a case, application should be made to the registrar, supported by appropriate affidavit evidence from the applicant for the grant of probate.

30.6   Completing the IHT account

30.6.1   Purpose of an IHT account

One of the first steps towards obtaining the grant of representation is the preparation of the appropriate IHT account and the calculation of any IHT payable.

If the estate is not an 'excepted estate' (see **30.7**), the PRs will prepare Form IHT 200 and whichever of the supplementary pages are relevant to the estate. For example, if there is a will, the PRs must complete the pages relating to wills.

The IHT 200 is an inventory of the assets to which the deceased was beneficially entitled and of his liabilities, and is the form for claiming reliefs and exemptions and calculating the IHT payable. It should usually be delivered within 12 months of the end of the month in which the death occurred. Usually PRs aim to deliver the account within six months to comply with IHT time-limits for the commencement of interest. Until the account is submitted no grant of representation can be issued.

As from 5 November 2007, it is necessary to apply for a reference number before submitting the IHT 200. Application can be made online or by post using Form D21.

Inheritance tax is payable on all property to which the deceased was beneficially entitled immediately before his death whether or not such property vests in his PRs. Certain types of property qualify for tax relief, for example business or agricultural property, or an exemption may apply because of the identity of the beneficiary (ie the surviving spouse or a charity) (see **4.6.3**).

Where surviving spouses or civil partners die on or after 9 October 2007, they can inherit any unused proportion of the nil rate band of the first spouse or civil partner to die. The PRs of the survivor must make a claim using IHT 216.

Example

Paul died in January 2008 (when the nil rate band was £300,000). He left £100,000 to his sister and everything else to his civil partner, Leo. Paul therefore had two-thirds of his nil rate band unused.

Leo dies in August 2008 leaving everything to his nephews and nieces. Leo's PRs can claim an additional two-thirds of the 2008/09 nil rate band. As a result the nil rate band available on Leo's death will be £312,000 + ($\frac{2}{3}$ x £312,000) = £520,000.

30.6.1.1 Paying the IHT

Inheritance tax on property without the right to pay by instalments (see **4.6.8**) must be paid within six months of the end of the month in which the death occurred. For example, if a person dies on 10 January, IHT is due on 31 July, or on delivery of the IHT 200 if this is earlier. Until this tax has been paid, no grant can issue to the deceased's estate.

Where there is property which qualifies for the right to pay the tax by instalments, none of the tax on that property is due until the expiry of the six-month period. If the option is exercised, only the first instalment of one-tenth must then be paid. In an estate where it is not possible to deliver the IHT 200 within that period, all tax on non-instalment option property plus the appropriate number of instalments on property with the option and interest must be paid on delivery of the account. Interest runs on all tax not paid on the due date.

The tax payable on the estate is apportioned between the instalment and non-instalment option property using the rate as described in **4.3.5**.

30.6.2 Valuations

30.6.2.1 General principles

Assets in the estate are valued at 'the price which the property might reasonably be expected to fetch if sold in the open market' immediately before the death (IHTA 1984, s 160).

30.6.2.2 Jointly owned assets

There is a special valuation rule where the deceased was the co-owner (as tenant in common or as beneficial joint tenant) of land at his death. The market value at the date of death may be discounted to reflect the virtual impossibility of selling a part interest in property. The probate value of the deceased's interest is the discounted market value at the date of death divided proportionately between the co-owners. A discount of 10–15% is normally considered reasonable.

> **Example**
>
> Mary and Nellie owned a house as joint tenants. The value of the house at Mary's death was £100,000. Apply a 10% discount.
>
> The discount is £100,000 × 10% = £10,000
>
> and her half share £100,000 – £10,000 = £90,000 ÷ 2 = £45,000.
>
> The probate value of Mary's share is £45,000.

The discount is not available where the co-ownership is of an asset other than land. For such assets, for example bank and building society accounts, the probate value is the account balance as at the date of death (plus interest) divided proportionately between the joint owners.

Where the co-owners of land are spouses or civil partners, the related property rules (see **4.3.2**) apply. HMRC has always refused to allow any discount in value. This normally means that each spouse or civil partner will be treated as owning a proportionate part of the value of the whole. *Arkwright v IRC* [2004] WLR 181 suggested that if one spouse or civil partner is terminally ill, the value of his or her share might be reduced. However, HMRC has announced that it thinks the decision is wrong.

30.6.3 Funding the IHT

Where there is IHT to pay on delivery of an IHT 200, the PRs must arrange for the appropriate amount of money to be sent to HMRC with the account. When this tax is paid, a receipted Form D18 is sent with the other documents (see **30.5**) to the appropriate Probate Registry so that the grant can issue. Funding the tax bill may be problematic as all the deceased's assets vesting in the PRs are 'frozen', and therefore may be untouchable, until the grant issues giving the proof of title to the PRs.

The options which may be available to raise funds to pay the IHT are set out below.

30.6.3.1 Direct payment scheme

HMRC has reached an agreement with the British Banker's Association and the Building Societies Association on a procedure allowing PRs to arrange payment of IHT to HMRC directly from the deceased's accounts.

The scheme is voluntary on the part of the institutions, so PRs must check whether the relevant banks and building societies are part of the scheme.

The procedure is as follows.

(a) PRs complete a separate D20 for each bank and building society from which money is to be transferred. They send the completed D20 forms to HMRC.

(b) HMRC will allocate a reference number and return the D20s duly noted.

(c) The PRs will send the D20s to the banks and building societies concerned.

(d) The bank or building society will send the money direct to HMRC. Once HMRC has received the money and is satisfied that the amount is correct, it will return the receipted Form D18 to the solicitor.

The process is not quick, so where there is an urgent need for a grant PRs will want to find an alternative source of funding.

Solicitors have for many years had private arrangements with banks and building societies under which the bank or building society provides the solicitor with a cheque made out to HMRC on the deceased's accounts. The solicitor can then send the cheque to HMRC with the other documentation. These arrangements can continue.

30.6.3.2   Life assurance

If there is sufficient cash payable on a policy of insurance on the deceased's life, the life assurance company may be willing to release funds to pay the IHT. If so, the funds will generally be paid directly to HMRC and not to the PRs or their solicitors.

30.6.3.3   Assets realisable without production of the grant

By applying the Administration of Estates (Small Payments) Act 1965 (see **30.4.1**), assets may, in some cases, be realised without production of a grant. The maximum value of any one asset that may be realised is £5,000. The Act gives discretion to the institution to allow assets to be realised in this way. Where an estate is reasonably large or complex, this discretion will often not be exercised. In such cases, a grant must first be obtained and produced to release the asset concerned.

30.6.3.4   Loans from beneficiaries

Wealthy beneficiaries may be prepared to fund the IHT from their own resources, on condition that they will be repaid from the deceased's estate once the grant issues. Alternatively, beneficiaries may already have received assets as a result of the death which they are prepared to use to pay the tax, such as money from a jointly held bank account, or the proceeds of a life policy vested in them under the Married Women's Property Act 1882. However, it is likely that the deceased arranged for such assets to provide financial assistance for that beneficiary while his estate was being administered and the beneficiary may not be able to afford to make a loan.

30.6.3.5   Bank borrowing

Banks which do not participate in the voluntary scheme will still usually lend against an undertaking to repay the loan given by the PRs. A bank may also require an undertaking from the solicitor to repay the loan from the proceeds of the estate. Whether or not the solicitor is a PR, any undertaking should be limited to 'such proceeds as come into the solicitor's control'. Undertakings to pay money should be carefully worded so as to ensure payment is not due from the solicitor personally.

Bank borrowing is expensive, because the bank will charge an arrangement fee and interest on the amount borrowed. Money borrowed should be repaid at the earliest opportunity so as to honour any undertaking and to stop interest running. Income tax relief is available to the PRs for interest paid on a separate loan account in respect of IHT payable on personalty vesting in them.

30.6.3.6   National Savings and Government stock

Payment of tax may also be made from National Savings Bank accounts or from the proceeds of National Savings Certificates, any Government stock held on the National Savings register or any other National Savings investment.

30.7 The requirement for an IHT account

30.7.1 Excepted estates

If the estate is an excepted estate, there is no need for an IHT 200 to be submitted, although HMRC can demand one within 35 days of the date of issue of the grant of representation. If an estate which initially appears to be excepted is subsequently found not to be so, the PRs must submit the IHT 200 within six months of the discovery.

The precise requirements for qualifying as an excepted estate change each year. For deaths on or after 1 September 2006 there are three categories of excepted estate and the requirements are as follows.

- *Category 1 – 'small' estates*

    Broadly, estates falling into this category are those where the gross value of the estate for IHT purposes, plus the chargeable value of any 'specified transfers' in the seven years prior to death, does not exceed the current IHT threshold. Where a surviving spouse or civil partner inherits a proportion of the nil rate band of the predeceased spouse or civil partner, the additional nil rate band is ignored for this purpose. The estate is excepted only if it falls within the deceased's own nil rate band.

    (For applications between 6 April and 1 August each year the threshold will be the threshold for the previous tax year.)

    In full, the new Regulations for this category provide as follows:

    (a) the deceased died, domiciled in the United Kingdom;

    (b) the value of the estate is attributable wholly to property passing:

    　(i) under his will or intestacy,

    　(ii) under a nomination of an asset taking effect on death,

    　(iii) under a single settlement in which he was entitled to an interest in possession in settled property, or

    　(iv) by survivorship in a beneficial joint tenancy or, in Scotland, by survivorship in a special destination;

    (c) of that property:

    　(i) not more than £150,000 represented value attributable to property which, immediately before that person's death, was settled property; and

    　(ii) not more than £100,000 represented value attributable to property which, immediately before that person's death, was situated outside the United Kingdom;

    (d) the deceased had not made any chargeable transfers in the seven years before death other than specified transfers where the aggregate value transferred (ignoring business or agricultural relief) did not exceed £150,000; and

    (e) the aggregate of:

    　(i) the gross value of the deceased's estate,

    　(ii) the value transferred by any specified transfers, and

    　(iii) the value transferred by any specified exempt transfers, did not exceed the IHT threshold. Only the deceased's own nil rate band is relevant for this purpose. Any nil rate band transferred from a deceased spouse or civil partner is ignored.

- *Category 2 – 'exempt' estates*

  These estates are excepted because the bulk of the estate attracts the spouse (or civil partner) or charity exemption. The gross value of the estate plus certain lifetime transfers must not exceed £1 million and the net chargeable estate after deduction of spouse and/or charity exemption must not exceed the IHT threshold. As with category 1 estates, only the deceased's own nil rate band is relevant for this purpose. Any inherited nil rate band is ignored.

  In full, the Regulations for this category provide as follows:

  (a) the deceased, domiciled in the United Kingdom;

  (b) the value of the estate is attributable wholly to property passing:

     (i)   under his will or intestacy,

     (ii)   under a nomination of an asset taking effect on death,

     (iii) under a single settlement in which he was entitled to an interest in possession in settled property, or

     (iv)   by survivorship in a beneficial joint tenancy or, in Scotland, by survivorship in a special destination;

  (c) of that property:

     (i)   not more than £150,000 represented value attributable to property which, immediately before that person's death, was settled property (settled property passing on death to a spouse or charity is ignored for this purpose); and

     (ii)   not more than £100,000 represented value attributable to property which, immediately before that person's death, was situated outside the United Kingdom;

  (d) that person died without having made any chargeable transfers during the period of seven years ending with his death other than specified transfers where (ignoring business or agricultural relief) the aggregate value transferred did not exceed £150,000;

  (e) the aggregate of:

     (i)   the gross value of that person's estate,

     (ii)   the value transferred by any specified transfers made by that person, and

     (iii) the value transferred by any specified exempt transfers made by that person,

     did not exceed £1,000,000; and

  (f) the net value of the deceased's estate and the specified transfers and specified exempt transfers after deduction of debts did not exceed the IHT threshold.

- *Category 3 – 'non-domiciled' estates*

  The third category is where the deceased was never domiciled or treated as domiciled in the United Kingdom, with only limited assets in the United Kingdom.

  In full, the new Regulations for this category provide as follows:

  (a) he was never domiciled in the United Kingdom or treated as domiciled in the United Kingdom by s 267 of the IHTA 1984; and

  (b) the value of the estate situated in the United Kingdom is wholly attributable to cash or quoted shares or securities passing under his will or intestacy or by survivorship in a beneficial joint tenancy or, in Scotland, by survivorship in a special destination, the gross value of which does not exceed £150,000.

For the purposes of the Regulations, a transfer is not a spouse (or civil partner) transfer if either spouse (or civil partner) was not domiciled in the United Kingdom at any time prior to the transfer. A transfer to a charity includes a transfer for national purposes within s 25(1) of the IHTA 1984. However, to qualify as a charity transfer, the transfer must be an outright gift; it is not sufficient if the transfer is to a settlement for the benefit of the charity.

Note that an estate cannot be excepted if one of the alternatively secured pension provisions applies to it. However, alternatively secured pensions are beyond the scope of this book and are not considered further.

30.7.1.1 Procedure

In England and Wales and Northern Ireland all applications for probate in relation to excepted estates must be accompanied by Form IHT 205 (or Form IHT 207 for those domiciled abroad).

The IHT 205 is a short form based on the document completed by applicants in person. The Probate Service will forward the forms to HMRC on a weekly basis.

HMRC will select a random sample to review. In addition, it 'will use other information sources to identify those estates nearer to the IHT threshold' where it feels that there is a risk that IHT may be payable.

Example 1

Adam has just died. His will leaves his estate to his wife Brenda and daughter Clare in equal shares. He is UK-domiciled and has made no lifetime transfers.

His estate consists of:	£
House owned jointly with Brenda (half share)	80,000
Building society a/c (sole name)	100,000
Personal chattels	2,000
Life interest in a trust fund set up in his father's will (value of capital assets)	30,000
Debts (funeral bill and credit cards)	(2,000)

Adam's estate satisfies the criteria and it has an IHT value of £212,000 gross (note that IHT exemptions and reliefs are ignored when ascertaining the gross IHT estate).

This is a category 1 ('small') excepted estate. This fact will also be noted on the oath.

Example 2

Davina has just died. Her will leaves £50,000 to her son, Ernst, and the residue to her husband, Ferdinand. She is UK domiciled. Her only lifetime transfer was made two years ago when she gave £100,000 to Ernst.

Her estate consists of:	£
House owned jointly with Fernando (half share)	400,000
Quoted Investments	100,000
Bank and building society accounts	50,000
Personal chattels	15,000
Debts (funeral bill and credit cards)	(5,000)

This is a category 2 ('exempt') excepted estate. The aggregate of the gross value of the estate, plus the chargeable value of permitted transfers in the seven years prior to death does not exceed £1 million; the net chargeable estate after deduction of liabilities and the spouse exemption does not exceed £312,000.

30.7.2 Form IHT 200

Form IHT 200 must be used whenever the deceased dies domiciled in the UK and his estate is not an 'excepted' estate.

The PRs must complete Form IHT 200 and relevant accompanying pages and sign a declaration that the contents are true. They must calculate the amount of any IHT payable and ensure that any IHT due on delivery of the account is paid. HMRC will receipt the accompanying Form D18.

When the PRs apply to the Probate Registry they must file the receipted Form D18 with the probate papers as proof that the relevant IHT has been paid.

30.8 Oaths: the background law

30.8.1 Types and purpose of oaths

Every application for a grant of representation must be supported by the appropriate form of oath. The three most common types of oath are as follows:

(a)   oath for executors;

(b)   oath for administrators with will annexed;

(c)   oath for administrators.

The oaths differ from each other in detail but they have a common purpose, namely:

(a)   to give details of the deceased;

(b)   to set out the basis of the applicant's claim to take the grant;

(c)   to require the applicant to swear that he will administer the estate correctly;

(d)   in the case of oaths for executors and oaths for administrators with the will annexed, to identify and exhibit the will and any codicils;

(e)   to swear to the value of the estate passing under the grant.

Unless the appropriate oath is accurately completed and submitted to the Probate Registry by, or on behalf of, those PRs who may properly make an application, no grant of representation will be issued.

30.8.2 Swearing or affirming the oath

Before the oath is submitted to the Probate Registry, the PRs must swear or affirm the truth of its contents. This must be done before a commissioner for oaths or a solicitor holding a current practising certificate, neither of whom is connected with the firm of solicitors acting for the PRs. The PRs may prefer to affirm, in which case they say 'I do solemnly sincerely and truly declare and affirm that ...'. A PR who swears the oath will be required to hold the New Testament or Bible whilst saying 'I swear by Almighty God that ...'.

Once the oath has been sworn or affirmed it should be sent to the Probate Registry with any will, the IHT account and the appropriate probate court fees.

There are proposals to remove the requirement to swear or affirm and to substitute a statement of truth.

30.8.3 The value of the estate passing under the grant

The oath must include the gross value of the property passing under the grant and the net value (ie after deduction of debts of the estate). The figures given will be repeated on the grant of representation issued by the Probate Registry.

The Probate Registry is not concerned with property passing otherwise than under the grant, so the value of joint property passing by survivorship or property passing under a trust is not included. The full value of property passing under the grant must be included. IHT exemptions and reliefs are irrelevant for this purpose.

If the estate is a category 1 ('small') excepted estate, the PRs must swear that it is not necessary to deliver an IHT account. They do not need to give the exact value of the property passing under the grant.

In relation to the gross value, they need only state that it does not exceed the nil rate band threshold.

In relation to the net value, they must round it up to the nearest whole thousand and state on the oath that it does not exceed that figure. This assists government departments such as the DWP that may need to check the deceased's eligibility for benefits received and charities that may want an indication of their likely entitlement where they are residuary beneficiaries.

If the estate is a category 2 ('exempt') excepted estate, the PRs again swear that it is not necessary to deliver an IHT account, but this time they must give the exact figures for the gross and net property passing under the grant.

30.9 Oath for executors

30.9.1 Entitlement to act

The oath for executors will lead to a grant of probate where they have been appointed by a valid will. One executor may obtain a grant and act alone.

Example 1

Alex by his will appoints Brian and Colin to be his executors and leaves his entire estate to a named charity.

Brian and/or Colin can apply for a grant of probate by lodging an oath for executors, and the will, with the Probate Registry.

The appointment of executors is not affected by the fact that the will may fail to dispose of some or all of the deceased's estate.

Example 2

Diana has just died. Her will appoints Eric as her executor and leaves her entire estate to Freda. Freda died before Diana whose estate will therefore be distributed according to the intestacy rules. Eric is alive and prepared to act as executor. Eric will apply for a grant of probate by swearing an oath for executors.

30.9.2 Capacity to act

Capacity to act as executor is judged at the time of the application for the grant.

30.9.2.1 Executor lacking capacity to act

A person appointed as an executor by the will but who, at the testator's death, does not have the mental capacity to act, may not apply for the grant.

30.9.2.2 Minors

There is no prohibition on a testator naming a minor as his executor. However, if the executor is still a minor at the testator's death he cannot act as an executor nor obtain a grant of probate until he attains majority.

Where one of several executors is a minor, the other(s) being adults, probate can be granted to the adult executor(s) with power reserved to the minor (for an explanation of 'power reserved', see **30.9.4**). If the administration of the estate has not been completed by the time the minor attains 18 years, he can then apply for a grant of double probate to enable him to act as executor alongside the other proving executor(s).

Example

George dies appointing his wife, Ingrid and his son Harry (aged 16) as his executors.

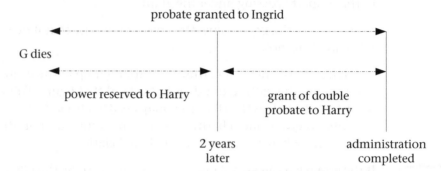

Where the minor is the only executor appointed by the will (or the adult executors are not able or willing to act), someone must take the grant on behalf of the minors as it would be impracticable to leave the testator's estate unadministered until the executor reaches 18 years. A grant of letters of administration with will annexed for the use and benefit of the minor will be made, usually to the parent(s) or guardian(s) of the minor, until the minor attains 18 years. On obtaining majority the executor may apply for a cessate grant of probate.

30.9.2.3   The former spouse or civil partner

If the testator appointed his spouse or civil partner as his executor and the marriage or civil partnership subsequently ends, that appointment will fail unless the testator has shown a contrary intention in the will (Wills Act 1837, s 18A: see **29.2.4**).

If the spouse or civil partner was one of several executors, the others may apply for the grant of probate without him or her. If she was the sole executrix, application should be made for a grant of letters of administration with will annexed. In either case, the oath to lead to the appropriate grant should cite the fact and date of the divorce.

30.9.3   Renunciation

Persons appointed as executors may renounce their right to take the grant, provided that they have not intermeddled in the estate. Intermeddling consists of doing tasks a PR might do, for example notifying the deceased's bank of the death. By intermeddling, executors accept their appointment. Once executors have intermeddled, they must take the grant.

Provided there has been no intermeddling, executors who do not wish to act can renounce their rights. Rights as executor then cease and the administration of the estate proceeds as if the executor had never been appointed.

The renunciation must be made in writing, signed by the person renouncing (the signature must be witnessed), and the renunciation must be filed at the Probate Registry. This is normally done by the PRs who are applying for a grant when they lodge their application at the Probate Registry.

30.9.4   Power reserved

There is no limit on how many executors can be appointed by the will, but probate will be granted to a maximum of four executors. Power may be reserved to the other(s) to take out a grant in the future if a vacancy arises.

Example 1

Alan's will appoints B, C, D, E and F to be his executors. All are willing and able to act. Probate is granted to C, D, E and F. 'Power is reserved' to B. If F dies before the administration is complete, B can then apply for a grant. B must apply; there is no automatic substitution.

If there is a dispute between the executors as to which of them should apply for a grant, this may be resolved by summons before a registrar (NCPR 1987, r 27(6)).

There is no need for every executor to act. A person appointed as one of several executors may not wish to act initially, but he may not want to take the irrevocable step of renouncing his right to a grant of probate.

Example 2

Alan appoints Ben and Charles as his executors. When Alan dies, Ben is working in Germany but is due to return to England in 12 months' time. Ben does not feel that he should act as executor whilst abroad and is happy to leave everything to Charles, but he does want to help in the administration if it has not been completed by the time he returns to England.

Charles should apply for the grant 'with power reserved' to Ben to prove at a later stage.

One executor is always sufficient. As we will see later, this is not the case for administrators.

30.10 Oath for administrators with will annexed

30.10.1 Entitlement to act

As the title of this oath suggests, it is used in an estate where there is a valid will but no executor willing and able to apply for a grant of probate.

There may be no executor because:

(a)   the will fails to appoint executors; or

(b)   the appointment was of the testator's spouse or civil partner and has failed as a result of the testator's divorce (Wills Act 1837, s 18A; see **29.2.4**);

(c)   the executor has predeceased the testator;

(d)   the executor has died after the testator but before taking the grant; or

(e)   the executor has renounced.

If there is a valid will but no executor and the will does not dispose of all the estate, the appropriate grant is still letters of administration with will annexed. The property undisposed of by the will is distributed according to the intestacy rules (see **29.4**).

30.10.2 NCPR 1987, r 20

The order of priority of the person(s) entitled to a grant of letters of administration with will annexed is governed by NCPR 1987, r 20. The rule states as follows:

Where the deceased died on or after 1 January 1926 the person or persons entitled to a grant in respect of a will shall be determined in accordance with the following order of priority, namely—

(a)   the executor...;

(b)   any residuary legatee or devisee holding in trust for any other person;

(c)   any other residuary legatee or devisee (including one for life) or where the residue is not wholly disposed of by the will, any person entitled to share in the undisposed of residue (including the Treasury Solicitor when claiming bona vacantia on behalf of the Crown), provided that—

(i)   unless a registrar otherwise directs, a residuary legatee or devisee whose legacy or devise is vested in interest shall be preferred to one entitled on the happening of a contingency, and

(ii)   where the residue is not in terms wholly disposed of, the registrar may, if he is satisfied that the testator has nevertheless disposed of the whole or substantially the whole of the known estate, allow a grant to be made to any legatee or devisee entitled to, or to share in, the estate so disposed of, without regard to the persons entitled to share in any residue not disposed of by the will;

(d)   the personal representative of any residuary legatee or devisee (but not one for life, or one holding in trust for any other person), or of any person entitled to share in any residue not disposed of by the will;

(e)   any other legatee or devisee (including one for life or one holding in trust for any other person) or any creditor of the deceased, provided that, unless a registrar otherwise directs, a legatee or devisee whose legacy or devise is vested in interest shall be preferred to one entitled on the happening of a contingency;

(f)   the personal representative of any other legatee or devisee (but not one for life or one holding in trust for any other person) or of any creditor of the deceased.

30.10.2.1   Clearing off

Each applicant is listed in priority in r 20. When applying for the grant, any person falling in categories (b) and below must explain on the oath why there is no applicant from a higher-ranked category. This is called 'clearing off'. A person in a lower-ranked category may apply only if there is nobody in a higher category willing and able to take the grant. The applicant must explain the basis of his own claim to the grant.

The categories will now be considered in detail with examples of clearing off.

'(a) the executor...'

NCPR 1987, r 20 in fact provides the 'order of priority for grant where deceased left a will'. This covers both grants of probate and letters of administration with the will annexed. An executor who has been appointed in the will and is able and willing to act has first right to a grant.

The remaining categories assume that, for whatever reason, no executor is available.

'(b) any residuary legatee or devisee holding in trust ...'

Example

Arthur has died leaving a will. Although he failed to appoint executors, he left his residue to Brian and Claire on trust for Debbie. Brian and Claire are the residuary legatees (or devisees, depending on the type of trust property) holding on trust and so they have first right to a grant. Clearly, Arthur was happy for them to deal with his property otherwise he would not have appointed them as trustees. They will have to state that 'no executor was appointed in the will and we are the residuary legatees holding on trust named in the will'.

'(c) any other residuary legatee or devisee ...'

Example 1

Amanda has died leaving a will appointing Boris as her executor and giving the residuary estate to Carol, ie Carol is the residuary legatee and devisee.

Carol can apply for a grant only if Boris is unable or unwilling to act. She must 'clear off' Boris by saying, 'the executor named in the will has [renounced probate] or [predeceased the deceased] and I am the residuary legatee and devisee named in the will' or as the case may be.

Note: strictly it is also necessary to clear off trustees of residue by stating that there is 'no residuary legatee or devisee holding on trust for any other person'. However, as the lack of appointment is apparent from the face of the will, this is often not done. Such practice is acceptable to the probate registrars.

Example 2

The facts are the same as in Example 1, but Boris was appointed 'executor and trustee' and the residue was given to Carol for life.

Carol must clear off Boris in both capacities by saying, 'the executor and trustee named in the will has [renounced probate] etc ...'.

'... or ... any person entitled to share in the undisposed of residue'

If a partial intestacy arises because the will fails to dispose of all or part of the residuary estate, those people entitled to the residue by virtue of the intestacy rules (see **29.4**) may apply for a grant under NCPR 1987, r 20, but they must show why they are entitled to the grant by clearing off all persons in higher-ranked categories.

Example

Damien's will appoints Errol to be his sole executor and residuary beneficiary. Errol died last month and Damien has just died. Damien's closest living relative is his mother, Florence.

As the sole residuary beneficiary has predeceased the deceased (and the gift is not saved by any substitutional gift), the residue is undisposed of and will be distributed according to the intestacy rules. Damien has left no spouse or civil partner and no issue but is survived by his mother, Florence, who is next entitled to the property.

Florence will apply for a grant of letters of administration with will annexed by clearing off the executor. She must also establish her entitlement to the undisposed of property and, therefore, to the grant. She will say 'the executor and residuary legatee and devisee has predeceased the deceased [and the deceased died a bachelor without issue] and I am the mother of the deceased'.

'(d) the personal representative of a deceased residuary legatee or devisee ...'

Where there is no proving executor and, for example, the residuary beneficiary survives the testator to take a vested interest in the estate but then dies without having taken the grant, that beneficiary's PR may apply for the grant. This is because the gift under the will forms part of the beneficiary's estate and needs to be collected by his PR.

Example

Gloria died last week leaving a will appointing Honor as executrix and giving the residuary estate to Ian absolutely. Honor has predeceased Gloria and Ian died yesterday. Ian's will appoints Janice as his sole executrix and beneficiary.

Janice may apply for a grant of letters of administration with will annexed to Gloria's estate. To do so the oath must clear off Honor and Ian by saying, 'the sole executrix predeceased the deceased and the sole residuary legatee and devisee named in the said will survived the deceased and has since died without having proved the said will and I am the executrix of the deceased residuary legatee and devisee'.

'(e) any other legatee or devisee ... or any creditor of the deceased ...'

This category covers any other beneficiary under the will, for example, a specific devisee who has been left the deceased's house, or a pecuniary legatee who has been left £5,000 by the deceased. It also covers creditors of the deceased.

'(f) the personal representative of any other legatee or devisee ... or of any creditor ...'

This category works on the same principles as category (d) above.

30.10.2.2   Beneficiary with vested interest preferred

Where there is more than one person of equal rank but one has a vested and one a contingent interest in the estate, the court generally prefers an application by the beneficiary with the vested interest.

Example

Keri's will leaves her residuary estate to her two children, Lisa and Matthew, contingent on their attaining 25 years of age. There is no executor appointed in the will and at Keri's death Lisa is 30 years old and Matthew 23 years old.

Lisa and Matthew can make a joint application, but if they were to apply separately the court would prefer Lisa because Matthew's interest is still contingent.

30.10.3   Minors

A minor cannot act as administrator with will annexed, nor can he apply for a grant. His parent(s) or guardian(s) may apply for a grant 'for his use and benefit' on his behalf. The grant is limited until he attains the age of 18.

If there is a person not under a disability who is entitled in the same degree as the minor then that person will be preferred to the guardian of the minor (NCPR 1987, r 27(5)).

30.10.4   The number of administrators

30.10.4.1   Maximum number

If there are several people entitled to act as administrators, the grant will not issue to more than four of them (Supreme Court Act 1981, s 114). It is not possible for an administrator to have power reserved to him.

If a person is entitled to act as administrator but does not obtain a grant (eg, because there are four other applicants), this does not affect that person's beneficial entitlement to the estate.

30.10.4.2   Number in the same category

Subject to the provisions of s 114 of the Supreme Court Act 1981 (see **30.14.1** below), where two or more people are entitled in the same degree, a grant can be made on the application of any one of them without notice to the other or others (NCPR 1987, r 27(4)).

Example

Jane dies leaving her residuary estate by will to her two adult brothers, Ken and Larry. Jane's will does not appoint an executor. Larry does not wish to act.

Ken can apply for a grant alone. This does not affect Larry's beneficial entitlement to half the estate.

30.10.4.3   Need for two administrators

Where there is a life interest, or property passes to a minor (whether the interest is vested or contingent), the court normally requires a minimum of two administrators to apply for the grant (Supreme Court Act 1981, s 114). The court may dispense with this and allow a single administrator in special limited circumstances.

Example 1

Max has just died leaving a valid will which:

(a)   appoints Nora his executor;

(b)   gives £1,000 to Olive (aged 6);

(c)   gives the residue of his estate to Peter and Paul.

Nora renounces probate.

Both Peter and Paul must apply for the grant because there is a minority interest, ie the legacy to Olive.

Example 2

Quentin's will fails to appoint an executor. He leaves his estate to his wife Rose for life, remainder to his adult son, Sam.

Both Rose and Sam must apply for the grant because of Rose's life interest.

Example 3

Tim's will leaves his residuary estate to his friend Una, whom he has also appointed executrix. Una has predeceased Tim. Tim is divorced and has three children, Victor (21), Wendy (19), and Zena (15).

Tim therefore dies partially intestate. By virtue of the intestacy rules his children take the residuary estate on the statutory trusts.

Victor and Wendy must both apply for the grant because part of the estate goes to Zena who is a minor.

30.10.5 Renunciation

Any person entitled to apply for a grant of letters of administration with will annexed can renounce in the same way as an executor, except that an administrator does not lose the right to renounce by intermeddling. Renunciation does not affect any beneficial entitlement of the administrator.

30.11 Oath for administrators

30.11.1 Entitlement to act

This oath is required if the deceased has died totally intestate.

The person or persons entitled to the grant are listed in NCPR 1987, r 22 as set out below. The order is the same as the order or entitlement on intestacy.

(1)   Where the deceased died on or after 1 January 1926, wholly intestate, the person or persons having a beneficial interest in the estate shall be entitled to a grant of administration in the following classes in order of priority, namely—

(a)   the surviving spouse or civil partner;

(b)   the children of the deceased and the issue of any deceased child who died before the deceased;

(c)   the father and mother of the deceased;

(d)   brothers and sisters of the whole blood and the issue of any deceased brother or sister of the whole blood who died before the deceased;

(e)   brothers and sisters of the half blood and the issue of any deceased brother or sister of the half blood who died before the deceased;

(f)   grandparents;

(g)   uncles and aunts of the whole blood and the issue of any deceased uncle or aunt of the whole blood who died before the deceased;

(h)   uncles and aunts of the half blood and the issue of any deceased uncle or aunt of the half blood who died before the deceased.

(2)   In default of any person having a beneficial interest in the estate, the Treasury Solicitor shall be entitled to a grant if he claims bona vacantia on behalf of the Crown.

(3)   If all persons entitled to a grant under the foregoing provisions of this rule have been cleared off, a grant may be made to a creditor of the deceased or to any person who, notwithstanding that he has no immediate beneficial interest in the estate, may have a beneficial interest in the event of an accretion thereto.

Some of the descriptions of relations require further explanation, as follows.

30.11.1.1   'Children'

On an intestacy, no distinction is drawn between those who have been born legitimate or have been adopted, or those whose parents were not married (subject to the qualification in the Family Law Reform Act 1987, s 18(2) – see **29.4.5.2**).

Equally entitled with the deceased's children are the children or grandchildren of any child who predeceased the deceased.

30.11.1.2   'Brothers and sisters'

Brothers and sisters of the deceased are also known as 'siblings'. A sibling is of the 'whole blood' where they share both parents in common with the deceased, and of the 'half blood' where they have only one common parent.

Example

Susan has been married twice. By Tom she had two children, Una and Victoria, and by Tony she had a daughter, Wendy.

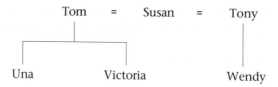

Una and Victoria are sisters of the whole blood.

Wendy is their sister of the half blood.

30.11.1.3   'Uncles and aunts'

Uncles and aunts of 'the whole blood' are the children of both grandparents of the intestate. Aunts and uncles of the 'half blood' are the children of only one of the deceased's grandparents.

Example

David has died recently and his closest living relations are his uncles, Ben and Charles. David's mother, Ann, and his uncle, Ben, were children of the same parents; Charles was the son of David's grandfather, Fred, and Fred's mistress, Joan.

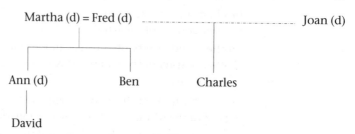

Ben is David's uncle of the whole blood.

Charles is David's uncle of the half blood.

30.11.2 Clearing off

Each category is listed in priority in NCPR 1987, r 22. Like the applicant under NCPR 1987, r 20 (see **30.10.2**), an applicant under r 22 must explain on the oath why nobody in a higher category is able to apply for the grant (again, this is called 'clearing off') and describe his own relationship to the deceased.

Where there is a surviving spouse and he or she is applying for the grant either alone or with others, there is nobody with a higher priority to clear off and therefore there is no need to add any clearing off words to the oath.

Where there is no surviving spouse, this fact must be stated by saying that the deceased died intestate, 'a bachelor', or 'a spinster', or 'a widower', or 'a widow', as the case may be.

Where the applicant needs to clear off categories of relation in addition to the spouse, he will do so by stating that the deceased died intestate 'without issue' or 'parents' or 'brothers and sisters of the whole blood' or 'their issue' etc.

Example 1

Alice has died intestate survived by her son. Her husband died five years ago.

The oath will read:

died INTESTATE a widow.

Example 2

Brian who never married has just died intestate aged 92 years. He is survived by his two brothers.

The oath will read:

died INTESTATE a bachelor without issue or parents.

Later in the oath the applicant will explain his own relationship to the deceased

30.11.3 The need for a beneficial interest in the estate

Unless the applicant is the Treasury Solicitor or a creditor, he must have a beneficial interest in the estate (or would have such an in interest if there was an accretion to the estate) by virtue of the intestacy rules; hence there is a similarity of entitlement under NCPR 1987, r 22 and under AEA 1925, s 46 (see **29.4**).

Example 1

Clara dies intestate survived by her mother and one brother.

Only the mother can apply for the grant because she is solely and absolutely entitled to Clara's estate under the intestacy rules.

Example 2

David dies intestate survived by his wife Eve and father Fred. David's estate is valued at £300,000.

As Eve and Fred share the estate by virtue of the intestacy rules, Fred can apply for the grant if Eve does not, although Eve ranks in priority and must be cleared off if Fred applies for the grant.

Example 3

The facts are the same as in Example 2 but David's estate is £90,000. Prima facie, Fred would seem to have no interest and would therefore be unable to apply for a grant if Eve failed to do so. But Fred can apply in these circumstances on the basis that if additional assets were found in David's estate Fred would then share the estate with Eve. It is irrelevant that David's estate never actually increases above £90,000. Again, Eve ranks in priority.

30.11.4 Minors

A minor cannot act as administrator, nor can he apply for a grant. The same rule as that discussed at **30.10.3** above should be applied.

30.11.5 Renunciation

A person entitled to a grant under NCPR 1987, r 22 can renounce his right to the grant in the same way as an administrator with the will annexed. If he is the only relative of the deceased with a beneficial entitlement, the grant will be made to a creditor of the deceased. Renunciation does not affect any beneficial entitlement of the administrator.

Example

Graeme dies intestate survived by one brother, Henry, and an uncle, Jack. Graeme owes Kirsty £100.

Henry has priority over Jack under r 22. As Jack has no beneficial interest in the estate, under the intestacy rules he cannot apply for the grant if Henry fails to do so. In that event Kirsty should apply for the grant of letters of administration.

It is common for a creditor to take the grant if the estate is insolvent.

30.11.6 The number of administrators

The rules applying to the number of administrators with will annexed apply equally to administrators of a totally intestate estate.

30.11.6.1 Maximum number

The grant will issue to a maximum of four administrators. If there are more than four people with an equal entitlement, it is not possible to have 'power reserved' to a non-proving administrator.

30.11.6.2 Number in the same category

Where two or more people are entitled in the same degree, a grant can be made on the application of any one of them without notice to the other(s).

30.11.6.3 Need for two administrators

A minimum of two administrators is generally required where the intestacy creates a life interest in favour of the surviving spouse and/or minority interests through property being held for minors on the 'statutory trusts'. The court may dispense with the need for two administrators in special circumstances.

Example 1

Grace dies intestate with an estate with a net value for probate purposes of £250,000. She is survived by her husband, Henry, and her adult daughter, Ingrid.

The grant must be taken by Henry and Ingrid because the intestacy rules give Henry a life interest in part of the estate.

Example 2

John dies intestate with a net estate for probate purposes of £300,000 and is survived by his wife, Karen and children, Laura (20) and Mike (16).

Karen and Laura must take the grant. Two administrators are needed because the intestacy creates a life interest and a minority interest. Mike cannot be an administrator because he is a minor.

Example 3

Nigel dies intestate, a bachelor without issue. Both his parents are dead.

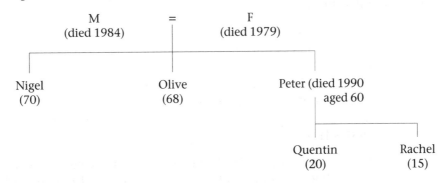

His sister and the issue of his deceased brother are equally entitled to apply for the grant as they share the estate under the intestacy rules. Both Olive and Quentin must apply because Rachel is a minor.

30.12 Effect of grant

30.12.1 Grant of probate

A grant of probate confirms the authority of the executor(s) which stems from the will and arises from the time of the testate's death (see **30.2**).

The grant provides conclusive evidence of the title of the executor(s) and of the validity and contents of the will.

30.12.2 Grant of administration (with or without will)

A grant of administration (with or without will annexed) confers authority on the administrator and vests the deceased's property in the administrator. Until the grant is issued, the administrator has no authority to act and the deceased's property is vested in the President of the Family Division.

The grant provides conclusive evidence of the administrator's title and of the validity and contents of any will (or intestacy). Normally, the grant is not retrospective to the date of the deceased's death.

30.13 Limited grants

A grant of representation is normally general, ie it is expressed to relate to 'all the estate which by law devolves to and vests in the personal representatives of the deceased'.

When necessary, a grant may be limited; for example, it may be:

(a) limited as to a specified part of the deceased's property. For example, a novelist might appoint literary executors to administer his literary estate; general executors would be responsible for his general estate;

(b) limited to settled land. Any settled land vested in the deceased is usually excepted from a general grant if the land remains settled after his death. The trustees of the settlement will submit an oath limited to the settled land;

(c) limited to a special purpose. For example, if the person entitled to apply for a grant is a minor then application should be made by his parent(s) or guardian(s) for a grant for his use and benefits. The practice in making such grants is governed by NCPR 1987, r 2.

30.14 The chain of representation and grant de bonis non administratis

30.14.1 Introduction

If there are several proving PRs administering an estate and one dies after taking the grant but before the administration has been completed, the surviving PRs continue to act. The continuing PRs' powers remain unaffected. Where the death leaves a sole surviving PR, the court may exercise its powers to appoint an additional PR. This might happen, for example, where there is a life or minority interest and the court wishes there to continue to be two PRs (Supreme Court Act 1981, s 114).

If a person entitled to be the PR (either as the executor under a will, or by virtue of NCPR 1987, r 20 or r 22) survives the deceased but then dies himself without taking out a grant of representation, AEA 1925, s 5 provides that his rights concerning the grant die with him (unless it is an exceptional case where his PR may apply for a grant under NCPR 1987, r 20).

Example 1

David dies, appointing Elizabeth as his executrix and leaving his estate to Richard. Elizabeth dies a few days after David and without having proved his will. Richard should apply for a grant of letters of administration with will annexed to David's estate.

The position is more complicated on the death of a sole or sole surviving PR if the administration is incomplete.

Example 2

Anthony died six months ago, appointing Edward as his sole executor.

Edward obtained a grant of probate to Anthony's estate and had begun to deal with the assets when he died. The house is on the market but unsold and the final IHT assessment cannot be agreed because tax is being paid on the house by instalments. The administration is therefore incomplete. What happens?

30.14.2 Chain of representation

The office of executor is personal to the executor appointed by the testator in his will. Because it is an office of personal trust an executor cannot assign that office (although he can appoint an attorney). However, AEA 1925, s 7 provides that in one case the office of executor will pass automatically to someone else. This is called the 'chain of representation'. This happens only where an executor who has taken out a grant of probate dies without completing the administration and appoints someone as his own executor. If that person takes out a grant of probate he will automatically become the executor of both estates.

30.14.2.1 Unbroken chain

The chain of representation is applicable only where there is an unbroken sequence of proving executors.

Example

Colin died, leaving a will appointing Diane as his executrix.

Diane proved the will and obtained a grant of probate.

Diane died before she had completed the administration of Colin's estate.

Diane's will appointed Eric to be her executor. If Eric applies for probate of Diane's will, he automatically becomes executor of Colin's estate.

It is not possible to accept the office of executor to Diane's estate and refuse to be executor by representation of Colin's estate.

30.14.2.2   AEA 1925, s 7

Section 7 provides that an executor by representation:

(a)   has the same rights in respect of the testator's estate as if he was the original executor; and

(b)   is, to the extent to which the testator's estate has come into his hands, answerable as if he was the original executor.

30.14.2.3   Broken chain

If for any reason there are no successive executors, the chain of representation will be broken.

Example 1

Fiona appointed Graham to be her executor. Graham obtained probate to Fiona's estate. Graham then died intestate. Graham's PR under NCPR 1987, r 22 is Ian, who obtains a grant of letters of administration to Graham's estate. Ian will not become the executor of Fiona's estate.

Example 2

John died intestate and Kelly obtained a grant of letters of administration to his estate. Kelly died leaving a will appointing Louise to be her executrix. Louise proved Kelly's will and obtained probate. Louise does not become the executrix of John's estate.

30.14.3   Grant de bonis non administratis

In situations where the chain of representation does not apply because there are no successive proving executors, a grant de bonis non administratis must be obtained to the original estate (usually known as a 'grant de bonis non'). The grant de bonis non may be one of administration with the will or one of simple administration, depending on the circumstances.

It is issued in estates where the sole, or sole surviving, PR has died after obtaining the grant but without having completed the administration, and it relates only to the unadministered part of the estate. Two requirements apply:

(a)   there must have been a prior grant of probate or letters of administration to a PR who has now died; and

(b)   the chain of representation must not apply.

The grant de bonis non will issue to the person who would have been entitled had the original PR never taken the grant. The order of priority will depend on NCPR 1987, r 20 or r 22, as appropriate.

30.15   Caveats and citations

Caveats and citations are available under the NCPR 1987 to assist in the event of a dispute over the right to take out a grant of representation to an estate. They are designed to resolve disputes without the expense and delay of contentious proceedings.

30.15.1   Caveats (NCPR 1987, r 44)

The effect of a caveat is to prevent the issue of a grant of representation. The person lodging or entering a caveat is called a 'caveator'. A caveat might be used, for example, where a beneficiary believes the executor named in the will lacks the mental capacity to act, or where the validity of the will is questioned.

Example 1

The will appoints Eric as executor, gives a legacy to Ann and the residue to Ben.

Eric wants to act as executor but Ann challenges his capability. Ann should enter a caveat before a grant of representation is issued so that the court can decide who should act as PR.

Example 2

On Dan's death a homemade will is found appointing Edward as executor and sole beneficiary. Freda would be entitled to Dan's estate under the intestacy rules and Freda believes the will is invalid. She should enter a caveat to prevent any grant of representation issuing until the court has decided the validity or otherwise of the will.

30.15.2   Citations (NCPR 1987, r 46)

Only executors or persons specified under NCPR 1987, r 20 or r 22 can take a grant of representation. If the person initially entitled to take the grant refuses to do so and also refuses to renounce, the estate would remain unadministered and the beneficiaries would be left waiting indefinitely for their inheritance. In such circumstances, a citation provides a remedy.

There are several types of citation which can be issued by the Probate Registry at the request of a beneficiary ('the citor').

30.15.2.1   Citation to take probate

A citation to take probate may be used where an executor has lost his right to renounce probate by intermeddling in the estate (eg, by advising the deceased's bank of his death, see **30.9.3**) but has not applied for a grant of probate within six months of the testator's death and shows no signs of so doing. Once cited, the executor must proceed with an application for a grant of probate. If he does not (without good reason) the citor can apply to the court for an order allowing the executor to be passed over and a grant of letters of administration with will annexed to issue to the person(s) entitled under NCPR 1987, r 20.

30.15.2.2   Citation to accept or refuse a grant

A citation to accept or refuse a grant is the standard method of clearing off a person with a prior right to any type of grant who has not applied, and shows no intention of applying, for a grant. If the person cited does not take steps to take out the grant, a grant may be issued to the citor.

Example

Adam's will appoints Bert his executor and Clare the residuary beneficiary. Bert takes no steps towards administering the estate or proving the will. Clare may cite Bert to act and, if Bert does nothing, Clare may apply by virtue of NCPR 1987, r 20 for a grant of letters of administration with will annexed.

30.16   An alternative to citation

To compel an unwilling person to take a grant is likely to produce more problems than it solves. If a person is unwilling to act as executor in the administration of an estate, it is often preferable to apply to the Probate Registry under the Supreme Court Act 1981, s 116 for an order passing over that person in favour of someone else. For example, in *Re Biggs* [1966] 1 All ER 358, an executor had intermeddled but then refused to have anything to do with the estate. The Probate Registry ordered that he be passed over.

Chapter 31

Administration of an Estate

31.1 The administration period

Once the PRs have obtained the grant, they have full power to undertake the administration of the estate. The work involved in administering an estate is broadly the same whether the deceased left a will or died intestate. However, in the latter case, the beneficiaries will be ascertained by application of the law of intestacy rather than from construction of the will.

The administration of an estate may be divided conveniently into five elements or stages, as follows:

(a) considering the duties of and powers available to the PRs in carrying out their task;

(b) collecting the deceased's assets;

(c) paying the deceased's funeral and testamentary expenses and debts;

(d) distributing the legacies; and

(e) completing the administration and distributing the residuary estate.

All five of the above elements in the administration occur within the 'administration period'. This is the period which commences at the moment immediately following the death and ends when the PRs are in a position to vest the residue of the estate in the beneficiaries, or the trustees if a trust arises under the will or the intestacy law.

31.2 Duties of the PRs

The Administration of Estates Act 1925 (AEA 1925), s 25 (as substituted by AEA 1971, s 9) states that the PRs of a deceased person shall be under a duty to 'collect and get in the real and personal estate of the deceased and administer it according to law'.

The duties to be undertaken by a PR are onerous. A PR who has accepted liability is personally liable for loss to the estate resulting from any breach of duty he commits as PR (although he is not generally liable for breaches committed by a co-PR). There are several types of breach of duty, including:

(a) failing to protect the value of assets;

(b) failing to pay the people entitled to assets.

The Trustee Act 1925 (TA 1925), s 61 gives the court power at its discretion to relieve a PR from liability for breach of duty if satisfied that the PR 'has acted honestly and reasonably and ought fairly to be excused for the breach'. Alternatively, an executor may be able to rely on a clause in the deceased's will providing protection from liability for mistakes made in good faith.

31.3 Protection against liability

As we saw at **30.3.5**, PRs can protect themselves against personal liability to unknown beneficiaries by complying with the requirements of TA 1925, s 27.

31.4 Missing beneficiaries

As we saw at **30.3.5**, the TA 1925, s 27 will not protect PRs against claims from beneficiaries whose existence is known but who cannot be traced. The only way they can fully protect themselves in such a case is to apply to court for a *Benjamin* order.

Before making an order, the court will require evidence that the fullest possible enquiries were made to trace the missing person. If the court considers the advertisements made in addition to the TA 1925, s 27 are insufficient, it will direct that further enquiry be made.

31.5 Inheritance (Provision for Family and Dependants) Act 1975

The PRs will be personally liable where an applicant under the I(PFD)A 1975 successfully obtains an order for 'reasonable financial provision' from the estate. They can protect themselves against such liability by waiting more than six months following the date of the grant of representation before distributing the assets. If earlier distribution is required, PRs should ensure they retain sufficient assets to satisfy an order should an applicant be successful within six months of the grant.

31.6 Administrative powers of PRs

31.6.1 Statutory powers of PRs and trustees

The PRs have a wide range of powers which they may exercise in carrying out the administration of an estate. These powers are largely conferred on them by statute. The AEA 1925 gives some powers specifically to PRs. The TA 1925 and the Trustee Act 2000 (TA 2000) confer powers on trustees for use in administering a trust. Since 'trustee' in the TA 1925 and TA 2000 includes a 'personal representative', PRs (executors and administrators) have these powers as well.

The TA 2000 modifies in various ways powers previously available to PRs and trustees. The main purpose of the Act is to remedy certain deficiencies by bringing the law into line with what has been regarded as good drafting practice for some years.

The TA 2000 deals with powers to invest trust property, appoint agents and nominees, remuneration of trustees (and PRs) and to insure trust property. A duty of care requires trustees (and PRs) when exercising many of their powers under the Act to exercise the skill and care reasonable in the circumstances, having regard to any special knowledge or expertise of the trustee.

The main changes made by the TA 2000 are noted in context in the paragraphs which follow.

31.6.2 Powers granted by a will

31.6.2.1 Modification of statutory powers

Many of the statutory powers may be modified by express provision contained within a will. If there are no executors who prove the will but the will is proved by administrators with the will annexed, they also have these modified powers available to them.

31.6.2.2 Additional powers

In addition to modification of statutory powers, a will often grants powers which are not available at law, for example power to advance capital to a person to whom a life interest has been given, or to lend capital to such a person; in the absence of any such express power, the executors have no implied power to advance or lend capital to a life tenant.

31.6.2.3 Will drafting

It is good drafting practice for a will to set out in full all the powers of the executors so that the position is clear on the face of the will, thus avoiding the possibility of a particular power available at law being overlooked. Whether the following powers are available to the PRs at all, or in modified form, will depend on the terms of the particular will and the circumstances of the estate.

31.6.3 Provisions concerning the administration of the estate

The provisions which follow may be included in the will to simplify the administration of the estate. However, if the terms of the will are short, the draftsman may have decided not to extend the executors' statutory powers.

31.6.3.1 Power to appropriate assets without consent of beneficiary

The statutory provisions

The AEA 1925, s 41 gives PRs the power to appropriate any part of the estate in or towards satisfaction of a pecuniary legacy or share in the residuary estate provided that the appropriation does not prejudice any specific beneficiary. Thus, if the will gives a pecuniary legacy to a beneficiary, the PRs may allow that beneficiary to take chattels or other assets in the estate up to the value of his legacy, provided that these assets have not been specifically bequeathed by the will. The section provides that the beneficiary (or his parent or guardian if he is a minor) must consent to the appropriation.

Specimen clause

> Power to exercise the power of appropriation conferred by s 41 of the Administration of Estates Act 1925 without obtaining any of the consents required by that section.

This provision is commonly included in order to relieve the PRs of the duty to obtain formal consent. Nevertheless, the PRs would informally consult the beneficiaries concerned.

There is no statutory power for trustees to appropriate assets so, if it is desired, an express clause must be included.

31.6.3.2   Power to insure

The statutory provision

The TA 1925, s 19 (as substituted by TA 2000, s 34) gives PRs and trustees power to insure trust property against any risks, to the full value of the property, and to pay premiums out of either capital or income.

Before the TA 2000, the statutory power of insurance was inadequate, and so it was normal to extend it by including an express power. However, this is no longer necessary.

The TA 2000 only provides trustees with a power to insure trust *property*. If trustees wish to be able to insure the *life* of a beneficiary or of the settlor (eg, where there is a risk of a charge to inheritance tax if death occurs within seven years) they will require an express power.

31.6.3.3   Power to accept receipts from or on behalf of minors

The statutory provision

Under the general law, an unmarried minor could not give a good receipt for capital or income. A married minor can give a good receipt for income only (LPA 1925, s 21). Parents and guardians used not to be able to give a good receipt on behalf of minors unless specifically authorised to do so in the will.

The Children Act 1989 provides that parents with parental responsibility have the same rights as guardians appointed under the Act. These rights are set out at s 3 and include the right to receive or recover money for the benefit of the child. Therefore, since the Children Act, parents and guardians have been able to give a good receipt to PRs.

Extended statutory power

There are often tensions within families and a client may not be happy for a parent or guardian to give a good receipt for a legacy. In such a case, it may be preferable to leave the legacy to another adult to hold on trust for the minor. Alternatively, the will should be drafted to leave a legacy to trustees to hold for the benefit of the minor rather than to the child directly. Alternatively, the will may include a clause allowing the PRs to accept the receipt of the child himself if over 16 years old. The provision may be incorporated into the legacy itself, or may be included in a list of powers in the will.

31.6.4   Provisions concerning the administration of a trust

At the end of the administration of an estate, the PRs may be able to distribute the residue to the beneficiaries, thus completing their task. However, in some cases distribution will be delayed and the PRs will hold the residue (or part of it) as trustees. This may happen:

(a)   where the beneficiary has a contingent interest, and so cannot be given the property until the interest vests; or

(b)   where the interests in the property are divided, for example between income and capital.

In either of these cases, the statutory powers of the trustees may also be extended.

31.6.4.1   Power to invest trust funds

The statutory provision

Under the general law, trustees have a duty to invest trust money. The TA 2000, s 3 gives trustees a 'general power of investment' enabling them to invest as if they were absolutely entitled to the trust property themselves. This wide power excludes investment in land, other than by mortgage, but further powers in relation to land are contained in s 8 (see **31.6.4.2**). In exercising the investment power, trustees are required to take proper advice and to review investments of the trust from time to time. They must have regard to the standard investment criteria, namely the suitability to the trust of any particular investment and to the need for diversification of investments of the trust.

An express investment clause can be included but is no longer necessary.

31.6.4.2   Power to purchase land

The statutory provisions

The TA 2000, s 8 gives trustees power to acquire freehold or leasehold land in the UK for 'investment, for occupation by a beneficiary or for any other reason'. When exercising their power, the trustees are given 'all the powers of an absolute owner in relation to the land'.

The statutory power does not authorise the purchase of land abroad, nor does it allow trustees to purchase an interest in land with someone else (eg, a beneficiary). An express power will be needed if the trustees are to have such powers.

Specimen clause

My trustees may apply trust money in
— the purchase of land or an interest in land anywhere in the world, and
— the improvement of such land.

31.6.4.3   Power to sell personalty

Trustees holding land in their trust have the power to sell it under their powers of an absolute owner. However, there is some doubt whether trustees who do not hold land have an implied power of sale. For this reason, some wills may continue to impose an express trust for sale over residue. The alternative solution is to include power in the will (among the administrative provisions) giving the trustees express power to sell personalty.

Specimen clause

Power to sell mortgage or charge any asset of my estate as it they were an absolute beneficial owner.

31.6.4.4   Power of maintenance

The statutory provisions

Where trustees are holding a fund for a minor beneficiary, the TA 1925, s 31 gives them power to use income they receive for the minor's maintenance, education or benefit.

The TA 1925, s 31 (as amended by TA 2000) states (inter alia):

(1) Where any property is held by trustees in trust for any person for any interest whatsoever, whether vested or contingent, then, subject to any prior interests or charges affecting that property—

    (i) during the infancy of any such person, if his interest so long continues, the trustees may, at their sole discretion, pay to his parent or guardian, if any, or otherwise apply for or towards his maintenance, education, or benefit, the whole or such part, if any, of the income of that property as may, in all the circumstances, be reasonable, whether or not there is—

        (a) any other fund applicable to the same purpose; or

        (b) any person bound by law to provide for his maintenance or education; and

    (ii) if such person on attaining the age of eighteen years has not a vested interest in such income, the trustees shall thenceforth pay the income of that property and of any accretion thereto under subsection (2) of this section to him, until he either attains a vested interest therein or dies, or until failure of his interest:

Provided that, in deciding whether the whole or any part of the income of the property is during a minority to be paid or applied for the purposes aforesaid, the trustees shall have regard to the age of the infant and his requirements and generally to the circumstances of the case, and in particular to what other income, if any, is applicable for the same purposes; and where trustees have notice that the income of more than one fund is applicable for those purposes, then, so far as practicable, unless the entire income of the funds is paid or applied as aforesaid or the court otherwise directs, a proportionate part only of the income of each fund shall be so paid or applied.

(2) During the infancy of any such person, if his interest so long continues, the trustees shall accumulate all the residue of that income by investing it, and any profits from so investing it, from time to time in authorised investments, and shall hold those accumulations ... .

(3) This section applies in the case of a contingent interest only if the limitation or trust carries the intermediate income of the property ... .

Application of section 31

Example – Trust 1

The trustees are holding £100,000 for Mary (16) who has a vested interest in the capital. Under s 31(1), the trustees have the power to pay all or part of the income to Mary's parent or guardian or 'otherwise apply' it for Mary's maintenance, education or benefit. This could include paying bills (eg, school fees) directly.

The power is limited to so much of the income as is 'reasonable'. The proviso directs the trustees to take into account various further points such as Mary's age and requirements and whether any other fund is available for her maintenance.

Section 31(2) directs the trustees to accumulate any income not used for maintenance and invest it.

Example – Trust 2

The trustees are holding £100,000 for Dora (14) who has a contingent interest in the capital. They may pay or apply the income for Dora's maintenance, education or benefit in the same way as the trustees of Trust 1.

The trustees are holding £100,000 for Charles (19) who also has a contingent interest in the capital. Section 31(1)(ii) directs them to pay all the income to Charles until his interest vests (ie until he is 21) when he will receive the capital, or fails (ie if he dies before he is 21). The same will apply to the income from Dora's share from her 18th birthday onwards.

Example – Trust 3

The trustees are holding £200,000 for Henry for life with remainder to Stephen (10). They have no power to use the income for Stephen's benefit as Henry is entitled to it. If Henry dies while Stephen is still a minor, s 31 will apply to allow the trustees to apply income for Stephen's maintenance, etc during the period from Henry's death until Stephen is 18 (when they will transfer the capital to Stephen).

Extending section 31 – specimen clause

> Section 31 of the Trustee Act 1925 shall apply to the income of my estate as if the words 'as the trustees shall in their absolute discretion think fit' were substituted for the words 'as in all the circumstances be reasonable' in paragraph (i) of subsection (1) thereof and the proviso to subsection (1) had been omitted and as if the age of 21 years were substituted for all references to the age of 18 wherever they occur in s 31 (references to 'infancy' being construed accordingly).

The clause begins by removing the 'reasonable' limitation in s 31. It gives the trustees complete discretion over whether to pay or apply income for minor beneficiaries and over how much income they pay or apply.

Secondly, it removes the right for a contingent beneficiary to receive all the income from the age of 18. The trustees' discretion under s 31 to pay or apply income for maintenance or to accumulate any surplus will continue until the beneficiary is 21. Thus in Trust 2 the trustees would have a discretion over the payment of income to Charles even though he is over 18.

31.6.4.5 Power to advance capital

The statutory provisions

The TA 1925, s 32 allows trustees in certain circumstances to permit a beneficiary with an interest in capital to have the benefit of part of his capital entitlement sooner than he would receive it under the basic provisions of the trust.

Section 32 states:

> (1) Trustees may at any time or times pay or apply any capital money subject to a trust, for the advancement or benefit, in such manner as they may, in their absolute discretion, think fit, of any person entitled to the capital of the trust property or of any share thereof, whether absolutely or contingently on his attaining any specified age ... and whether in possession or in remainder or reversion ...
>
> Provided that—
>
> (a) the money so paid or applied for the advancement or benefit of any person shall not exceed altogether in amount one-half of the presumptive or vested share or interest of that person in the trust property; and
>
> (b) if that person is or becomes absolutely and indefeasibly entitled to a share in the trust property the money so paid or applied shall be brought into account as part of such share; and
>
> (c) no such payment or application shall be made so as to prejudice any person entitled to any prior life or other interest, whether vested or contingent, in the money paid or applied unless such person is in existence and of full age and consents in writing to such payment or application.

Application of section 32

Example – Trust 1

Mary has a vested interest in £100,000 capital. Section 32 allows the trustees to release some of the capital for Mary's benefit. 'Benefit' is widely construed: money could be used to pay educational or living expenses. The amount the trustees may advance is limited to one half of Mary's entitlement, ie £50,000.

Example – Trust 2

Charles and Dora have contingent interests in capital, their presumptive shares being £100,000 each. Section 32 applies to allow the trustees to release up to £50,000 for the benefit of either beneficiary. The trustees could give money directly to Charles as he is old enough to give a valid receipt. The power applies even though the interests of Charles and Dora are contingent. If either beneficiary dies before the age of 21 there is no right to recover any advance even though that beneficiary's interest in capital has failed.

Section 32(1)(b) requires advances to be brought into account on final distribution. If the trustees give £50,000 to Charles now, he will receive £50,000 less than Dora when the fund is finally distributed to them.

Example – Trust 3

Henry has only an interest in income and s 32 does not permit the release of capital to him. The section does apply to Stephen's vested interest in remainder, and permits the trustees to apply up to £100,000 (half his interest) for Stephen's benefit.

Such an advance would prejudice Henry since his income would be substantially reduced. Section 32(1)(c) provides that no advance may be made without Henry's written consent.

Extending section 32 – specimen clause 1

> Power to apply for the benefit of any beneficiary as my trustees think fit the whole or any part of the share of my residuary estate to which that beneficiary is absolutely or presumptively entitled and I leave it within the discretion of my trustees whether and to what extent the beneficiary shall bring into account any payments received under this clause.

This clause extends the limit in s 32(1)(a) to the full amount of the beneficiary's share. Up to £100,000 could be advanced for Mary (in Trust 1) or for Charles and Dora (in Trust 2). In Trust 3, the whole fund could be advanced for Stephen, provided that Henry consents.

The second part of the clause supersedes s 32(1)(b) and means that, if in Trust 2 £50,000 was advanced to Charles, the trustees could on distribution still divide the remaining fund equally between Charles and Dora.

Extending section 32 – specimen clause 2

> Power to pay or apply capital money from my residuary estate to any extent to or for the benefit of my husband.
>
> Power to advance capital money from my residuary estate to my husband by way of loan to any extent upon such terms and conditions as my trustees may in their absolute discretion think fit.

These provisions would permit the trustees in Trust 3 to give or lend capital from the fund to Henry even though he has only an interest in income, not capital. Such a clause may be included to give more flexibility in case the income proves insufficient for Henry's needs. Henry still remains dependent on the discretion of the trustees.

31.6.4.6 Power to accept receipts from and on behalf of minors

The statutory provisions

Where a trust arises in favour of a beneficiary who is a minor, the trustees have statutory powers of maintenance and advancement under ss 31 and 32 of the TA 1925. Section 31 specifically allows the trustees to pay income to the child's parent or guardian or 'otherwise apply' it for the child's maintenance, education or benefit. Similarly, s 32 empowers the trustees to pay 'or apply' capital for the beneficiary's advancement or benefit. Thus, even before the Children Act 1989, the trustees had no difficulty in obtaining a good receipt when exercising these powers.

31.6.4.7 Control of trustees by beneficiaries

The Trusts of Land and Appointment of Trustees Act 1996 (TLATA 1996), s 19 provides that where beneficiaries are sui juris and together entitled to the whole fund, they may direct the trustees to retire and appoint new trustees of the beneficiaries' choice. This means that in a case where the beneficiaries could by agreement end the trust under the rule in *Saunders v Vautier* (1841) 4 Beav 115, they now have the option of allowing the trust to continue with trustees of their own choice. The provision may be expressly excluded by the testator. If, under the terms of the trust, the position could arise where all the beneficiaries are in existence and aged over 18 but the trust has not ended, the testator may wish to prevent the beneficiaries from choosing their own trustees.

Specimen clause

> The provisions of section 19 of the Trusts of Land and Appointment of Trustees Act 1996 shall not apply to any trust created by this will so that no beneficiary shall have the right to require the appointment or retirement of any trustee or trustees.

31.6.4.8 Trusts of land

The TLATA 1996 gives special powers (see below) to a beneficiary under a trust of land who has an interest in possession. If, under the terms of the will, a trust with an interest in possession could arise the will may amend those powers. The Act does not define 'interest in possession', so it presumably has its usual meaning; a beneficiary has an interest in possession if he is entitled to claim the income of the fund as it arises (normally either because he has a life interest, or because he is over 18 and entitled to claim income under the TA 1925, s 31).

Duty to consult beneficiaries

Trustees exercising any function relating to the land must consult any beneficiary who is of full age and beneficially entitled to an interest in possession in the land and, so far as consistent with the 'general interest of the trust', give effect to the wishes of any such beneficiary (TLATA 1996, s 11). The duty to consult may be excluded by the will.

Specimen clause

> The provisions of section 11 of the Trusts of Land and Appointment of Trustees Act 1996 shall not apply so that it shall not be necessary for my trustees to consult any beneficiaries before carrying out any function relating to land.

Beneficiary's rights of occupation

A beneficiary with a beneficial interest in possession, even if not of full age, has the right to occupy land subject to the trust if the purposes of the trust include making the land available for occupation by him, or if the trustees acquired the land in order to make it so available (TLATA 1996, s 12). There is no power to exclude s 12, but a declaration that the purpose of the trust is not for the occupation of land may be included in the will.

Specimen clause

> The purposes of any trust created by this will do not include making land available for occupation of any beneficiary [although my trustees have power to do so if they wish].

31.6.4.9   The apportionment rules

One of the duties of trustees is to ensure that a fair balance is kept between the interests of the beneficiaries. This is particularly important where different beneficiaries are entitled to income and capital, for example where property is left on trust for X for life with remainder to Y, as in Trust 3 at **31.6.4.5** above. The trustees must ensure that the investments they choose produce a reasonable income for X, the life tenant, and preserve the capital reasonably safely for Y, the remainderman.

The equitable rules

The equitable rules to preserve a fair balance between a life tenant and a remainderman derive from *Howe v Dartmouth* (1820) 7 Ves 137 and *Allhusen v Whittell* (1867) LR 4 Eq 295. Although the even-handed result of applying these rules may be desirable, in practice the calculations required by the rules are complex and the time and expense involved is rarely justified. Thus it is usual to exclude the rules when drafting life interest trusts.

Apportionment Act 1870

The Apportionment Act 1870, s 2 provides that income such as rent and dividends is to be treated as accruing from day to day and apportioned accordingly. Thus, where assets in the estate produce income (such as dividends on shares) which is received after death but relates to a period partly before and partly after death, the income must be apportioned. The part accruing before death is capital, while that accruing after death is income.

It is desirable to exclude the Act whenever a life interest trust is created.

It is also desirable to exclude it where an income-producing asset is left to one person and residue to another. For example, 'My shares to X, my residue to Y'.

Unless the Act is excluded income attributable to the pre-death period is Y's and income attributable to the post-death period is X's.

It is also desirable to exclude the Act where there is a trust with contingent interests. Beneficiaries will fulfil the contingency at different times (or fail to fulfil it), and unless the Act is excluded there will have to be an apportionment of income each time there is a change in beneficial entitlement.

Excluding the apportionment rules – specimen clause

> Power to treat as income all the income from any part of my estate whatever the period in respect of which it may accrue and to disregard the Apportionment Act 1870 [and the rules of equity relating to apportionment including those known as the rules in *Howe v Dartmouth* and *Allhusen v Whittell* in all their branches].

This clause is appropriate in a will which creates a life interest trust. It is intended to exclude the application of all the apportionment rules described above. In a will containing a specific gift of an income-producing asset or a contingent gift of residue, the clause could be included with the omission of the words in square brackets.

31.6.5   Miscellaneous additional powers

31.6.5.1   Charging clause

Background law

The rule of equity that a trustee may not profit from his trust applies both to trustees and executors. Its effect is that an executor or trustee may claim only out-of-pocket expenses and may not charge for time spent in performing his office unless expressly authorised.

The TA 2000, ss 28–31 have made various changes to the general rule of law governing the remuneration of 'professional' trustees.

Professional trustees are defined as those whose business includes the provision of services in connection with the management or administration of trusts.

A professional trustee charging for services is now entitled to charge for all services, even if they are services which are capable of being provided by a lay person (TA 2000, s 28(2)). Previously, express authority was required.

Where a will or trust instrument does not contain a charging clause, a professional trustee acting in a non-charitable trust can charge reasonable remuneration *if authorised to do so in writing by each of the co-trustees* (s 29(2)). This means that it is still desirable to include a charging clause as a sole trustee will be unable to charge and a co-trustee will be able to do so only with the permission of co-trustees.

A charging clause used to be regarded as a legacy, but this is no longer the case (s 28(4)). This means that a partner in a firm authorised by the will to charge can witness the will without losing the entitlement to charge. If there are insufficient funds to pay the pecuniary legacies in full, the legacies will abate proportionally unless the will provides otherwise. As a charging clause is no longer a legacy, it is not necessary to provide that the charges be paid in priority to other legacies.

Note that, if a person engaged in a profession or business not connected with the administration of trusts is to have power to charge for time spent dealing with the trust, there must be express authority in the trust instrument.

In any case where a professional executor or trustee is appointed such as a bank, a firm of solicitors, an individual solicitor or an accountant, a power to charge should be included in the will so that the testator is aware of the position.

Power to charge – specimen clause

> Any of my trustees being a solicitor or other person engaged in any profession or business may charge and be paid his usual professional charges for work done by him or his firm in the administration of my estate and the trusts arising under my will including acts which a trustee not engaged in any profession or business could have done personally.

Power to appoint a trust corporation – specimen clause

> Power to appoint a trust corporation to be the sole trustee or one of the trustees of my will upon such terms and conditions in all respects as may be acceptable to the corporation so appointed.

Provision of this latter kind is not commonly included in practice. Its purpose is to ensure that, if individual trustees wish to retire and no substitutes can readily be found, a bank (or other trust corporation) may be appointed even though there may be minor beneficiaries who are unable to give the required consent to the bank's usual terms and conditions, particularly in relation to charging.

31.6.5.2 Power to carry on business

Where an estate includes a business which was run by the deceased as a sole (unincorporated) trader, the powers of the PRs to run the business are limited. For example, they may only run the business with a view to selling it as a going concern and may use only those assets employed in the business at the date of death. These powers may be extended by will, although in practice PRs are unlikely to wish to involve themselves in the detailed running of a business. It may be preferable to bequeath the business by specific legacy and to appoint the legatee as a special PR of the business.

31.7 Collecting the deceased's assets

31.7.1 Duty of the PRs

As we have seen already at **29.1**, some assets pass independently of the will and intestacy rules. The PRs have no obligation, or indeed power, to deal with these assets.

Assets which pass under the will or intestacy rules devolve on the PRs, who are under an obligation to collect and administer it for the benefit of those entitled.

In order to collect the property, the PRs generally produce their grant of representation to whoever is holding the various assets, for example to the deceased's bank or building society. If the bank is holding share certificates or documents of title to land, these also will be handed over to the PRs once the grant has been produced. In most cases, an office copy grant will be accepted as evidence of title.

In some cases, a grant is not required to collect certain assets. As explained at **30.4.1**, it may be possible to realise assets without production of a grant under the Administration of Estates (Small Payments) Act 1965.

31.7.2 Property not devolving on the PRs

The following examples illustrate types of property which do not devolve on the PRs and which therefore will not pass under any will or under the intestacy law.

31.7.2.1   Life interest

Example

Terry died some years ago having by his will left property to Henry and Ian on trust for sale 'for Andrew for life, remainder for Ben'. Andrew has recently died. Assuming Ben is of full age and capacity, Henry and Ian will transfer the property to him in accordance with the terms of Terry's will.

31.7.2.2   Joint tenancy

Example

Alan and Brian own property as beneficial joint tenants at law and in equity. On Alan's death his interest passes by operation of the right of survivorship to Brian the surviving joint tenant.

31.7.2.3   Policy held in trust for others

As explained at **29.1.3**, any proceeds of an insurance policy written in trust for third parties, or written under the Married Women's Property Act 1882, s 11 for the benefit of the deceased's spouse and/or children, will be paid to the trustees of the policy on proof of death, usually by production of the death certificate. The trustees will then distribute the proceeds among the beneficiaries in accordance with the trusts of the policy.

31.7.2.4   Pension schemes

Death in service benefits payable under an occupational pension scheme established by the deceased's former employers, where the trustees have a discretion as to whom to pay the benefits, do not devolve on the deceased's PRs and do not form part of his estate for succession purposes. In exercising their discretion as to payment, the trustees will have regard to any 'letter of wishes' given to them by the deceased person during his lifetime; however, they are not bound to give effect to these wishes (see **30.4.3**).

31.8   Paying the deceased's funeral and testamentary expenses and debts

31.8.1   Preliminary considerations

31.8.1.1   Immediate sources of money

As soon as monies can be collected from the deceased's bank or building society, or realised through insurance policies etc, the PRs should begin to pay the deceased's outstanding debts and the funeral account. Administration expenses, for example estate agents' and valuers' fees, will arise during the course of administration of the estate and will have to be settled from time to time while the administration is proceeding.

31.8.1.2   Repayment of loan to pay IHT

It may be necessary to raise money to repay a loan from the deceased's bank to pay IHT to obtain the grant. If an undertaking has been given to the bank in connection with the loan, it will probably be a 'first proceeds' undertaking. This means that the PRs must use money first realised by them during the administration to repay the bank. Failure to do so will be a breach of the terms of the undertaking.

31.8.1.3 Which assets to sell?

The PRs must take considerable care when deciding which assets they will sell to raise money for payment of the various outgoings from the deceased's estate. A number of points must be addressed when making their decision, including the matters set out below.

Provisions of the deceased's will

The will may direct from which part of the deceased's estate the debts, funeral account, testamentary and administration expenses should be paid; usually they will be paid from the residue. In the absence of such direction, the PRs must follow the statutory rules for the incidence of liabilities as outlined below. In any event, it will be generally incorrect for PRs to sell property given specifically by will (eg, a gift of the testator's valuable stamp collection to his nephew) unless all other assets in the estate have been exhausted in payment of the debts, etc.

The beneficiaries' wishes

Where possible, the wishes of the beneficiaries of the residuary estate should be respected by the PRs. Although the PRs have power to sell any assets in the residuary estate, it is clearly appropriate that the residuary beneficiaries should be consulted before any sale takes place. Generally, beneficiaries have clear views as to which assets they desire to be retained for transfer to them; other assets may be sold by the PRs to raise the necessary money, possibly following receipt of professional advice as to particular sales.

Tax consequences

Before selling assets, the PRs should consider the amount of any capital gains (or losses) likely to arise as a result of the sale, and the availability of any exemptions, etc. Full use should be made of the annual exemption for CGT. If assets are to be sold at a loss (compared to their value at the date of death) CGT loss relief may be available for the PRs, as may 'loss relief' for IHT purposes. An explanation of these reliefs is contained at **31.10.6**.

31.8.2 Funeral and testamentary expenses and debts

31.8.2.1 Funeral expenses

Reasonable funeral expenses are payable from the deceased's estate. In all cases, it is a question of fact what funeral expenses are reasonable.

31.8.2.2 Testamentary expenses

The phrase 'testamentary and administration expenses' is not defined in the AEA 1925, but it is generally considered to mean expenses incident to the proper performance of the duties of a PR. The phrase will include:

(a)   the costs of obtaining the grant;

(b)   the costs of collecting in and preserving the deceased's assets;

(c)   the costs of administering the deceased's estate, for example solicitors' fees for acting for the PRs, valuers' fees incurred by PRs in valuing the deceased's stocks and shares or other property; and

(d)   any IHT payable on death on the deceased's property in the UK which vests in the PRs (IHTA 1984, s 211).

31.8.3 Administration of assets: solvent estate

The rules applying to the payment of funeral and testamentary expenses and debts depend on whether the estate is solvent or insolvent. The insolvent estate is considered at **31.8.4**.

31.8.3.1 The statutory order for payment of debts

Section 34(3) of the AEA 1925 states:

> Where the estate of a deceased person is solvent his real and personal estate shall, subject to rules of court and the provisions hereinafter contained as to charges on property of the deceased, and to the provisions, if any, contained in his will, be applicable towards the discharge of the funeral, testamentary and administration expenses, debts and liabilities payable thereout in the order mentioned in Part II of the First Schedule to this Act.

Part II of the First Schedule lays out an order which the PRs must follow when deciding which part of the deceased's estate should be used for the purposes of payment of the funeral and testamentary expenses and debts. Under the order generally, assets forming part of the residue are to be used before using property given to specific legatees.

'Subject ... to'

However, the effect of the proviso 'subject to' is that the operation of s 34(3) is expressly subject to two important rules or provisions, as follows:

(a)   The AEA 1925, s 35, which deals with secured debts, ie debts owing by the deceased which are charged on particular items of property. A common example is a loan secured by legal mortgage on the deceased's house. The effect of this rule is that a beneficiary taking the asset takes it subject to the debt and will be responsible for paying the debt.

(b)   The deceased's will can vary the provisions implied by the AEA 1925, ss 34(3) and/or 35. To vary s 35 it is necessary to have an express reference to the mortgage. A direction to pay 'debts' from residue is not sufficient to vary s 35.

31.8.4 The insolvent estate

31.8.4.1 Meaning of insolvency

An estate is insolvent if the assets are insufficient to discharge in full the funeral, testamentary and administration expenses, debts and liabilities. In such cases, the creditors will not be paid in full (or at all) and the beneficiaries under the will or the intestacy provisions may receive nothing from the estate. In doubtful cases, the PRs should administer the estate as if it is insolvent. Failure to administer an insolvent estate in accordance with the statutory order is a breach of duty by the PRs.

In the case of an insolvent estate which is being administered by the deceased's PRs out of court (this being the most common method of administration), the order of distribution in the Administration of Insolvent Estates of Deceased Persons Order 1986 (SI 1986/1999) should be followed.

Secured creditors, for example those holding a mortgage or charge over the deceased's property, are in a better position than unsecured creditors in that they may (inter alia) realise the security, ie sell the property by exercising a power of sale as mortgagee or chargee.

31.9   Paying the legacies

31.9.1   Introduction

Once the funeral, testamentary and administration expenses and debts have been paid, or at least adequately provided for by setting aside sufficient assets for the purpose, the PRs should consider discharging the gifts arising on the death, other than the gifts of the residuary estate. They may also consider making interim distributions to the residuary beneficiaries on account of their entitlement.

31.9.2   Specific legacies

It is unusual for property given by specific bequest or devise to be needed for payment of the deceased's funeral and testamentary expenses and debts. Once the PRs are satisfied that the property will not be so required, they should consider transferring it to the beneficiary, or to trustees if a trust arises, for example if the property is given to a beneficiary contingently on attaining a stated age and the beneficiary has not yet reached that age.

The method of transferring the property to the beneficiary or trustee will depend on its particular nature. For example, the legal estate in a house or flat should be vested in a beneficiary by a document known as an assent. If the specific legacy is of company shares, a stock transfer form should be used.

In the case of specific gifts only, the vesting of the asset in the beneficiary is retrospective to the date of death, so that any income produced by the property, for example dividends on a specific gift of company shares, belongs to the beneficiary. He is not entitled to the income as it arises but must wait until the PRs vest the property in him. As the beneficiary is entitled to the income he will be liable to be assessed for any income tax due on that income since the death.

Any costs of transferring the property to a specific legatee, and the cost of any necessary insurance cover taken to safeguard the property are the responsibility of the legatee who should reimburse the PRs for the expenses incurred (subject to any contrary direction in a will indicating that such expenses should be paid from residue). If the deceased's title to the asset is disputed by a third party, the specific legatee will be responsible for the cost of litigation to establish ownership.

31.9.3   Pecuniary legacies – provision by will for payment

An example of a clause dealing expressly with the payment of pecuniary legacies is clause 4 of Tom Smith's will, first mentioned in connection with the payment of debts in **31.8.4.1**.

The clause reads as follows:

> I GIVE all my estate both real and personal whatsoever and wheresoever not hereby or by any codicil hereto otherwise specifically disposed of (hereinafter called 'my residuary estate') unto my trustees UPON TRUST to raise and discharge thereout my debts and funeral and testamentary expenses and all legacies given hereby or by any codicil hereto and any and all taxes payable by reason of my death in respect of property given free of tax and subject thereto UPON TRUST to pay and divide the same equally between …

There is clear intention shown by the testator to pay the pecuniary legacies from the fund of general residue described as 'my residuary estate'. The result would be the same if the clause gave the residuary estate 'subject to' or 'after payment of' the pecuniary legacies. In both cases the legacies should be paid from the fund of residue before the division of the balance between the residuary beneficiaries.

31.9.4 Pecuniary legacies – no provision by will for payment

Where the will makes no provision for the payment of pecuniary legacies, they are paid primarily from residuary personalty.

> #### Example
>
> A will leaves a legacy of £5,000 to Dawn. There is no direction as to payment of the legacy. Residue consisting of personalty and realty is given by the will to 'Edward if he shall survive me by 28 days'. He does so survive the testator, and residue is, therefore, fully disposed of. The PRs should pay the legacy from the personalty, with the proceeds of the realty being used afterwards if necessary.

If a partial intestacy arises, for example where part of a gift of residue fails because one of the beneficiaries dies before the testator, it is often unclear as a matter of law which is the appropriate part of the estate for the payment of the pecuniary legacies. It is preferable, therefore, to make express provision for payment of legacies (as in **31.9.3**).

31.9.5 Time for payment of pecuniary legacies

31.9.5.1 The executor's year

The general rule is that a pecuniary legacy is payable at the end of 'the executor's year', ie one year after the testator's death. The AEA 1925, s 44 provides that PRs are not bound to distribute the estate to the beneficiaries before the expiration of one year from the death. It is often difficult to make payment within the year and, if payment is delayed beyond this date, the legatee will be entitled to interest by way of compensation. The rate of interest will either be the rate prescribed by the testator's will, or, in default of such provision, the rate payable on money paid into court. If the testator stipulates that the legacy is to be paid 'immediately following my death', or that it is payable at some future date, or on the happening of a particular contingency, then interest is payable from either the day following the date of death, the future date or the date the contingency occurs, as may be appropriate.

31.9.5.2 Interest payable from the date of death

There are four occasions when, as an exception to the normal rule, interest is payable on a pecuniary legacy from the date of the death. These occur when legacies are:

(a) payable in satisfaction of a debt owed by the testator to a creditor;

(b) charged on/and owned by the testator;

(c) payable to the testator's minor child (historically this was so that provision was made for maintenance of the child, and interest is not payable under this provision if other funds exist for the child's maintenance); or

(d) payable to any minor (not necessarily the child of the testator) where the intention is to provide for the maintenance of that minor.

31.10 Completing the administration and distributing the residuary estate

31.10.1 Introduction

Once the PRs have paid the deceased's funeral, testamentary expenses and debts and any legacies given by the will, they can consider distribution of the residuary estate in accordance with the will or the intestacy rules.

The PRs may have made interim distributions to the residuary beneficiaries on account of their entitlements, at the same time ensuring that they have retained sufficient assets to cover any outstanding liabilities, particularly tax.

Before drawing up the estate accounts and making the final distribution of residue, the PRs must deal with all outstanding matters. Such matters relate mostly to IHT liability, but there will also be income tax and CGT to consider.

31.10.2 Adjusting the IHT assessment

Adjustment to the amount of IHT payable on the instalment and non-instalment option property in the estate may arise for a number of reasons, including:

(a) discovery of additional assets or liabilities since the HMRC account was submitted;

(b) discovery of lifetime transfers made by the deceased within the seven years before death;

(c) agreement of provisionally estimated values, for example with the shares valuation division of HMRC (in the case of shares in private companies) or the district valuer (in the case of land). The shares valuation division and the district valuer are official agencies established for the formal agreement of valuations on behalf of HMRC with PRs and others. Especially in the case of private company shares, but also in the case of land, valuations may require long negotiations and can often delay reaching a final settlement of IHT liabilities;

(d) agreement between the PRs and HMRC of a tax liability or repayment, in relation to the deceased's income and capital gains before the death;

(e) sales made by the PRs after the deceased's death which have given rise to a claim for IHT 'loss relief'.

31.10.2.1 IHT loss relief

Where 'qualifying investments' are sold within 12 months of death for less than their market value at the date of death (ie 'probate value'), then the sale price may be substituted for the market value at death and the IHT liability adjusted accordingly (IHTA 1984, ss 178–189). 'Qualifying investments' include shares or securities which are quoted on a recognised stock exchange at the date of death and also holdings in authorised unit trusts.

There are similar provisions relating to the sale of land within four years of a death at a loss (IHTA 1984, ss 190–198).

31.10.3 PRs' continuing IHT liability

31.10.3.1 IHT by instalments

The PRs may have opted to pay IHT by instalments on the property in the deceased's estate attracting the instalment option. By the time they are ready to transfer the assets to those entitled, probably only one or two instalments will have been paid. The PRs continue to be liable for the remaining instalments. They would be foolish to transfer all the assets to the beneficiaries in reliance on a promise that the beneficiaries will pay the tax. If the beneficiaries become insolvent or disappear, the PRs will be liable for the unpaid tax but will have no assets of the estate to meet the liability. They should consider retaining sufficient assets in the estate. Details of the instalment option facility are discussed at **4.3.7**. If any instalment option property is sold, any outstanding IHT on the property sold becomes due immediately.

31.10.3.2   IHT on lifetime transfers

If the deceased dies within seven years of making either a potentially exempt transfer (PET), or a chargeable transfer, IHT (if a PET) or more IHT (if a chargeable transfer) may become payable. Although the general rule is that the donees of lifetime transfers are primarily liable for the tax, the PRs of the donor's estate may become liable if the tax remains unpaid by the donees 12 months after the end of the month in which the donor died. However, the PRs' liability is limited to the extent of the deceased's assets which they have received, or would have received in the administration of the estate, but for their neglect or default.

In addition, if the deceased gave away property during his lifetime but reserved a benefit in that property, such property is treated as part of his estate on death (see **4.3.1**). The donee of the gift is primarily liable to pay the tax attributable, but if the tax remains unpaid 12 months after the end of the month of death, the PRs become liable. Again the PRs should consider how they can protect themselves in case this liability materialises.

31.10.4   Corrective account

When all variations in the extent or value of the deceased's assets and liabilities are known, and all reliefs to which the estate is entitled have been quantified, the PRs must report all outstanding matters to HMRC. This report is made by way of a corrective account on Form D3, although, in a case where there are only minor adjustments to be made, a letter will generally suffice. The form is signed by the PRs as disclosing all matters relevant to the IHT position of the estate, but it does not require self-assessment of IHT by the PRs, unlike the original Form IHT 200. Submission of the form results in HMRC issuing the final IHT assessment. The assessment should be checked carefully. If it is correct the PRs should arrange to pay any further IHT which is due, or seek a repayment of any overpaid IHT.

31.10.5   IHT clearance

31.10.5.1   Certificate of clearance

The last step for the PRs to take in relation to IHT is to obtain confirmation from HMRC that there is no further claim to IHT. If HMRC is satisfied that IHT attributable to a chargeable transfer has, or will be, paid, it can, and if the transfer is one made on death must, give a certificate. The effect of the certificate is to discharge all persons, thus in particular the PRs, from further liability to IHT (unless there is fraud or non-disclosure of material facts). The same certificate also extinguishes any charge imposed by HMRC on the deceased's property for the IHT.

31.10.5.2   Closing letter from HMRC

In April 2007 HMRC announced that handling the many applications for formal clearance certificates was placing a significant strain on its limited resources. It therefore announced that as from 30 April 2007 it would treat its final letter as having the same effect as a formal clearance certificate.

The final letter will provide confirmation that HMRC's enquiries are settled and that either:

(a)   no tax is due; or

(b)   all the tax has been paid; or

(c)   all the tax has been paid except for any tax being deferred (eg on timber) or being paid by instalments.

31.10.6   Income tax and CGT

31.10.6.1   The deceased's liability

Immediately following the death, the PRs must make a return to HMRC of the income and capital gains of the deceased for the period starting on 6 April before the death and ending with the date of death. Even though the deceased died part way through the income tax year, the PRs, on his behalf, may claim the same reliefs and allowances as the deceased could have claimed had he lived throughout the whole year. Any liability to tax must be paid by the PRs during the administration. It will represent a debt due at death deductible by them when calculating the amount of IHT. Alternatively, if a refund of tax is obtained, this will represent an asset, so increasing the size of the estate for IHT purposes.

31.10.6.2   The administration period

For each income tax year (or part) during the administration period, the PRs must make a return to HMRC of the income they receive on the deceased's assets, and any gains they make on disposals of chargeable assets for administration purposes, for example to raise money to pay IHT or the pecuniary legacies. These returns for the estate are distinct from the PRs' returns of their own income and capital gains.

31.10.6.3   Income tax

Rate of tax

The rates at which PRs pay income tax depends on the type of income they receive. For 2008/09, this is:

dividends	10%
other (gross) income	20%

PRs do not pay income tax at any higher rate(s).

In many cases, the PRs will have no tax to pay since income is often received after bearing income tax at the relevant rate. This applies to interest received (20%) and to dividends (non-recoverable 10% tax credit). If gross income is received, PRs will be assessed to tax at 20%.

Calculation of PRs' liability

In calculating any income tax liability on the income of the administration period, the PRs may be able to claim relief for interest paid on a bank loan to pay IHT. If the PRs use this loan to pay the IHT on the deceased's personal property in the UK which devolves on them in order to obtain the grant, income tax relief is generally available to them.

Example

PRs' only income is gross interest of £4,000 for a tax year in the administration period. They pay £1,000 interest to the bank on a loan to pay IHT to obtain their grant.

Gross income	£4,000
Less: interest paid	£1,000
Taxable income	£3,000
Less: tax (20%)	£600
Net income for the beneficiaries	£2,400

Beneficiary's income tax liability

Once the PRs' tax position has been settled, the remaining net income will be paid to the beneficiary. The grossed up amount of this income should be included by the beneficiary in his return of income for the income tax year to which it relates.

Example

PRs have completed the administration of an estate and there is bank deposit account interest which, after payment of tax at 20% by the PRs, amounts to £800. That sum is paid by the PRs to the residuary beneficiary.

When the beneficiary makes his return of income he must declare the estate income grossed up at 20%, ie

$$£800 \times \frac{100}{80} = £1,000.$$

The PRs must supply the beneficiary with a certificate of deduction of tax, on Form R185, which the beneficiary should send to his own inspector of taxes as evidence of the payment of the tax by the PRs.

31.10.6.4 Capital gains tax

No disposal on death

On death, there is no disposal for CGT purposes, so that no liability to CGT arises. The PRs acquire all the deceased's assets at their probate value at death. This has the effect of wiping out gains which accrued during the deceased's lifetime so that these gains are not charged to tax. Although there is no disposal, the probate value becomes the PRs' 'base cost' of all the deceased's assets for future CGT purposes.

Calculation of PRs' liability

If the PRs dispose of chargeable assets during the administration of the deceased's estate to raise cash (eg, to pay IHT, or other outgoings or legacies), they are liable to CGT on any chargeable gains that they make. The PRs (like trustees) pay CGT at the rate of 18% (2008/09) whatever the size of the gains made.

In addition to deducting their base cost (probate value), the PRs may deduct from the disposal consideration the incidental costs of disposal (eg, stockbroker's commission on sale of shares). In addition, they may deduct a proportion of the cost of valuing the deceased's estate for probate purposes. Calculations may be based either on a scale published by HMRC, or on the actual expenditure incurred if this is higher.

The PRs may claim the annual exemption for disposals made in the tax year in which the deceased died and the following two tax years only (if the administration lasts this long). The exemption is the same as for an individual (ie, £9,600 for 2008/09). Maximum advantage will be taken from this exemption if the PRs plan sales of assets carefully so that gains are realised in stages in each of the three tax years for which it is available.

Example

PRs need to raise £50,000 to pay administration expenses. The investments they are advised to sell will realise a net gain of £18,000. They have no unused losses. Ignore indexation and taper.

(1)   If all sales occur in the same tax year, their CGT position is as follows:

	£	
gain	18,000	
annual exemption	9,600	
taxable	8,400	at 18% = £1,512

(2)   If the sales are spread evenly over two tax years, their CGT position is as follows:

		£
Year 1	gain	9,000
	annual exemption	9,600
	taxable	nil
Year 2	gain	9,000
	annual exemption	9,600
	taxable	nil

Sales at a loss

If the PRs sell assets for less than their value at death, an allowable loss for CGT will arise. This loss may be relieved by setting it against gains arising on other sales by the PRs in the same, or any future, tax year in the administration period. Any loss which is unrelieved at the end of the administration period cannot be transferred to the beneficiaries. In view of this limitation, the PRs should plan sales carefully to ensure they can obtain relief for all losses which they realise. If there is a possibility of losses being unused, the PRs should either plan sales of other assets, or consider transferring the assets worth less than their probate value to the beneficiaries (see below).

Transfer of assets to the 'legatees'

If, instead of selling assets, the PRs vest them in the 'legatees', ie in the beneficiaries or trustees if a trust arises, no chargeable gain arises. The beneficiary or trustee is assumed to acquire the asset transferred at its probate value. This 'base cost' of the asset will be relevant to the CGT calculation on a future disposal.

Example 1

A testator by will leaves his residuary estate to Phil. Among the assets forming residue are 1,000 shares in XYZ plc. Probate value of these was £5,100. By the time they were transferred to Phil the value had risen to £10,000. Five years after death Phil sells them for £18,000.

	£
Disposal consideration	18,000
Less: acquisition (probate) value	5,100
Gain	12,900
Less: annual exemption	9,600
Chargeable gain	3,300

Example 2

If he sells the shares for £3,100, ie £2,000 less than their probate value, his position would be as follows:

	£
Disposal consideration	3,100
Less: acquisition (probate) value	5,100
Loss	(2,000)

The loss of £2,000 is available to Phil to set against chargeable gains he may have in the same, or any future, tax year.

31.10.7 Transferring assets to residuary beneficiaries

31.10.7.1 Interim distributions

Once the outstanding tax, legal costs and other matters have been disposed of, PRs should consider transferring any remaining assets to the residuary beneficiaries. In doing so they must remember that payments may have been made already to the beneficiaries as interim distributions on account of their entitlement. If so, these will be taken into account when determining what and how much more should be transferred to those beneficiaries. These interim distributions will also be shown in the estate accounts.

31.10.7.2 Adult beneficiaries

If the beneficiaries are adults, and have a vested entitlement to property in the residuary estate, their entitlement can be transferred to them. If they have a contingent entitlement, the property cannot be transferred to them but will instead be transferred to trustees to hold on their behalf until the contingency is satisfied.

31.10.7.3 Minor beneficiaries

If any beneficiaries are under 18 years of age, whether the interest enjoyed is vested or contingent, the property will usually be held in trust for them until the age of majority is reached or the contingency is satisfied. If a minor beneficiary has a vested interest the PRs may be able to transfer his entitlement to him (if expressly authorised in the will), or to parents and guardians on behalf of the minor.

31.10.7.4 Transferring property to the residuary beneficiaries

The manner in which the property is transferred to residuary beneficiaries, or to trustees of their behalf, will depend on the nature of the property remaining in the estate.

Personal property

The PRs indicate that they no longer require property for administration purposes when they pass title to it by means of an assent. Generally, no particular form of assent is required in the case of personalty so that often the property passes by delivery. The beneficiary's title to the property derives from the will; the assent is merely the manner of giving effect to the gift by the PRs. Company shares are transferred by share (stock) transfer form. The PRs must produce their grant to the company as proof of title to the shares. They, as transferors, transfer the shares 'as PRs of X deceased' to the beneficiary (the transferee), who then applies to be registered as a member of the company in place of the deceased member.

Freehold or leasehold land

Personal representatives vest the legal estate in land in the person entitled (whether beneficially or as trustee) by means of an assent, which will then become a document of title to the legal estate. If PRs are to continue to hold property in their changed capacity as trustees under trusts declared by the will, or arising under the intestacy law, an assent will again be appropriate. The PRs should formally vest the legal estate in themselves as trustees to hold for the beneficiaries.

By the AEA 1925, s 36(4), an assent must be in writing, it must be signed by the PRs, and it must name the person in whose favour it is made. It then operates to vest the legal estate in the named person. A deed is not necessary to pass the legal estate, but PRs may chose to use a deed, for example if they require the beneficiary to give them the benefit of an indemnity covenant. If the title to the land is registered, the assent must be in the form specified by the Land Registration Rules 2003.

Any person in whose favour the PRs make an assent or conveyance may require notice of it to be endorsed on the original grant of probate or administration. In view of this entitlement, it is good practice that the endorsement should be made by the PRs, or solicitors on their behalf, as a matter of routine at the same time as the assent is given. Indeed, if the PRs have made an assent where the title is unregistered in favour of a beneficiary, endorsement is essential for that beneficiary's protection in view of the provisions of the AEA 1925, s 36(6) benefitting any later purchaser from the PRs.

If the title to the land is registered, two options are open to the PRs:

(a)   they can apply to be registered as proprietor in place of the deceased, in which case they must produce the grant of representation when making the application; or

(b)   they can transfer the property by assent without being registered as proprietor themselves, in which case the beneficiary must be given a certified copy of the grant of representation so that he can present it with his application for registration.

As the register is conclusive as to title, the provisions in the AEA 1925 regarding endorsements on the grant are of no relevance.

31.10.8   Estate accounts

31.10.8.1   Purpose of the accounts

The final task of the PRs is usually to produce estate accounts for the residuary beneficiaries. The purpose of the accounts is to show all the assets of the estate, the payment of the debts, administration expenses and legacies, and the balance remaining for the residuary beneficiaries. The balance will normally be represented by a combination of assets transferred to the beneficiaries in specie, and some cash. The residuary beneficiaries sign the accounts to indicate that they approve them. In the absence of fraud or failure to disclose assets, their signatures will also release the PRs from further liability to account to the beneficiaries.

31.10.8.2   Presentation of the accounts

There is no prescribed form for estate accounts. Any presentation adopted should be clear and concise so that the accounts are easily understood by the residuary beneficiaries. If interim distribution payments were made to the residuary beneficiaries during the administration period, these must be taken into account and shown in the estate accounts.

Vertical presentation

Estate accounts may be presented vertically, disclosing assets less liabilities, etc, and a balance for the beneficiaries, or on a double-sided basis, disclosing receipts opposite the payments. It is customary to use the probate values of the assets for accounting purposes.

Narrative introduction

The accounts generally start with a narrative statement of the date of death, the date of the grant of representation, a summary of the will or succession under the intestacy law, and the value of the deceased's gross and net estate. All this information is provided to make the understanding of the accounts easier for the beneficiaries.

Capital and income accounts

Normally accounts show capital assets, and income produced by those assets during the administration period, in separate capital and income accounts. In small estates this may not be necessary, so that one account showing both capital and income will be sufficient. However, it is always necessary to prepare separate accounts if the will (or the intestacy rules) creates a life or minority interest, since the different interests of the beneficiaries in the capital and income need to be distinguished throughout the period of the trust, and when it ends.

Part V Summary – Probate and Administration

Topic	Summary	References
What happens to property when someone dies?	People usually think that where property goes depends on whether or not there is a will. However, many assets pass independently of a will. For example, property held as beneficial joint tenants passes by survivorship; trust property passes under the terms of the trust. Money due from a pension scheme will be subject to the terms of the scheme which normally give the trustees power to choose who to pay it to. Often, the bulk of a person's wealth passes independently of any will.	See **29.1**.
What are the requirements of a valid will?	A testator must be at least 18 and have testamentary capacity. The testator must know and approve the contents of the will and must not have been subjected to undue influence, force, fear or fraud. The will must be signed and witnessed in accordance with s 9 of the Wills Act 1837.	See **29.2**.
How are wills revoked?	Wills can be revoked by a later will or codicil, by destruction or by the formation of a later civil partnership.	See **29.2.4**.
Failure of legacies	A gift in a will fails if the beneficiary predeceases the testator, witnesses the will or is a spouse or civil partner of a witness. A gift of a specific item will fail if the testator no longer owns the item at death. A gift to a spouse or civil partner fails if the marriage or civil partnership ends.	See **29.3**.
What if there is no valid will?	If there is no valid will or if there is property undisposed of by the will, the undisposed of property passes under the intestacy rules. The deceased's personal representatives hold the property on trust. They pay any debts and inheritance tax due and then pay what is left to the closest members of the deceased's family following the order set out in s 46 of the Administration of Estates Act 1925.	See **29.4**.

Topic	Summary	References
What if a family member or dependant is inadequately provided for?	Family members and dependants can apply to the court under the Inheritance (Provision for Family and Dependants) Act 1975 for a redistribution of assets if they feel that the deceased did not make reasonable provision for them. The court is limited to providing for the reasonable maintenance of the applicant except in the case of spouses and civil partners who can claim a reasonable share of the deceased's assets.	See **29.5**.
Who deals with the estate of a deceased person?	Someone has to deal with the assets of the deceased. The generic name for people doing this job is 'personal representatives'. There are two types: executors and administrators. Executors are people appointed in the will. If there are no executors able and willing to act then beneficiaries of the estate will act as administrators. The order of entitlement for administrators is set out in Rules 19 and 20 of the Non-contentious Probate Rules 1987. Both executors and administrators need proof that they are entitled to act. They need to apply to the Probate Registry for a grant of representation. Executors get a grant of probate; administrators get a grant of administration. Note that personal representatives deal only with assets capable of passing by will. Other assets such as property held as beneficial joint tenants pass directly to the person entitled.	
Procedure for applying for a grant of representation	This varies depending on what type of grant is involved, but all personal representatives must swear an oath and pay any inheritance tax due.	See **30.5– 30.11**.
What do the personal representatives do once they have obtained the grant of representation?	Once the grant is obtained, the personal representatives must pay the debts, finalise the IHT position and distribute the assets to the people entitled. This is a burdensome task as personal representatives are personally liable for errors in payment. They can get limited protection under s 27 of the Administration of Estates Act 1925 by advertising for claimants to the estate.	See **Chapter 31**.

Index